Distant Voices

To the Adkins Family.

May God Bless you all.

Isaiah 54:17

Distant Voices

✦

Listening to the Leadership Lessons
of the Past

Napoleon Bonaparte's
Maxims, Quotes and Life in His Own Words

Compiled and Edited
With Commentary
by
Michael B. Colegrove, Ph.D.

iUniverse, Inc.
New York Lincoln Shanghai

Distant Voices
Listening to the Leadership Lessons of the Past

Introduction, Summary and Editorial Materials
Copyright © 2005 by Michael B. Colegrove, Ph.D.

iUniverse books may be ordered through booksellers or by contacting:

iUniverse
2021 Pine Lake Road, Suite 100
Lincoln, NE 68512
www.iuniverse.com
1-800-Authors (1-800-288-4677)

ISBN: 0-595-34849-1

Printed in the United States of America

To Donna, whose love means the entire world to me.
You are my best friend, and I love you.

Contents

viii   Distant Voices

Preface

Messiahs, diplomats, intellectuals, and philosophers have contributed to the twists and turns of history, but they have flourished only when protected by military leaders who could ensure the survival of their way of life. The most influential leaders in world history have come not from the church, the halls of governments, or the scholastic centers but from the ranks of soldiers and sailors.

Throughout time, peoples fortunate enough to have great military leaders and innovators in warfare among their numbers have prospered, controlling their territory and dominating their neighbors. Civilizations without strong military leaders have found themselves subjugated or annihilated. In other instances, military leaders have proved to be tyrannical despots to their own people as well as to their enemies.

Who do you think was the greatest military leader in world history? Your criterion for what "greatest" is may vary. Whether it be lasting influence, strategic intelligence, leadership ability, or the number of victories won, you would have to decide.

Some on your list lived centuries ago, and the test of time has validated their perpetual influence through the ages. The status of the more recent military figures included on your list is subject to the passage of time, world events, and the emergence of other new leaders.

Napoleon wrote: "The Gauls were not conquered by the Roman legions, but by Caesar. It was not before the Carthaginian soldiers that Rome was made to tremble, but before Hannibal. It was not the Macedonian phalanx which reached India, but Alexander. It was not the French army that reached Weser and the Inn; it was Turenne. Prussia was not defended for seven years against the three most formidable European powers by the Prussian soldiers but by Frederick the Great."

This work is the first in a planned series dealing with the writings of great military and political leaders. Prehaps listening to the "Distant Voices" will guide and inspire leaders of the present and the future.

Mike Colegrove

Acknowledgements

I could not possibly list all the people who have been a positive influence in shaping my philosophy of leadership and love of military history, but I would like to thank certain special people for their support, love, and prayers. To my wife and best friend, Donna, our daughter, Kimberly, and her husband, Matt. Also, to my colleagues, past and present, at Cumberland College and all the soldiers with whom I have served. Above all, I give thanks to my Heavenly Father for His inspiration and daily guidance.

Napoleon Bonaparte: An Introduction

The most famous Frenchman in history was born at Ajaccio, Corsica on 15 August, 1769. Consequently Napoleon Bonaparte was not, in fact French. He was, though, a French subject as a result of the ceding of Corsica to France by the Genoese in 1768. His family was upper-middle class. His father Carlo was a political opportunist who gained acceptance into the French aristocracy.

At the age of 10 Napoleon entered the military academy at Brienne, France. His first few months there were a nightmare with the other children teasing him for his strange name, his foreign accent and his small size. Napoleon coped by concentrating on his studies. In 1784 he won a place at the prestigious Ecole Militaire in Paris. A year later he graduated and was commissioned a second lieutenant of artillery. He was garrisoned at Valence. He spent the next six years as a struggling soldier in an isolated outpost.

Napoleons regiment was stationed in Auxonne when the French Revolution broke out. Napoleon approved of the Revolution in principal but he deplored the violence of the common people. On 10, 1792 August he witnessed the second storming of the Tuileries and the arrest of King Louis XVI. He also saw the slaughter of the Swiss Guards that followed. From this point on Napoleon both hated and feared the common people of France.

Between 1790 and 1791 Napoleon spent 18 months in his homeland of Corsica, helping to consolidate French rule. In 1793, he rejoined his regiment who were stationed in Italy. He was here given his first military command at the siege of Toulon. In 3 days Napoleon bombarded the city into submission, gaining control of this important Harbour city. He was rewarded by a speedy promotion to brigadier-general and an appointment as commander of planning for the army of Italy.

In 1795 he was recalled to Paris to help quell mobs under royalist leadership that were preparing to storm the Tuileries. Napoleon was placed as second in command of the defence. He ordered the storming crowds to be annihilated with forty cannon. This act established Napoleon as a hero of the Revolution and gained him entrance into Parisian society. Through such connections he met Josephine de Beauharnias. On March 9, 1796 the two were married. His brides connections were evident two days later when Napoleon became commander of the Army of Italy.

In quick succession Napoleon achieved victories over the Italians, Austrians and Sardinians at Matenotte, Dego, Millesimo, Mondovi and Lodi, Milan, Castiglione and Arcola. In February 1797 he marched across the Alps toward Vienna. The Austrians sued for an Armistice before a single shot was fired.

His return to France was triumphant. At just 28 years of age Napoleon had established himself as the greatest French general of all time. In honour of his achievements he was elected to the prestigious Institut. He set his sights on achieving total power.

First though there was the ongoing sea war with Britain. He decided on a rearguard action to attack Britains resources by occupying Egypt and cutting off her trade routes with India and the Far East. On June 10, 1798 his forces took the island fortress of Malta. Three weeks later they sieged Alexandria. Within days the entire Nile Delta was in French hands. Napoleons first defeat, however, came on August 1 when his entire naval fleet was destroyed by the British navy. In February, 1799 the French were again defeated, this time on land at the battle of Acre. Napoleon retreated to Egypt. Here he handed his command over to General Jean Baptiste Kleber and sailed for France.

When he arrived back in Paris, Napoleon was dismayed to find that France had lost control of most of the territories he had won in Italy. The Directory was, in fact, in a state of chaos. The young General was seen as the last hope for the country. Two of the directors approached him with a plan to overthrow the Directory. A coup detat was executed on 10 November 1799. The directors were forced to resign and the Directory was abolished. A new Government was established consisting of three consuls. Napoleon Bonaparte was meant to be one of the three equal members of this consul but it didnt take long for him to assert himself as de facto dictator of France.

Napoleon set about reforming local and national government, education and legislature, proving himself a brilliant statesman and administrator. In 1802 Napoleon was voted consul for life. This, however, was not enough for him, and he set about paving the way for himself to be crowned Emperor of the French. In May, 1804 he got his wish.

In 1803 the British declared war on France once more. In December of that year the Grand Armee assembled in preparation of an invasion of Britain. The destruction of his fleet, combined with the Spanish, by the British off Cape Trafalgar, however, ended any plans of a British invasion. In August, 1805 Napoleon invaded Germany. French victories followed at Ulm, and Austerlitz. Napoleon was crowned king of Italy. His relations were made kings of Naples and Holland. In 1806 Prussia declared war on France and was soundly defeated. Napoleon now introduced The Cotinental System which forbade all Europoean nations trading with his age old enemy, Britain. In June, 1807 he gained victory over the Russians at the Battle of Friedland. A year later Charles IV ceded his rights in Spain to Napoleon. Napoleons brother Joseph took the throne of Spain.

The beginning of the end came in December, 1810 when the Russians announced that they would no longer observe the Continental System. Napoleons response was to invade Russia. Making it to Moscow the French forces were decimated by a massive fire. The Russian winter then took its toll on the French. More than half a million men had been reduced to less than 10,000. Napoleon retreated to Paris.

Europe now believed that France could be beaten. In 1813 the Prussians joined forces with Russia in an alliance against France. When Austria joined the alliance, Napoleon knowing he couldnt prevail, sued for an armistice. He soon reneged on the conditions, however and an allied invasion of France was put in motion. By January, 1814 France was under attack from all sides. In March, 1814 Paris fell to the allies. Napoleon had moved his army east. The Parisian authorities had, however, abandoned him and they came to terms with the allies.

Napoleon was determined to hold out to the bitter end. But after his General defected he finally faced the inevitable. On 6 April, 1814 Napoleon Bonaparte announced his abdication. Under the Treaty of Fontainebleau he was exiled to the island of Elba. Just a year later, however, he returned to Paris and, with the masses rallying around him, was reinstated as head of state. The allies, of course, retaliated by marching once more on France. Initially Napoleons forces gained the victory but the final defeat came when the British forces, reinforced by the Prussians, met the French at Waterloo. Napoleon had fought his last battle.

For a second time the Emperor abdicated. Deciding what to do with him, the allies finally decided on exile to the rocky island of St. Helena in the south Atlantic. Situated a thousand miles off the African Coast Napoloen was now well and truly out of the way. On 5 May, 1821 Napoleon Bonaparte died on his island prison. He was just fifty one years of age.

Napoleon's Maxims

1.) The frontiers of nations are either large rivers, or chains of mountains, or deserts. Of all these obstacles to the march of an army, deserts are the most difficult to surmount; mountains come next; and large rivers hold only the third rank.

2.) A plan of campaign should anticipate everything which the enemy can do, and contain within itself the means of thwarting him. Plans of campaign may be infinitely modified according to the circumstances, the genius of the commander, the quality of the troops and the topography of the theater of war.

3.) An army invading a country may either have its two wings resting on neutral countries or on natural obstacles, such as rivers or chains of mountains; or it may have only one of its wings thus supported; or both may be without support. In the first case, a general has only to see that his line is not broken in front. In the second case, he must rest on the wing which is supported. In the third case, he must keep his different corps resting well on his centre and never allow them to separate from it; for if it is a disadvantage to have two flanks in the air, the inconvenience is doubled if there are four, tripled if there are six; that is to say, if an army is divided into two or three distinct corps.

The line of operations in the first case, may rest on the left or the right wing, indifferently. In the second case, it should rest on the wing which is supported. In the third case, it should fall perpendicularly on the middle of the line formed by the army in marching. But in all the cases above mentioned, it is necessary to have at every five or six days' march, a fort or entrenched position, where magazines of provisions and military stores may be established and convoys organized; and which may serve as a centre of motion and a point of supply, and thus shorten the line of operations.

4.) It may be laid down as a principle that in invading a country with two or three armies, each of which has its own distinct line of operations extending towards a fixed point at which all are to unite, the union of the different corps should never be ordered to take place in the vicinity of the enemy, as by concentrating his forces he may not only prevent their junction but also defeat them one by one.

5.) All wars should be systematic, for every war should have an aim and be conducted in conformity with the principles and rules of the art. War should be undertaken with forces corresponding to the magnitude of the obstacles that are to be anticipated.

6.) At the commencement of a campaign, the question whether to advance or not requires careful deliberation; but when you have once undertaken the offensive, it should be maintained to the last extremity. A retreat, however skillful the maneuvers may be, will always produce an injurious moral effect on the army, since by losing the chances of success yourself you throw them into the hands of the enemy. Besides, retreats cost far more, both in men and materiel, than the most bloody engagements; with this differerence that in a battle the enemy loses nearly as much as you, while in a retreat the loss is all on your side.

7.) An army should be every day, every night, and every hour, ready to offer all the resistance of which it is capable. It is necessary, therefore, that the soldiers should always have their arms and ammunition at hand; that the infantry should always have with it its artillery, cavalry and generals; that the different divisions of the army should be always in a position to assist, support and protect each other; that whether encamped, marching or halted, the troops should be always in advantageous positions, possessing the qualities required for every field of battle that is to say, the flanks should be well supported and the artillery so placed that it may all be brought into play. When the army is in column of march, there must be advanced guards and flank guards to observe the enemy's movements in front, on the right and on the left; and at sufficient distances to allow the main body of the arm to deploy and take up its positions.

8.) A general should say to himself many times a day; If the hostile army were to make its appearance in front, on my right, or on my left, what should I do? And if he is embarassed, his arrangements are bad; there is something wrong; and he must rectify his mistake.

9.) The strength of an army, like the momentum of its mechanics, is estimated by the weight multiplied by the velocity. A rapid march exerts a beneficial moral influence on the army and increases its means of victory.

10.) When your army is inferior in numbers, inferior in cavalry and in artillery, a pitched battle should at all cost be avoided. The want of numbers must be supplied by rapidityin marching, the want of artillery by the character of the maneuvers; the inferiority in cavalry by the choice of positions. In such a situation, it is often of great importance that confidence should prevail among the soldiers.

11.) To operate upon lines remote from each other and without communications between them, is a fault which ordinarily occasions a second. The detached column has orders only for the first day. Its operations for the second day depend on what has happened to the main body. Thus, according to circumstances, the column wastes its time in waiting for orders or it acts at random. It ought then to be adopted as a principle that the columns of an army should be always kept united, so that the enemy cannot thrust himself between them. When for any reason this maxim is departed from, the detached corps should be independent in their operations. They should move towards a fixed point at which they are to unite. They should march without hesitation and without new orders, and should be exposed as little as possible to the danger of being attacked separately.

12.) An army should have but a single line of operations which it should carefully preserve, and should abandon only when compelled by imperious circumstances.

13.) The intervals at which the corps of an army should be from each other in marching, depend on the localities, the circumstances and the object in view.

14.) Among mountains there are everywhere numerous positions extremely strong by nature, which you should abstain from attacking. The genius of this kind of war consists in occupying camps either on the flank or the rear but to withdraw from this position without fighting; and to move him farther back, or to make him come out and attack you. In mountain warfare the attacking party acts under a disadvantage. Even in offensive warfare, the merit lies in having only defensive conflicts and obliging your enemy to become the assailant.

15.) In giving battle a general should regard it as his first duty to maintain the honor and glory of his arms. To spare his troops should be but a secondary consideration. But the same determination and perseverance which promote the former object are the best means of securing the latter. In a retreat you lose, in addition to the honor of your arms, more men than in two battles.

For this reason you should never despair while there remain brave men around the colors. This is the conduct which wins, and deserves to win, the victory.

16.) A well-established maxim of war is not to do anything which your enemy wishes and for the single reason that he does so wish. You should, therefore, avoid a field of battle which he has reconnoitered and studied. You should be still more careful to avoid one which he has fortified and where he has entrenched himself. A corollary of this principle is, never to attack in front a position which admits of being turned.

17.) In a war of marches and maneuvers, to escape an engagement with a superior enemy, it is necessary to throw up entrenchments every night and to place yourself always in a good position for defense. The natural positions which are commonly met with cannot secure an army against the superiority of a more numerous one without the aid of artillery.

18.) An ordinary general occupying a bad position, if surprised by a superior force, seeks safety in retreat; but a great captain displays the utmost determination and advances to meet the enemy. By this movement he disconcerts his adversary; and if the march of the latter evinces irresolution, an able general, profiting by the moment of indecision, may yet hope for victory or at least employ the day in maneuvering; and at night he can entrench himself or fall back on a better position. By this fearless conduct he maintains the honor of his arms, which forms so essential a part of the strength of an army.

19.) The passage from the defensive to the offensive is one of the most delicate operations of war.

20.) Your line of operations should never, as a general rule, be abandoned; but changing it when circumstances require, is one of the most skillful of military maneuvers. An army which changes its line of operations skillfully, deceives the enemy, who no longer knows where his antagonist's rear is, or what are the weak points to threaten.

21.) When an army is encumbered with siege equipage and large convoys of wounded and sick, it should approach its depots by the shortest roads and as expeditiously as possible.

22.) The art of encamping on a position is nothing else than the art of forming in order of battle on that position. For this purpose the artillery should all be in readiness and favorably placed; a position should be selected which is not commanded, cannot be turned, and from which the ground in the vicinity is covered and commanded.

23.) When you occupy a position which the enemy threatens to surround, you should collect your forces quickly and menace him with an offensive movement. By this maneuver you prevent him from detaching a part of his troops and annoying your flanks, in case you should deem a retreat indispensable.

24.) A military maxim, which ought never to be neglected, is to assemble your cantonments at the point which is most remote and best sheltered from the enemy, especially when he makes his appearance unexpectedly. You will then have time to unite the whole army before he can attack you.

25.) When two armies are in order of battle, and one, if obliged to retire, must effect its retreat by a bridge, while the other can withdraw towards all points of the compass, the latter has greatly the advantage. A general so situated should be enterprising, strike vigorously and maneuver against the flanks of his adversary; and victory is his.

26.) It is a violation of correct principles to cause corps to act separately, without communication with each other, in the face of a concentrated army with easy communications.

27.) When you are driven from your first position, the rallying point of your columns should be so far in the rear that the enemy cannot get there before them. It would be the greatest of disasters to have your columns attacked one by one before their reunion.

28.) No detachment should be made the day preceding a battle, for during the night the state of things may change, either by a retreat of the enemy or by the arrival of strong reinforcements, which would put him in condition to assume the offensive and render the premature dispositions which you have made ruinous.

29.) When you have it in contemplation to give battle, it is a general rule to collect all your strength and to leave none unemployed. One battalion sometimes decides the issue of the day.

30.) Nothing is more rash or more opposed to the principles of war than a flank march in presence of an army in position, especially when that army occupies heights at the foot of which you must defile.

31.) When you intend to engage in a decisive battle, avail yourself of all the chances of success; more especially if you have to do with a great captain; for if you are beaten, though you may be in the midst of your magazines and near your fortified posts, woe to the vanquished!

32.) The duty of an advance guard does not consist in advancing or retreating, but in maneuvering. It should be composed of light cavalry supported by a reserve of heavy, and by battalions of infantry, with artillery to support them. The advance guard should be formed of choice troops; and the generals, officers and soldiers, according to the requirements of their respective rank, should be thoroughly acquainted with the peculiar tactics necessary in this kind of service. An untrained company would be only a source of embarrassment.

33.) It is contrary to the usages of war to cause your parks or heavy artillery to enter a defile, the opposite extremity of which is not in your possession; since, in the event of a retreat, they will embarrass you and be lost. They ought to be left in position, under a suitable escort, until you have made yourself master of the termination of the defile.

34.) It should be adopted as a principle never to allow intervals through which the enemy can penetrate between the different corps forming the line of battle, unless you have laid a snare into which it is your object to draw him.

35.) The camps of the same army should be always so placed as to be able to sustain each other.

36.) When a hostile army is covered by a river on which it has several bridgeheads, you should not approach it in front, for in doing so your forces would be too little concentrated and in danger of being broken into detached parts, if the enemy should sally from one of the bridgeheads. You should approach the river you wish to cross in columns disposed in echelon, so that there may be only a single column the foremost one which the enemy can attack without exposing his own flank.

Meanwhile the light troops will line the bank; and when you have fixed on the point at which to pass, you must proceed rapidly to the spot and throw the bridge across. You must take care that the bridge shall always be at a distance from the leading echelon in order to deceive the enemy.

37.) The moment that you become master of a position which commands the opposite bank, you obtain many facilities for effecting the passage of a river, especially if that position has sufficient extent to admit of your planting a large number of pieces of artillery upon it. This advantage is less if the river is more than six hundred yards wide, as the grape no longer reaches the other shore; and consequently the troops that oppose the passage can, by suitable precautions, easily render your fire of little effect. Hence if the grenadiers charged with the duty of passing the river to protect the bridge, succeed in crossing to the other side, they will be swept off by the enemy's grapeshot; as his batteries established four hundred yards from the termination of the bridge are near enough to pour in a very destructive fire, although more than a thousand yards distant from the batteries of the army which is endeavouring to pass. Therefore he has all the advantage of the artillery. So in such a case a passage is not practicable unless you either contrive to take the enemy by surprise, or are protected by an intervening island, or avail your self of a deep re-entrant bend, which enables you to erect batteries crossing their fire just in advance of the point where a landing is to be effected. Such an island or re-entrant forms a natural bridgehead and gives the advantage of the artillery to the attacking army.

When a river is less than a hundred and twenty yards in breadth and you can command the opposite bank, the troops that are thrown over to the other side derive such advantages from the protection afforded by the artillery that, however slight the re-entrant formed by the river may be, it is impossible for the enemy to prevent the establishment of the bridge. Under such circumstances, the most skillful generals, when they have been able to foresee the designs of their antagonist and arrive with their army at the point at which he was making his attempt, have contented themselves with disputing the passage of the bridge. A bridge being in fact a defile, you should place yourself in a half-circle around its extremity and take measures to shelter yourself at the distance of six or eight hundred yards from the fire of the other bank.

38.) It is difficult to prevent an enemy provided with bridge equipage from crossing a river. When the object of the army which disputes the passage is to cover a siege, the commanding general, as soon as he is certain that he cannot successfully oppose the passage, should take measures to arrive in advance of the enemy at a position between the river and the place whose siege he is covering.

39.) In the campaign of 1645, the forces of Turenne were hemmed in before Philipsburgh by a very numerous army. There was no bridge over the Rhine, but Turenne established his camp on the ground lying between the river and the place. This should serve as a lesson to officers of the engineer department in regard to the construction of bridgeheads as well as of fortresses. There should be left, between the fortress and the river, a space in which an army may be rallied and formed; as the entrance of the troops into the place itself would endanger it. An army pursued and retiring upon Mayence, must necessarily be in a precarious situation, since it would require more than one day to pass the bridge, and the works surrounding Cassel are too small to contain an army without crowding and confusion. Four hundred yards should have been left between the works and the Rhine. It is essential that bridgeheads before large rivers should be constructed on this plan; otherwise they will be of little utility in protecting the passage of an army in retreat. Bridgeheads, as they are taught in the schools, are good only before small rivers where the defile is not long.

40.) Fortresses are useful in offensive as well as defensive war. Undoubtedly they cannot of themselves arrest the progress of an army, but they are excellent means of delaying, impeding, enfeebling and annoying a victorious enemy.

41.) There are only two modes of prosecuting a siege successfully. One is to begin by beating the hostile army employed to cover the place, driving it from the field of operations and forcing its remains beyond some natural obstacle, such as a chain of mountains or a large river. This first difficulty overcome, you must place an army of observation behind the natural obstacle until the labors of the siege are finished and the place is taken.

But if you wish to take the place in the face of an army of relief without hazarding a battle, you must be provided with siege equipage, ammunition and provisions for the time during which the siege is expected to continue; and must form lines of contravallation and circumvallation, turning, meanwhile, the peculiarities of the ground such as heights, woods, marshes and overflows to the best account.

As there is then no necessity for keeping up any communication with your depots, you have only to hold in check the army of relief To this end you should form an army of observation which must never lose sight of the enemy and which, while shutting him out from all access to the place, may always have time to fall upon his flanks or rear, if he should steal a march upon you. By taking advantage of your lines of contravallation you can employ a part of the besieging forces in giving battle to the army of relief.

A siege therefore, in the presence of a hostile army requires to be covered by lines of circumvallation.

If your army is so strong that, after leaving before the place a body four times the number of the garrison, it is still equal to the army of relief, it may move to a greater distance than one day's march.

If, after making the detachment, it remains inferior to the army of relief, it should be posted at one short day's march from the place besieged, so as to be at liberty to fall back on the lines or receive succor in the event of sustaining an attack.

If the two armies of siege and of observation, united, are equal only to the army of relief, the besieging army must remain altogether within or near its lines and employ itself in pushing the siege with all possible activity.

42.) Feuquieres has said that you should never wait for the enemy in your lines of circumvallation, but should go out and attack him. The maxim is erroneous. No rule of war is so absolute as to allow no exceptions, and waiting for the enemy in the lines of circumvallation ought not to be condemned as injudicious in all cases.

43.) They who proscribe lines of circumvallation and all the aid which the art of the engineer can furnish, gratuitously deprive themselves of auxiliaries that are never injurious, almost always useful and often indispensable. The principles of field fortification, however, need improvement. This important branch of the art of war has made no progress in modern times. It is even at this day in a lower state than it was two thousand years ago. Officers of the engineer department ought to be encouraged to perfect this branch of their art and raise it to a level with others.

44.) When you have a hospital and magazines in a fortified town, and circumstances are such as not to admit of your leaving a sufficient garrison to defend it, you should at least make every possible exertion to put the citadel in security from a coup de main.

45.) A fortified place can protect a garrison and arrest the enemy only a certain length of time. When that time has elapsed and the defences of the place are destroyed, the garrison may lay down their arms. All civilized nations have been of one opinion in this re-spect, and the only dispute has been as to the greater or less degree of resistance which the governor should offer before capitulating. Yet there are generals Villars is of the number—who hold that a governor ought never to surrender, but that in the last extremity he should blow up the fortifications and take advantage of the night to cut his way through the besieging army.

In case you cannot blow up the fortifications, you can at any rate sally out with your garrison and save your men. Commanders who have pursued this course have rejoined their army with three-fourths of their garrison.

46.) The keys of a fortified place are ample compensation for permiffing the garrison to retire unmolested, whenever the latter evince a determination to die rather than accept less favorable terms. It is always better, therefore, to grant an honorable capitulation to a garrison which has resisted vigorously than to run the risk of an attempt to storm.

47.) The infantry, cavalry and artillery cannot dispense with each other. They ought not be quartered in such a manner as always to be able to support each other in case of surprise.

48.) Infantry formed in line should be in two ranks only, for the musket cannot otherwise be used with equal effect. It is admitted that the fire of the third rank is very imperfect and even injurious to that of the first two.

But though the great body of the infantry should be drawn up, as has just been said, in two ranks, the absence of a regular third rank should be supplied by supernumeraries composed of one soldier out of nine or one every two yards.

49.) The practice of mingling companies of horse and foot together is bad; it produces nothing but trouble. The cavalry is deprived of its capacity for rapidity of motion; it is cramped in all the movements; it loses its impulse.

The infantry, too, is exposed; for, at the first movement of the cavalry, it remains without support. The best mode of protecting cavalry is to suport its flank.

50.) Charges of cavalry are equally serviceable in the beginning, the middle and the end of a battle. They should be executed whenever they can be made on the flanks of the infantry, particularly when the latter is engaged in front.

51.) It is a function of the cavalry to follow up the victory and prevent the beaten enemy from rallying.

52.) Artillery is more necessary to cavalry than to infantry, because cavalry does not fire and can fight only in close conflict. It is to supply this deficiency that horse-artillery has been resorted to. Cavalry, therefore, should always be accompanied by cannon, whether attacking, resting in position or rallying.

53.) The principal part of the artillery should be with the divisions of infantry and of cavalry, whether marching or in position, and the rest should be placed in reserve. Each piece should have with it three hundred charges of powder and ball, besides the contents of the ammunition box. That is about the quantity consumed in two battles.

54.) Batteries should be placed in the most advantageous positions and as far in advance of the lines of infantry and cavalry as is possible without endangering the guns. It is desirable that the batteries should have a command over the field equal to the full height of the platform. They must not be masked on the right or left, but should be at liberty to direct their fire towards every point.

55.) A general should avoid putting his army into quarters of refreshment, so long as he has the opportunity of collecting magazines of provisions and forage, and thus supplying the wants of his soldiers.

56.) A good general, good officers, commissioned and noncommissioned, good organization, good instruction and strict discipline make good troops independently of the cause for which they are fighting. But enthusiasm, love of country and the desire of contributing to the national glory may also animate young troops with advantage.

57.) It is very difficult for a nation to create an army when it has not already a body of officers and non-commissioned officers to serve as a nucleus, and a system of military oranization.

58.) The first quality of a soldier is constancy in enduring fatigue and hardship. Courage is only the second. Poverty, privation and want are the school of the good soldier.

59.) There are five things which a soldier ought never to be without: his musket, his cartridge-box, his knapsack, his provisions for at least four days and his pioneer hatchet. Reduce his knapsack, if you deem it necessary to do so, to the smallest size, but let the soldier always have it with him.

60.) You should by all means encourage the soldiers to continue in the service. This you can easily do by testifying great esteem for old sol diers. The pay should also be increased in proportion to the years of service. There is great injustice in giving no higher pay to a veteran than to a recruit.

61.) It is not by harangues at the moment of engaging that soldiers are rendered brave. Veterans hardly listen to them and recruits forget them at the first discharge of a cannon. If speeches and arguments are at any time useful, it is during the course of the campaign by counteracting false reports and causes of discontent, maintaining a proper spirit in the camp and furnishing subjects of conversation in the bivouacs. These several objects may be attained by the printed orders of the day.

62.) Tents are injurious to health. It is much better for the soldier to bivouack, because he can sleep with his feet to the fire, which quickly dries the ground on which he lies. A few boards or a little straw shelter him from the wind.

Tents, however, are necessary for the leaders, who have to write and consult the map. They should be given therefore to the superior officers, who should be ordered never to lodge in a house.

Tents attract the observation of the enemy's staff and make known your numbers and the position you occupy. But of an army bivouacking in two or three lines, nothing is perceived at a distance except the smoke, which the enemy confounds with the mist of the atmosphere. He cannot count the fires.

63.) The information obtained from prisoners ought to be estimated at its proper value. A soldier seldom looks beyond his own company and an officer can, at most, give account of the position or movements of the division to which his regiment belongs. A general, therefore, should not allow himself to be confirmed in his conjectures as to the enemy's position, by attaching any weight to the statements of prisoners, except when they coincide with the reports of the advance guards.

64.) Nothing is more important in war than unity in command. When, therefore, you are carrying on hostilities against a single power only, you should have but one army acting on one line and led by one commander.

65.) The effect of discussions, making a show of talent, and calling councils of war will be what the effect of these things has been in every age: they will end in the adoption of the most pusillanimous or (if the expression be preferred) the most prudent measures, which in war are almost uniformly the worst that can be adopted. True wisdom, so far as a general is concerned, consists in energetic determination.

66.) There are certain things in war of which the commander alone comprehends the importance. Nothing but his superior firmness and ability can subdue and surmount all difficulties.

67.) To authorize generals and officers to lay down their arms by virtue of a special capitulation under any other circumstances than when they constitute the garrison of a fortified place, would unquestionably be attended with dangerous consequences. To open this door to cowards, to men wanting in energy or even to misguided brave men, is to destroy the military spirit of a nation. An extraordinary situation requires extraordinary resolution. The more obstinate the resistance of an armed body, the more chances it will have of being succored or of forcing a passage. How many things apparently impossible have nevertheless been performed by resolute men who had no alternative but death!

68.) No sovereign, no people, no general can be secure, if officers are permitted to capitulate on the field and lay down their arms by virtue of an agreement favorable to them selves and to the troops under their command, but opposed to the interests of the remainder of the army. To withdraw from peril themselves, and thus render the position of their comrades more dangerous, is manifestly an act of baseness. Such conduct ought to be proscribed, pronounced infamous and punishable with death. The generals, officers and soldiers who in a battle have saved their lives by capitulating, ought to be decimated. He and who those who obey him, are alike traitors, and deserve capital punishment.

69.) There is but one honorable way of being made a prisoner of war; that is by being taken separately and when you can no longer make use of your arms. Then there are no conditions__for there can be none, consistently with honor__but you are compelled to surrender by absolute necessity.

70.) The conduct of a general in a conquered country is encompassed with difficulties. If he is severe, he exasperates and increases the number of his enemies; if he is mild, he inspires hopes which, since they cannot be realized, cause the abuses and vexations unavoidably incident to war only to stand out in bolder relief. A conqueror should know how to employ by turns severity, justice and leniency suppressing or preventing disturbances.

71.) Nothing can excuse a general who avails himself of the knowledge he has acquired in the service of his country to give up its bulwarks to a foreign nation. That is a crime abhorrent to the principles of religion, morality and honor.

72.) A general-in-chief cannot exonerate himself from responsibility for his faults by pleading an order of his sovereign or the minister, when the individual from whom it proceeds is at a distance from the field of operations, and but partially, or not at all, acquainted with the actual condition of things. Hence it follows that every general-in-chief who undertakes toexecute a plan which he knows to be bad, is culpable. He should communicate his reasons, insist on a change of plan and finally resign his commission rather than become the instrument of his army's ruin.

Every general-in-chief who, in consequence of orders from his superiors, gives battle with the certainty of defeat, is equally culpable.

In this latter case, he should refuse to obey; for an order requires passive obedience only when it is issued by a superior who is present at the seat of war. As the superior is then familiar with the state of affairs, he can listen to objections and make the necessary explanations to the officer who is to execute the command.

But suppose a general-in-chief were to re ceive from his sovereign an order to give battle with the injunction to yield the victory to his adversary and permit himself to be beaten. Would he be bound to obey? No! If the general comprehended the utility of so strange an or-der, he ought to execute it; but, if not, he should refuse to obey.

73.) The first qualification of a general-in-chief is to possess a cool head, so that things may appear to him in their true proportions and as they really are. He should not suffer himself to be unduly affected by good or bad news.

The impressions which are made upon his mind successively or simultaneously in the course of a day, should be so classified in his memory that each shall occupy its proper place; for sound reasoning and judgment result from first examining each of these varied impressions by itself, and then comparing them all with one another.

There are some men who, from their physical and moral constitution, deck everything in the colors of imagination. With whatever knowledge, talents, courage or other good qualities these may be endowed, nature has not fitted them for the command of armies and the direction of the reat operations of war.

74.) To be familiar with the geography and topography of the country; to be skillful in making a reconnaissance; to be attentive to the despatch of orders; to be capable of exhibiting with simplicity the most complicated movements of an army__these are the qualifications that should distinguish the officer called to the station of chief of the staff.

75.) A general of artillery should be acquainted with all the operations of the army, as he is obliged to supply the different divisions of which it is composed with arms and ammunition. His communications with the artillery officers at the advanced posts should keep him informed of all the movements of the troops, and the management of his great park must be regulated by this information.

76.) To reconnoiter rapidly defiles and fords; to obtain guides that can be relied upon; to interrogate the clergyman and the postmaster; to establish speedily an understanding with the inhabitants; to send out spies; to seize the letters in the mails, to translate and make an abstract of their contents; in short, to answer all the inquiries of the general-in-chief on his arrival with the whole army such are the duties which come within the sphere of a good general of an advanced post.

77.) Commanders-in-chief are to be guided by their own experience or genius. Tactics, evolutions and the science of the engineer and the artillery officer may be learned from treatises, but generalship is acquired only by experience and the study of the campaigns of all great captains. Gustavus Adolphus, Turenne and Frederic, as also Alexander, Hannibal and Caesar have all acted on the same principles. To keep your forces united, to be vulnerable at no point, to bear down with rapidity upon important points these are the principles which insure victory.

It is by the fear which the reputation of your arms inspires that you maintain the fidelity of your allies and the obedience of conquered nations.

78.) Read over and over again the campaigns of Alexander, Hannibal, Caesar, Gustavus,Turenne, Eugene and Frederic. Make them your models. This is the only way to become a great general and to master the secrets of the art of war. With your own genius enlightened by this study, you will reject all maxims opposed to those of these great commanders.

79.) The first principle of a general-in-chief is to calculate what he must do, to see if he has all the means to surmount the obstacles with which the enemy can oppose him and, when he has made his decision, to do everything to overcome them.

80.) The art of a general of the advance guard or of the rear guard is, without compromising himself, to contain the enemy, to delay him and to force him to take three or four hours to advance a mile. Tactics supplies the only means to attain such great results. It is more necessary for the cavalry than for the infantry, for an advance guard or for a rear guard, than for any other position.

81.) It is exceptional and difficult to find all the qualities of a great general combined in one man. What is most desirable and distinguishes the exceptional man, is the balance of intelligence and ability with character or courage. If courage is predominant, the general will hazard far beyond his conceptions; and on the contrary, he will not dare to accomplish his conceptions if his character or his courage are below his intelligence..

82.) With a great general there is never a continuity of great actions which can be attributed to chance and good luck; they always are the result of calculation and genius.

83.) A general-in-chief should never allow any rest either to the conquerors or to the conquered.

84.) An irresolute general who acts without principles and without plan, even though he lead an army numerically superior to that of the enemy, almost always finds himself inferior to the latter on the field of battle. Fumblings, the mezzo termine (the middle course) lose all in war.

85.) A general of engineers who must conceive, propose and direct all the fortifications of an army, needs good judgment and a practical mind above all.

86.) A cavalry general should be a master of practical science, know the value of seconds, despise life and not trust to chance.

87.) A general in the power of the enemy has no more orders to give: whoever obeys him is a criminal.

88.) The heavy cavalry should be with the advance guard, with the rear guard and on the wings and in reserve to support the light cavalry.

89.) To wish to hold the cavalry in reserve for the end of the battle, is to have no idea of the power of combined cavalry and infantry charges either for attack or for defense.

90.) The power of cavalry is in its impulsion. But it is not only its velocity that insures success: it is order, formation and proper employment of reserves.

91.) The cavalry should compose a quarter of the army in Flanders or Germany; in the Pyrenees or in the Alps, a twentieth; in Italy or in Spain, a sixth.

92.) In a battle like in a siege, skill consists in converging a mass of fire on a single point: once the combat is opened, the commander who is adroit will suddenly and unexpectedly open fire with a surprising mass of artillery on one of these points, and is sure to seize it.

93.) The better the infantry is, the more it should be used carefully and supported with good batteries.

Good infantry is, without doubt, the sinew of an army; but if it is forced to fight for a long time against a very superior artillery, it will become demoralized and will be destroyed. It is possible that a general who is more skillful and a better maneuverer than his adversary, having better infantry, will gain success during a part of the campaign although his artillery park is very inferior; but, on a decisive day in a general action, he will feel his inferiority in artillery cruelly.

94.) A good army of 35,000 men should in a few days, especially when supported by a fortress or a large river, make its camp unassailable by an army double in force.

95.) War is composed of nothing but accidents, and, although holding to general principles, a general should never lose sight of everything to enable him to profit from these accidents; that is the mark of genius.

In war there is but one favourable moment; the great art is to seize it.

96.) A general who retains fresh troops for the day after a battle is almost always beaten. He should, if helpful, throw in his last man, because on the day after a complete success there are no more obstacles in front of him; prestige alone will insure new triumphs to the conqueror.

97.) The rules of fighting require that a part of an army should avoid fighting alone against an entire army that has already been successful.

98.) When a general has laid siege to a place by surprise and has gained a few days on his adversary, he should profit from this by covering himself with lines of circumvallation; from this moment he will have improved his position and will have acquired a new element of power and a new degree of force in the general framework of affairs.

99.) In war the commander of a fortress is not a judge of events; he should defend the fortress to the last; he deserves death if he surrenders it a moment before he is forced to.

100.) Agreements to surrender made by surrounded bodies, either during a battle or during an active campaign, are contracts with all the advantageous clauses in favor of the individuals who contract them, and all the onerous clauses against the prince and the other soldiers of the army. To avoid peril oneself, while making the position of the rest more dangerous, is an act of cowardice.

101.) Defensive war does not exclude attacking, just as offensive war does not exclude defending, although its aim may be to force the frontier and invade the enemy's country.

102.) The art of war indicates that it is necessary to turn or envelop a wing without separating the army.

103.) When they are thoroughly understood, field fortifications are always useful and never injurious.

104.) An army can march anywhere and at any time of the year, wherever two men can place their feet.

105.) Conditions of the ground should not alone decide the organization for combat, which should be determined from consideration of all circumstances.

106.) Flank marches should be avoided; and when they must be undertaken, they should be as short as possible and made with the greatest speed.

107.) Nothing can be designed better to disorganize and destroy an army than pillage.

108.) Praise from enemies is suspicious; it cannot flatter an honorable man unless it is given after the cessation of hostilities.

109.) Prisoners of war do not belong to the power for which they have fought; they all are under the safeguard of honor and generosity of the nation that has disarmed them.

110.) Conquered provinces should be maintained in obedience to the conquerors by moral means, such as the responsibility of local governments and the method of organization and administration. Hostages are among the most powerful means; but to be effective, they should be many and chosen from the preponderant elements, and the people must be convinced that immediate death of the hostages will follow violation of their pledges.

111.) The geographical conditions of a country, life in plains or mountains, education or discipline, have more influence than climate on the character of the troops.

112.) All great captains have done great things only by conforming to the rules and naturalprinciples of the art; that is to say, by the wisdom of their combinations, the reasoned balance of means with consequences, and efforts with obstacles. They have succeeded only by thus conforming, whatever may have been the audacity of their enterprises and the extent of their success. They have never ceased to make war a veritable science. It is only under this title that they are our great models, and it is only in imitating them that one can hope to approach them.

113.) The first law of naval tactics should be that as soon as the admiral has given the signal that he is going to attack, each captain should make the necessary movements to attack an enemy ship, take part in the combat and support his neighbors.

114.) War on land, in general, consumes more men than naval warfare; it is more dangerous. The sailor in a fleet fights but once during a campaign; the ground soldier fights every day. The sailor, whatever may be the fatigues and dangers of the sea, suffers much less than the soldier. He is never hungry nor thirsty; he always has a place to sleep, his kitchen, his hospital and his pharmacy. There are fewer sick in the English and French fleets, where discipline maintains cleanliness and experience has discovered all the means of preserving health, than in armies. Besides the perils of battle, the sailor risks those of tempests; but seamanship has so much diminished the latter that it cannot be compared with those on land, such as popular uprisings, partial assassinations and surprises by hostile light troops.

115.) An admiral commanding a fleet and a general commanding an army are men who need different qualities. One is born with the qualities proper to command an army, while the necessary qualities to command a fleet are acquired only by experience. The art of war on land is an art of genius, of inspiration. On the sea everything is definite and a matter of experience. The admiral needs only one science, navigation. The general needs all or a talent equal to all, that of profiting by all experience and all knowledge. An admiral needs to divine nothing; he knows where his enemy is and he knows his strength. A general never knows anything with certainty, never sees his enemy clearly and never knows positively where he is.

When armies meet, the least accident of the terrain, the smallest wood, hides a portion of the army. The most experienced eye cannot state whether he sees the entire enemy army or only three quarters of it. It is by the eyes of the mind, by reasoning over the whole, by a species of inspiration that the general sees, knows and judges. The admiral needs only an experienced glance; nothing of the enemy force is hidden from him. What makes the general's function difficult is the necessity of nourishing so many men and animals; if he permits himself to be guided by administrators, he will never budge and his expeditions will fail. The admiral is never bothered since he carries everything with him. An admiral has neither reconnaissances to make, terrain to examine nor fields of battle to study. Indian Ocean, American Ocean or North Sea it is always a liquid plain. The most skillful will have no advantage over the least, except for his knowledge of prevailing winds in such and such coastal waters, by foresight of those which should prevail or by atmospheric signs: qualities which are acquired by experience and by experience only.

The general never knows the field of battle on which he may operate. His understanding is that of inspiration; he has no positive information; data to reach a knowledge of localities are so contingent on events that almost nothing is learned by experience. It is a faculty to understand immediately the relations of the terrain according to the nature of different countries; it is, finally, a gift, called a coup d'oeil militaire (the ability to take in the military situation at a glance) which great generals have received from nature. However the observations that can be made from topographic maps and the facility which education and habit give in reading maps, can be of some assistance.

An admiral depends more on the captains of his ships than a general on his generals. The latter has the opportunity to take direct command of the troops himself, to move to any point and to repair false movements. An admiral can influence personally only the men on the vessel on which he finds himself; smoke prevents signals from being seen and winds change or vary over the space occupied by his line. It is thus of all professions that in which subalterns should use the largest initiative.

Napoleon's Quotes

On Britain

- (The English Channel) is a mere ditch.

- England is a nation of shopkeepers.

- Masters of the Channel for six hours, we are masters of the world.

- Two powers like France and England, with a good understanding between them, might govern the world.

On Nations

- When a Nation is in war, the presence of a deliberative body is injurious and often fatal. The turbulent, the ambitious greedy of distinction, of popularity, of power, erect themselves by their own authority into advocates of the people, defending those who are not attacked, as advisers of the Prince, they will know all, rule all, direct all, they become successively censors, factious and rebels.

- There is no Nation however small which had the right to set itself free, that has not rescued itself from the dishonour of obeying the Prince imposed by an enemy in the hour of victory.

- Patriotism is a word which represents a noble idea.

- The fate of a Nation may sometimes depend upon the position of a fortress.

- It strengthens the bonds between nations to have the same civil laws and the same monetary system.

- In a conquered country benevolence is not humanitarianism. It is a general political axiom that a conqueror must not inspire a good opinion of his benevolence until he has demonstrated that he can be severe with malefactors.

- Agriculture is the soul and chief support of empires; industry produces riches and the happiness of the people; exportation represents the superabundance, and good use of both.

- Nothing renders a nation so despicable as religious despotism.

- Equality should be the chief basis of the education of youth.

- A nation recruits men more easily than it can retrieve its honour.

- Liberty and equality are magical words.

- We should wash our dirty linen at home.

- We are nothing but by the law.

- Military despotism represses generous sentiments, priestly tyranny stifles them.

- Timid and cowardly soldiers cause the loss of a nation's independence; but pusillanimous magistrates destroy the empire of the laws, the rights of the throne, and even social order itself.

- To extraordinary circumstances we must apply extraordinary remedies.

- In these days the invention of printing, and the diffusion of knowledge, render historical calumnies a little less dangerous: truth will always prevail in the long run, but how slow its progress!

On Politics & Power

- Good and decent people must be protected and persuaded by gentle means, but the rabble must be led by terror.

- Every beggar shall be arrested. But to arrest a beggar merely in order to put him in jail would be barbarous and absurd. He should be arrested for the sole purpose of teaching him how to earn a living by his work.

- I have come to realise that men are not born to be free.

- Ten people who speak make more noise than ten thousand who are silent.

- A man will fight harder for his interests than for his rights.

- God! How men of letters are stupid.

- Time is the great art of man.

- It is the success which makes great men.

- Doctors will have more lives to answer for in the next world than even we generals.

- Never interrupt your enemy when he is making a mistake.

- Public opinion is the thermometer a monarch should constantly consult.

- Secrets travel fast in Paris.

- Men are more easily governed through their vices than their virtues.

- Men take only their needs into consideration, never their abilities.

- Men are moved by only two levers: fear and self interest.

- Be successful! I judge men only by the results of their actions.

- I like honest men of all colors.

- I start out by believing the worst.

- Our hour is marked, and no one can claim a moment of life beyond what fate has predestined.

- The herd seek out the great, not for their sake, but for their influence; and the great welcome them out of vanity or need.

- The stupid speak of the past, the wise of the present, and fools of the future.

- We must laugh at man to avoid crying for him.

- The French complain of everything, and always.

- He who fears being conquered is sure of defeat.

- A people that is able to say everything, becomes able to do everything.

- The crowd which follows me with admiration, would run with the same eagerness were I marching to the Guillotine.

- The public spirit is in the hands of the man who knows how to make use of it.

- Public esteem is the recompense of honest men.

- Public opinion is a mysterious and invisible power, to which everything must yield. There is nothing more fickle, more vague, or more powerful; yet capricious as it is, it is nevertheless much more often true, reasonable, and just, than we imagine.

- To attach no importance to public opinion, is a proof that you do not merit its suffrage.

- What is the government? Nothing, unless supported by opinion.

- Power is founded upon opinion.

On War

- Read over and over again the campaigns of Alexander, Hannibal, Caesar, Gustavus, Turenne, Eugene and Frederic…. This is the only way to become a great general and master the secrets of the art of war.

- How many things apparently impossible have nevertheless been performed by resolute men who had no alternative but death.

- Two armies are two bodies which meet and try to frighten each other.

- I love a brave soldier who has undergone the baptism of fire.

- The secret of war lies in the communications.

- To have good soldiers, a nation must always be at war.

- The moral is to the physical as three to one.

- Victory belongs to the most persevering.

- The torment of precautions often exceeds the dangers to be avoided. It is sometimes better to abandon one's self to destiny.

- Every soldier carries a marshal's baton in his pack.

- If they want peace, nations should avoid the pin-pricks that precede cannon-shots.

- Doctors will have more lives to answer for in the next world than even we generals.

- An army marches on its stomach.

- You must not fight too often with one enemy, or you will teach him all your art of war.

- There are only two forces in the world, the sword and the spirit. In the long run the sword will always be conquered by the spirit.

- In war there is but one favorable moment; the great art is to seize it!

- One bad general is worth two good ones.

- Soldiers generally win battles; generals get credit for them.

- There are certain things in war of which the commander alone comprehends the importance. Nothing but his superior firmness and ability can subdue and surmount all difficulties.

- He that makes war without many mistakes has not made war very long.

- The most important qualification of a soldier is fortitude under fatigue and privation. Courage is only second; hardship, poverty and want are the best school for a soldier.

- In time of revolution, with perseverance and courage, a soldier should think nothing impossible.

- God is on the side with the best artillery

- An army's effectiveness depends on its size, training, experience, and morale, and morale is worth more than any of the other factors combined.

- Between a battle lost and a battle won, the distance is immense and there stand empires.

- If you had seen one day of war, you would pray to God that you would never see another.

- In war, three-quarters turns on personal character and relations; the balance of manpower and materials counts only for the remaining quarter.

- Strategy is the art of making use of time and space. I am less concerned about the later than the former. Space we can recover, lost time never.

- Courage is like love: it must have hope for nourishment.

- It would be a joke if the conduct of the victor had to be justified to the vanquished.

- In war, as in politics, no evil—even if it is permissible under the rules—is excusable unless it is absolutely necessary. Everything beyond that is a crime.

- Remember, gentlemen, what a Roman emperor said: The corpse of an enemy always smells sweet.

- If you wage war, do it energetically and with severity. This is the only way to make it shorter and consequently less inhuman.

- There are in Europe many good generals, but they see too many things at once. I see one thing, namely the enemy's main body. I try to crush it, confident that secondary matters will then settle themselves.

- There is no man more pusillanimous than I when I am planning a campaign. I purposely exaggerate all the dangers and all the calamities that the circumstances make possible. I am in a thoroughly painful state of agitation. This does not keep me from looking quite serene in front of my entourage; I am like an unmarried girl laboring with child. Once I have made up my mind, everything is forgotten except what leads to success.

- It should not be believed that a march of three or four days in the wrong direction can be corrected by a countermarch. As a rule, this is to make two mistakes instead of one.

- In war, moral factors acount for three quarters of the whole; relative material strength accounts for only one quarter.

- The basic principle that we must follow in directing the armies of the Republic is this: that they must feed themselves on war at the expense of the enemy territory.

- Sometimes a single battle decides everything and sometimes, too, the slightest circumstance decides the issue of a battle. There is a moment in every battle at which the least manoeuvre is decisive and gives superiority, as one drop of water causes overflow.

- You do not get peace by shouting: Peace. Peace is a meaningless word; what we need is a glorious peace.

- What my enemies call a general peace is my destruction. What I call peace is merely the disarmament of my enemies. Am I not more moderate than they?

- If the art of war were nothing but the art of avoiding risks, glory would become the prey of mediocre minds. I have made all the calculations, fate will do the rest.

- He who makes war for National independence must be enabled to count upon the union of all resources, all the wishes, and the concurrence of all the National authorities.

- An Emperor confides in national soldiers, not in mercenaries.

- The fate of a Nation may sometimes depend upon the position of a fortress.

- Men soon get tired of shedding their blood for the advantage of a few individuals, who think they amply reward the soldiers' perils with the treasures they amass.

- It is the business of cavalry to follow up the victory, and to prevent the beaten army from rallying.

- The keys of a fortress are always well worth the retirement of the garrison when it is resolved to yield only on those conditions. On this principle it is always wiser to grant an honorable capitulation to a garrison which has made a vigorous resistance than to risk an assault.

- Charges of cavalry are equally useful at the beginning, the middle and the end of a battle. They should be made always, if possible, on the flanks of the infantry, escpecially when the latter is engaged in front.

- An army ought to only have one line of operation. This should be preserved with care, and never abandoned but in the last extremity.

- When you determine to risk a battle, reserve to yourself every possible chance of success, more particularly if you have to deal with an adversary of superior talent, for if you are beaten, even in the midst of your magazines and your communications, woe to the vanquished!

- When you have resolved to fight a battle, collect your whole force. Dispense with nothing. A single battalion sometimes decides the day.

- The transition from the defensive to the offensive is one of the most delicate operations in war.

- The first qualification of a soldier is fortitude under fatigue and privation. Courage is only the second; hardship, poverty, and want are the best school for a soldier.

- In war, the general alone can judge of certain arrangements. It depends on him alone to conquer difficulties by his own superior talents and resolution.

- Never lose sight of this maxim, that you should establish your cantonments at the most distant and best protected point from the enemy, especially where a surprise is possible. By this means you will have time to unite all your forces before he can attack you.

- Artillery is more essential to cavalry than to infantry, because cavalry has no fire for its defense, but depends on the sabre.

- A general-in-chief should ask himself several times in the day, 'What if the enemy were to appear now in my front, or on my right, or my left?"

- In war, the moral element and public opinion are half the battle.

- Unity of command is essential to the economy of time. Warfare in the field was like a siege: by directing all one's force to a single point a breach might be made, and the equilibrium of opposition destroyed.

- War must be made as intense and awful as possible in order to make it short, and thus to diminish its horrors.

- I believe one bad general to be worth two good ones.

- War is like government, a matter of tact.

- The art of war is to gain time when your strength is inferior.

- An army which cannot be regularly recruited is a doomed army.

- A soldier will fight long and hard for a bit of colored ribbon.

- Generals who save troops for the next day are always beaten.

- A man like me troubles himself little about a million men.

- Great battles are won with artillery.

- I have destroyed the enemy merely by marches.

- In war you see your own troubles; those of the enemy you cannot see. You must show confidence.

- My generals are a parcel of post inspectors.

- My enemies make appointments at my tomb.

- The worse the troops the greater the need of artillery.

- The spectacle of a field of battle after the combat, is sufficient to inspire Princes with the love of peace, and the horror of war.

- Much shedding of blood, many great actions, and triumphs, toil and perseverance are the end of all things human.

- Revolutions are good times for soldiers of talent and courage.

- It is easier to brave and threaten, than to conquer an enemy.

- Reprisals are but a sad resource.

- We should always go before our enemies with confidence, otherwise our apparent uneasiness inspires them with greater boldness.

On Genius

- Imagination rules the world.

- To do all that one is able to do, is to be a man; to do all that one would like to do, is to be a god.

- The first method is that of a schemer and leads only to mediocre results; the other method is the path of genius and changes the face of the world.

- Even when I am gone, I shall remain in people's minds the star of their rights, my name will be the war cry of their efforts, the motto of their hopes.

- Men of genius are meteors, intended to burn to light their century.

- Adversity is the midwife of genius.

- Genius is an infinite capacity for taking pains.

- The herd seek out the great, not for their sake, but for their influence; and the great welcome them out of vanity or need.

On Greatness

- Great men seldom fail in their most perilous enterprises.

- A great people may be killed, but they cannot be intimidated.

- Great men, for good, or for bad, resemble each other. Thus it were no sophistry to say: that the soul of Cartouche had something of the Great Condé in it. The revolution produced all sorts of ambitious characters.

- Great men are those who can subdue both good luck and fortune.

- He who fears being conquered is certain of defeat.

- Better not to have been born than to live without glory.

- All men are equal before God: wisdom, talents, and virtue are the only difference between them.

The Corsican:
A Diary of Napoleon's Life in His Own Words

1769–1795

August 15th, 1769. Birth at Ajaccio.
I was called Napoleon; that, for centuries past, had been the name given to the second son in our family.

April, 1779. Military school at Brienne.
I entered Brienne, and was happy. My mind was beginning to work; I was anxious to learn, to know, to get on; I devoured books. I soon became the talk of the school. I was admired, envied; I was conscious of my powers; I enjoyed my superiority.

October 12th, 1783. (To Charles Buonaparte.) My dear father: Your letter, as you may well imagine, gave me little enough pleasure; but as your return to Corsica is necessitated by your illness and by that of a family that is so near to me, I can but approve, and must try to console myself.

June 25th, 1784. My brother lacks the courage to face the dangers of action, and regards the military profession from the garrison point of view.

July 7th. My dear father arrived here on the 21st with Luciano and the two young ladies. Joseph is in the class of rhetoric, and could do better if he would only work.

October 29th. (At Brienne) every one said of me: That boy is no good except at geometry. I was not very popular. I was dry as parchment.

October 30th. Leaves Brienne for the Military College at Paris.

March 28th, 1785, Paris:
We have lost our father, the sole support of our youth. Our country has lost a keen, enlightened, and honest citizen. It was so decreed by the Supreme Being!

(To Madame Buonaparte.) My dear mother: It is for you to console us, the event demands it. Our affection, our devotion, will be doubled, to make you forget, so far as it is possible, the incalculable loss of a beloved husband.

October 30th. Second lieutenant of artillery, regiment of La Fère.

April 26th, 1786, Valence:
To-day Paoli enters his sixty-first year. The Corsicans have already, in a just cause, shaken off the yoke of the Genoese; they can do as much with that of the French. Amen!

May 3d. Always solitary among men, I am here, within doors, dreaming, and giving full vent to all my melancholy. To what will it drive me to-day? To thoughts of death. Still at the dawn of life, I may hope for many days to come. It is now six or seven years since I last saw my country. What madness, then, drives me to self-destruction? Doubtless it is the hollowness of life. If one is to die, why not kill one's self? What spectacle awaits me when I return to my own people? My compatriots laden with chains, and kissing in fear the hand that strikes them!

9th. Virtue and the love of truth are not enough to enable a man to argue against Rousseau. He was human; and so, one may easily believe, liable to error.

July 29th. (To M. Borde, bookseller, Geneva.) Sir:
This is to request you to forward me the Memoirs of Mme. de Valens (sic), sequel to the Confessions of J. J. Rousseau. Pray send me also the History of the Revolutions of Corsica, and a list of books you may have relating to the island of Corsica, or that you could get for me quickly. I will remit the correct amount on hearing from you. Address your letter: Monsieur Buonaparte, Officer of artillery, regiment of La Fère, Valence, Dauphiné.

September 20th, Lyons:
I leave Lyons with even more reluctance than I did Valence. I like the place so much, I would be content to spend the rest of my days here; but a man must follow his fate, and must accept the conditions of his profession. A soldier can be constant to nothing but his flag.

April 2d, 1787. Napoleone Buonaparte, second lieutenant in the regiment of La Fère artillery, begs Msgr. Marshal de Ségur for leave of absence for five and a half months from the 16th of May next.

November 22d, Paris:
I had just left the Italian Opera and was facing the walks of the Palais Royal. I had reached the iron gates when my eyes fell on a woman. The time of day, her appearance, her youth, all showed clearly enough what she was. I stared at her; she stopped. Her hesitation encouraged me, and I spoke to her...I spoke to her, I, who so loathe her vile trade, I, who have always felt myself contaminated by a single glance!...You will be cold, I said, how can you go out there?—Ah, Monsieur, hope keeps me warm. I must finish my evening.—The indifference with which she spoke, the calmness of her reply, aroused my interest, and I turned back with her.—You don't look very strong; I am surprised that you can stand doing what you do.—Well, Monsieur, one must do something for one's living.—That may be, but surely you could find some employment suited to your health?—No, Monsieur, I must earn the money.

I was interested, pleased; here at last was a woman who would answer my questions, a result which previously I had not always attained!

July 1st, 1788, Auxonne:
I have no interests outside my work. I get into full dress only once a week. Since my illness I sleep very little, incredibly little! I go to bed at ten, and am up at four. I have but one meal a day, a practice that agrees well with me.

April 1st, 1789. This year has begun hopefully for right thinkers. and after all these centuries of feudal barbarism and political slavery it is surprising to see how the word Liberty sets minds on fire that appeared to be demoralized under the influence of luxury, indulgence, and art. While France is being regenerated, what will become of us unfortunate Corsicans?

16th, Ajaccio:
My shattered health will prevent my return to the regiment before the 15th of October.

July 14th. Capture of the Bastille, French Revolution.

August 28th, 1790. Friday night a gibbet was erected on the quay with this inscription over it: La Lanterne de Paris.

February 6th, 1791, St. Vallier:
Ivy will cling to the first met tree, that, in a few words, is the whole history of love. What is love? The realization of his weakness that sooner or later pervades the solitary man, a sense both of his weakness and of his immortality:—the soul finds support, is doubled, is fortified; the blessed tears of sympathy flow,—there is love.

8th, Serve:
Everywhere the peasants stand firm; in Dauphiné, specially so. They are ready to die for the Constitution. The women are royalist. This is not surprising, for Liberty is lovelier than any of them and eclipses them all!

The Patriotic Club would do well to present Mirabeau with a complete Corsican dress, that is to say, cap, coat, breeches, dagger, pistol, and gun; it would make a fine impression.

April 24th, Auxonne:
Louis is studying hard, learning to write French; I am teaching him mathematics and geometry. He reads history. He will turn out extremely well. He has already acquired quite the French manner, polish, vivacity; he can enter an assembly, bow gracefully, propound the customary questions with all the seriousness and dignity of a man of thirty. I see well enough that he will turn out the best of us four. It must be said, however, that none of us has had so good an education.

June 1st. The royalist orators have undoubtedly done much towards overturning the monarchy, for after spending all their breath in empty argumentation, they invariably finish up by declaring that a republican government is impossible because it is impossible!

July 27th, Valence:
Is it to be war?

The country is full of zeal, of enthusiasm. Two weeks ago, in a meeting of twenty-two clubs from the three Departments, a petition was drawn up demanding that the king be brought to trial. At the banquet on the 14th, I proposed the health of the patriots of Auxonne.

September 20th, Corte, in Corsica:
M. Volney is here, and in a few days we shall start together on a tour of the island. M. de Volney's reputation in the republic of letters is founded on his Voyage in Egypt.

February 1st, 1792, Ajaccio:
In these stormy days the duty of a good Corsican is to remain at home. The general in command has offered me a commission as adjutant major of a volunteer battalion.

April. War of the First Coalition.

May 29th, Paris:
I arrived yesterday. Paris is in a state of grave agitation. The national guards on duty to protect the king at the Tuileries have been doubled.

There is a vast amount of desertion among army officers. From every point of view the situation is most critical.

June 14th. The country is distracted by fanatical parties; it is difficult to seize the thread of such complex events; how it will all turn out is more than I can guess, but the aspect of things is very revolutionary.

18th. No news of the army.

20th. Let us follow this rabble! Seven to eight thousand men, armed with pikes, axes, swords, guns, spits, pointed sticks, marched to the Assembly to present a petition. Thence they proceeded to the king. The garden of the Tuileries was closed, and was guarded by 15,000 national guards. They broke down the gates, entered the palace, placed guns in position opposite the king's lodging, smashed through four doors, and presented to the king two cockades, one white, the other tricolour. Choose,—they said,—reign here, or at Coblentz! The king stood it well, and placed a red cap on his head.

How could they let the rabble in (to the Palace yard)? They ought to have mowed down four or five hundred of them with cannon, and the others would still be running.

When I was told that Louis had put a red cap on his head I concluded that his reign was over, for in politics an act that degrades can never be lived down.

July 3d. I am bound to say that our leaders are a poor lot of men. Seeing the whole business close to, shows clearly enough how little worth while it is to attempt to win the favour of the people. Each one pursues his individual interest and tries to excel in horrors; intrigues are to-day as base as ever they. were. It is enough to destroy all ambition.

August 7th. All the symptoms are that violence will break out; many people are leaving Paris.

I have been working a good deal at astronomy during my stay here. It's a splendid amusement, and a superb branch of science; with my knowledge of mathematics it required very little effort to learn. It is a great acquisition.

10th. I lodge Rue du Mail, Place des Victoires. At the sound of the tocsin, and at the news that the Tuileries were attacked, I started for the Carrousel. Before I had got there, in the Rue des Petits Champs, I was passed by a mob of horrible looking fellows parading a head stuck on a pike. Thinking I looked too much of a gentleman, they wanted me to shout Vive la Nation! which I promptly did, as may easily be imagined.

The palace was being attacked by the vilest rabble. After the palace had been captured and the king had withdrawn to the Assembly, I ventured cautiously into the gardens. Never since that day, no, not on all my battlefields, have I had such an impression of masses of dead men as the Swiss then produced on me.

As I witnessed the storming of the Tuileries and the capture of the king, I was far from thinking that I should one day stand in his place, and that that palace would be.

After the victory of the Marseillais, I came across one who was on the point of killing a Garde du Corps. I said to him: Man of the South, let us save this unfortunate fellow!—Are you a Southerner?—Yes!—All right, we will save him!

September 22d. Proclamation of the French Republic.

October 18th, Ajaccio:
I wanted to get to Bonifacio to restore order, but the general has sent for me, and I shall have to go to Corte.

The latest news is to the effect that the enemy have evacuated Verdun and Longwy; our men are not going to sleep. Savoy and Nice are ours, Sardinia will soon be attacked.

January 11th, 1793, Olmette:
(To the municipal officials of Bonifacio.) We shall reach your city to-morrow, under orders from General Paoli. I shall have two companies with me. I know your good will and patriotism, and do not doubt you will bestir yourselves to provide for the troops.

Buonaparte,
Lieutenant-Colonel of the
National Volunteers of Ajaccio.

July. Revolt of southern France against the Republic.

August. The supper at Beaucaire.
I happened to be at Beaucaire on the last day of the fair, and chanced to sup with two merchants from Marseilles, one from Nimes, and a Montpellier manufacturer.

(The Soldier.) You see what civil war means; we rend, we hate, we kill one another! Why should you fear the army? The army respects Marseilles because no city has sacrificed more for the general good. Think better of us, and you will have no better friends. Believe me, shake off the yoke of the handful of rascals who are carrying you straight down the path of counter-revolution; reëstablish your old authorities; accept the constitution; and the army will immediately march off to make the Spaniards, who are too much puffed up with a few successes, dance the Carmagnole.

218th. Occupation of Toulon by the British.

September 16th, in front of Toulon.
It is the guns capture fortresses.

19th. Three days after my arrival the army had its artillery organized.

October 25th. The guns are beginning to do things.

November 14th. The plan for the capture of Toulon which I have presented to the generals is the only practical one.

28th. This is the battery of the men without fear!

29th. What is this young man's name?
(Junot!)
He will get on.
30th. The enemy, realizing the importance of the battery, attacked it in strong force, carried it, and spiked the guns. Half an hour later we recaptured it. General Dugommier fought with truly republican courage.

December 7th. We are much in the same position. The army is 30,000 strong.

17th. Go and rest, we have captured Toulon; day after to-morrow you shall sleep there.

24th. The enemy beat a very hasty retreat. We have captured most of their baggage. If the wind had held them up another four hours, they were lost.

January 4th, 1794, Marseilles:
I shall have guns placed at the fort so as to command the city. The batteries are in an absurd state.

20th. Within a fortnight I hope to get the coast from the Rhine to the Var in good shape.

February 12th. They have spent lots of money on the coast and made a bad job of it.

April 1st. In command of the artillery, army of the Alps.

2d. We open the campaign with 30,000 men.

June 20th. The army's objective is the valley of the Stura.

July 23d. Revolution of Thermidor.

August 7th, Antibes:
(To the representatives Albitte and Saliceti.) You have relieved me from duty and ordered me under arrest. You have branded me without a sentence, or sentenced me without a hearing. Have I not, ever since the Revolution began, constantly shown my devotion to right principles? Have I not taken my share in the struggle both against the internal foe and, as a soldier, against the foreigner? I have sacrificed everything for the republic. I served at the siege of Toulon with some distinction, and with the army I earned my share of laurels at the capture of Saorgio.

Saliceti, you have known me five years. What have you seen in me that is suspect to the Revolution?

14th. (To the representatives of the people.) Citizens, herewith you will find my replies to your four questions. Since appearing to have forfeited the esteem of free men, my conscience enables me to remain calm, but my heart is torn, and I feel that, with a cool head but a warm heart, I cannot endure a life that is under the cloud of suspicion.

19th. (To Junot.) I appreciate all the friendliness of the offer you make me, my dear Junot; you know long since all the friendship I feel for you, and that you can count on it. Men may be unjust to me, but my innocence remains. My conscience is easy, therefore do nothing; you would only compromise me.

March 22d, 1795, Paris:
(To Junot.) You have nothing, save your lieutenant's shoulder-strap. Paulette hasn't even that. Sum up; you have nothing; she has nothing; what is the total?—Nothing. You therefore cannot marry just at present; we must wait. Perhaps we shall see better days, my friend!

April 1st. Saliceti has done me a grievous injury. He broke my career just as it was opening out. He withered my ideas of glory on their stem. That man is my evil genius. No, I can forgive; but forget,—that is another matter.

May 18th. Day of the 1st of Prairial.
If we continue to drag our revolution through the mud in this way, one will soon be ashamed of being a Frenchman. (Barras) is at this moment at the end of the boulevard with a considerable body of troops, and intends, so he told me, to open with shell. I advised him not to do it.

June 22d. I am appointed brigadier-general in the army of the West. I am ill, which compels me to ask for leave.

To-day the Constitution is being read in the Convention.

July 1st. In the present situation of Europe the King of Sardinia obviously must want peace. We must carry the war into his country, and manœuvre the Austrians into such a position that we can eventually operate against them. The army of Italy must drive the enemy from Loano, threaten Piedmont, conquer Lombardy, penetrate into the Tyrol, and effect its junction with the army of the Rhine.

12th. There is an astounding revival of luxury, pleasure, and art. The women are everywhere.

18th. Junot is here, going the pace, and spending as much of his father's money as he can. Marmont is at the siege of Mainz.

24th. The news from the South is distressing. Let us hope for a strong and well-organized government that will put a stop to all this.

25th. (To Joseph Buonaparte). It must be on purpose that you make no mention of Desirée (Clary); I don't even know if she is still alive.

August 17th. I have been ordered for duty in the army of the Vendée: I refused.

20th. I am appointed to the topographical bureau of the Committee of Public Safety. I could, for the asking, get sent to Turkey as general to reorganize the artillery of the Grand Seignior.

Everything is quiet here for the moment, but it may be that a storm is brewing.

25th. (To Joseph.) I hope a consulship can be obtained for you.

The primaries are to be convened to elect a third of the legislature.

29th. The army of the Interior has accepted the Constitution. Some of the Sections of Paris are demanding that the troops be withdrawn, and the decree repealed.

September 5th. The Committee thinks that I cannot leave France so long as the war continues. I shall be reinstated in the artillery.

If I stay here, I may possibly get bitten with the notion of getting married.

6th. (To Joseph.) The consulship of Chio is vacant; but you told me you had no use for an island. I hope for something better.

To-day the primary assemblies for Paris are meeting; there are many posters, but we hope all will go off quietly. I am very pleased with Louis; he fulfils all my hopes; he's a good fellow, but then he is built after the same fashion as I am: vivacity, wit, health, talent, trustworthiness, benevolence,—he has everything for him. You know, my dear fellow, that I live only for the happiness of my own family.

7th. All is quiet. It is a mistake to view the situation tragically. The Republic, powerful abroad, will soon succeed in reëstablishing order at home.

11th. The primary assemblies refuse to accept the decree.

27th. There is considerable uneasiness, and much inflammable material.

October 3d. (11 Vendémiaire.)
Paris is ablaze since this morning. I must be cautious. I have little enough influence.

4th. (12. Vendémiaire.)
I am going out to get news.

I found several deputies in a state of great alarm, among others Cambacérès. They expected to be attacked next day, and didn't know what to do; my reply was, Give me cannon. This suggestion paralyzed them.

The night passed, and no decision come to.

5th (13 Vendémiaire), morning:
The news was very bad. They then put the matter in my hands, and set to discussing whether they had the right to repel force by force. Do you intend to wait,—said I,—until the people give you permission to fire at them? You have appointed me, and I am compromised; it is only fair that I should do the business my own way.—On that I left the lawyers to drown themselves in their own flood of words, and got the troops on the move.

6th, 2 a. m.:
(To Joseph.) At last, it's all over, and my first thought is to send you the news. The royalists were getting bolder every day. The Convention had ordered the Section Lepelletier to be disarmed; but the Section resisted the troops. Menou was immediately relieved from duty. The Convention appointed Barras to command the army; and the Committees selected me as second in command. We made our arrangements; the enemy attacked us; we killed great numbers of them. We have disarmed the Sections. Good fortune is with me. My love to Eugénie and to Julie.

11th. I am appointed general second in command of the army of the Interior.

20th. A citoyen Billon has asked for Paulette's hand; he has no money; I have written to Mamma that it is out of the question.

25th. I am appointed to command in chief the army of the Interior.

1796

March 9th. This nineteenth day of the month of Ventôse in the fourth year of the Republic, this deed of marriage between Napoleone Buonaparte, general-in-chief of the army of the Interior, twenty-eight years of age, born at Ajaccio, Department of Corsica domiciled in Paris, Rue d'Antin, son of Charles Buonaparte, gentleman, and of Letizia Ramolini; and Marie Joseph Rose Detascher, twenty-eight years of age, born in the island of Martinique, in the Windward Islands, domiciled in Paris, Rue Chantereine, daughter of Joseph Gaspard Detascher, captain of dragoons, and of Rose Claire Desvergers de Lannois, his wife.

11th. (To the Directoire.) I had asked citoyen Barras to inform the Directoire of my marriage with the citoyenne Tascher Beauharnais. The trust which the Directoire has reposed in me made it a duty to inform it of all my actions. This is one more bond that draws me to our country; it is a pledge of my firm resolve to seek salvation only in the Republic.

21st. Departure for Italy.

27th, Nice:
Soldiers! you are naked and starving; the Government owes you much and can give you nothing. Among these rocks, your patience, your courage, are admirable; but not one ray of glory can shine down on you. I will lead you into the most fertile plain of the earth. Wealthy cities, great provinces, will be in your power; and there await you honour, glory, and riches. Soldiers of Italy, will your courage, will your constancy fail?

28th. (To the Directoire.) I joined the army a few days ago; yesterday I assumed command. I have informed the troops, in your name, of your satisfaction with their conduct and their patience. This pleased the men, and especially the officers, very much. One battalion has mutinied, because it had neither boots nor pay. I ordered the grenadiers under arrest.

29th. General Alexandre Berthier is appointed chief of staff to the army of Italy.

April 6th, Albenga:
I have shifted headquarters to Albenga. This movement has drawn the enemy out of winter quarters. They have moved their outposts up to Dego. The King of Sardinia is displaying much activity.

The destitution of the army is alarming. I have many difficulties to overcome, but it can be done. The absolute misery of the army has broken its discipline, and without discipline there can be no victories. The Piedmontese are 40,000 strong in infantry; the Austrians have 34,000. I have actually 45,000 men.

At Oneglia I found some statuary of considerable value. I ordered an auction, from which we may derive 30,000 or 40,000 francs.

11th. Fighting began at eight o'clock this morning. I shall attack. To-morrow we will advance on the enemy all along our right.

12th, Carcare:
Vive la République! This day, 23d of Germinal, the divisions of General Masséna and of General Laharpe attacked the Austrians, who, under the command of General Beaulieu, numbered 13,000, and occupied the important position of Montenotte. The republicans defeated the Austrians completely, killing and wounding 3000 men.

At night:
I have just been over the battlefield; there were prisoners and dead on all sides.

14th. (To the Directoire.) The campaign of Italy has begun. I owe you an account of the battle of Montenotte.

General Beaulieu, with one division, attacked the right of our army. On the (12th) at daybreak, Beaulieu and Laharpe engaged, when Masséna appeared on the enemy's flank and rear, spreading destruction and panic. The rout of the enemy was complete.

15th. (To the Directoire.) To-day I have to inform you of the battle of Millesimo. The enemy, surrounded on all sides, had no time even to surrender; our columns scattered death, panic, and flight. General Provera, with the body he commanded, surrendered at Cosseria. Our soldiers pursued the enemy on all sides unflaggingly. We have in this glorious battle taken 7000 to 9000 prisoners, 22 guns, and 15 flags.

The chef de brigade of the 39th having been killed, I have appointed citoyen Lannes to replace him.

16th. (To the Directoire.) To-day I must render you an account of our action at Dego. We estimate the enemy's loss at 2000 men. Major Murat contributed largely to our success.

The enemy are much stronger than we anticipated, fight well, and outnumber us in cavalry and artillery. I have not a single engineer officer to reconnoitre Ceva, and must go there myself.

22d, Lesegno:
(To the Directoire.) I have to render account of the action at Mondovi and of our occupation of that city. Driven from Ceya, the Piedmontese army took up a position at the confluence of the Corsaglia and the Tanaro, their right on Vico, their centre on the Bicocca. General Serrurier attacked their right, crossed the bridge under fire, and after three hours' fighting drove them from the village. The enemy's position was very strong. We spent the day making demonstrations so as to cover our real intentions. My object was to throw myself on Mondovi. However, at two in the morning, General Colli began his retreat in the direction of that city. At daybreak the struggle began in the village of Vico. The enemy lost 1800 men, 11 flags, and 8 guns. The 20th dragoons, led into action by citoyen Murat, distinguished itself.

(To the army.) The general in command congratulates the army on its courage, and on its daily successes against the enemy; but he has seen with horror the frightful pillage committed by degraded individuals who rejoin their corps after the battle is over to indulge in excesses that disgrace the army and France. It is therefore ordered: the generals shall, within twenty-four hours, hand in a report on the conduct of all commanding officers under their orders. The generals are empowered to relieve from duty all officers who, by their example, have countenanced the horrible pillage of these last few days. Their names shall be sent to their Departments so that they may incur the contempt of their fellow citizens.

23d, Carrù:
(To General Colli.) Sir: The Directoire has reserved to itself the right of negotiating peace; the plenipotentiaries of the king your master must therefore proceed to Paris. The military and moral situation of the two armies makes an armistice pure and simple entirely out of the question. I must decline, on vague presumptions, to suspend my march. There is, however, a way of attaining your object; it is by placing me in possession of Coni, Alessandria, and Tortona. This proposal is a very moderate one.

24th. An armistice for one month, guaranteed by the possession of two fortresses, would be of great service to the Republic. It would give me time enough to over-run Austrian Lombardy.

(To the Directoire.) You cannot conceive the state that this army is in,—it has no bread, no discipline. Our lack of carts, our bad horses, our rapacious commissaries, have reduced us to absolute destitution. The life I lead is unbelievable; worn out with my day's work, I have to sit up all night to administer, and to proceed in person everywhere to restore order. Our starving soldiers commit excesses that make one ashamed to he a man. I shall make some terrible examples. I will restore order, or cease to command these bandits. I have to face 100,000 men with only 34,000 infantry and 3500 cavalry.

Citoyen Junot, my aide-de-camp, will present 21 flags to you. The army of Italy in sending you these standards, certificates of its valour, charges me to assure you of its devotion to the Constitution.

26th, Cherasco:
All goes well. The pillage has decreased. This first excess of an army that lacked everything is wearing off. The wretched men are excusable; they have reached the promised land, and cannot but be at it. To-morrow some of the men who have rifled a church will be shot. It is a painful thing to have to do, and costs me many pangs; horrors have been committed that make me shudder; fortunately the Piedmontese army in its retreat behaved even worse. This splendid country will be of great help to us; from Mondovi alone we can raise a million.

(To the army.) Soldiers! In fifteen days you have won six victories, captured twenty-one flags, fifty-five guns, several fortresses, conquered the richest part of

Piedmont; you have made 15,000 prisoners; you have killed or wounded nearly 10,000 men.

Until now you have fought for barren rocks. Lacking everything, you have accomplished everything. You have won battles without cannon, crossed rivers without bridges, made forced marches without boots, bivouacked without brandy, and often without bread. Only the phalanx of the Republic, only the soldiers of Liberty, could endure the things that you have suffered.

But, soldiers, you have really done nothing, if there still lies a task before you. As yet, neither Milan nor Turin is yours. Our country has the right to expect great things of you; will you be worthy of that trust? There are more battles before you, more cities to capture, more rivers to cross. You all burn to carry forward the glory of the French people; to dictate a glorious peace; and to be able, when you return to your villages, to exclaim with pride: "I belonged to the conquering army of Italy!

Friends, that conquest, I promise, shall be yours; but there is a condition you must swear to observe: to respect the people you are liberating; to repress horrible pillage. All plunderers will be shot without mercy.

People of Italy, the French army is here to break your chains; you may greet it with confidence.

28th. (To the Directoire.) You will find herewith the armistice agreed on last night between General La Tour, commanding the Piedmontese army, and myself. Ceva, Coni, and Alessandria are in our power. If you should fail to come to a settlement with Sardinia, I can hold these fortresses and march on Turin. Meanwhile, to-morrow I move against Beaulieu. I shall seize Lombardy, and before a month has passed I expect to be in the mountains of the Tyrol. As to Sardinia, you can dictate whatever conditions of peace you choose, since I am in possession of the chief fortresses. If you will continue to trust me and to give my plans your approval, success is certain: Italy is yours.

(To General Laharpe.) Start for Acqui at once, and pursue the Austrians; they are withdrawing and will cross the Po.

29th. (To the Directoire.) My columns are moving; Beaulieu is retreating; I hope I shall catch him. I shall raise several millions from the Duke of Parma. He will send you proposals for peace, but don't be in a hurry; give me time to make him pay the expenses of the campaign. If you should not conclude peace with the King of Sardinia, if your intention is to dethrone him, you must play with him for several weeks, and notify me at once; I can then seize Valenza and march on Turin.

May 1st, Acqui:
(To Faypoult, at Genoa.) We are at Acqui since yesterday. Beaulieu's retreat is so rapid that we have failed to reach him. Send me a memorandum, geographical, historical, political, and topographical, on the imperial fiefs in the neighbourhood of Genoa. Send me a memorandum on the Dukes of Parma, of Piacenza, and of Modena, their troops, fortresses, and resources; send me also a schedule of the pictures, statues, cabinets, and curios of Milan, Parma, Piacenza, Modena, and Bologna. The Duke of Parma was to have concurred in the peace we made with Spain; how was it this was not done?

Send 6000 pairs of boots to Tortona immediately.

6th, Tortona:
(To the Directoire.) Yesterday we were cannonading the Austrians beyond the Po. This river is wide and very difficult to cross. My plan is to cross it as near Milan as possible, so as to leave no further obstacle between me and that capital. To-day we march on Piacenza. If I were to wait for a couple of pontoon bridges, I am certain we should not get over in July; my plan is to cross with rafts and flying bridges.

It would be of advantage if you could send me three or four artists of repute to select the things we want to send to Paris.

Since the campaign opened, General Berthier, chief of staff, has been constantly by my side in action, and at night at his desk; it is impossible to display greater energy, together with zeal, courage, and technical knowledge.

7th. Castel San Giovanni:
The Austrian army had intrenched itself to cover the Milanese. After various military and diplomatic feints to persuade it that I intended to cross at Valenza, I

have made a forced march with 5000 grenadiers and 1500 horse on Castel San Giovanni.

9 a. m. At the crossing of the Po.
We have reached the crossing of the Po, where the enemy shows about 150 cavalry; the infantry must still be in the direction of Valenza. The general-in-chief is therefore determined to cross at once with the advance guard.

We jumped into the boats. Chef de brigade Lannes, brave and intelligent, was first on the bank. The divisions of the army are hurrying their march, since our movement is now unmasked.

Afternoon:
All the advance guard and Laharpe's division are across the Po.

8th. Beaulieu, perceiving our movement, realizes too late that his fortifications at Pavia are useless, and that the French republicans are not so foolish as was Francis I!

9th. (To Carnot.) Beaulieu has been surprised; his moves are weak, and he constantly walks into the traps that are set for him. What we have captured from the enemy is incalculable. I am sending you twenty pictures by the greatest masters, Correggio, Michael Angelo. I owe you special thanks for your attentions to my wife; I commend her to your care; I love her madly. I hope, if all goes well, to send about ten millions to Paris, which might be useful for the army of the Rhine. Since Stengel's death I have not one single general officer of artillery who fights. I need two or three adjutant-generals who have dash and a firm resolve not to execute scientific retreats.

At night:
The enemy is retreating on Lodi.

11th, Lodi:
We made our way into Lodi, and found the bridge swept by 30 guns. The fire was very hot. As soon as the troops got up they were formed in solid column, supported by the grenadier battalions, the men cheering for the Republic. The bridge, 200 yards in length, was at tacked. The enemy's fire was terrible. The head of our column appeared to waver. Generals Berthier, Masséna, Lannes,

rushed to the front and carried uncertain fortune with them. Our stalwart column broke down all resistance; in a flash, the hostile army was scattered.

The battle of Lodi has conquered Lombardy for the Republic.

Evening: (The grenadiers acclaim General Bonaparte as the little corporal.)

14th. (To the Directoire.) Yesterday I sent one division to Milan; Beaulieu is at Mantua.

I think it unwise to divide the army of Italy in two; it is against the interests of the Republic to give it to two generals. The move on Rome, Leghorn, Naples, is a small matter. There should not only be a single general, but he should be unfettered in his judgment and operations. I have conducted this campaign without consulting any one; I should have done no good had I been guided by another's opinions. I have had some measure of success because my moves have been as quick as my thoughts. If you put shackles on me, you must be prepared for poor results. Every man has his own fashion of making war. General Kellermann has had a longer experience and will do better than I; but he and I together will only make a mess of it. If I am to render real service to the country, I must have your absolute confidence. I feel that it requires much courage to write you this letter; it would be so easy to accuse me of ambition or pride.

17th, Milan:
The tricolour flag floats over Milan, Pavia, Como, and all the cities of Lombardy. Orders are issued to equip the divisions with all they need, so that they may soon resume active operations and carry them through with the rapidity and dash that have given us our victories.

I have sent off to Tortona at least two millions' worth of jewels and silver ingots.

20th. Soldiers! You have rolled down from the Apennines like a torrent; you have overthrown and scattered all that opposed your advance. Milan is yours, and the republican flag floats over Lombardy. The Po, the Ticino, the Adda, could not stay your advance for a single day. Yes, soldiers, you have accomplished much; but is there nothing left to do? Come, forward! We have more forced marches to make, more enemies to conquer, more laurels to win, more wrongs for which to claim revenge.

21st. We have imposed 20 millions of francs on the Milanese.

22d. The troops are marching towards the passes of the Tyrol. The Austrian army receives reinforcements daily.

25th, 2 a. m.:
(To General Berthier.) I am just back from halfway to Pavia. We met about a thousand peasants at Binasco, and defeated them. After killing a hundred or so, we burned the village, a terrible example which will have the desired effect; in an hour we shall start for Pavia, where the report is that our men are still holding out.

(To the inhabitants of Lombardy.) A misguided mob, with no real means of defence, has committed acts of violence in several districts. Such incredible folly deserves compassion; this unhappy people is misled and drawn to its own destruction. Those who do not lay their arms down within 24 hours will be treated as rebels; their villages will be burnt. May their eyes be opened by the terrible example of Binasco! Every city and village that continues in rebellion will meet with the same fate.

General Despinoy will immediately assemble a court-martial to sentence, in the course of the day, persons caught with arms in their possession during the riot that has occurred in Milan, and to have those who are convicted of participation in the insurrection shot. The execution is to be carried out within 24 hours.

26th, Pavia:
At daybreak I marched on Pavia. The city appeared to be defended by a large mass of people, and to be in a state of defence; the citadel had been captured and our soldiers were prisoners. I ordered the guns up. General Dommartin formed the 6th grenadiers in solid column, axe in hand, and two field pieces at the head. The gates were broken in; the mob scattered to the cellars and to the roofs, at tempting in vain, by throwing down tiles, to prevent our entering the streets. I had the town councillors shot. To-day everything is quite calm.

28th, Brescia:
Any village in which the tocsin is rung shall be burned down.

We are now on the territory of the Venetian republic, a neutral country, in which individuals and property must be rigidly respected.

30th, Valeggio:
To-day Masséna's and Augereau's divisions attacked the passage of the Mincio. The enemy have been completely defeated along the line of this river, which was crossed by a part of our troops with water up to their armpits. The enemy left us five guns and the store of medicines for their ambulances. They are in full retreat all along the line.

(To Carnot.) I am in despair; my wife doesn't come, some lover keeps her in Paris. I curse all women, but I embrace my excellent friends.

31st, Peschiera:
The enemy has crossed the Adige, and only the garrison of Mantua remains, which will soon be destroyed by the unhealthiness of its marshes! Vive la République! The Austrians are driven entirely out of Italy.

June 1st. (To the Directoire.) I could not name all the soldiers who have distinguished themselves for courage. Nothing could equal their bravery. You would suppose that once at their bivouac they would at least sleep; nothing of the sort,—every man sets to work spinning yarns or drawing up the next day's plan of operations. The other day I was watching a demi-brigade filing by, a light infantryman steps up to my horse: General,—says he,—we must do so and so.—Rascal, I answered, shut your mouth, will you?—He promptly vanished; I sent for him in vain; what he had said was precisely what I had given orders to do.

I am sending off from Milan to-morrow one hundred carriage horses, the finest that could be found in Lombardy; they will replace the mediocre backs that draw your carriages at present.

5th, Roverbella:
The general-in-chief has gone to Milan; headquarters remain at Roverbella.

7th, Milan:
(To the Directoire.) When Beaulieu perceived that we were marching on the Mincio, he seized the fortress of Peschiera, which belongs to the Venetians. Two days later, the action at Borghetto and the passage of the Mincio placed it in our

hands. The proveditore came to offer me hasty explanations; I received him stiffly, and declared that I would march on Venice in person to protest to the Senate against so patent an act of bad faith. There was great alarm in Venice. If you wish to extract 5 or 6 millions from Venice, here is a pretext all ready to your hand. If your policy goes beyond this, my advice would be to keep the matter open and to wait for a favourable moment, for we must not have everybody on our hands at once.

I shall soon be at Bologna. Is it your wish that I should then grant an armistice to the Pope, in return for 25 millions in money, 5 millions in foodstuffs, 300 pictures, statues and MSS. in proportion?

8th. We have surrounded the city of Mantua. This fortress is unapproachable for the moment because of the flooded state of the rivers.

11th. Lombardy is perfectly quiet. Political songs are in every mouth. The people are becoming used to Liberty. It might be worth while to form a Lombard battalion.

The general-in-chief understands that, notwithstanding his repeated orders, looting still continues. Such infamous conduct makes it impossible longer to delay employing drastic methods. It is therefore ordered that any soldier, of whatsoever rank, caught in the act, shall be shot.

15th, Tortona:
The Emperor is saying to everybody that in August he will reënter Italy. His troops are everywhere on the march, even in Poland.

(To Faypoult, at Genoa.) I am sending you General Murat, my aide-de-camp; please take him to the Senate immediately so that he may present the letter which he will show you. If you were to present it, it would take two weeks to get an answer, and it is necessary to communicate after a fashion that is more likely to electrify these gentlemen.

20th, Bologna:
We are in Bologna since yesterday. We have made 700 prisoners and found 40 guns. The Cardinal Legate is a prisoner of war. Chef de brigade Lannes commands the infantry of the advance guard; General Murat the advance guard itself.

21st. The Modena pictures have started. Citoyen Barthélemy is now engaged selecting the Bologna ones. He expects to take about fifty. Monge, Berthollet, and Thouin are at Pavia, at work adding to our natural history specimens. I hope they will not overlook a complete collection of snakes which seemed to be well worth the journey.

An intercepted letter from Vienna states that General Wurmser will command the army in Italy. One division has already occupied the passes of the Grisons.

I have given the Cardinal Legate leave to proceed to Rome. I told him that if the Pope would send us peace proposals and would pay a contribution of war promptly, he might perhaps find a support yet in the French Republic. The heat is excessive; and we have not one moment to spare for recrossing the Po and concentrating our troops against the Austrians. I shall be at Leghorn on the 29th; I hope we shall have concluded an armistice with the Pope by then. As we shall have concluded this armistice more with the dog days than with the Pope, my feeling is against making peace, so that in September, if we prosper, we can seize Rome.

26th, Pistoja:
(To the Directoire.) You will find herewith the conditions of the armistice with the Pope. M. D'Azara had the impudence to offer us five millions in money and three millions in foodstuffs. Seeing he could get no abatement out of me, he turned to the Government Commissioners, and worked them so well that he discovered our secret, which is the impossibility of our marching to Rome. On that we could only get 20 millions out of him, by making a march on Ravenna. I had always stipulated that we should get the treasure of Our Lady of Loretto, which, I thought, was agreed; but he so twisted and turned that we had to accept one million instead. This manner of negotiating three handed is very prejudicial to the interests of the Republic. This negotiation, in which the Republic has lost 10 millions, has been extremely disagreeable to me. There was no difficulty as to the other conditions save for the MSS., which they did not want to give up; on that score, too, we had to come down from two or three thousand to five hundred.

July 2d, Bologna:
I saw at Florence the famous Venus, for which there should be room in our Museum, and a collection of anatomical models in wax which it would be desir-

able to acquire. Fontana is willing to undertake having these copied for us. It would cost little, and would be of advantage to us in a matter so useful to humanity.

Our art commissioners behave well and work hard. The scientists have garnered a fine harvest at Pavia.

I am starting for Mantua. I expect to open the trenches on the 9th. The enemy will probably manœuvre to relieve the fortress; we shall then engage, if necessary.

5th, Roverbella:
(To General Despinoy.) Hurry on the artillery; don't go to sleep among the pleasures of Milan; and whatever you do, don't write letters to upset our poor chief of staff, who, ever since you mentioned a lovely actress who awaits him in Milan, is dying of impatience to get there.

(To Josephine.) I am dead tired. Please start at once for Verona; I need you, for I feel as though I were going to be seriously ill. A thousand kisses. I am in bed.

9th, Verona:
(To General Despinoy.) I am in a rage with every one at Milan. Nothing gets here, no artillery, no officers, no gunners. I am sending you an aide-de-camp to stir things up. In the present situation days equal centuries. There is a company of artillery I have been expecting this last century; it has stopped on the way. I had ordered 600 horses to Coni; they are all dead on the road I suppose, as I haven't heard a word of them.

11th, Marmirolo:
(To Faypoult.) I have not yet seen M. Cattaneo; when I do I shall not forget to put him to sleep, and to inspire the Senate with a little more confidence. The hour of Genoa has not struck, because the Austrians are growing in numbers and we shall soon have a battle. The policy of the Directoire as to Genoa does not as yet seem quite clear.

12th, Verona:
(To the Directoire.) Would it not be as well to start a little quarrel at once with the Minister of Venice in Paris, so that as soon as I have taken Mantua I can make an opportunity for asking them, as you desire I should, for several millions?

17th, Marmirolo:

(To Josephine.) I have received your letter, adorable friend, and it has filled my heart with joy. I thank you for troubling to send me news of yourself. Since leaving you, I have been constantly sad. Your kisses, your tears, your playful jealousy, haunt my mind; and the charms of the incomparable Josephine set a bright and burning flame blazing in my heart and in my senses. When shall I be free from all worries, from all business, so as to spend my hours near you, with nothing to do but to love you, and nothing to think of but to tell it and to prove it you? Since I first knew you, I adore you more and more every day, which proves the untruth of La Bruyère's maxim, that love comes suddenly. All things in nature run their course, and vary in their growth. Ah! I implore you, let me witness some of your defects; be less beautiful, less amiable, less tender, less good,—above all, above all, never be jealous, never weep; your tears affect my reason and scorch my blood.

18th. I passed the night under arms. A bold and fortunate stroke would have given me Mantua; but the waters in the lake began to go down rapidly, so that the column in the boats was not able to disembark. I was in the village of Virgil, on the shore of the lake, by a silvery moonlight; and I could not cease thinking of Josephine for one moment.

19th. We attacked Mantua yesterday. We warmed it up with two batteries firing red-hot shot, and with mortars. All through the night the wretched city was blazing, a horrible but grand spectacle. We captured several outworks, and shall open our trenches to-night. I start tomorrow for Castiglione with headquarters, and expect to sleep there.

22d, Castiglione:

(To Josephine.) The situation of the army makes my presence here necessary; it is out of the question for me to go so far as Milan. Come, quickly, and join me; be happy and without fear.

29th, Montechiaro, morning:

The enemy have forced our positions at La Corona. An effort will be made for their recapture. We must attack them, and defeat them.

Afternoon: General Augereau is to retreat on Roverbella.

Roverbella, evening:
The fighting at La Corona makes it necessary to move the heavy baggage of the
army back to Milan by Cremona. I am expecting Berthier impatiently. The situation is decidedly critical. To-morrow will, I hope, turn out better for us.

Part of Masséna's division has been driven in. I am starting for Castelnovo with a
few demi-brigades. Perhaps we can reëstablish things.

30th, Castelnovo:
The army's unfortunate position is this: that the enemy have broken through our
lines at three points; they hold Rivoli; Masséna and Joubert have had to retreat;
Sauret has fallen back on Desenzano; the enemy have seized Brescia. Our communications with Milan are cut.

31st, Roverbella:
(To General Kilmaine.) It is absolutely necessary that you should attack the
enemy at Montechiaro. As I am in great baste, send a copy of this order to General Masséna..

Generals Augereau, Rampon, Cervoni, are marching on Montechiaro, which
their advance guard will reach at 4 a. m. The attack on Brescia must be renewed.
General Serrurier on receiving the order to evacuate (the lines of) Mantua will
occupy Marcaria.

August 2d, Brescia:
(To Saliceti.) For a moment fortune appeared to have turned against us. So much
has happened these last five or six days, that I can render you no complete
account; but at last, thanks to the battle of Lonato and my vigorous measures,
things are beginning to look better. I have raised the siege of Mantua, and am
here with nearly the whole army. I shall seize the first opportunity of engaging the
enemy, and thereby settling the fate of Italy. We are worn out; I have killed five
horses.

We have had reverses, but victory is inclined to rejoin our standards.

6th, Castiglione:

All through the 2d Wurmser was concentrating, drawing all the troops he could from Mantua, ranging them between Solferino and the Chiese. He brought together 25,000 men. The fate of Italy was still in suspense.

I also gave orders for concentrating my columns. I proceeded in person to Lonato; imagine my surprise when a flag came in summoning the commandant of Lonato to surrender because, so it was said, he was surrounded! There were, in point of fact, columns in touch with our outposts, and the Brescia road was cut. I realized that these troops could be only the débris of a division that had been cut off and was trying to force its way through our lines. The position was an awkward one, as I had not more than 1200 men with me. I ordered the officer with the flag to be brought before me and his eyes unbandaged. I informed him that if, within the space of eight minutes, his division had not surrendered, I should give no quarter. The officer was astounded at seeing me there, and a moment later his column laid down their arms; it was 4000 strong.

On the 3d, at daybreak, the armies were in presence. I ordered our troops to fall back so as to draw the enemy towards us while Serrurier was turning Wurmser's left.

The moment we saw Serrurier's division, I ordered Adjutant-General Verdier to attack. After a heavy cannonade the enemy's left was routed. Augereau attacked their centre; Masséna their right. We were victorious all along the line.

We have, therefore, in five days, fought another campaign. Wurmser has lost 70 guns, all his transport, 12,000 to 15,000 prisoners, 6000 killed and wounded.

At night, on the battlefield:

The moonlight was lovely; suddenly, from out the deep solitude of the night, a dog, crawling from under a dead man's clothes, dashed at us, but only to return quickly to his lair, howling plaintively. He licked his master's face, then turned on us again; it seemed as though he both asked for help and cried out for vengeance. Whether it was my mood, or the place, the hour, the incident itself, or something unaccountable, yet I can truly say that never anything on a field of battle moved me so much. Involuntarily I stopped to watch. Perhaps, said I to myself, the man has friends, and he lies here abandoned by all except his dog! What a lesson for nature to read us through the act of a dog!

8th, Verona:
Here we are, back in our old positions. The enemy's retreat has carried them far into the Tyrol. The Austrian army has vanished like a dream, and threatened Italy is at peace once more.

13th, Brescia:
The Court of Rome believed we were lost, and sent a legate to Ferrara. I have ordered this Cardinal to come to headquarters.

14th. (To the Directoire.) I think it as well, Citoyens Directeurs, to give you my opinion of the generals on duty with this army:

Berthier: talent, energy, courage, force, everything.

Augereau: strong character, courage, firmness, energy; has much experience of war, is liked by the soldiers, and is fortunate in what he undertakes.

Masséna: active, indefatigable; has boldness, instinct, and decision.

Serrurier: fights like a soldier; lacks initiative; firm; has too low an opinion of his men; is ill.

Despinoy: flabby, no energy, no boldness; is not made for warfare; is not liked by his men, and won't lead them into action; but high-minded, intelligent, and sound in politics; good for a home command.

Sauret: good, very good soldier; not enough education for a general; not lucky.

Abbatucci: not fit to command fifty men.

Garnier, Meunier, Casabianca: incapable; not fit to command a battalion in so lively and difficult a campaign as this.

Macquart: a good fellow; no talent; dash.

Gaultier: good for office work; has never seen active service.

How many blunders Murat has committed for the sake of placing his headquarters in a castle where there were women!

18th. My wife has arrived.

In four or five days the invincible army of Italy will open a new campaign. We shall force the passes of the Tyrol and conclude the war in Germany.

31st. (To Josephine.) I am just starting for Verona. I had expected a letter from you; it makes me most anxious. You were not very well when I left you; I beg of you don't keep me in such anxiety. Three days and no letter; I have written several. Your absence is horrible, the nights are long, boresome, dull, the days are monotonous.

To-day, alone with my thoughts, my work, my business, with men and their vain projects, I have not a single line from you to press to my heart.

The headquarters have moved; I start in an hour.

September 3d, Ala:
(To Josephine.) We are on the march, adorable friend. We have swept back the enemy's outposts. The troops are gay and in high spirits.

No letters from you,—I am really worried; however, I am told you are well, that you have even made an excursion on the lake of Como. Every day I am waiting impatiently a letter with news from you; you know how precious it will be. Away from you I don't exist; the happiness of life is at the side of my gentle Josephine. Think of me! Write often, very often; it's the only cure for absence.

6th, Trent:
6000 or 7000 prisoners, 25 guns, 7 flags, these are the results of the battle of Roveredo, one of the most successful of the campaign. At eight o'clock in the morning of the 5th Masséna occupied Trent. Wurmser abandoned the city to seek refuge towards Bassano. General Vaubois is pursuing the enemy. I shall reach Bassano on the 8th. If the enemy stand their ground, there will be a battle.

9th, Bassano:
Our march of twenty leagues in two days has completely disconcerted the enemy. We have captured five flags; chef de brigade Lannes took two with his own hand. We are pursuing a division of 8000 men, all that is left of the formidable army which, a month ago, threatened to drive us from Italy. In six days we have fought two battles and four engagements. We have captured 21 flags, and have taken 16,000 prisoners. We have covered more than 45 leagues.

Chef de brigade Lannes to be brigadier-general.

10th, Montebello:
(To Josephine.) We have never met with such great and steady successes. Italy, the Friuli, the Tyrol, are safe for the Republic. In a few days we shall meet; that will be the sweetest reward for all my troubles and labours. A thousand burning and loving kisses.

15th, Verona:
I like the Poles. The partition of Poland was an iniquitous deed that cannot stand. When I have finished the war in Italy, I will lead the French myself and force the Russians to reëstablish Poland.

17th. (To Josephine.) I write frequently, dear friend, and you very seldom. You are perverse, and wicked, very wicked, and your conduct is frivolous. Don't you think it's a little too bad to deceive a poor husband, a tender lover? Must he lose every claim because he is at a distance, loaded with work, fatigue, and care? Without his Josephine, without her love, what would there be left on earth? What could he live for? Adieu, adorable Josephine, one of these nights your door will burst open; the rush of a jealous man, and I am in your arms!

26th, Milan:
To Cardinal Mattei.) Sir, I am persuaded because of your high character, which is praised by every one, to permit you to return to Ferrara, and to draw the veil over your conduct last month.

I shall assume that you merely forgot for a moment a principle which your knowledge of the Scriptures will recall to you: that the priest who intervenes in political matters forfeits the privileges of his position. Return to your bishopric; practise virtue; and don't ever meddle in politics.

October 1st. The army of observation is 18,000 strong; the blockading army 9000. The Emperor will have 50,000 men in six weeks.

2d. (To the Directoire.) Venice is alarmed, and is hatching something with the King of Naples and the Pope. We can do nothing with them till Mantua is ours. The King of Naples has 60,000 men on foot.

The Grand Duke of Tuscany is a cipher, from every point of view.

The Duke of Parma behaves fairly well; he also is a cipher, from every point of view.

Rome is strong on the score of fanaticism.

If you insist on making war against Rome and Naples, we must be reinforced with 45,000 men. Keep negotiations with Rome open until we are ready to march on that proud city.

(To His Majesty the Emperor of Germany.) Your Majesty, Europe wants peace. This disastrous war has lasted too long. I have the honour of warning your Majesty that unless plenipotentiaries are sent to Paris, my orders from the Directoire are to fill in the port of Trieste. I hope that your Majesty will restore peace and repose to the world.

(To General Kellermann, at Lyons.) However much the 40th may be needed at Lyons, it is indispensable that it should be sent here. On the whole, I think it will pay better to risk some fisticuffs in Lyons, but to maintain our conquest of Italy.

Think this over, my dear general, with your usual patriotic sentiments; send us help as promptly as you can, if you want us to continue sending you 700,000 francs.

8th. (To the Directoire.) My health is so shattered that I must ask you to find me a successor.

11th. The national colours of the Lombard legion are green, white, and red.

Large bodies of the Emperor's troops are moving in the Tyrol.

The rains still cause much sickness in our ranks.

12th. (To the Directoire.) You doubtless assumed that your commissaries would steal, but do their work; they steal so impudently that had I a month to spare, there is not one I could not have shot. I am constantly having them arrested; but the judges are bought up: this is a fair, everything is for sale.

Thévenin is a thief; he flaunts his extravagance in our faces; he has sent me several fine horses that I needed; I took them, but cannot make him accept payment. Have him arrested; keep him six months in prison; he is good for 500,000 francs in cash.

The transport service is full of émigrés; they call themselves Royal-Charrois, and sport green collars under my very eyes. As you may imagine, I am constantly ordering arrests, but they have a habit of being where I am not.

The new agent appears to be an improvement on Thévenin. This, you understand, refers only to the thieves on a large scale. Would you believe that attempts are made to bribe my secretaries in my very office?

This denunciation is on my soul and conscience, as member of the jury. They are all spies. There is not an army agent who is not hoping for our defeat. and corresponding with the enemy; most of them are émigrés; it is they reveal our numbers; and I have to be more careful of them than of Wurmser.

17th, Modena:
Bologna, Modena, Reggio, and Ferrara have convened a congress. They are animated with the greatest enthusiasm and the purest patriotism; they see already Italy new made. A legion of 2500 men is being organized, equipped, clothed, and paid at their own expense, and without our intervention. Should these troops make a good showing, the consequences might be very important.

(To Josephine.) I was in the saddle all yesterday; to-day I am in bed. Fever and a bad headache have prevented me from writing to my adorable friend; but her letters have reached me, I have pressed them to my heart and to my lips, and the pangs of absence have vanished. For a moment I could imagine you at my side, no longer capricious and vexed, but gentle, tender, with all that graciousness and goodness that belong only to Josephine. It was a dream; guess whether it cured my fever. Your letters are as frigid as fifty years old; they suggest fifteen years of marriage. They convey the friendship, the sentiments, of the winter of life. Fie, Josephine! It is wicked, it is bad, it is treasonable of you! What more can you do to make me unhappy? Love me no more? Eh! That's already done! Hate me?—Well, let it be! Everything degrades save hatred. But indifference, with its marble pulse, its steady stare, its even step…!

21st, Ferrara:
(To Cardinal Mattei.) The Court of Rome has declined the offers of the Directoire; it is arming, it wants war; it shall have it. But I owe to my country, to humanity, to myself, one last effort to bring the Pope to sentiments more moderate and more in keeping with his sacred office. Go to Rome, see the Holy Father, enlighten him as to his true interests. An arrangement is still possible.

24th, Verona:
The bishop cardinal of Ferrara, a Roman prince with a revenue of 150,000 francs, gives all to the people and lives in his church. I have sent him to Rome on the pretext of negotiating, but really to get rid of him: he was delighted with his mission.

The Pope's folly is incredible. My intention is to get as far as Ancona under cover of the armistice, and there to declare myself. The art of the thing will be to keep on juggling for the present, so as to deceive the old fox.

25th. (To Carnot.) You will have seen by my brother's (Lucien) letter, what a hothead he is. He got himself compromised several times in '93, notwithstanding my constant advice. He was bound he would be a Jacobin.

As Corsica is now free you would oblige me by ordering him there, since his wrongheadedness makes his stay with the army of the Rhine no longer possible.

26th. I have appointed Muiron, Sulkowsky, and Duroc my aides-de-camp.

November 2d. (To Masséna.) Send me a galloper every three hours with news. We are ready to move forward.

3d. The enemy have crossed the Piave.

5th. Last night General Vaubois fell back on Roveredo.

7th, Rivoli:
Soldiers! I am no longer proud of you! You have shown no discipline, no steadiness, no courage; you have abandoned every position. Men of the 39th and of the 85th, you are no longer French soldiers. Chief of staff,—put on their flags: They are no longer of the army of Italy!

13th, Verona:
I am doing my duty, so is the army. My feelings are torn, but my conscience is at rest. Send us help! Send us help! The Minister of War sends me 6000 effectives, 3000 present; when they reach Milan, they number 1500.

At 3 o'clock in the morning of the 11th, hearing that the enemy had camped at Villanova, we marched from Verona. On the 12th, at dawn, we found the enemy.

They had 22,000 men, and we 12,000. General Augereau got possession of the village of Caldiero, and Masséna of the hill on the enemy's flank. But the rain was all for our opponents, (and they remained) masters of the position.

The weather is still bad. The army is harassed with fatigue and short of boots. I have led it into Verona, which we have just reached. For to-day we must rest the troops. To-morrow we can act.

The pick of the army is wounded; all our generals are off duty. The army of Italy, now a handful of men, is at the last gasp. Joubert, Lannes, Lanusse, Victor, Murat, Chabot, Dupuy, Rampon, Pijon, Chabran, St. Hilaire, are wounded. The few who are left feel death inevitable with such depleted ranks. Perhaps the knell of brave Augereau, of indomitable Masséna, of Berthier, my own, is about to ring.

We shall make one last effort.

(To Josephine.) I love you no longer; indeed, I hate you. You are a wicked woman, stupid, tactless, and foolish. You have stopped writing to me; you don't love your husband; you know how much pleasure your letters give him, and you don't write him so much as six haphazard lines.

How is your day spent, madame? What are the important matters that give you no time to write to your good lover? What passion stifles the love, the tender and constant love, that you promised him?

Seriously, I am anxious, dear friend, at not hearing from you. Quick, write me four pages, and some of those sweet things that fill my heart with sentiment and pleasure.

Soon I hope to clasp you in my arms, and to cover you with a million kisses as burning as the equator.

14th, Villafranca:
Should General Vaubois be attacked at Rivoli, he is to resist stiffly, and hang on till night. The army is making a movement to cross the Adige and attack the enemy to-morrow.

19th, Verona:
(To the Directoire.) I am so exhausted that I cannot give you the detail of the movements preceding the battle of Arcola, which has just decided the fate of Italy.

Getting information that Marshal Alvintzy was marching on Verona, I slipped away along the Adige with Augereau's and Masséna's divisions. At Ronco, I threw a bridge of boats. I hoped to strike at Villanova and capture the artillery and baggage of the enemy, and attack their rear. The enemy, however, had thrown several regiments into the village of Arcola, in the midst of the marshes and canals. This village held our advance guard in check all day. Generals Verdier, Bon, Verne, and Lannes were put out of action.

Augereau, seizing a flag, carried it to the end of the bridge. Cowards,—he shouted to his men,—do you fear death?—He staid there several minutes. We had got to carry the bridge. I went to the front myself. I asked the soldiers if they were still the victors of Lodi. My appearance produced such an impression on the men that I decided to attempt the passage once more. General Lannes, already twice wounded, returned and received a third wound. General Vignolle was wounded. We had to give up the frontal attack on the village, and wait for the arrival of General Guieu's column from Albaredo. It did not come up till night.

At earliest dawn the fighting was renewed with great spirit. On the left Masséna routed the enemy and pursued them to Arcola. The trophies of the battle of Arcola are 4000 or 5000 prisoners, 4 flags, 18 guns. Two of my aides-de-camp were killed, Elliot and Muiron, both officers of great promise.

(To Carnot.) There was never a more desperate fight than at Arcola. I have hardly any generals left; their devotion and courage are unparalleled. Lannes came to the battlefield from a sick-bed. On the first day he was twice wounded; he was lying on a bed of suffering when he was informed that I myself had gone to the head of the column. He jumped out of bed, got on a horse, and sought me out. As he couldn't stand on his feet, he had to remain on horseback; and at the head of the bridge of Arcola a shot struck him down senseless. I can assure you that all that was needed to give us a victory. You must send us reinforcements promptly, for we cannot repeat what we have already accomplished. You know what the French temperament is,—rather inconstant. Our splendid demi-brigades, weakened by so many victories, are now but ordinary troops.

22d. (To Josephine.) I am just off to bed, dear little Josephine, my heart full of your adorable face, and in bitter sorrow at being kept so long from your side; but I hope to be better situated in a few days, and to be able to give you proof of the ardent love with which you have filled me. Cruel woman! You no longer write to me, you no longer think of your good friend. Don't you know that, deprived of you, of your love, there is no peace, no happiness, no life for your husband? Heavens! how happy I should be watching you making your charming toilet; a little shoulder, a little white breast, so firm and so soft, and above it all that fascinating little face in its Creole handkerchief! Life, happiness, pleasure, are only what you make them. To live with Josephine is to live in Elysium,—kisses on your mouth, your eyes, your shoulder, your breast....
27th, Milan:
(To Josephine.) I arrive at Milan, I rush to your room; I had left everything to see you, to press you in my arms,—you were not there, you were junketing in other cities; you run away when I come; you care no more for your dear Napoleon. Your love was a caprice; inconstancy makes you indifferent.

Accustomed as I am to danger, I know where to find a remedy for the worries and woes of existence. My misfortune is incalculable; I was entitled not to expect it.

I shall stay here till the afternoon of the 29th. That need not interfere with your arrangements; amuse your self; happiness was made for you. All the world is happy if it can please you; your husband alone is unhappy. Ah! Josephine! Josephine!

December 5th. (To Lalande.) I have received your letter. I have immediately forwarded the one inclosed for the Milan astronomer. Whenever I am able to render a service to science, I gratify my own feelings and am sure that I am acquiring honour. Among all the sciences astronomy is the one which has rendered the greatest services to reason and to commerce. To share the night between a beautiful woman and a lovely sky; to spend the day checking observation by calculation,—that is happiness on earth.

8th. (To the Proveditore of the Republic of Venice.)
Sir: I have failed to recognise in the note which you have handed me the conduct of French troops, but have rather seen that of those of the Emperor, who have everywhere committed horrors at which I shudder.

The style of the note issued from Verona is that of a poor student of rhetoric. Eh! good God! Mr. Proveditore, the evils of war are bad enough, I assure you, not to magnify them a hundred fold, and to broider on them ridiculous fairy tales!

I give the lie in due form to any one who dares assert that there has been one single woman raped by the French troops in Venetian territory. One would imagine, from the ridiculous note handed to me, that not one church, not one woman, in the provinces of Verona and Brescia, has been respected! You threaten me with rioting and the rising of the cities. This looks very like defiancé. Are you authorized to take this step by your government? Does Venice wish to declare against us?

21st, Verona:
The general-in-chief has reviewed Masséna's and Augereau's divisions. He has seen with pleasure the good condition of the troops, but with regret the scarcity of bayonets.

I had sooner see a soldier without his breeches than without his bayonet.

28th, Milan:
Alvintzy's army is on the Brenta and in the Tyrol. The army of the Republic is along the Adige, an advance guard in front of Verona and of Legnago. Mantua is closely blockaded.

The art of war lies in calculating odds very closely to begin with, and then in adding exactly, almost mathematically, the factor of chance. Chance will always remain a sealed mystery for average minds.

1797

January 3d, Milan:
(To General Berthier.) Give General Lannes orders to start for the 19th demi-brigade in two hours, to take command. All the officers must march with their companies, and not in postchaises; they must look like a demibrigade of the army of Italy, and not like a demi-brigade of the King of Persia. I will cashier any officer who travels by stage and is not with his company.

6th. The more I study, in my leisure moments, the hopeless defects in the army service, the more I am convinced something must be done quickly. Everything is bought and sold. The army consumes five times as much as is necessary. The leading actresses of Italy are kept by the employés of the French army; extravagance, immorality, and graft have reached their limit. There is only one remedy,—a judicial body that can sentence any army administrator to be shot. Marshal Berwick hanged his commissary because his army was short of food; and we, we are often short. It is not that I am weak; I have employés arrested every day, but nobody backs me up.

12th, Roverbella:
Orders for the reserve cavalry to march to-night to Legnago, and for General Masséna to be ready to move to-night so as to check the enemy's possible plan of crossing the Adige. General Joubert, who has 10,000 men with him, is undisturbed; in any case, even if he were beaten while we are at Legnago, we should still have time.

13th, 9 a. m., Verona:
(To General Joubert, at Rivoli.) Let me know as soon as you can if the enemy in front of you number more than 9000 men. It is very important I should be able to judge whether it is a minor movement, meant to deceive us. The enemy show about 6000 men in the direction of Verona.

3 p. m.:
The enemy's movement is unmasked; his forces are moving on Rivoli.

Night:
General Joubert having concentrated to defend the plateau of Rivoli, the general-in-chief is moving the greater part of Masséna's division to support him.

17th, Roverbella:
(To the Directoire.) On the 14th we won the battle of Rivoli. We captured 13,000 prisoners, several flags, and some guns. On the 14th General Augereau, attacked the enemy at Anghiari. He captured 2000 prisoners and 16 guns; but in the night the enemy got away towards Mantua. Augereau got within cannon-shot, attacked St. George, but failed to carry it. I arrived in the night with reinforcements, which led to the battle of La Favorita, from which battlefield I am writing. The results of this battle are 7000 prisoners. So here, in three or four days, is the fifth army of the Emperor destroyed.

18th, Verona:

I reached Rivoli (on the 14th) at 2 a. m. I immediately ordered the important position of San Marco to be reoccupied; and lined the plateau of Rivoli with artillery. At daybreak the fighting was fast and furious. Joubert with the 33d supported his light infantry. Alvintzy didn't suspect that I had arrived in the night. Our left was briskly attacked, it fell back, and the enemy pushed in on our centre. The 14th held them up with great pluck.

On the 16th brave General Provera asked to surrender. The army of the Republic has therefore in the space of four days made nearly 25,000 prisoners, taken 20 flags, 60 guns, and killed or wounded at least 6000 men. All our demi-brigades covered themselves with glory. It is said that the Roman legions could march 24 miles a day; our brigades cover thirty, and do some fighting in between times.

19th. A regiment is never destroyed by the enemy, sir; it is immortalized!

20th. (To the Directoire.) I move 5000 men over the Po to-morrow, who will march straight on Rome. I send you 11 flags taken from the enemy in the battles of Rivoli and La Favorita. Bessières, who will hand them to you, is a brave and distinguished officer.

22d. (To Cacault, at Rome.) Citoyen Ministre: Pray leave Rome six hours after receiving this letter. They have made you stand endless humiliations; now you can leave.

(To Cardinal Mattei.) The words of peace with which I sent you to the Holy Father have been stifled. It is time the curtain fell on this ridiculous comedy. Whatever happens, the Holy Father may stay in Rome in full security. As chief priest of religion he is assured of protection, both for himself and his church. I shall see that no attempt is made to touch the religion of our fathers.

28th. Nothing new at Mantua. On the 3d we shall open with shell.

The weather is horrible,—rain in buckets for 48 hours.

February 1st, Bologna:

The armistice has been broken by the Roman government; I therefore declare that the armistice of the 2d of Messidor is at an end.

The French army is entering Papal territory; it will be true to its principles and will protect religion and the people.

2d. Capitulation of Mantua.

3d, Faenza:
I have made a point of displaying French generosity towards Wurmser, a general 70 years of age who has been very unfortunate. Besieged in Mantua, he made two or three sorties; they were all unlucky; he led them all in person.

4th, Forli:
Soldiers of Victor's division, I am not pleased with you! The only glory you can reap in our present expedition is that which comes of good conduct. I therefore order: every soldier convicted of any injury to persons or property of the conquered shall be shot at the head of his battalion.

10th, Ancona:
(To Josephine.) We have been at Ancona these last two days. I have never been so bored as by this sorry campaign.

15th, Macerata:
(To the Directoire.) Ancona is a very good port, within 24 hours of Macedonia and ten days of Constantinople.

We must keep Ancona when peace is made, and maintain it under the French flag; it will give us a hold on Turkey.

The treasure of Loretto amounted to three millions francs. They left about one million behind. I am sending you in addition the Madonna and all the relics. The Madonna is made of wood.

Our troops will reach Foligno to-night. Here is what I expect to do: I will grant the Pope peace provided he cedes Bolona, Ferrara, Urbino, and Ancona, and that he pays us three millions for the treasure of Loretto and fifteen millions that he owed us on the armistice treaty. If he doesn't accept, I shall go for Rome.

16th. (To Josephine.) You are sad; you are ill; you have stopped writing; you want to go to Paris. Do you love your friend no longer? This thought makes me wretched. Sweet friend, life has become unbearable since hearing that you are sad.

Perhaps I can get a peace with the Pope soon, and be back at your side; it is my most ardent wish.

A hundred kisses. Nothing equals my love save my anxiety.

17th, Tolentino:
The army is within three days' march of Rome; I am negotiating with the gang of priests; doubtless St. Peter will once more save the capitol!

18th. I hear from Venice that Prince Charles has reached Trieste, and that the Austrians are everywhere in motion.

19th. (To the Directoire.) Herewith the treaty of peace which has just been signed between the French Republic and the Pope. I start to-night for Mantua. We shall soon be across the Piave.

March 6th, Mantua:
(To the Directoire.) When you receive this letter we shall be in active operations again. A ten days' armistice has been proposed to me, which I have declined.

The Pope has ratified the treaty of peace concluded at Tolentino. Our situation in Italy appears very satisfactory. This is not yet the moment for carrying out your instructions as to Venice.

10th, Bassano:
Soldiers of the army of Italy! The capture of Mantua gives you an eternal claim to the gratitude of our country. You have been victorious in fourteen pitched battles and seventy engagements; you have captured more than 100,000 prisoners and 2500 guns; you have fed, supplied, and paid the army; you have remitted 30 millions to the Public Treasury. You have enriched the Museum of Paris with three hundred objects, the products of 30 centuries.

But your work is not complete. A great destiny is yours: the country reposes in you its dearest hopes. Of all our foes the Emperor alone still faces us; he has accepted the wages of the merchants of London; his policy has become that of those perfidious islanders who, immune from the dangers of war, laugh at the woes of the continent.

The Directoire has made every effort to restore peace to Europe. But Vienna has turned a deaf ear. The house of Austria, which for three centuries past has lost in every war some portion of its power, will be reduced at the close of this sixth campaign to accept the peace it shall please us to grant, and will fall to the rank of the lesser powers, which it already touched when it accepted the salary of England.

11th. Our advance guard reached Felke yesterday, but found no enemy.

13th, Conegliano:
We are over the Piave. The enemy is retreating and is apparently taking position behind the Tagliamento.

16th, 11.30 p.m., Valvasone:
This morning we reached the Tagliamento, and found Prince Charles with 16,000 men in line. Serrurier and Bernadotte forced their way over. We captured 8 guns.

17th. The passage of the Tagliamento is auspicious; but the further I advance into Germany, the more troops will be accumulated against me. I can't do everything with 50,000 men.

20th, Palmanova:
We have forced the line of the Isonzo.

21st, Goritz:
Write to Boudet to approve placing on the flag of the 57th demi-brigade: "The terrible 57th demi-brigade, that nothing can stop."

It is easy enough to say to a general, go to Italy, win battles, and sign peace at Vienna. But the doing of it is not so easy. I have never paid the least attention to the plans sent to me by the Directoire. Only fools could take stock in such rubbish. As to Berthier, you see what he is: he's an ass! Well, he it is who does everything, he it is who reaps a large share of the glory of the army of Italy!

22d. In a week I may reach Klagenfurt, fifteen post-houses from Vienna. If the Rhine is not crossed soon, we shall be unable to maintain ourselves.

25th. Are we over the Rhine yet? My movement has got to be unmasked, and the enemy will at once realize the danger. They will withdraw everything from the Rhine to concentrate on me.

28th, Villach:
The demi-brigades are expressly forbidden to carry with them more women than the laundresses the law provides for. Every woman found with the army and not duly authorized shall be publicly whipped.

31st, Klagenfurt:
(To the Archduke Charles.) Brave soldiers wage war, but hope for peace. Has not this one now lasted six years? Have we not killed enough people? Europe, which had taken up arms against the French Republic, has laid them down. Is there no hope, then, of coming to terms, and must we continue to cut each other's throats?

If the overture I have the honour of making can save the life of one single individual, I shall be more proud of the civic crown I should earn than of the sad glory that comes of military success.

April 1st. I have sent off the letter to Prince Charles Should his reply be favourable, and the Court of Vienna be inclined for peace, I shall take it on myself to sign a convention. With 20,000 men more, I would have carried the army through to Vienna almost posthaste.

3d, Friesach:
Prince Charles is drawing in all the troops he can to cover Vienna.

Masséna and Guieu are pursuing the enemy on the Mür. Yesterday we made 600 prisoners, and killed and wounded a number of their rear guard, which Prince Charles commanded in person.

4th, Scheifling:
Masséna's division will advance along the road to Leoben.

5th, Judenburg:
The enemy appear to be retreating more hastily. Prince Charles has sent in a staff officer to ask for a suspension of hostilities for four hours,—an absolutely inadmissible proposal.

7th, morning:
(To Generals Merveldt and Bellegarde.) In the present situation of the two armies a suspension of hostilities is all against the interests of the French army; but if it is intended as a step towards the peace that is so needed by both peoples, I readily accede to your wishes.

6 p. m.:
Order for General Masséna to start with his whole division for Leoben, which he is to occupy.

Midnight :
An armistice is agreed on until the 13th of April.

8th, Judenburg:
(To the Directoire.) You will find herewith the note handed me by Generals Merveldt and Bellegarde. I have told them that the condition preliminary to a treaty of peace is the cession of all territory to the Rhine. They asked for an explanation as to Italy, but I declined. We are here about 20 leagues from Vienna; the army of Italy is therefore isolated and exposed. Our armies have not yet crossed the Rhine.

Everything leads me to think we have reached the moment for concluding peace, and we must do so. If, contrary to my expectations, the negotiations went off, I should be very embarrassed as to what to do next.

9th. All goes well.
(To the Most Serene Doge of Venice.) All the Venetian mainland is in arms. The watchword of the peasants you have armed is: "Death to the French!" Is it your belief that because I am in the centre of Germany I am unable to compel due respect for the greatest Power in the world? Do you think the legions of Italy will quietly submit to the massacres you have stirred up? The blood of my comrades shall be avenged. I send you this letter by my first aide-de-camp. War or peace! We are not living in the days of Charles VIII!

(This) letter is for Junot to take to Venice, and to get answere d within 24 hours. It would be dangerous to give time for the Venetian troops to assemble.

16th, Leoben:
(To the Directoire.) I am sending you by Adjutant-General Leclerc this dispatch on the negotiations. Pray send him back at once. All the officers I send to Paris stay there too long; they spend their money, and kill themselves with fast living.

General Merveldt and Count di Gallo are great sticklers for etiquette; they always want to put the Emperor before the Republic; I have declined flatly.

We have reached the matter of recognition. I told them the Republic did not want to be recognised; it is in Europe what the sun is on the horizon; those who can't see it must take their chances.

On the 15th M. di Gallo came to see me at eight in the morning: he said he desired to have some spot neutralized so that we could continue our negotiations in correct form. We selected a garden with a summer-house in the middle; we have declared the place neutral, a farce which I took part in to soothe the childish vanity of these people. This so-called neutral spot is in the midst of the bivouacs of our divisions.

When one wants to open a campaign there is nothing can stand as an obstacle, and a river has never been a real obstacle. If Moreau wants to cross the Rhine, he will cross; if he had already crossed it, we could dictate our conditions of peace imperiously; but the man who fears for his reputation is certain to lose it. I have crossed the Julian Alps over three feet of ice; I have carried my artillery through places where never a cart has passed. Had I thought only of the repose of my army and my private interests, I should have stopped on the banks of the Isonzo; I threw myself into Germany to disengage the army of the Rhine. I am at the gates of Vienna, and its haughty court has sent its plenipotentiaries to my headquarters.

18th, Castle of Eggenwald:
His Majesty the Emperor and the Directoire have concluded peace preliminaries.

19th. (To the Directoire.) I expect to send you within three days, by General Masséna, the Emperor's ratification. I shall quarter the army in Venetia. As for myself, I ask for rest. I have justified the trust you confided in me. I have accounted myself as nothing in all I have done; and now I have thrown myself on Vienna, having won more glory than should make me happy, and with the splendid plains of Italy behind me, just as I began the previous campaign by seeking bread for an army which the Republic could no longer feed. I insist, therefore, that together with the ratification of the peace preliminaries you should send me leave to return to France.

30th, Trieste:
The conduct of the Venetians gets each day worse and worse; we are really in a state of war. The Senate has sent me a deputation; I treated it as it deserved. I told them to drive out the English minister; to hand us twenty millions, and all merchandise belonging to the English.

May 3d, Palmanova:
I can see no other course than to obliterate the Venetian name from the earth.

13th, Milan:
Order to General Baraguay d'Hilliers to enter Venice and seize all military positions.

14th. I have just received from the Directoire the ratification of the peace preliminaries.

The citizens of Venice are under the protection of the French Republic.

I am organizing the Cisalpine Republic; I have four committees working hard at framing the Constitution.

(To the national guards of the Cisalpine Republic.) Yours is the task, brave comrades, of consolidating the liberty of your country.

It is the soldier who founds republics, it is the soldier who maintains them. Without armies, without force, without discipline, neither political independence nor civil liberty can exist.

15th. Heavens! how scarce men are! There are in Italy 18 millions of men, and I can barely find two, Dandolo and Melzi!

20th, Mombello:
General Baraguay d'Hilliers has occupied Venice.

June 30th. (To the Directoire.) I have this moment received (a copy of) Dumolard's resolution. This motion, which the Assembly has ordered to be printed, is directed against me. I had a right, after concluding five treaties of peace, and after dealing the last blow to the Coalition, to expect, if not a civic triumph, yet at least to be left in peace; but I see myself denounced, persecuted, hounded down by every means, I whose reputation is part of that of my country!

After having earned a decree that I had deserved well of my country, I should not have been subjected to such absurd and atrocious accusations. I repeat the demand I have already made to retire. I want to live in peace, if the daggers of Clichy spare me.

I understand why Bonaparte is accused; it's for concluding peace. But I warn you, I speak in the name of 80,000 men; the time when cowardly lawyers and low chatterers could send soldiers to the guillotine has passed, and if you drive them to it, the soldiers of Italy will march to the Clichy gate with their general: but, if they do, look out for yourselves!

The general-in-chief appoints citoyen Eugène Beauharnais supernumerary sub-lieutenant in the 1st hussars, and his aide-de-camp. This young and talented citizen is the son of General Beauharnais, whose loss will long be mourned by his country.

July 4th. I am receiving so many letters from all parts of the Republic that I cannot answer them all. The esteem of his fellow citizens is the only worthy reward for the services rendered by a soldier to his country.

14th, Milan:
Soldiers! I know that you feel deeply the misfortunes that threaten our country; but it will not run any real danger. Mountains lie between us and France; you would surmount them as rapidly as the eagle, to maintain the Constitution, to defend liberty, to protect the government and all republicans.

Soldiers, dismiss all uneasiness, and let us swear on our new standards: Eternal war on the enemies of the Republic and of the Constitution!

17th. The Emperor is trying to gain time. What is his motive? It is difficult to imagine, unless it lies in the direction of the Clichy Club, and the return of the royalists. What is the use of our constant victories? The blood we have shed for the country is made useless by internal factions.

23d. Without question the Court of Vienna hopes everything from time, and expects to make a useful diversion in favour of England.

27th. (To the Directoire.) General Augereau has asked leave to proceed to Paris, where he has business to attend to. He will inform you verbally of the absolute devotion of the soldiers of Italy to the Constitution and to the Directoire.

28th. The tone of the notes handed to the French plenipotentiaries, the protests, the extraordinary demands they contain, the movements of Austrian troops, every-thing, in a word, points to war.

29th. There is much dissension between the Council of Five Hundred and the Directoire.

It appears that Hoche is about to embark for Ireland.

August 1st. The agitation in Paris continues; the gentlemen are divided among themselves. The army of Sambre et Meuse has declared itself vigorously. General Desaix is here; he assures me that the army of the Rhine is at one with the army of Italy. General Serrurier has just arrived; he is indignant at the royalist agitation.

16th. The Emperor is apparently concentrating all his forces on Italy. The large number of recruits, together with the prisoners we have sent back, will enable him to place a formidable army in line against me.

The time is fast coming when we shall realize that really to destroy England we must seize Egypt.

General Augereau has been appointed to command the 17th (Paris) military division.

28th. (To citoyenne Marie Dauranne, laundress of the 51st of the line.) Worthy citoyenne: The general-in-chief, in making public your civic and courageous deed at the crossing of the Piave, in saving at the risk of your own life one of our brave companions in arms, has awarded you a civic crown. You will find engraved on it the record of a deed that honours not you only but your sex; you may add to it your own name, and that of the brave man whose life you saved, but whose name we do not know.

September 4th. Revolution of Fructidor; Barras and Augereau.

6th. (To the Minister of Foreign Affairs.) It would be impossible to carry on so weighty a discussion with more timid negotiators, worse logicians, or men less influential with their own court. When they have said: Those are our instructions,—they have done their utmost. I said to them: If your instructions stated that it is now actually night-time, would you ask us to accept it?—Yesterday they proposed that we should give them Romagna, Mantua, and the Venetian state. I asked them how many miles from Paris their army was, and I got vigorously angry at the impertinence of such proposals.

In private conversation I told them that I would give them my opinion confidentially,—to them, because they knew better than outsiders that I was not given to gas-conading,—and that it was that two weeks after the campaign opened I should be very close to Vienna.

7th. The army is warned to be ready to move on the 24th.

8th. The plenipotentiaries continue willing nilling, saying unsaying,—somewhat disconcerted by my measures. I have moved Dumas' cavalry forward.

12th. (To the Directoire.) Herewith you will find my proclamation to the army announcing the events of the 18th of Fructidor. You may reckon that here are 100,000 men who can by their own effort safeguard the measures you have taken to place liberty on solid foundations.

13th. Why not seize the island of Malta? If, when we conclude peace with England, we have to give up the Cape of Good Hope, we should take Egypt.

16th. (To the sailors of Admiral Bruey's fleet.) Comrades: As soon as we have pacified the continent, we will join you in conquering the liberty of the seas. We will recall the horrid spectacle of Toulon in ashes, and victory will attend our efforts. Without you we could only carry the glory of the French name to a small part of the continent; with you, we will cross the seas and our national glory shall be witnessed by the most distant shores.

19th. Notwithstanding our pride, our thousand and one pamphlets, our endless speechifyings, we are very ignorant in political and social science. We have not yet defined what we mean by the executive, legislative, and judicial powers. Montesquieu's definitions are false.

In fifty years I can see but one thing that we have defined clearly, which is the sovereignty of the people; but we have done no more towards settling what is constitutional than we have in the distribution of powers. The organization of the French nation is, therefore, still incomplete.

This legislature, without eyes or ears for what surrounds it, should no longer overwhelm us with a thousand laws passed on the spur of the moment, that negative one absurdity by another, and that leave us, with three hundred folios of laws, a lawless nation.

Here, I think, is a political creed which our present circumstances render excusable. What a misfortune for a nation of 30 millions of people, and in the eighteenth century, to be driven to the support of bayonets to save the country!

25th. (To the Directoire.) An officer arrived from Paris day before yesterday; he has let it be known that he left Paris the 12th, and that there was anxiety there as to how I would take the event of the 18th of Fructidor; he was armed with a sort of circular to all the divisional generals of the army.

From this it clearly appears that the Government is acting towards me very much as it acted towards Pichegru after Vendémiaire. I ask you, Citoyens Directeurs, to replace me and to accept my resignation. No power on earth can make me continue to serve the Government after this horrible display of ingratitude, which I was entitled not to expect.

I am also in need of tuning my mind once more to the opinion of the public. I have too long wielded exceptional power. I have always used it for the good of the country, despite what those may think who doubt my rectitude. My reward must lie in my own conscience and the opinion of posterity. Now that the country is pacified and freed from danger, I can leave the post confided to me without any ill effects.

Great events hang by a thread. The able man turns everything to profit, neglects nothing that may give him one chance more; the man of less ability, by overlooking just one thing, spoils the whole.

October 1st. After dinner I had a private conversation with Count Cobenzl. He said that the Emperor might give us the Rhine, if we made great concessions in Italy; his proposals were absurd. My health is ruined, and nothing can replace good health, which is essential to carrying on war. I can barely get into the saddle, and need two years' rest.

6th. The negotiations are at a standstill; the Austrians ask for too much. In twelve days we shall be in the field.

10th. At last the peace negotiations look like coming to a head. To-night peace will be signed, or the negotiations will be broken off.

Then a war with England will open for us a wider, more essential, more splendid field of opportunity. The English nation is worthier than the Venetian, and its liberation will forever consolidate the liberty and the happiness of France; or if we can compel the government to make peace, the advantages which we shall secure for our commerce all over the world will mark a great step in the consolidation of liberty and national prosperity. As for me, there is nothing left but to return from whence I came, to take up the plough of Cincinnatus, and to set the example of obedience to the laws and of aversion from military rule, which has destroyed so many republics.

16th, Campo Formio:
Count Cobenzl and I met for our concluding session in a room where, according to Austrian custom, a dais had been installed with a chair of state representing that of the Austrian Emperor. On entering I asked what this meant, and (on being told), I said to the Austrian minister: Come, before we begin, you had better have that chair taken away, because I have never yet seen a chair set higher than others without immediately wanting to get into it.

Count Cobenzl, is that your ultimatum? Before three months are over I shall have smashed your monarchy, as I now smash this tray of glasses.—I break off negotiations.

18th, Passariano.
Peace was signed one hour after midnight at Campo Formio. I am quite sure there will be much criticism and carping.

November 2d. The army of England is already formed.

5th. General Hoche had some good maps of England, which might be got from his heirs.

9th. About half the troops will pass through Milan on the 11th of December on their way to France to form the nucleus of the army of England.

Order for Generals Masséna, Bernadotte, Brune, Joubert, Victor, Rampon, Gardanne, Belliard, Lannes, to be ready to start to take up commands in the army of England.

13th. I am off to-morrow for Rastadt, to exchange ratifications, to execute the clauses of the treaty, and to take part in the Congress of the Empire.

My wife expects to start on a trip to Rome in two or three days.

26th, Rastadt:
(To the Directoire.) As you perceive, I have travelled at breakneck speed, and I am not a little surprised to find that the Emperor's booby plenipotentiaries are not here yet, except General Merveldt. General Berthier has handed me the treaty of peace, which this time, I am sure, will please the plenipotentiaries of the Emperor, for it is all splendour and gilt edges!

30th. To-morrow we complete everything relating to the secret clauses; in which case I shall start that very night.

December 26th, Paris:
(To the President of the National Institute.) I am honoured by the vote of the distinguished members of your society. I am only too conscious that before becoming their equal I must long remain their pupil. Were there any stronger way of expressing the esteem in which I hold them, I would use it.

The real conquests, those that leave no regrets behind, are those made over ignorance. The most honourable occupation, that which is most useful to nations, is to help on the diffusion of humane ideas. Henceforth the real strength of the French Republic must consist in not failing to make every new idea her own.

31st. On my return from Italy I took up my abode in a little house, Rue Chantereine. The Municipality of Paris ordered its name changed to Rue de la Victoire.

1798

January 13st, Paris:

Paris has a short memory. If I remain longer doing nothing, I am lost. In this great Babylon one reputation quickly succeeds another. After I have been seen three times at the theatre, I shall not be looked at again; I shall therefore not go very frequently.

9th. I have laid a number of proposals before the Directoire relating to the composition of the army of England.

11th. All goes well. We are working hard at the reorganization of our navy, and at the formation of the army of England. Kléber, Desaix, Gouvion Saint-Cyr, Lefebvre, Championnet, are to be of the army. Joubert has gone to Holland.

29th. I will not remain here; there is nothing to be done. They will listen to nothing. I realize that if I stay my reputation will soon be gone. All things fade here, and my reputation is almost forgotten; this little Europe affords too slight a scope; I must go to the Orient; all great reputations have been won there. If the success of an expedition to England should prove doubtful, as I fear, the army of England will become the army of the East, and I shall go to Egypt.

The Orient awaits a man!

February 7th. I leave to-morrow to inspect the Atlantic coast. I shall be back in twelve days.

12th, Dunkirk:

It is said that the Dutch have numbers of fast-sailing flatboats; we must obtain from 150 to 250, with as many gunboats as possible. We must then get these vessels to Dunkirk at once, so as to be able to leave that port a month hence, with 50,000 men, artillery, supplies, etc.

23d, Paris:
Whatever we do, we cannot command the sea for several years to come. To effect a landing in England without controlling the sea is the boldest and most difficult military operation ever attempted. It would seem, then, that the expedition to England is not feasible. We must therefore merely keep up the pretence of it, and concentrate our attention and our resources on the Rhine, or else undertake an expedition to the Levant so as to threaten the trade with India. And if none of these operations is feasible, I can see no other course than to make peace with England.

March 26th. (To the Minister of the Interior.) Please give positive orders that all the Arabic type we have be packed immediately, and that citoyen Langlès take charge of it. I also beg you to give orders that the Greek type be packed; I know we have some, as Xenophon is being printed; and it won't matter so very much if Xenophon is held up for three months.

30th. I have just heard from Admiral Brueys; he left Corfu on the 25th of February with six French and five Venetian men of war. I hope these ships can start again two weeks after their arrival.

April 5th. (To Monge.) We shall take one third of the Institute and many scientific instruments with us. I place the Arabic printing-press under your special care.

14th. I should like to take with me citoyen Piveron, who was for many years the king's agent at the court of Tippoo Sahib. We could try to get him through to India.

17th. (To Vice-Admiral Brueys.) I expect to join you during the first week of Floréal. Have a good bed for me, as I expect to be sick during the whole journey. Get good supplies.

18th. (To Eugène Beauharnais.) You will start at four o'clock on the 3d of Floréal. You should reach Lyons on the 4th before noon. Travel in mufti, and don't let it be known that you are my aide-de-camp. You will give out everywhere that I am going to Brest.

(To General Kléber.) Orders for General Kléber and his staff to proceed at once to Toulon, where he will receive further instructions.

28th. Bonaparte, member of the National Institute, general-in-chief of the army of England, orders General Régnier to embark the men of his division at Marseilles on the 6th of May on the transports that will be there ready for him.

May 10th, Toulon:
Soldiers of the army of the Mediterranean!

You are a wing of the army of England! You have fought among mountains, in plains, before fortresses; but you had yet to carry out a naval campaign. The Roman legions that you have sometimes rivalled, but never equalled, fought Carthage on this very sea and on the plains of Zama. Victory never forsook them.

Soldiers! Europe is watching you!

11th. (To Admiral Brueys.) As the fleet is made up of 15 of the line, 12 frigates, and over 200 transports, you are to assume the rank and fly the flag of Admiral.

17th, on board the Orient:

We have been riding at anchor these last three days ready to start, but a strong wind continues to blow from the wrong quarter.

19th, 7 a. m.:
The frigates are at sea; the convoy is standing out; we are weighing anchor; the weather is lovely.

23d, between Corsica and Elba:
English ships have been reported cruising off Sicily. I cannot believe they are in sufficient force to interfere with our plans.

27th. We have been becalmed these two days, ten leagues from the strait of Bonifacio. Our dispatch boat, Le Coreyre, chased an English brig, which was run on to the Sardinian coast and burnt. The crew of this brig speak of an English fleet.

28th, 8 p. m.:
We are carrying full sail and heading for our goal.

June 13th, Malta:
(To the Directoire.) At dawn on the 10th we sighted the island of Gozzo. At night I sent one of my aides-de-camp to ask for the Grand Master's leave to water in the bays of the island. Our consul at Malta brought me his answer, which was a flat refusal. The need of the army was pressing, and placed the duty on me of employing force. General Lannes and chef de brigade Marmont landed within cannon-shot of the works. At daybreak our troops had landed at all points, notwithstanding a brisk but ill-directed cannonade. On the 12th I began sending guns ashore. We have few fortresses in Europe so strong and scientifically planned as Malta. The Grand Master asked for a suspension of hostilities on the morning of the 12th. At midnight his representatives came aboard the Orient and concluded the convention, which I inclose you herewith.

16th, on board the Orient:
The fleet is working out of the harbour, and we expect to be on our way once more on the 19th.

22d, at sea:
(Proclamation to the army.) Soldiers! You are about to attempt a conquest, the effect of which will be incalculable on civilization and the commerce of the world! You are about to deal England the most certain and telling blow she can suffer, until the time comes when you can strike her death-stroke. Not many days after our arrival, the Mameluk beys, who have exclusively favoured English commerce, who have injured our merchants and tyrannized over the wretched inhabitants of the Nile, will have ceased to exist.

The people among whom we are going are Mahometans; the chief article of their creed is: God is God, and Mahomet is his prophet. Do not contradict them; deal with them as we have dealt with the Jews, with the Italians; show respect for their muftis and their imams, as you have for rabbis and bishops. The legions of Rome protected all religions. You will meet with customs different from those of Europe; you must learn to accept them.

The first city we shall see was built by Alexander. Our every step will evoke memories of the past worthy of the emulation of Frenchmen.

30th. (To the Pasha of Egypt.) The Directoire of the French Republic has on several occasions requested the Sublime Porte to punish the beys of Egypt for the damage which they have caused to French merchants.

The French Republic has decided to send a powerful army to put a stop to the piracy of the beys of Egypt. You, who should be the master of the beys, but whom they hold powerless and without authority at Cairo, should greet my arrival with joy. Come and meet me, therefore, and join me in cursing the unholy race of the beys.

July 1st, off Alexandria:
The expedition was off Alexandria at dawn. An English fleet, described as very strong, was here three days ago, and left a packet for transmission to India.

Admiral, we have not one moment to lose. Fortune has given me three days; if I don't profit by it we are lost.

To-morrow I must be in Alexandria.

The wind was very strong and the sea very rough; I decided, however, to land at once. We spent the day in preparations.

The coast near Alexandria, 11 p. m.:
I disembarked with General Kléber and a part of the troops at 11 p. m. We immediately began our march on Alexandria.

July 2d. At daybreak we caught sight of Pompey's column. The walls of the Arab city were lined with men.

General Kléber picked out the point of the wall at which his grenadiers were to scale it, but received a shot in the head that stretched him senseless. The grenadiers of his division, spurred by this event, fought their way into the town.

The old harbour of Alexandria can shelter a fleet, however large; but there is a place in the channel where there is no more than 15 feet of water, which makes the sailors doubt whether the 74's can get in. This affects my plans very seriously.

(Proclamation.) Bonaparte, member of the National Institute, general-in-chief,—

People of Egypt: You will be told that I have come to destroy your faith; believe it not! Answer that I am here to maintain your rights, to punish usurpers, and that I respect even more than do the Mameluks, God, his Prophet, and the Koran!

Tell them that in the eyes of God all men are equal; wisdom, talent, and virtue alone make the inequality of mankind. And what wisdom, what talent, what virtue, distinguish the Mameluks and entitle them to the exclusive enjoyment of all that makes life lovely and pleasant?

To whom belong the great estates? To the Mameluks. To whom belong lovely slaves, splendid horses, fine houses? To the Mameluks. If Egypt, then, is their farm, let them display the lease that God has granted them. But God is just and merciful unto his people. All Egyptians will be called on to fill public stations; the most wise, the most virtuous, the best educated, will govern the country, and the people will be happy.

Is it not we who destroyed the Pope who urged war against all Mussulmans? Is it not we who destroyed the Knights of Malta because they foolishly believed that God had bidden them wage war against all Mussulmans? Is it not we who in centuries past have befriended the Grand Seignior,—may God fulfil his wishes,—and been the enemy of his enemies? Have not the Mameluks, on the contrary, always revolted against the authority of the Grand Seignior, which they still refuse to recognise? They act merely at their own pleasure.

Let those who arm on behalf of the Mameluks and fight against us beware, and three times beware! For them there is no hope: they will perish!

It is a bit quackish!

3d, Alexandria:
(To General Desaix.) You will probably not meet more than a few squadrons of cavalry; mask your cavalry; don't use your fieldpieces. Save them for the day when we shall have to fight four or five thousand horse.

(To Admiral Brueys.) The general-in-chief feels certain that you have already had the channel sounded. He wants the fleet to be brought into port. It is essential that the fleet should be sheltered from the superior forces that the English may have in these seas. The Admiral is to notify the general-in-chief to-morrow whether the fleet could defend itself against a superior force of the enemy if it were anchored across the bay of Aboukir.

10th, El Ramanyeh:
Desaix had a skirmish with about a thousand mounted Mameluks this morning. The country is splendid.

12th. The general-in-chief's intention is to attack the enemy reported in Chobrakyt at daybreak.

15th, Châbour:
We met and defeated the enemy yesterday. Murad Bey with 3000 or 4000 mounted Mameluks, twenty guns, and a few gunboats attempted to hold the crossing at Chobrakyt. The army was drawn up with each division in battalion squares, baggage in the centre, the guns in the battalion intervals.

21st, The Pyramids:
At dawn we met their advance guard, which we drove back from village to village. At two in the afternoon we discovered the intrenchments and the enemy's army.

Soldiers! Forty centuries behold you!

The instant Murad Bey perceived Desaix' movement he decided to attack. One of his bravest beys at the head of a picked body of cavalry charged down like lightning on our two divisions. We let them come to within fifty paces, and mowed them down with a hail of bullets and grape that stretched great numbers on the battlefield. They pushed right into the intervals between the two divisions, where they were caught by a crossfire that completed their defeat.

Our columns of attack, under the command of brave General Rampon, rushed on the intrenchments, in the face of a heavy artillery fire, with their usual dash, when the Mameluks (again) charged them. They came out of the earthworks at full gallop; our columns had just time to halt, face outwards, and receive them with their bayonets and a storm of bullets. In a flash the field was covered with their bodies. Our troops soon carried the intrenchments.

22d, Gyzeh:
(To the Sheiks and Notables of Cairo.) You will judge of my sentiments by the proclamation which I inclose. Yesterday the Mameluks were for the most part killed or made prisoners, and I am in pursuit of the few who survive. Send over to this bank what boats you have, and a deputation to announce your submission. Have bread, meat, straw, and forage collected for my army, and be without uneasiness, for no one could wish you better than I.

26th, Cairo:
No news from France since our departure.

(To Joseph.) Be kind to my wife. Go and see her occasionally. I am asking Louis to give her good advice. I wish Désirée all happiness if she marries Bernadotte. She deserves it. I embrace your wife and Lucien. I am sending a handsome shawl to Julie. Don't be quite so unfaithful to her; she is an excellent woman; make her happy.

28th. Perrée should be sent out with three frigates, having on board: a company of actors; a corps de ballet; three or four marionette showmen for the people; a hundred or so French women; the wives of all who are employed here; 20 surgeons, 30 chemists, 10 physicians.

I will colonize this country. I am twenty-nine now, and shall then be thirty-five; that's nothing; six years gives me long enough, if all goes well, to reach India.

31st. Severity is needed to govern the Turks; I order five or six heads to be sliced off every day in the streets of Cairo. Up till now we have had to behave mildly so as to counteract the reputation of terror that preceded us; at present it is, on the contrary, better to assume the tone that commands obedience with these people, for with them obedience signifies fear.

August 1st. Battle of the Nile; Nelson and Brueys.
Adjutant-General Bribes is to occupy Damanhour. He will disarm the city, and will have the heads of five of the chief inhabitants cut off; one chosen from the lawyers who have behaved worst, and the four others from the most influential people. He is specially enjoined to see to the clearing of the canal to Alexandria that begins at El Ramanyeh so that the Nile may enter it.

15th. (To Rear-Admiral Ganteaume.) The account of what you have been through is truly horrible. If you have come out alive, it is clearly that you are destined by fate to avenge our navy and our friends; on this I congratulate you. This is the only cheering thought that has occurred to me since I received your report day before yesterday, thirty leagues from Cairo. You are to assume command of all that is left of our naval forces in Egypt. You will do your utmost to withdraw from the Bay of Aboukir anything we may have left there. I imagine that by this time the English have moved their shattered ships away.

(To General Kléber.) I have just received the news of the battle of the 1st. I promptly returned to Cairo. Things are not quite settled yet in these parts; but every day there is a perceptible improvement, and I am justified in thinking that very soon we shall be really masters of the country. Our enterprise demands more than one sort of courage.

19th. (To the Directoire.) Fate has ordained, in this event as in so many others, that if we are given a great preponderance on the continent, to our rivals is given the dominion of the seas. However great our defeat, it is not attributable to the inconstancy of Fortune, for she has not yet abandoned us; far from it, she has favoured us more than ever before in our present undertaking.

Collect all our ships from Toulon, Malta, Ancona, Corfu, Alexandria, to form a new fleet.

Had I been master of the sea, I should have been lord of the Orient.

22d, Cairo:
There shall be an Institute for Science and Art in Egypt, established in Cairo:

The chief object of this Society shall be, to develop and encourage learning in Egypt. All general officers of the French army shall be entitled to attend its sessions. The proceedings of the Society shall be printed.

23d. The Egyptian Institute held its first session on the 6th of Fructidor; citoyen Bonaparte propounded the following questions:

Can the ovens used for baking army bread be improved in regard to expense or fuel, and if so, how?

Does Egypt afford any substitute for hops in the brewing of beer?

How can Nile water best be filtered and sweetened?

What means are there in Egypt for manufacturing gunpowder?

How is Egypt situated in the matter of jurisprudence, of civil and criminal judges, of education?
What improvements, approved of by the people, can be introduced in these matters?

(To General Menou.) Don't put the sailors forward. Try to inspirit them and to dispel their belief in the superiority of the English.

September 8th. (To the Directoire.) I await news from Constantinople. I cannot be back in Paris, as I had promised, in October; but it is only a matter of a few months. Everything here is going well. The country is quiet and getting used to us. For the rest, let time work. Since our departure I have not heard one word from you, nor from the ministers, nor from a single person who is related to me. My dispatches have, I expect, been more fortunate than yours.

October 4th. No news from Europe.
(To General Kléber.) I regret to hear you are not well. Desaix has reached Syout. He drove the Mameluks into the desert, and part of them have reached the oases. Ibrahim Bey is at Gaza, and threatens invasion; it will not come to anything; but we, who are not threatening anybody, might very well dislodge him from where he is.

Believe me when I say that I hope for your speedy cure, and that I rate high your good-will and your friendship. I fear that we have had a little misunderstanding; you would be doing me an injustice if you doubted that this gives me much concern. In the land of Egypt, clouds, when we have any, pass away in six hours; if there should seem to be any between us, they will pass in three. My high regard for you is at least equal to that which you have on occasion manifested for me.

(To the French Commissioners to the Divan.) The object for which the Divan has been convened is tentative, the intention being to accustom the notables of

Egypt to the idea of assemblies and legislation. You must tell them that I have convened them to obtain their advice, and to ascertain what can be done for the benefit of the people, and what they themselves would do had they the power which conquest has given us.

7th. (To the Directoire.) The Porte has appointed Djezzar pasha of Acre and general-in-chief of all Syria. He has taken no notice of the overtures I have made. Our consuls have been arrested everywhere, and the Ottoman Empire is full of martial sounds. You will not abandon your army in Egypt; you will send us help and news; and you will do all that I have urged to place a large fleet in this sea. When I know for certain what the Porte intends, when the country is more settled and our fortifications are completed, which will be before long, I may decide to return to Europe; especially if news reaches me that the continent is not at peace.

16th. (To General Manscourt.) Pray forward me the report that mentions the rumour of an insurrection in the garrison. If a demi-brigade under my orders mutinies, I will disband it, and I will have every officer who fails to maintain discipline shot.

18th. Not the least bit of news from France. Bourrienne! what am I thinking of?

(Bourrienne: In truth that's rather difficult, you think of so many things!)

I don't know whether I shall ever see France again, but if I do, my sole ambition is to fight one great campaign in Germany, in the plains of Bavaria, to win a great victory, and to avenge France for her defeat at Blenheim. After that I will retire to the country and live quietly.

21st. The Turkish army is concentrating at Damascus, and, it is reported, will amount to 60,000 men.

22d. (To General Bon.) It is essential for us to attack the insurgent quarters. Bombard the mosque. All armed men caught in the streets are to be killed at sight.

23d. Order for levelling the grand mosque in the course of the night by breaking down some of the pillars if possible.

(To General Berthier.) Please order the commandant of the town to have the heads of all prisoners caught in arms cut off. They are to be taken to-night to the bank of the Nile between Boulâq and old Cairo; the bodies can be thrown into the river.

(To Louis Bonaparte.) I inclose you an order for the commandant at Alexandria to send you off on a brig, the Vif or the Indépendant.

We have been busy these last two days appeasing a revolt in Cairo. I was compelled to throw shells into a quarter which the insurgents had barricaded. About a thousand Turks have been killed. To-day everything is calm and orderly again. Good-bye, good health; a prosperous journey.

November 20th. (To General Desaix.) We have got French and English gazettes to the 10th of August; up till then there was no new development in Europe; I am sending them on.

December 10th. (To General Dommartin.) The general-in-chief acknowledges receipt of the request of chef de brigade Grobert to return to France. The general-in-chief's reply is that in view of the fact that citoyen Grobert got his step as chef de brigade in Paris, and without even having heard a shot fired, his intention is that you should keep this officer continuously on outpost duty.

21st. (Order.) At noon each day the regimental bands shall play in the public square, opposite the hospital, pieces of music that will cheer the patients and recall the great events of former campaigns.

23d. I leave to-morrow.

29th, Suez:
Order for the commanding officers of engineers and artillery to accompany the general-in-chief on a survey of the Suez Canal.

1799

January 12d, Paris:

I am working to determine the line along which a water-way can be run to join the Nile and the Red Sea. This waterway once existed, for I have found traces of it at several points.

8th, Cairo:

(Order.) Citoyen Boyer, surgeon, who has been so cowardly as to refuse help to some wounded because they were supposed to be infected, is unworthy of being a French citizen. He is to be dressed in women's clothes, and paraded through the streets of Alexandria on a donkey, with a board on his back, on which shall be written: *Unworthy of being a French citizen—he fears death.* After which he is to be placed in prison, and sent back to France by the first ship.

25th. (To Tippoo Sahib.) You have already learned of my arrival on the shores of the Red Sea with an innumerable and invincible army, anxious to free you from the iron yoke of England.

I take the first opportunity of letting you know that I am anxious that you should send me information through Moka and Muscat as to your political situation. I hope you can send to Suez or to Cairo, some able and trustworthy person with whom I can discuss matters.

28th. (To General Marmont.) I can't understand Commissary Michaud's obstinacy in remaining in a house when the plague is in it; why doesn't he go into camp out towards Pompey's column? Put the 75th in the grove where you camped so long with the 4th light infantry; it can be barracked there, and all communication with Alexandria cut off. As to the unlucky demi-brigade of light infantry, have the men strip and take sea-baths; they must be rubbed from head to heel; they must wash their clothes and keep themselves clean. Give orders to have the men wash their feet, their hands, their faces, every day.

February 5th. I have just heard of the arrival at Alexandria of a merchantman from Ragusa with a cargo of wine, and with letters for me from Genoa and from Ancona; it is the first news from Europe since eight months.

The troops are now on the march across the desert.

(To Kléber.) At last we have news from France. Jourdan has left the Legislative Assembly and is in command of the army of the Rhine. Joubert has the army of Italy. Steps have been taken to recruit the armies; it appears that all young men of eighteen years of age are called on, and are known as conscripts. Europe is arming on all sides.

10th. I have observed the Ramadan, which began yesterday, with the greatest ceremony; I carried out the duties which formerly devolved on the Pasha.

(To the Directoire.) When you read this letter I may be standing among the ruins of the temple of Solomon. Djezzar Pasha, an old man 70 years of age, is a ferocious person, who has unbounded hatred of the French. He has treated with disdain the friendly advances which I made.

On the 29th of Brumaire I sent him a letter; he had the messenger's head chopped off. Egypt was inundated with firmans that revealed Djezzar's hostile intentions and announced his arrival. His advance guard occupied El Arych, where there are a few good wells and a fort in the desert.

There was therefore no choice. I was challenged; I promptly decided to carry the war into the enemy's country.

17th, in front of El Arych:

The divisions of the army started from different points to meet at El Arych, where we have now established contact with the enemy. The Mameluks, supported by a body of Djezzar Pasha's troops, were there. Régnier's division came up and immediately attacked the Mameluks, killed about 400, and now holds the rest blockaded in the fort.

You are not my friend!—The women!—Josephine!—If you were my friend, you would long ago have told me what I have just learned from Junot,—there is a true friend. Josephine!—and I am six hundred leagues away—you ought to have told me!—Josephine!—to deceive me in such a fashion!—she!—Let them beware! I will wipe out these dandies and exquisites!—As for her—a divorce. Yes, a divorce, publicly, scandalously! I must write, I know everything!—It's your fault, you ought to have told me!

My reputation? Eh! I don't know what I wouldn't give if only what Junot has told me were not true—I love that woman so! If Josephine is guilty, a divorce must separate us forever. I will not be the laughing-stock of all the wastrels of Paris! I will write to Joseph, he will get me a divorce.

18th. The artillery is having great difficulties owing to the quicksands, and the army is so placed that the least delay may be fatal.

The capture of El Arych makes a good beginning for the campaign.

26th, Gaza:

We are in water and mud up to our knees; the cold and weather are just what we get at Paris at this season. The country is finer than we supposed, and we have unexpectedly found stores of provisions and war material, including many cannon-balls of European make.

(To General Marmont.) Send the three ships to Jaffa; their cargoes may help us in besieging St. John of Acre.

(To General Menou.) I have learned with pleasure that you have been attending worship in the mosque.

27th. We crossed 70 leagues of desert with much fatigue; the water was brackish, when there was any. We eat dogs, donkeys, and camels.

March 6th, in front of Jaffa:

At eight o'clock to-morrow morning Delignette's battery will open. General Bon will support the mortar battery. General Lannes will place six companies of grenadiers at the breaching battery before daylight. When the firing between the town and our light infantry is well developed, two columns, each of three companies of grenadiers, will move on the breach and carry it. Battalions will be pushed up successively in support of the grenadiers and light infantry.

7th. (To Abdallah-Aga, commandant of Jaffa.) God is merciful and longsuffering!

Bonaparte, general-in-chief, informs you that he is in Palestine for no other purpose than to drive out the troops of Djezzar Pasha. Jaffa is completely blockaded, and in two hours our batteries will break down your walls and shatter your fortifications. His heart is touched by the suffering that would result to the city were it captured by assault. He offers his safeguard to the garrison and protection to the city, and will therefore delay opening fire until seven o'clock this morning.

8th. At dawn, I summoned the governor to surrender: he had my messenger's head cut off, and made no reply. At seven, we opened fire; at one, I judged the breach to be practicable. General Lannes made the arrangements for the attack; Adjutant Netherwood with ten riflemen led the way. At five, we were in possession of the city, which was sacked for twenty-four hours and given up to all the horrors of war, which never appeared more hideous.

9th. (To General Berthier.) Summon the artillery colonel, get from him the names of the twenty principal artillery officers; have him take them with him to the village where the battalion is that is going to Cairo. There they are to be placed in the fort until further orders. When they have started for the village, order the adjutant-general on duty to take the artillerymen down to the coast, and to have them all shot, taking every precaution to prevent their escaping.

18th, Mount Carmel:
Captain Smith, with two English men-of-war has arrived at St. John of Acre from Alexandria. Acre will be surrounded to-night.

23d, in front of Acre:
(To Sidney Smith.) Do not doubt my desire of showing you every courtesy and of making myself useful to any of your compatriots who may be victims of the mischance of war.

29th. Since our arrival in front of Acre, plenty reigns in our camp. We have opened trenches against the city, and the work is being pushed on energetically.

We have established a breaching battery, and have opened fire on the wall; we hope to carry the place very quickly.

April 4th. (Order.) All soldiers who in the course of to-day and to-morrow bring in cannon-balls found in the open will receive 20 sous for each cannon-ball.

5th. We are very short of cannon-balls. Commodore Smith with his two ships, the *Theseus* and the *Tiger,* has just returned after being away ten days.

8th. We have now been a fortnight in front of Acre, where we hold Djezzar Pasha blockaded. The great quantity of artillery which the English have thrown into the town, with a reinforcement of gunners and officers, together with our own lack of guns, has delayed its capture. But yesterday the two English men-of-war got annoyed with us, and fired more than 2000 shot, which has given us a good supply.

14th. The siege progresses. We have run a gallery beyond the counterscarp, 30 feet below the ditch, which is now only 18 feet from the wall. We have not fired a shot for two weeks; the enemy blaze away like mad; and we merely pick up their cannon-balls humbly, pay 20 sous for them, and pile them up so that we already have about 4000. That will be enough to pour in a hot fire for twenty-four hours, and to batter a fine breach. I am waiting before giving the signal for the sappers to be ready to blow up the counterscarp at the end of a double sap that runs straight to a tower; we are still 50 feet from the counterscarp, which is a matter of a couple of nights. There are many French *émigrés* and English in the town; we are dying to get at them; the chances are it will be on the 21st.

18th. The Janissaries of Damascus, with the cavalry of Djezzar, the Arabs, and the Mameluks of Ibrahim Bey, crossed the Jordan to relieve Acre; they have been completely defeated in engagements at Nazareth, Safed, and Cana, and in the battle of Mount Thabor.

19th. (To citoyen Fourier.) Tell the Divan that when this letter reaches you, Acre will be ours, and that I shall be on my way to Cairo. I am as anxious to be there as you are to see me. One of the first things I shall do will be to convene the Institute and to see whether we cannot do something to extend the bounds of human knowledge.

21st. Mr. Smith is firing away hot and heavy.

(Order.) The general-in-chief, as a mark of his great satisfaction with the 300 brave men commanded by Brigadier-General Junot, who, in the engagement at Nazareth, held in check 5000 cavalry, captured 5 flags, and covered the battle-field with dead, orders:—

A medal worth 500 louis is offered for the best picture representing the battle of Nazareth.

In this picture the French shall be shown in the uniforms of the 2d light infantry and 14th dragoons.

The staff will have sketched by our artists in Egypt, dresses of the Mameluks, of the Janissaries of Damascus, of the Arabs, and will send them to the Minister of the Interior at Paris so that copies may be made and sent to the best artists of Paris, Milan, Florence, Rome, and Naples, and that a day may be set and judges chosen for the competition.

This order shall be communicated to the communes of all the brave soldiers present at the battle of Nazareth.

23d. (To General Lannes.) The mine can be fired at the moment when our guns have silenced the enemy's; the general-in-chief will give the order himself.

As soon as the mine is fired, the breach is to be stormed. Have a band placed in the 1st parallel, and have it strike up the instant our men have got into the breach. I am ordering all the grenadiers to report at your quarters before 4 o'clock in the morning.

25th. More than 300 men were blown up by the mine. It did not (however) produce all the effect the engineers expected; part of the earthworks caved in; the ditch was completely filled for twenty feet on either side.

Several burning barrels of gunpowder which the enemy threw into the breach demoralized the thirty grenadiers we had lodged there, and we had to abandon our lodgment before morning. General Caffarelli is dead.

May 2d. Our 18-pounders have been at work these last two days. The tower is now a ruin. The enemy have only one gun left with which they can fire; realizing that they cannot defend their walls much longer, they are crowning their glacis with parapets. The day after tomorrow we shall get our 24-pounders up so as to make a breach, and as soon as it is practicable we shall deliver a general assault *en masse*.

8th. Last night at ten o'clock we captured the breach tower.

9th. This wretched clump of hovels has cost me many lives and much time. But things have gone so far that we must make a last attempt. If I succeed, as I hope and believe, I shall raise and arm all Syria. I shall march on Damascus and Aleppo. As I advance, I shall swell my ranks with all the discontented; I shall announce the end of slavery and of the tyrannous rule of the pashas. I shall reach Constantinople at the head of an armed multitude. I shall establish in the East a new and great Empire. If I fail in the last assault I mean to deliver, I shall leave at once, as time is pressing. I cannot reach Cairo before the middle of June.

As Kléber's division is on the point of arriving, the intention of the general-in-chief is that as soon as this division is rested it shall move to the breach to attack and capture the city.

Night:
The troops will leave camp at two o'clock in the morning and march to the positions allotted to them in the plan of attack.

10th. We have carried the principal parts of the wall, (but) the enemy have built a second wall abutting on Djezzar's palace. We should have to sap through the town, to open trenches before every house, and to lose more lives than I am willing to lose. In any case, the season is too far spent. My object is accomplished; Egypt calls me.

I am planting a battery of 24-pounders to raze Djezzar's palace and the principal buildings of the town; I shall blaze away about a thousand shells, which, in so small a space, will do considerable damage. With Acre reduced to a heap of stones, I shall recross the desert, so as to be ready for any European or Turkish army that attempts to disembark in Egypt in July or August.

16th. We have razed the palace of Djezzar and crushed the city under our shell fire.

17th. Soldiers! With the swiftness of an Arab host you have crossed the desert that separates Africa from Asia. The army that was marching to invade Egypt is destroyed; you have captured its general, its material, its waterskins, and its camels. On the battlefield of Mount Thabor, you dispersed a horde that had gathered from the extreme parts of Asia for the pillage of Egypt.

A few days more and you hoped to capture the pasha himself in his palace; but at this season of the year the citadel of Acre is not worth the loss of even a few days; the brave lives its capture would cost are needed for more important operations.

20th. (To the Divisional Generals.) The assembly will be beaten at seven o'clock at night by one drum only for each company. General Murat with all the cavalry will not start until eleven o'clock at night.

I have been through some trying moments. I allowed my imagination to interfere with my practice; but I think St. John of Acre has killed it. I shall take good care not to let it run away with my judgment again!

27th, Jaffa:
We reached Jaffa on the 25th. Detachments have been starting on the march to Egypt these last two days. I shall stay here a few more days to have the fortifications blown up.

28th, Jaffa:
There were fourteen or sixteen ill of the plague. I assembled a medical board,—they said the sick would die in twenty-four hours. I determined to wait that time rather than leave them to the Turks, who would cut off their noses and ears. At the end of the time only one or two were alive, and they were dying when my army marched.

June 9th, Salheyeh:
We got over the desert pretty well. The English commodore who has summoned Damietta to surrender is a lunatic. As he has always been in command of fire-ships, he has no notion of the manners that are called for in an important command. The allied army of which he speaks was destroyed in Acre.

15th, Cairo:
My entry took place in the midst of an immense throng that lined the streets, of all the muftis riding on their mules, because the Prophet had a preference for riding these beasts, of all the bodies of Janissaries, of the agas of police, of the descendants of Abou Bekr, of Fatima, and of the descendants of many saints revered by true believers. The chief merchants walked in front, as well as the Coptic Patriarch; the procession was closed by the Greek auxiliaries.

(To General Desaix.) I am here with part of the army. We have reached the season when a landing is possible. I shall lose not one hour in making ready.

Why don't you wear a flannel vest? It's the only way to protect yourself against eye-trouble.

19th. Still no news from France.

28th. The French army has lost 5,344 men since its arrival in Egypt. Next season we shall be reduced to 15,000 effectives, from which deduct 2,000 in hospital, 500 veterans, 500 artificers who don't go into action, and we have 12,000 left.

29th. (To citoyen Poussielgue.) Kindly let me know the ages of the three male slaves that have just come in from Upper Egypt; I want to buy them.

July 15th. On the 13th a Turkish fleet made up of 5 ships of the line, 3 frigates, 50 or 60 transports, anchored in the bay of Aboukir.

20th, El Ramanyeh:
(To General Kléber.) We have reached El Ramanyeh. Adjutant-General Jullien informs me that your advance guard has reached Rosetta, and that you are close up with the rest of your division.

It appears certain that the enemy have landed at Aboukir. My line of front will be Alexandria, Birket, and Rosetta. I shall hold Birket in person with the main body. General Marmont will be at Alexandria, you at Rosetta, each with about the same number of troops; so that you are my right, General Marmont my left. If the enemy are in force, I shall fight them on good ground, bringing either my right or my left in to me. I shall hope that the wing that is not with me can get up fast enough to act as my reserve. Birket is one league off the parallel of Leloha, and one league from Besentonay. Get all the information you need, and try to place yourself so that instantly on my order you can march rapidly on Edkou or Birket; and as it is quite likely that communications will be cut, get plenty of men out reconnoitring so as to know what I am doing and where I am; and should circumstances point to a movement that you are free to make, and you think it likely from your information that I would have ordered you to make it, you can go ahead.

21st. (To the Divan of Cairo.) They are beginning to disembark at Aboukir; I am not interfering with them. There are Russians on the fleet, people who hold in horror those who believe in the unity of God because, according to their lies, they believe that there are three Gods.

22d. The enemy's fleet has been reinforced by 30 ships. Their army is in position in front of Aboukir; I am starting in two hours to reconnoitre.

24th. At the well between Alexandria and Aboukir.
(To General Murat.) Take command of all the cavalry. The advance guard will march on the enemy at two o'clock in the morning; no drums will be beaten.

25th, near Aboukir:
At seven o'clock we were in presence of the enemy, who were in position one league in front of the fort of Aboukir. We attacked them, completely defeated them, captured their redoubts, intrenchments, and camp. The enemy ran into the sea in an attempt to reach their ships three quarters of a league away. They were all drowned,—the most horrible sight I ever witnessed. We have captured the general-in-chief who is wounded, his name is Mustafa Pasha; I shall take him to Cairo with me. We had 100 killed and 400 wounded, among the latter General Murat. The battle of Aboukir is one of the most successful I have seen. Of the army which the enemy disembarked, not a man has escaped. This victory, which will have so much influence on the fortunes of the Republic, is due chiefly to General Murat.

27th. (Order.) The general-in-chief, as a mark of his satisfaction with General Murat's cavalry brigade, which covered itself with glory at the battle of Aboukir, directs the commanding officer of the artillery to hand over to this brigade the two English fieldpieces which had been sent by the Court of London as a present to Constantinople, and that were captured in the battle.

The names of each of the three regiments of this brigade, the 7th hussars, the 3d and 4th dragoons, and the names of General Murat and of Adjutant-General Roize, shall be engraved on each gun; on the breach shall be inscribed: *Battle of Aboukir.*

August 11th, Cairo:

I have English gazettes to the 10th of June. France declared war against the Emperor on the 13th of March. Jourdan has been defeated at Feldkirch and has withdrawn across the Rhine. Scherer, who had been given the army of Italy, has been beaten at Rivoli, and is back across the Mincio. Mantua is blockaded.

If ever I have the luck to set foot in France again, the reign of chatter is over.

16th. (Order.) The commandants of provinces will make known by a circular in Arabic sent to all villages, the pomp with which the festival of the Prophet has been observed in Cairo. All the army, carrying a great number of torches, proceeded to the house of Sheik El Bekry; the general-in-chief had dined with him, as had Mustafa Pasha and the principal officers made prisoners at the battle of Aboukir. The general-in-chief was present at the reading of various Arabic poems in honour of the Prophet, after which, surrounded by the principal sheiks, he attended worship and ordered the genealogy of the Prophet to be read. The Pasha and the Turkish prisoners could not overcome their surprise at seeing the respect professed by the French for Islam and the law of the most holy of Prophets.

19th, Menouf:
(To General Kléber.) I am convinced that there is no hostile fleet of any size in the Mediterranean. Please start for Rosetta at once. I have to confer with you on matters of extreme importance.

22d, Alexandria:
I leave to-night for France.

(To General Kléber.) You will find herewith an order for assuming command of the army. I am taking with me Generals Berthier, Lannes, Murat, Andréossy, and Marmont, citoyens Monge and Berthollet.

I inclose you the English papers to the 10th of June. You will see that we have lost Italy; that Mantua, Turin, and Tortona are besieged. I have reason to expect that the first named fortress will hold out until the end of November. I hope, if fate is propitious, to reach Europe before the beginning of October.

Accustomed as I am to view the good opinion of posterity as the fit reward for the pains and labours of life, I leave Egypt with the deepest regret. The interests of our country, her destiny, my duty, the extraordinary events that are occurring, have decided me to pass through the enemy's fleets to return to Europe. In mind and in heart I shall be with you; I will value your successes as highly as if I were still among you, and I shall reckon ill-employed every day on which I do nothing to help the army I place under your orders. The army I am leaving you is made up of my children, who have at all times, even in the greatest affliction, given me constantly tokens of their affection; maintain them in these sentiments; it is your duty because of the esteem and affection I have for you, and because of my real attachment to them.

(To General Junot.) When you receive this letter I shall be far away from Egypt. I regretted not being able to take you with me; you were too far from our starting-point. I have left orders with Kléber to send you off in October. In any case, wherever and however we may be situated, believe in the continuance of my devoted friendship.

October 7th, Ajaccio:
At Ajaccio we got news of our continued reverses in Italy, the capture of Mantua, the battles of Novi and La Trebbia, the landing of the Anglo-Russians in Holland, and the events of Prairial.

8th, Frejus:
At nightfall we sighted the French coast. Universal enthusiasm broke out on its becoming known that General Bonaparte was on board the frigates. As in Corsica the two ships were at once invaded by a crowd, notwithstanding repeated and pressing warnings of the danger of not observing the laws of quarantine.

9th. The quarantine officers gave us a clean bill, and at noon we went ashore, the forty-seventh day since our departure from Alexandria.

On the same day General Bonaparte started for Paris; on his way he was received with demonstrations of joy that showed the political effect of his unexpected return.

10th, Aix:
Citoyens Directeurs: Since leaving France I have received only one dispatch from you; it found me in front of Acre, and from that moment I judged that I could not remain absent from France much longer. I obtained copies of the English gazettes to the 6th of June, and from them learned of the defeats of Jourdan in Germany and of Scherer in Italy. I started immediately, that very hour, with the frigates *La Muiron* and *La Carrère,* although both slow sailers. I did not stop to reckon the risk; my duty was to proceed wherever I might be most useful. That being my view, I would have wrapped myself in my cloak and started in an open boat, if I had had no frigates. I have made my way through the English cruisers. I have landed at Fréjus safely. I shall be in Paris nearly as soon as my letter.

15th. *Arrival in Paris, rue de la Victoire.*
No further relations between us! She shall not set foot in my house! What do I care what people will say? They will gossip for one or two days, and talk of something else the third. Forgive her? Never!

Well! well! She is here! Don't believe that I have forgiven her;—never while I live. I wanted to doubt!—Her truthfulness! I drove her out when I arrived. And that fool Joseph who was here!

But what could I do? As she came down the staircase in tears, I saw Eugène, Hortense, who were following her sobbing. I was not given a heart for nothing, and I cannot remain unmoved when I see tears flowing. Eugène followed me to Egypt; I have accustomed myself to look on him as my adopted son; he is so brave, he is such a good boy! Hortense is just coming out; all who know her speak highly of her. I confess, I was deeply moved, I couldn't resist the sobs of those two poor children; I said to myself: Are they to be the victims of their mother's ill conduct? I stopped Eugène. Hortense turned back with her mother; I said nothing. How could I help it? Every man is weak!

17th. So you believe that the thing can be done?

22d. I have already learned a good deal: but we shall see. I think I shall have Bernadotte and Moreau against me. I am not afraid of Moreau; he is soft, has no energy. But Bernadotte! He has Moorish blood in his veins; he is bold and enterprising; he is related by marriage to my brothers; he dislikes me; I am pretty sure he will be against me. Well, we have only just arrived, we'll see.

24th. Patience! The pear is nearly ripe.

November 1st. Well, Bourrienne, I'll bet that you can't guess with whom I breakfasted to-day, eh? With Bernadotte, and the joke is that I invited myself. Yes. You would have seen the whole business if you had come to the Théâtre Français with me last night. I ran right into Bernadotte as we were coming out, and upon my word, not knowing what on earth to say to him on the spur of the moment, I asked him if he would join our party to-day. He replied that he would, and as we were then in front of his house in the rue Cisalpine, I plain asked him for a cup of coffee and said I should be delighted to have some talk with him. He made himself quite pleasant to me. What do you think of it, Bourrienne? No, no, I was right, you may be sure; it will compromise him with (the Directeur) Gohier. Remember one thing: always take the first step towards your enemies and put on a good countenance, otherwise they think you are afraid and are encouraged.

6th. (Brumaire 15.)
To subvert a representative form of government is a criminal proposal in this century of enlightenment and liberty. (Vive Bonaparte! Peace! Peace!) I raise my glass to the union of all Frenchmen!

7th. (Brumaire 16.)
Well, general, what is your opinion as to the state of the Republic?

(Jourdan: Unless some more stable order can be evolved we shall have to despair of saving the country.)

We need a stronger government. Don't be uneasy; all will be done in the interests of the Republic.

8th. (Brumaire 17.)
When it comes to conspiracy, everything is permissible.

I have accepted an invitation to dine with Gohier to-morrow: but you may be sure I shan't go. I regret his obstinacy, however. To reassure him a little my wife is inviting him to breakfast. I have seen Barras this morning, and he was in a state of great anxiety when I left him. He begged me to call this evening: I promised him I would, but I don't want to; to-morrow it will all be over. That's not a great while to gain. Come, good-night; be here at seven o'clock in the morning.

9th. (Brumaire 18.)
The army has come to me, and I have come to the legislative body.

What have you done with France which I left in your hands so prosperous? I left you peace, I find war! I left you victories, I find defeats! I left you millions, I find beggary! This state of things must cease.

Citoyens Représentants: The Republic was perishing, you perceived it, and your decree has saved it. Let those who seek to foment disorder beware! I will arrest them with the help of my companions in arms. Your wisdom has framed this decree; our arms will carry it out. We want a Republic founded on real liberty, on civil liberty, on national representation; we will succeed, we swear it.

(To the Army.) Soldiers! The extraordinary decree of the Council of Ancients has placed me in command of the city and army. For two years past the Republic has been badly governed. You had hoped that my return would bring our afflictions to an end; you have hailed it with an unanimity that imposes on me the obligation I am now fulfilling; you will fulfil yours and support your general with energy and firmness, and with that same confidence which I have always reposed in you.

Liberty, victory, and peace will restore to the French Republic the rank she formerly held in Europe, and that only ineptitude or treason could make her lose. *Vive la République!*

Night:
It is peace we have conquered: that is what must be said in every newspaper, every theatre; what must be repeated in prose, in verse, even in ballads.

Things went pretty well to-day. We'll see to-morrow.

10th. (Brumaire 19.) *The two Councils meet at Saint Cloud.*

9 a. m., Place de la Concorde:
To-morrow we shall sleep in the Luxembourg, or finish here.

2 p. m., Saint Cloud:
The wine is drawn, we must drink it. Augereau, remember Arcola!

(To the Council of Ancients.) *Citoyens Représentants:* The existing circumstances are extraordinary; you are on a volcano. Yesterday I was living quietly in Paris when you charged me to carry out your decree for transferring (the session of the Legislature to Saint Cloud). I immediately called together my comrades, and we flew to your help. Well, to-day, I am already overwhelmed with calumny. Caesar, Cromwell, a military government, are spoken of. Had I aimed at a military government, would I have lent my support to the national representatives? The Republic is without a government. The Council of Five Hundred is divided against itself. There is only the Council of Ancients. It is from that Council I derive my powers: it is for you to take steps,—speak, I am here to carry out your measures. Let us save liberty; let us save equality!

(A voice: And what about the Constitution?)

The Constitution? You yourselves have torn it up. You broke it on the 18th of Fructidor; you broke it on the 22d of Floréal; you broke it on the 30th of Prairial. Not a soul respects it any longer. I will speak out. Since my return, I have been surrounded with intrigues. Every faction has approached me. And men who arrogantly describe themselves as the only patriots have urged me to thrust the Constitution aside.

(Several voices: Names! names!)

Outspokenness of a soldier—agitation—(increasing confusion and noise) victories—Constitution broken—Cæsar, Cromwell, tyrant—that's all I have to say to you.—Liberty! Equality!—You forget the Constitution!—Hypocrites, intriguers—I am not—I will abdicate from power the instant the Republic is free from danger.—The God of War and the God of Fortune is with me!

(Bourrienne: Come away, general: you don't know what you are saying.)

My friends will follow me!

And you, brave grenadiers, if any speaker dares to apply the word *outlaw* to your general, let the thunders of war crush him instantly.

So I talked a lot of nonsense, did I?

(Well, yes, general.)

I had rather talk to soldiers than to lawyers. Those…made me nervous. I am not accustomed to assemblies; it may come in time.

4 p. m.:
I entered the Council of Five Hundred, alone, unarmed. The daggers of the deputies are at once raised against their liberator. Twenty assassins rush at me.

(Down with the tyrant! Dictator! Dictator! Outlaw him!)

4.30 p. m.:
To arms! My horse! Soldiers! can I trust you? I will bring them to reason!

(Murat: Grenadiers, forward! Vive la République! Vive Bonaparte!)

5 p. m.:
The Council of Five Hundred is cleared by the troops.

11 p. m.:
I have tried not to be the man of a party. Conservative, paternal, liberal ideas have been restored to their rightful place among us.

(Proclamation.) On my return to Paris I found the Government divided, and all men agreed on this truth, that the Constitution was half ruined and could not save the cause of liberty. All parties came to me, told me their plans, revealed their secrets, and asked for my support: I refused to be the tool of any party.

The Council of Ancients summoned me; I answered its appeal. I thought it my duty to my fellow citizens, to the soldiers who are dying with our armies, to the national glory purchased with their blood, to accept the command. The Councils met at Saint Cloud; the troops guaranteed the maintenance of order outside, but inside a gang of assassins establish terror. Several deputies of the Council of Five Hundred, armed with daggers and firearms, uttered threats of death. I laid my complaints before the Council of Ancients; I called on it to insure the execution of its beneficent decrees; it joined me by renewed demonstrations of its unaltered resolve. I entered the Council of Five Hundred, alone, unarmed, my head uncovered. Daggers are at once raised against me; twenty assassins fly at me and strike at my breast. The grenadiers of the legislative body, whom I had left at the door, rush in to interpose between the assassins and me. They drag me out. At the same moment cries of *Outlaw* are raised against the protector of the law. They crowd around the president (Lucien Bonaparte) with threats in their mouths, and arms in their hands; they call on him for a declaration of outlawry; word is sent out to me; I give orders to have him saved from their rage, and six grenadiers bring him out. Immediately after this the grenadiers of the legislative body charge into the hall and clear it. Alarmed, the factions disperse and go away.

People of France, you will doubtless recognize in my conduct the zeal of a soldier of liberty, of a citizen devoted to the Republic.

11th, Paris:
Have you no muster rolls at the war office? At all events, you must have an account of the pay, which will give us the same result?—An account of the stores? Of the clothing?

You have worked a long time in the Ministry of Finance?

(Gaudin: Twenty years, general.)
We need your help. Come, take the oath, we are in a hurry.

12th. People of France: Swear with us to be true to the Republic one and indivisible, founded on equality, liberty, and the representative system.

The Consuls of the Republic:
Bonaparte, Roger Ducos, Sieyès.

15th. Every day must be marked by one step forward in the creation of a general system of finance.

24th. (To General Jourdan.) I have received your letter of the 20th. You were vexed at the events of the 10th. But the worst is over now, and I am more than anxious to see the victor of Fleurus remain in the path that will lead us to organization, true liberty, and happiness.

You must rally to the mass of citizens. Is not the plain designation French citizen equal to that of royalist, of *Clichien,* of *Jacobin,* of *Feuillant,* and of those thousand and one denominations born of a factious spirit that for ten years past have threatened to plunge the nation into an abyss from which it is time it should be drawn forever.

Sieyès thinks that he alone can arrive at truth; when an objection is raised, he replies as though he were inspired, and there's an end to the matter.

(Sieyès: Do you want to be king, then?)

December 1st. The Minister of War will take steps for having at least 100 field-pieces of the army of Italy horsed and made ready for active service as rapidly as possible.

Have a plan drawn up for placing all flags captured from the enemy under the dome of the *Invalides;* have the chronology of the victories of the Republic engraved on marble tablets.

4th. The Minis ter of War will send for Generals Moreau and Clarke to draw up a plan of operations for the new army of the Rhine. It will be reinforced.

5th. Concentrate at Lyons the remnants of the demi-brigades of the 8th military division that were formerly with the army of Italy, and reorganize them so that in three or four months we can form an army of reserve.

6th. If Sieyès goes to the country, draw up the plan of a constitution quickly; I will push it through.

7th. Inform General Moreau that the Consuls think there is urgent need he should join the army.

14th. *The Constitution is being drawn up.*

Citoyen Daunou, Sit down there, (and write.)

The decision of the First Consul shall be sufficient! (Sieyès: my only wish is to retire.)

15th. A constitution should be short and obscure.

(To the People of France.) A constitution is submitted to you. It will bring to an end the uncertainties which attended the provisional government in all its dealings, exterior, military, and interior.

The Constitution is based on the true principles of representative government, on the sacred rights of property, of equality, of liberty.

The powers it provides for are strong and stable, as they should be to guarantee the rights of citizens and the interests of the State.

Citizens, the Revolution is now anchored to the principles which gave it birth. The Revolution is finished.

Bonaparte, Roger Ducos, Sieyès.

18th. I trust that the ensuing campaign will be more honourable to the French arms than the last.

21st. The object of the Republic in prosecuting the war is to bring about a peace. It is on the army comanded by General Moreau that rests the Republic's chief hope of peace for the moment. The Government has absolute confidence in the zeal and military capacity of General Moreau.

22d. Considering the present condition of the army of Italy, the Consuls of the Republic declare: that General Masséna is intrusted with extraordinary powers. He may suspend and dismiss any general who has lost his confidence. He may disband corps and cashier officers for insubordination.

25th. (To His Majesty the King of Great Britain and Ireland.) Called by the wishes of the French nation to the first magistracy of the Republic, I think it proper, on taking up my duties, to notify Your Majesty of the fact in person.

Is the war that for eight years past has devastated the four quarters of the world to be eternal? Is there no possibility of coming to an agreement? How can the two most enlightened nations of Europe, both more powerful than is needed to secure their safety and independence, sacrifice to some vague notion of superiority the interests of commerce, internal prosperity, and the happiness of families? How can they fail to see that peace is the first of necessities and the greatest of glories?

Your Majesty must see in this overture nothing but my sincere desire by prompt action to contribute efficaciously for the second time to a general pacification.

(To His Majesty the Emperor, King of Hungary and of Bohemia.) Once more in Europe after an absence of eighteen months, I find war raging between the French Republic and Your Majesty. The French nation has summoned me to its chief magistracy. Far as I am from any sentiments of vainglory, my greatest desire is to prevent the effusion of the blood that is about to flow. Your Majesty's reputation leaves me no doubt as to your most heartfelt desire. If that sentiment is given its course, I do not doubt that we can conciliate the interests of the two countries.

(To the army of Italy.) Soldiers! The circumstances that have placed me at the head of the Government prevent me from being in your midst.

Soldiers! Several corps have abandoned their positions, have refused to listen to the voice of their officers. The 17th light infantry is one of them. Are the brave soldiers of Castiglione and of Rivoli all dead, then? They would have perished rather than abandon their flags.

Soldiers of Italy! A new general commands you. He was always in the front rank in the days of your glory. Give him your confidence; he will bring victory back to your standards.

I shall have a daily account rendered me of the conduct of all the corps, especially of the 17th light infantry and of the 63d of the line. Let them remember how I once trusted them!

26th. (To Lucien Bonaparte, Minister of the Interior.)

If war were not a necessity, my first care would be to found the prosperity of France on the communes. It is a much simpler matter, when reconstructing a nation, to deal with one thousand of its inhabitants at a time instead of striving romantically for the individual happiness of every one. In France a commune stands for 1000 inhabitants. To work at the prosperity of the 36,000 communes is to work at the prosperity of the 36,000,000 inhabitants, while simplifying the question, and reducing the difficulty by the proportion that exists between 36,000 and 36,000,000.

The Minister of the Interior will carefully consider the following ideas:

Before the Revolution the commune belonged to the lord and to the priests; the vassal and the parishioner had no right to the roads; no ditches, nor fields for pasturing their cows or their sheep. Since 1790, when, suddenly and righteously, these common rights of communication and pasturage were snatched from the hands of the feudal lord, each municipality has, under the protection of the laws, become a real person, having the right to hold, to acquire, and to sell property, and to perform every deed known to our law for the benefit of the municipal community. France was therefore suddenly divided into 36,000 individualities, each one of which was subject to all the instincts of the proprietor, which are to increase his possessions, to improve his products, to swell his revenue. The root of the prosperity of France, therefore, lay at that point.

The reason why nothing has grown from this root is this: that an individual proprietor is always alive to his interests, while a community is, on the contrary, sleepy and sterile; the interests of an individual are a matter of simple instinct; those of a commune demand virtue, and virtue is rare. Since 1790 the 36,000 communes are but 36,000 orphans, heiresses of the old feudal privileges, neglected or plundered these ten years by the municipal tutors of the Convention and of the Directoire. They have stolen from the roads, from the pathways, from the trees, from the churches. What would become of the communes if this went on another ten years? The first duty of a Minister of the Interior is to stop an evil which will otherwise infect these 36,000 members of the social body.

The first condition, when dealing with a great evil, is to diagnose carefully its gravity and its incidents. The Minister of the Interior will therefore begin by drawing up a general schedule of the situation of the 36,000 communes of France. We have never had such a schedule. Here are the principal heads to be set down.

There will be three classes: Communes that are in debt; communes whose accounts balance; communes with assets. The last two classes are not numerous, and their case is not pressing. The real question is how to clear the communes that are in debt.

The Schedule will show:

1°. Details of property accruing to the commune after the division of communal property.
2°. Details of the loans, of outstanding debts, and of dates of payment.
3°. Valuation of revenues under specified heads, as rents, leases, etc.
4°. Charges other than those that are strictly communal, as payments to hospitals, charities, etc.
5°. Details of the roads with a general indication of those that are useful and those that might be sold.
6°. Condition of the rectories, churches, and annexes.
7°. Details of rebates to be got from owners of foreshore who have plundered the commune.
8°. Timber, and of what kind, that might profitably be sold.
9°. Whether leases, rights of fishery and of pasturing might be made more remunerative.

When this schedule is drawn up, the prefect will be notified that the whole effort of the administration must be brought to bear on the communes that are in debt, and that the mayors who do not come into line with these ideas of communal improvement must be removed. The prefect is to visit these communes at least twice a year, and the sub-prefect four times a year, under penalty of removal from office. A monthly report shall be sent to the minister of what is being done and of what remains to be done in these communes.

Suggestions may be sent in to me for a prize to be awarded to mayors who free their communes from debt within two years, and the Government will appoint a special Commissioner to administer every commune that is not free in five years.

In five years, therefore, there will be only two classes of communes in France: Communes with assets; communes whose accounts balance. Having reached this first levelling up, the efforts of the minister and of the communes will be directed towards bringing up the communes whose accounts balance into the class of the communes with assets, so that in ten years France will have none but the latter class. Then the trend towards prosperity resulting from 36,000,000 individual efforts will be intensified by the power of 36,000 communal entities, all acting under the guidance of Government in the line of greater and greater improvement.

Every year the fifty mayors who have done most to free their communes, or to increase their resources, shall be brought to Paris at the expense of the State and presented ceremonially to the three Consuls. A column erected at the expense of the Government at the principal entrance of the city or village will hand the name of the mayor down to posterity. On it shall be inscribed: "A grateful country to the guardian of his commune!"

29th. (To General Berthier.) You will find herewith a proclamation and several decrees of the Government relating to the Vendée. You will note that the inhabitants are free to practise their religion; that unsold churches are handed over to the communes; that the priests are to be asked for no other oath than that of fidelity to the Constitution; and that the priests are at liberty to celebrate mass whenever they wish.

1800

January 12d, Paris:
On the first day of each decade there shall be held a gen-eral council of finance; on the fourth day a council of military administration; on the sixth day a council of naval administration. On the 8th day of each month there shall be a council of judicial administration; on the 18th, one for foreign affairs; and on the 28th, one for internal and police matters. These Councils will meet at the First Consul's at half-past nine in the evening.

When I want to close off one matter, I push in its file, and pull out another. I never get them mixed up, and they never bother nor fatigue me. If I want to sleep, I push in all the files at once, and I'm asleep.

13th. Four millions are all important to us in the present situation. Perhaps we could raise them at Hamburg.

14th. (To citoyen Gaudin.) General Moreau complains that his drafts on Bâle have not been honoured. His army is in absolute want. It is urgent to send him money. Couldn't you get some drafts on Marseilles or Corsica?

15th. (To brave Léon.) I have received your letter, my brave comrade; there was no necessity to remind me of your deeds. Since the death of brave Benezette you are the bravest grenadier of the army. One of the hundred swords I am giving to the army goes to you. All the men agreed that you were the model of your regi-ment. I am anxious to see you; the Minister of War will issue an order to that effect. I regard you as my son.

General Murat will give him a brevet as sub-lieutenant in the Consular Guard, and will write him a letter.

25th. I intend to organize a Reserve army, of which the command will go to the First Consul.

February 7th. (Order.) Washington is dead. That great man fought against despotism. He established the liberty of his country. His memory will always be treasured by the French people, as it will by the free men of both continents, and especially by the French soldiers who, like him and the American soldiers, are fighting for equality and liberty.

The First Consul therefore orders that, for the space of ten days, a black crape shall be draped on the standards and guidons of the Republic.

13th. (To General Hédouville.) Inform Bourmont that he must surrender his guns within twenty-four hours of your summons, and 3000 muskets within three days. On his refusal put yourself at the head of your troops and don't take your boots off till you've destroyed him.

18th. At the palace of the Tuileries:

To be here is nothing, we've got to stay here!

(To General Brune.) From what you write about Georges (Cadoudal) I shall be glad to see him in Paris. Send me a list of the leaders. Frotté has been captured with all his staff; I had refused to negotiate with him. At this writing he should be shot; so that peace is pretty well established in Normandy.

27th. Announce the Civil Code for next session. Give me the names of men who can carry through the work, and draw up a decree.

March 1st. There will be a grand parade of all the troops of the garrison in the Court of the Tuileries every decade.

5th. I saw Georges this morning; he looks a burly Breton who might be turned to some useful account for his country.

Will it be peace? Or will it be war? That is still very uncertain. However, the Emperor negotiates with some politeness; so far as manners go it all looks well.

8th. (Proclamation.) People of France, you want peace. Your Government desires it even more ardently than you. Our first hopes, our constant endeavours, have been to secure it. The English Government has betrayed the secret of its horrible policy. To tear France asunder; to destroy her navy and her ports; to efface her name from Europe; to reduce her to the rank of a second rate power; to divide the nations of the continent so as to seize their commerce and enrich herself with their spoils: these are the hideous successes for which England lavishes her gold, her promises, and her intrigues. If any Power still insists on attempting the fate of arms, the First Consul has promised peace; he will conquer it at the head of those warriors he has more than once led to victory. With them he will know how to find once more the fields of their former exploits; but in the midst of battle he will invoke peace, and he swears to fight for nothing but the happiness of France and the repose of the world.

12th. (To General Masséna.) The campaign will soon open on the Rhine. Melas, who is against you, is not very deep. He is far from having your military ability, or your activity. I am very distressed at your situation, but I count on your zeal and on your talent.

15th. The first division of the Reserve army, about 12,000 strong, will start from Paris to-morrow. The two other divisions left Nantes and Rennes on the 12th.

16th. (To General Moreau.) I have become a sort of lay figure, having lost my liberty of action and happiness. I envy you your lucky fate. At the head of brave men you will accomplish great things. I would willingly trade off my consular purple for the stripe of a chef de brigade under your orders.

I hope that circumstances will allow me to come to your help. In any case, I have the fullest confidence in you.

(To a journalist.) I am trying my strength against Europe; you are trying yours against the spirit of the Revolution. Your ambition is greater than mine, and I have more chances of success than you.

20th, Malmaison:
I was here last Sunday, walking, alone with the silence of nature. The sound of the church-bell of Rueil suddenly struck my ear; it gave me a sharp sensation. So strong is the power of early habit and education over us! I said to myself: How great must that impression be on simple and credulous men! Let the philosophers and rationalists get over that! The people need a religion.

April 4th. General Berthier is starting for the Reserve army; I have appointed Carnot minister of war. I have not yet sent my baggage off; I am daily expecting decisive information from Vienna.

5th. The First Consul would be gratified by the suppression of the couplet that alludes to him in the *Tableau des Sabines.*

(To citoyen Fouché.) The Consuls intend that the journals *Le Bien Informé, Les Hommes libres,* and *Les Dé-fenseurs de la Patrie* be suppressed. Inform Mr. (Tom) Paine that the police are aware that his conduct is not good; at the first complaint he will be sent to America, his own country.

9th. (To General Berthier.) The Reserve army which you command is to establish harmony between the armies of the Rhine and of Italy in view of the operations that are about to take place. It is to be the centre of a grand line of which the right is at Genoa and the left on the Danube.

(To General Masséna.) The army of the Rhine will open the campaign between the 10th and 20th of this month. As soon as this is done, General Lecourbe will be transferred to the command of General Berthier; he will cross the St. Gothard and descend into Italy. At the same moment part of the Reserve army will enter the Valais, and thence cross into Italy, either by the Simplon or by the St. Gothard.

21st. (Proclamation to the youth of France.) Young Frenchmen: If you are burning to belong to an army that is intended to bring the wars of the Revolution to a close, by securing the independence, the liberty, and the glory of the great nation: to arms! to arms! Rush to Dijon!

Generally speaking, the best way to praise me is to do all things that inspire the nation, the youth, the army, with heroic sentiments.

24th. (To Carnot.) The army of Italy is in contact with the Austrian army. The Reserve army must not lose a single hour. Therefore pray order General Berthier to move the army as rapidly as possible to Geneva. I have nothing new by the semaphore from Bâle to-day. Repeat the order to General Moreau to attack the enemy.

25th. (To General Berthier.) Everything is going smoothly here, and the instant you think my presence necessary because of events either on the Rhine or in Italy, I can start one hour after receiving your letter. I regret to see that residing in Dijon makes you melancholy. Cheer up!

27th. (To General Berthier.) My plan is no longer to cross the St. Gothard; I think that move possible and within the bounds of prudence only if General Moreau should win some success over the enemy. Besides, Milan may not be our objective after all, for we may have to hasten to Tortona to relieve Masséna, who, if he has been defeated, has doubtless shut himself up in Genoa, where he has food for thirty days. We shall therefore have to cross by the St. Bernard.

There is no greater coward than I when I am drawing up a plan of campaign. I magnify every danger, every disadvantage that can be conceived. My nervousness is painful; not but that I show a cool face to those who are about me. I am like a woman in the throes of childbirth. When once my decision is made, however, I forget all, except what may carry it through to success.

I love power; but I love it as an artist, as a musician loves his violin. I love to draw sounds from it, chords, harmony!

Midnight:

I am waiting impatiently for news from the Rhine and from Italy.

May 1st. (To Carnot.) Please send an intelligent staff or engineer officer to General Suchet and then on to General Masséna. He will inform them that the Reserve army is in full march for the passes of the Alps, and will debouch in Piedmont on the 11th of May.

2d. (To Berthier.) The enemy is far from suspecting your march. I have sure information that at Vienna and in Italy they are laughing at our Reserve army; they think August will be here before it is ready, and that it is merely a levy of conscripts to fill the ranks of the army of the Rhine.

3d. (To the Presidents of the Tribunals of the Department of the Seine.) While France was torn by factions, justice was badly administered, as was indeed inevitable. For ten years have these conditions lasted; it is for you to bring them to an end. You are never to ask to what party the man who demands justice belongs; but you are to weigh the rights of all men with severe impartiality. It is for the army to secure peace with foreign countries; it is for Justice to secure peace between our citizens. You are appointed for life; no one has the right to remove you; you are responsible for your judgments only to your conscience; you will be as impassive as the law.

With laws that actually interfere with the action of justice, I myself am compelled to prosecute disorders that affect the security of the state and to repress them arbitrarily.

Penal laws should read as though engraved on tables of marble, and should be as concise as the Decalogue.

A law should always lay down a general principle; it would be futile to attempt to foresee all possible cases.

4th. (To General Berthier.) I have just received your dispatch. The last news from Italy is that on the 23d Masséna was at the bridge of Cornigliano; he is therefore really blockaded in Genoa. It may happen: that Masséna will capitulate and evacuate Genoa; (or that) Masséna's positions at Genoa will be carried. In either case, you must see that General Melas can move from Genoa to Aosta in eight days, and if he reached there before you could debouch with 20,000 men, the odds would be much in his favour in attempting to hold the passage into Italy. Therefore try to get General Chabran's (command), together with a thousand cavalry, to Aosta by the 10th of May, and the rest by the 12th and 13th. I leave to-morrow night, and will be at Genoa on the 18th.

5th. (To Berthier.) I have just learned by semaphore that Moreau has been engaged with the enemy at Stockach, that he has made 7000 prisoners, captured nine guns, and large magazines. All is going well. Masséna's aide-de-camp has reached me; he assures me they have rations for twenty-five days. Order forced marching.

(To Moreau.) I was starting for Geneva when the semaphore brought me news of your victory over the Austrians: glorious, and three times glorious!

The situation of the army of Italy is somewhat critical; Masséna is cooped up in Genoa with rations that will last till the 25th or 26th. The army of Melas appears to be quite large. I greet you cordially.

(To Masséna.) The Reserve army is marching fast. I leave to-night. I count on you to hold out as long as you can, but at the least until the 30th.

9th, Geneva:
(To the Consuls of the Republic.) I reached here at midnight. The whole army is moving and in good order. I note with pleasure that Paris is calm. But in any case, I repeat, strike hard at any one, whoever he may be, who shows the first signs of wabbling.

What I witnessed on my journey through France is indescribable. Had I not frequently changed my route I would have been another eight days getting here.

11th. (To Saliceti.) Write to Malta by every ship, and give them news from Europe, insisting on the fact that France and Europe confidently expect them to hold their posts to the last mouthful of bread.

19th, Lausanne:
(To General Dupont.) Give orders that, beginning to-morrow, in every demi-brigade the conscripts shall be made to fire a few shots, shall be shown with which eye to aim, and how to load a musket

13th. I have news from Masséna up to the 30th. He was completely surrounded in Genoa, and fighting every day.

14th. (To General Desaix.) My dear Desaix: I receive your letter this very moment. Here you are at last; splendid news for the whole Republic, but especially for me who hold you in the esteem due to men of your talent, and in a friendship which my heart, so old now and knowing mankind but too well, feels for no one else.

On my arrival in France I found the Republic lost; the Vendée was at the gates of Paris; the fleet instead of being at Toulon was at Brest, and dismantled; Brest was even threatened by the English. I have had to destroy the Vendée, find money, refit the fleet. But don't let us talk of those things; come and join me as quickly as you can.

(To the Consuls of the Republic.) I wish you to have printed in the *Journal Officiel* that Generals Desaix and Davout have arrived at Toulon, with a few words added to the effect that these generals maintained, after my departure, the reputation they had won in the campaigns of Holland and the Rhine.

15th. (To the Consuls.) The advance guard commanded by General Lannes is at this moment crossing the St. Bernard. Hold back the news from the army for a few days; merely say that it is in full march.

16th. (To Josephine.) I am just starting for St. Maurice, where I shall sleep. I have had no letters from you; that's not nice; I write to you by every courier. A thousand tender things, my good little Josephine, for you and for yours.

17th, Martigny:
I have just arrived at Martigny. I shall stay the night here in hopes of getting news of the capture of Fort Bard to-morrow morning.

18th. We are struggling against ice, snow, storms, and avalanches. The St. Bernard, amazed at the sight of so great a multitude attempting to pass so rapidly, places obstacles in our way. Not since Charlemagne has so large an army been seen here. A third of our fieldpieces are over. General Berthier is at Aosta. In three days the whole army will have crossed.

19th. (To the Consuls.) I hear from General Suchet that the enemy are showing signs of being disturbed at the movement of the Reserve army, and that they have sent a detachment towards Berthier. I see that I am reported in the papers as writing to my mother that I should be in Milan in a month. It doesn't sound like me. I often don't say what I know, but I never prophesy what will happen. I wish you to send a note to the *Moniteur* on this subject, written in a bantering tone.

20th. On the St. Bernard:
The St. Bernard was covered with snow, and the climb was very stiff. General Marmont, in command of the artillery, employed two methods. The first was to take a tree-trunk hollowed out like a trough in which the 8-pounders and howitzers were placed; a hundred men hitched to a cable dragged it, taking two days to

cross the St. Bernard. In the worst places the men were cheered on by the drums beating the charge,—a striking spectacle! The First Consul descended the St. Bernard sitting on the snow, crossing precipices and sliding over torrents by this means.

24th, Aosta:

On the 19th, Melas was at Nice, still unsuspecting. Our artillery continues crossing the St. Bernard. Fort Bard, at the mouth of the valley, makes the passage of the artillery very difficult.

(To Joseph Bonaparte.) Please give 30,000 francs to my wife. We have dropped here like a thunderbolt; the enemy didn't expect it, and hardly believe it yet.

27th, Ivrea:
I reached Ivrea last night. Everything is going as well as possible. I shall be back in Paris before the end of Prairial.

29th. At Chivasso the First Consul reviewed the advance guard. He said to the 28th of the line:—You have spent two years on these mountains, often deprived of everything, and you have always done your work without a murmur. That is a good soldier's first duty.—The First Consul ordered that as a sign of his satisfaction with the good appearance of this demi-brigade it should be placed in the van at the next engagement. Two couriers have been intercepted, and it is clear that General Melas is still at Turin. The greater part of his army, which was tucked away at Nice, is making forced marches towards the Po.

30th, Vercelli:
I leave to-night for Novara. To-morrow I shall reach the banks of the Ticino to see how we can get across; the river is very large and swift.

The advance guard remained at Chivasso the whole of the 29th. The enemy have moved all their available infantry from Turin along the right bank of the Po, opposite Chivasso. In the meanwhile, General Murat was completing his bridge over the Sesia, crossed that river, reached Novara, and took up a position along the right bank of the Ticino. The inhabitants of Milan could hear the guns at our outposts to-day.

June 1st, Novara:
The First Consul arrived at the Ticino on the morning of the 31st. The enemy showed a considerable force of cavalry and a few guns on the left bank. General Murat got a battery in position, and a cannonade followed for an hour. After six hours' work we got nearly 1500 men and two guns over.

Murat is now halfway to Milan.

3d, Milan:
General Murat reached Milan on the 2d. He immediately surrounded the citadel. Three hours later the First Consul and his staff made their entry, surrounded by a crowd displaying the greatest enthusiasm.

Night:
Our movement has been so rapid that it was only twenty-four hours before our entry that the people of Milan knew the French were in Italy.

4th. (To Talleyrand.) Please have a pamphlet printed with the following title: *Letter of a patriotic member of the Germanic body on the policy of the House of Austria.* The object is to show that Austria has always striven to enlarge herself at the expense and to the detriment of the Empire. It would be a good thing to have this letter printed in German and to have it distributed broadcast in Germany.

I see no objection to your sending some dresses to the Queen of Spain; you may spend about a thousand louis for this purpose. However, see that proprieties are observed and that nothing ridiculous is done.

(To General Bernadotte.) I will say nothing more, my dear General, than that we are in Milan, that we have captured the enemy's train, 300 field and siege guns, all their hospitals and magazines.

Moreau is holding his own near Ulm.

Capture that rascal Georges dead or alive. If you ever catch him, have him shot within 24 hours.

5th. (Speech to the priests of Milan.) It was my wish to meet you here so as to be able to inform you in person of my sentiments towards the Roman, Catholic and

Apostolic faith. Convinced as I am that it is the only faith that can assure real happiness to a well-ordered society and strengthen the foundations of good government, I assure you that at all times and in every way I shall en-deavour to protect and defend it. Ministers of a religion which is also mine, I regard you as my dearest friends. My firm intention is that the Christian religion, Catholic and Roman, shall be maintained untouched. Now that power is in my hands I am resolved to put everything in operation to secure and guarantee the faith. Have no alarm because of the way in which the late Pope was treated: the misfortunes of Pius VI were partly due to the wretched intrigues of his advisers and partly to the cruel policy of the Directoire. When I am able to discuss matters with the new Pope I hope I shall be fortunate enough to remove every obstacle that may still remain in the way of a reconciliation between France and the head of the Church.

6th. Our men are over the Po and hold the position of Stradella; the enemy's army is therefore cut off.

7th. Most of the army will be concentrated by to-morrow. There is nothing Melas can do but to offer battle, and he has no retreat open save the fortresses of Alessandria and of Tortona.

8th. (To General Berthier.) General Murat has sent me some intercepted dispatches that give us interesting particulars. A letter from Melas to the Aulic Council of the 5th of June from Turin states that Masséna capitulated on the 4th. It looks as though the enemy could not complete their concentration at Alessandria before the 12th or 13th. Send detachments forward rapidly and crush everything you come across. The advance guard can move as far as Voghera.

9th. (To Carnot.) I still fail to see bow Melas can get out of it: either he must attack us at Stradella, and be de-feated and destroyed; or he can attempt to get over the Po, the Sesia, and the Ticino, and will get no better result. His position is somewhat amusing, and if Genoa had held out only 72 hours more but little of his army would ever have got away.

I start in an hour to cross the Po on my way to Stradella.

10th, Stradella:
General Ott got from Genoa to Voghera in three forced marches with 15,000 of the besieging troops. He was reinforced by 4000 or 5000 men detached by General Melas to guard the Po. The advance guards of the two armies met about noon. The enemy held the heights in front of Casteggio. Determined fighting took place and lasted all day. The 96th decided the long uncertain result with a bayonet charge. The enemy left 3000 killed and wounded, 6000 prisoners, and 5 guns on the field. Their rout was complete.

14th. *Battle of Marengo.*

15th. Torre dei Garoffoli:
(To the Consuls of the Republic.) All the news from the army is very good. I shall be in Paris soon. I can write no more, I am prostrated by the death of the man whom I most loved and esteemed.

(Bulletin.) After the battle of Montebello the army marched to cross the Scriva. The enemy appeared to have no plan and was making uncertain movements.

On the 14th at daybreak the enemy crossed the Bormida on three bridges, determined to cut their way through; they debouched in force, surprised our advance guard, and briskly opened the celebrated battle of Marengo which has at last decided the fate of Italy and of the Austrian army.

Four times during the battle we were falling back, and four times we were moving forward. At different moments and at one point and another, more than sixty guns were captured and recaptured. More than twelve charges of cavalry were delivered, with varied success.

At 3 in the afternoon 10,000 cavalry outflanked our right in the splendid plain of San Giulano. They were supported by a line of infantry and many guns. The grenadiers of the Guard stood like a granite redoubt in the midst of this immense plain; nothing could shake them.

This desperate resistance contained the enemy's left, and supported our right until General Mounier got up, and carried the village of Castel Ceriolo at the point of the bayonet. The enemy's cavalry now made a rapid movement on our left, which was already shaken; this attack hastened our retreat.

The enemy were advancing along the whole line, pouring grape from a hundred guns. The roads were packed with fugitives and wounded: the battle appeared to be lost. The enemy were allowed to continue their advance as far as the village of San Giulano, where Desaix'division had been deployed, with eight fieldpieces on its front, and two battalions thrown back and in column on the wings. All the fugitives were rallying behind. The enemy were already making mistakes that presaged their catastrophe, they were extending their wings too much. The presence of the First Consul was restoring the morale of the troops:—My lads, he called out, remember that my habit is to sleep on the battlefield!—

With shouts of *Vive la République! Vive le Premier Consul!* Desaix moved forward by his centre at the charge. In a moment the enemy's line was broken. General Kellermann, who, with his brigade of heavy cavalry, had been protecting the retirement of our left wing all day, charged at just the right moment, and so hard that 6000 grenadiers, with General Zach, chief of staff, were made prisoners, while several generals were killed.

The whole army followed up this attack. The enemy's right was cut off; surprise and panic seized their ranks. The Austrian cavalry moved to the centre to protect their retreat. Brigadier-General Bessières, at the head of the *Cassecous* and the grenadiers of the Guard, bravely and promptly charged them and broke through them, which completed the rout of their army.

We have captured 15 flags, 40 guns, and 6000 or 8000 prisoners. More than 6000 of the enemy remained on the battlefield. General Berthier had his clothes full of bullets and several of his staff were unhorsed. But a grave loss for the army, and for the whole Republic takes all rejoicing from our hearts: Desaix was struck by a bullet just as his division went into action; he was killed on the spot. He lived just long enough to say to young Lebrun who was near him: "Go tell the First Consul that I die regretting I have not lived long enough to be known to posterity!" He had joined headquarters only three days before; he was ardent for the fray, and the day before he had several times repeated to the officers of his staff. "It is long since I fought in Europe. The bullets will have forgotten me; something will happen." When, in the midst of heavy firing, the news of Desaix' death was brought to the First Consul, he merely said: "Why may I not weep?"—His body has been removed to Milan for embalming.

Little Kellermann made a very lucky charge; it was in the nick of time; we owe him a lot. To think that great events turn on such things!

(To Kellermann.) Your charge was pretty good!

16th, Marengo:
(To the Consuls.) The day following the battle of Marengo General Melas sent a request to our outposts that he might send General Skal to confer with me, and in the course of the day the inclosed convention was agreed on, and was signed in the night by General Berthier and General Melas. I hope the French people will be pleased with its army. I shall be at Milan to-night.

(To His Majesty the Emperor and King.) I have the honour of writing to Your Majesty to communicate the wish of the French people to bring to an end the war that desolates our countries. It is on the battlefield of Marengo, in the midst of suffering and surrounded by 15,000 corpses, that I beg Your Majesty to listen to the cry of suffering. It is for me to urge Your Majesty, as I am nearer the field of conflict. The arms of Your Majesty have earned enough glory, and control enough territory. What reasons can Your Majesty's ministers allege for continuing hostilities?

I think it my duty to propose to Your Majesty: that the armistice be extended to all the armies; and that negotiators be instructed on both sides.

17th, Milan:
I have just reached Milan, somewhat fatigued.

Some Hungarian grenadiers and German prisoners passing by, who had already been prisoners in the campaigns of 1796 and 1797, recognized the First Consul. Many began to shout, with apparent enthusiasm: "Vive Bonaparte!"

What a thing is imagination! Here are men who don't know me, who have never seen me, but who only knew of me, and they are moved by my presence, they would do anything for me! And this same incident arises in all centuries and in all countries! Such is fanaticism! Yes, imagination rules the world. The defect of our modern institutions is that they do not speak to the imagination. By that alone can man be governed; without it he is but a brute.

18th. To-day, whatever our Paris atheists may say, I am going in full state to the *Te Deum* that is to be sung in the Cathedral of Milan.

An imposing and splendid ceremony!

21st. (To the Consuls.) I have sent a courier to the Emperor, with a letter which the Minister of Foreign Affairs will transmit to you. You may think it rather informal in style, but it was written on a battlefield. Part of the Guard started for Paris to-day with the flags captured at Marengo. Their route is arranged so that they shall reach Paris on the 14th of July. You must work at making the celebration a brilliant one, and don't ape previous ones. Fireworks would be effective. Chariot races are all right for Greece, where chariots were implements of war; with us they mean nothing.

25th. I am starting for Paris.

26th, Turin:
The Reserve army and the army of Italy are united as the army of Italy. General Masséna will be commander-in-chief.

29th, Lyons:
I have reached Lyons. I am stopping to lay the cornerstone of the *place Bellecour,* which is being rebuilt. I am told that we may hope to have it finished in two years. I hope that before then the trade of this great city, once the pride of Europe, will have recovered its prosperity.

I shall arrive in Paris unexpectedly. I wish no triumphal arches, no ceremonies. I have too good an opinion of myself to put any value on such flim-flam. The only real triumph is the satisfaction of the public.

July 2d, Paris, the Tuileries:
Well, citizens, here we are. Come, have you been hard at work since I left?

(Not as hard as you, general!)

I only gain battles, but Josephine by her sweetness, wins every heart.—Josephine the most amiable and the best of women!—

4th. I! a royal maggot! I am a soldier, I come from the people, I have made myself! Am I to be compared with Louis XVI? I listen to everybody, but my own mind is my only counsellor. There are some men who have done France more harm than the wildest revolutionaries,—the talkers, and the rationalists. Vague and false thinkers, a few lessons of geometry would do them good!

My policy is to govern men as the great number wish to be governed. That, I think, is the way to recognise the sovereignty of the people.

14th. To the 14th of July! To the French people, the sovereign of us all!

24th. (To His Majesty the Emperor.) I have received the letter which Your Majesty has sent me by Count St. Julien. The peace preliminaries it contains will soon, I hope, be followed by a final peace.

25th. When a Frenchman has to choose between a policeman and the devil, he is for the devil, but when it is between the devil and fashion, he follows fashion, and providing the government does well, all that it does will be in the fashion.

28th. At Marengo Desaix had a presentiment of his death. I could see that he was gloomy, and as at the crisis there was much anxiety, I got off my horse and said to him, let us sit down here for a moment on the grass to show our confidence. It was at that moment that Desaix said to me,—the bullets don't recognise me now.

30th. Well, Junot, so you were fool enough to get caught by those...English. What do you want to do? Shall I send you to the army of the Rhine? You need to put on another ten years.

The impact of an army, like the total of mechanical coefficients, is equal to the mass multiplied by the velocity.

A battle is a dramatic action which has its beginning, its middle, and its conclusion. The result of a battle depends on the instantaneous flash of an idea. When you are about to give battle concentrate all your strength, neglect nothing; a battalion often decides the day.

In warfare every opportunity must be seized; for fortune is a woman: if you miss her to-day, you need not expect to find her to-morrow.

There is nothing in the military profession I cannot do for myself. If there is no one to make gunpowder, I know how to make it; gun carriages, I know how to construct them; if it is founding a cannon, I know that; or if the details of tactics must be taught, I can teach them.

The presence of a general is necessary: he is the head, he is the all in all of an army. It was not the Roman army conquered Gaul, but Cæsar; it was not the Carthaginians made the armies of the Republic tremble at the very gates of Rome, but Hannibal; it was not the Macedonian army marched to the Indus, but Alexander; it was not the French army that carried war to the Weser and to the Inn, but Turenne; it was not the Prussian army that defended Prussia during seven years against the three strongest Powers of Europe, but Frederick the Great.

Concentration of forces, activity, activity with the firm resolve to die gloriously: these are the three great principles of the military art that have always made fortune favourable in all my operations. Death is nothing; but to live defeated and ingloriously, is to die every day.

I am a soldier, because that is the special faculty I was born with; that is my life, my habit. I have commanded wherever I have been. I commanded, when twenty-three years old, at the siege of Toulon; I commanded in Paris at Vendémiaire; I carried the soldiers of the army of Italy with me as soon as I appeared among them; I was born that way.

August 12th. (Decree.) The Minister of Justice will call together at the ministry citoyens Tronchet, Bigot de Préameneu, and Portalis, to confer on the draft of the Civil Code.

13th. Wealth cannot confer a privilege. I have no intention of preaching collectivism; I am speaking between ourselves; I even want to have rich men, for that is the only way of supporting the poor; but I cannot admit that wealth is entitled to social or political distinction.

How can a state be well governed without the aid of religion? Society cannot exist save with inequality of fortune, and inequality of fortune cannot be supported without religion. When a man dies of hunger by the side of another who is gorged, he cannot accept that disparity without some authority that shall say to him: "God has decreed it thus: there must be rich and poor in the world; but in the hereafter, and for all eternity, it will be the other way about."

It was by becoming a Catholic that I pacified the Vendée, and a Mussulman that I established myself in Egypt; it was by becoming ultramontane that I won over public opinion in Italy. If I ruled a people of Jews, I would rebuild the temple of Solomon! Paradise is a central spot whither the souls of men proceed along different roads; every sect has a road of its own.

September 6th. A monument shall be erected to the memory of Generals Desaix and Kléber, who died on the same day, at the same moment: one in Europe, at the battle of Marengo, which reconquered Italy for the Republic; the other in Africa, after the battle of Heliopolis, which reconquered Egypt for France.

7th. The King is at Mittau; let him stay there!

(To the Comte de Provence (Louis XVIII).) I have received your letter, sir, and I thank you for the polite expressions it contains. You must give up all hope of returning to France; you would have to step over 100,000 dead bodies. Sacrifice your personal interest to the peace and happiness of France. History will remember you for it. I am not unmindful of the misfortunes of your family. I would be glad to contribute to the comfort and security of your retirement.

My poor Cambacérès, I can't help it, but your case is clear; if ever the Bourbons return, you will be hanged!

10th. (To Lucien Bonaparte, Minister of the Interior.) Please send me a list of our ten best painters, of our ten best sculptors, of our ten best composers, of our ten best musicians, of our ten best architects, and the names of any artists in other lines who deserve public recognition.

23d. The Government notifies the King of England that it would raise no objection to admit his envoys to the Congress of Lunéville, on the basis of a truce at sea.

October 17th. To govern France, after ten such extraordinary years, is no easy task!

November 22d. (To Savary.) Kindly start for Brest tomorrow. You will take with you citoyen Jerome Bonaparte, whom you will put on board Admiral Ganteaume. Stay there until that rear-admiral has made sail and is out of sight.

(To Rear-Admiral Ganteaume.) I am sending you citoyen Jerome Bonaparte, to serve his apprenticeship at sea. You know that he needs a firm hand, and has lost time to make up. Insist on his carrying out every one of the duties of the profession he has entered.

December 1st. If I die four or five years hence, the machine will be in order, it will run. If I die before then, I don't know what would happen.

(Devaismes: We should make some general First Consul.)

You don't want a general in that position; you want a civilian. The army will obey a civilian better than it will a soldier. If three or four years from now I were dying in my bed, of a fever, and if to crown my romance I were to make my will, I would warn the nation against a military government; I would tell it to choose a civilian for its first magistrate.

9th. Order salutes of all the artillery in the shore batteries and ships at Calais and Boulogne to announce the victory of Hohenlinden.

24th. I had been greatly occupied with business all day, and in the evening was sleepy and tired. I threw myself on a sofa in my wife's salon, and fell asleep. Josephine came down some time after, awoke me, and insisted that I should go to the theatre. You know that when women take a thing into their heads, they will go through with it, and you must gratify them. Well I got up much against my inclination, and went in my carriage, accompanied by Lannes and Bessières. I was so drowsy that I fell asleep in the coach. I was asleep when the explosion took place; and I recollect when I woke experiencing a sensation as if the vehicle had been raised up, and was passing through a great body of water. The contrivers of this were a man named St. Régent, Imolan, and some others. They got a cart and barrel resembling that with which water is supplied through the streets of Paris, with this exception, that the barrel was put crossways. This he had filled with gunpowder, and placed it nearly in the turning of the street through which I was to pass. Possibly my coachman may have assisted by driving furiously round the corner, as he was drunk and not afraid of anything. He was so far gone that he thought the report of the explosion was that of a salute fired in honour of my visit to the theatre.

25th. They want to attack the Revolution by destroying me; I will defend it because I am the Revolution!

31st. (General, you are taking longer over your meals!) Already!—The corruption of power!

1801

January 2d, Paris:
Moreau is not more than five days' march from Vienna, and in control of all the magazines of the enemy.

M. de Cobenzl, the Emperor's plenipotentiary at Lunéville, has declared, in a note dated the 31st of December, that he was prepared to negotiate a separate peace. Austria is thus free from the influence of the English Government.

9th. (To General Moreau.) I need not express how much interest I have taken in your skilful and beautiful manœuvres; you have surpassed yourself this campaign. The wretched Austrians are very obstinate; they were counting on the ice and snow; they don't really know you yet.

13th. (To Forfait.) Citoyen Ministre: Kindly draw me up a report on Madagascar. Pray order Vice-Admiral Bruix to The Hague. His special business will be to concert measures with the Dutch Minister of the Navy for the expedition to the Cape of Good Hope.

15th. The great thing is to support (the army in) Egypt.

19th. (To Talleyrand.) Please prepare the draft of a treaty with Switzerland, so as to obtain the cession of the Valais up to Brieg.

21st. A courier arrived from Russia yesterday, who had done the journey in fifteen days; he brought me a very friendly letter in the Emperor's own hand. Russia is inclined to be hostile to England.

(To Forfait.) I inclose your report on Madagascar; I find it insufficient.

25th. Are you rich, Maret?

(No, general.)

So much the worse for you, a man ought to be independent.

(General, I wish never to be dependent on any one but you.)

Hem!—Not so bad!

Maret is a good fellow, he's no fool; he answered me cleverly.

February 10th, St. Quentin:
I arrived at St. Quentin yesterday, at four in the afternoon. I was on horseback all the morning inspecting the canal. The weather is cold, and there has been much snow. All I have seen of the plans and the preliminary works of the St. Quentin canal appears satisfactory. I went down the stairway into the tunnel. The manufactures of the city, which formerly gave employment to 70,000 work-people and brought fifteen millions of money into France, have gone down five sixths. The hope of restoring one of our most important and exclusive manufactures, and of giving a livelihood to so many French families, is just the thing to bring cambric into fashion again.

13th, Paris:
Peace has been signed for the continent at Lunéville; its terms are such as the French people desired.
By our secret treaty with Spain, she is to give us six men-of-war.

25th. General Murat is sending a division of 10,000 men to occupy Taranto, Brindisi, and all the smaller ports of the peninsula beyond the line Taranto Brindisi.

27th. (To the Emperor of Russia.) The pride and arrogance of the English are unparalleled. I will bring together, as Your Majesty appears to wish, 300 or 400 gunboats in the ports of Flanders, where I will collect an army. I have given orders for concentrating an army in Brittany that can be put on board ship at Brest.

The English have attempted to land in Egypt. The interest of all the Mediterranean and Black Sea Powers is that Egypt should remain in the possession of France. The Suez canal, which would join the Indian Ocean to the Mediterranean is already surveyed; the work is easy and will not take long, it will confer incalculable benefits on Russian commerce.

March 1st. Lafayette is an obstinate political monomaniac; he cannot understand me; I regret it, because he is an honest man. I wanted to make him Senator; he refused. Let him go his own way then, I can get on without him.
4th. There shall be held in Paris, each year, an exhibition of the products of French industry.

20th. Do you know why I allow such free discussion in the Council of State? It's because I'm the best of them all in an argument. I let them attack me because I know how to defend myself.
I am a doctor of laws!

(To a Tribune.) Why don't you come and discuss things with me in my study? We might have little fireside conversations.

21st. If the minutes of the Council of State are well drafted, they will constitute a document worthy of posterity. If we turn over the minutes of the reign of Louis XVI, we find only chatter. The little slips our jurists make must not appear in ours, for during protracted sessions inattention may occur at times. As for me, a man of the sword and of finance, not a jurist but a legislator, my opinions matter little. In an argument I may say things that fifteen minutes later I disapprove; but I do not wish to be made to appear any better than I am.

The woman owes obedience to her husband. The civil magistrate should have a formula covering the woman's oath of obedience and faithfulness. She must be instructed that on passing out of the care of her family she enters under that of her husband. The civil magistrate celebrates marriage without any solemnity, which is too arid. There should be some moral appeal;—look at the priests.

(A Councillor of State: Did the old laws prescribe obedience?)

The angel declared it to Adam and Eve. In the marriage ceremony it was said in Latin, so the woman understood nothing. But the word is well suited to Paris, where the women think they can do what they like. I don't say that it will have any effect on all of them, but it will on some.

(To Portalis.) If you were in power, you would permit no divorce, for it comes to the same thing to make it so degrading to apply for it that none but a man with a brazen face would do so. That's your scheme, isn't it?

(Portalis: If we were dealing with a brand new people I would not admit divorce.)

If the marriage is unhappy, should not the civil law, which has no cognizance of the lofty sacramental theory, provide for the happiness of the individuals?

(Portalis: Man is sociable, and marriage is in nature.)

I deny that! Marriage does not derive from nature, but from society and from morality. I do not accept the opinion that the family proceeds from civil law, and civil law from the law of nature.

Divorce was bound to come into our legislation, freedom of religion implied it; but it would be a great misfortune if it became a national habit. What becomes of the family when it is broken asunder? What are husbands and wives who, after having lived in the closest union that nature and law can tie, suddenly become strangers, yet unable to forget one another? What are children without a father, who cannot join in the same embrace their disunited parents? Ah! let us do nothing to encourage divorce! Of all social habits it would be the most fatal. Let us not brand with shame the man who demands it; but let us rather pity him as the victim of a great misfortune. And custom must frown down the sad resource which the law cannot refuse to the unfortunate.

2 A.M.
Come, come, citoyens, wake up; it's only two o'clock; we must earn the money the French people pay us!

March 22d. (To General Murat.) Should the negotiations drag, enter the Neapolitan state, place your headquarters at Aquila, and raise all obstacles. If on your arrival the King declines to accept the moderate terms proposed by citoyen Alquier, march on Naples.

April 12th. The Emperor of Russia died on the night of the 24th or 25th of March of an attack of apoplexy. The lively sorrow I feel at the death of a prince whom I valued so highly prevents my entering into details. His eldest son has succeeded and has been recognised by the army and the capital.

26th. (To the Emperor of Russia.) M. de Kalitchy has handed us the letter in which Your Majesty announces his accession to the throne of all the Russias and the death of his father. We have been profoundly affected by the unexpected loss which Your Majesty has suffered. Our only consolation is in learning the accession of Your Majesty to the Empire.

July 10th. (To Talleyrand.) I have read the note of General the Prince of Peace; it is so ridiculous that it is not worth a serious answer. But if this Prince, paid by England, should persuade the King and Queen into steps contrary to the dignity and interests of the Republic, the last hour of the Spanish monarchy has rung.

20th. (To Joseph Bonaparte.) Please continue your negotiations with Cardinal Consalvi and your other colleagues. I would like the bull to be published in France as soon as possible, so that I can make nominations to the archbishoprics and bishoprics at once. I would like it if we could publish the bull in Paris on the 15th of August.

August 6th. (To Fouché.) The First Consul wants you to inform the journalists, political and literary, that they must abstain from discussing religion, its priests and ceremonies.

16th. (To Jerome Bonaparte.) I learn with pleasure that you are becoming accustomed to the sea; there only can the greatest glory he won.

25th. (To the men of the 1st Artillery.) Soldiers, your conduct in the citadel of Turin is known throughout Europe. You forced your way into a fortress in a disorderly and tumultuous manner, disregarding the French flag which floated there. You killed the brave officer whose duty it was to defend it. You passed over his body. You are all guilty! The officers who failed to keep you under control are unfit to command you. The flag which you have deserted, to which you refused to rally, will be placed in the temple of Mars and hung with crape. Your regiment is disbanded!

30th. Cardinal Caprara is coming to Paris as papal legate.

October 6th. (To Talleyrand.) I inclose the ratifications of the peace preliminaries signed at London on the 1st, and of the secret clause.

10th. (To His Holiness the Pope.) I have received Cardinal Caprara, Your Holiness' legate, with great pleasure. Peace has been signed with England, Portugal, Russia, and the Porte. I hasten to send this information, well knowing the interest. Your Holiness takes in the happiness and peace of nations.

(To the Emperor of Russia.) In the peace preliminaries happily signed between France and England it is provided that Malta shall be restored to the Order under the protection of a great Power. Will Your Majesty let me know your views relatively to the island and to the Order of Malta, of which your, august father was recognised as Grand Master.

December 1st. (To Lucien Bonaparte.) I can't in the least make out the conduct of the Cabinet of Madrid. Please express to Their Majesties my extreme dissatisfaction with the wrongful and illogical action of the Prince of Peace. During these six months past this minister has not spared us insulting notes and rash steps; all that could be done against France, he has done; speak out and tell the Queen and the Prince of Peace that if things go on this way the end will come like a thunderbolt.

1802

January 7th, Paris:
(To Joseph Bonaparte.) To-morrow, at midnight, I start for Lyons. I think General Bernadotte has gone to Amiens. Whether he has or not, I want him to tell you if it would suit him to go to Guadeloupe as captain-general.

13th, Lyons:
I took sixty-nine hours to get to Lyons; from Lyons to Paris everything is covered with snow. I arrived at nine o'clock at night, and have every reason to be satisfied with the marks of attachment that the people of Lyons are giving me, and of the activity I find in their workshops, and in their minds, to restore the prosperity of the chief manufacturing city of the Republic.

14th. The cold here is excessive. I am spending my mornings, from six till twelve, receiving the prefects and notables of the neighbouring departments. In conferences of this sort one has to talk at length. To-night the City gives a concert and a ball; I am starting in an hour.

My satisfaction with all I see of the people of Lyons and of southern France continues.

16th. It is very fine but very cold. The internal improvement of the Republic is very apparent since two years ago. Lyons must have increased its population by 20,000 people in 1800 and 1801. All the manufacturers of St. Etienne and of Annonay with whom I talked reported that their works were in full swing. On the 18th I shall review six demi-brigades of the army of the West.

18th. (To the Consul Cambacérès.) Your letter of the 15th has posted me on the debates in the Senate. I trust that you will not fail to have the twenty and sixty undesirable members in our constitutional bodies promptly removed. The will of the Nation is that this Government shall not be hindered in its beneficent work, and that the Head of Medusa shall not be permitted to appear again in our assemblies. The conduct of Sieyès at this juncture shows conclusively that after taking a hand in the destruction of every constitution since 1791, he wants to have a go at this one. It is very curious that he can't see the folly of it. He ought to be glad to burn a candle at Notre Dame for having so happily and unexpectedly come through. But the older I get the more clearly I perceive that a man must accomplish his destiny!

The cold is less intense.

21st. I went for an hour to the ball given to my wife by the Commerce (of Lyons); it was very fine.

25th. Held a parade to-day, *place Bellecour.* The weather was splendid, the sun as in Floréal. The generals who were in Lyons thought it proper to give a grand ball to-night, for my wife; I shall look in for half an hour.

February 19th, Paris:
If by ill luck peace should not be maintained, what could be undertaken?

(To Fouché.) As the reëstablishment of peace with the Powers gives me time to pay special attention to the police, I want to be posted in the smallest details, and to work with you at least once, sometimes twice a day, when necessary. The most convenient hours for me are in the morning at eleven and at night at eleven.

April 9th. (To Portalis.) The intention of the First Consul is to present each archbishop and bishop, at his consecration, with a cross, a crozier, and a mitre. You will therefore arrange to have these articles ready in time, and bought as cheaply as possible.

12th. Note the insolence of the priests who, in the division of authority with what they call the temporal power, reserve for themselves the dominion of the mind, of the noble part of man, and have the pretension of leaving me dominion over the body. They keep the soul and throw me the carcase!

There will be no stable political conditions until we have a teaching body acting on fixed principles. So long as men are not taught from childhood whether to be republican or monarchist, Catholic or freethinking, the state will not be a nation.

May 4th. In every country force bows to the civilian virtues. The bayonets fall before the priest who speaks in the name of religion, and before the man of science. I foretold that a military government would never take in France unless the nation were degraded by fifty years of ignorance. Every attempt would fail, and their authors would be the first victims. It is not as a general that I govern, but because the nation believes that I have civilian qualities that make me fit for governing, otherwise the government could not maintain itself. I knew what I was about when, as a general, I assumed the title of Member of the Institute; my meaning was clear even to the last drummer of the army.

We cannot argue on the analogy of the dark ages. We are thirty millions of men held together by enlightenment, property, and commerce; three or four hundred thousand soldiers are nothing in such a mass. The soldiers themselves are the children of the citizens. The army is the nation.

The distinctive mark of the soldier is that all his desires are despotic; that of the civilian is that he submits everything to discussion, to truth, to reason.

7th. The bishops who have not yet taken the oath will take it Sunday next in the chapel of the First Consul. This chapel shall be arranged in the First Consul's study. The Archbishop of Paris will consecrate it at ten; at eleven he will say mass. The bishops will take the oath after the gospel has been read.

9th. *The Consulate renewed for ten years.*

Senators: The testimonial of your esteem contained in your debate of the 8th will remain forever engraved in my heart. My reputation and my happiness would seem to have marked as the term of my public life a moment when the peace of the world has been attained. But the glory and the interests of the private citizen must be subdued when the interest of the State and the good opinion of the public call on him. You have decided that I owe a new sacrifice to the people; I will make it.

12th, Saint Cloud:
Gobain, a grenadier, has committed suicide because of a love affair; he was, however, a good soldier. This is the second incident of this nature in the regiment within a month. The First Consul directs that there shall be inserted in the Guard's orders: That a soldier must overcome grief and the melancholy of love; that there is as much courage in supporting with firmness the afflictions of the soul as there is in standing steady under the grape of a battery of guns. To give

one's self up to grief without resistance, to kill one's self to escape it, is to abandon the battlefield defeated.

14th, Paris:
By virtue of clause 87 of the Constitution concerning military rewards, and to recompense distinction and service among civilians, a Legion of Honour shall be instituted.

Where is the republic, ancient or modern, that has not granted honours? Call them trifles if you like, but it is by trifles that men are influenced. I would not utter such a sentiment as this in public, but here, among statesmen and thinkers, things should be spoken of as they are. In my opinion the French do not care for liberty and equality; they have but one sentiment, that of honour. Therefore that sentiment must he gratified; they must be given distinctions. Do you suppose you can persuade men to fight by a process of analysis? Never; that process is valid only for the man of science in his study. The soldier demands glory, distinction, rewards.

August 6th. The Minister of the Interior is directed, apart from the Simplon, to build roads over the Mont Cenis, and the Mont Genèvre, and to improve the one over the Pass of Tenda.

(To Jerome.) I have received your letter, Mr. Midshipman. I am anxious to hear that you are aboard your corvette, on the high seas, which you must make your road to glory. I am willing you should die young, but not if you live ingloriously, useless to your country, without leaving a trace of your existence, for that is not to have lived.

7th. We must bear in mind to help the trade of Nice; for instance, Piedmont can get its sugar, coffee, and other colonial produce through Nice, and in the same way soap and every other article that Marseilles and our manufactories can supply.

(To Talleyrand.) Let me know within twenty-four hours of its reception the contents of every dispatch from an ambassador or minister plenipotentiary. At the time I was opening the bag of the ministry of foreign affairs I realized that you received official reports on matters that I have often tried to get knowledge of by indirect means.

13th. (To Fouché.) Keep all English papers out of France, and in particular prevent their circulating in public places and reading-rooms.

15th. (To Talleyrand.) Citoyen Lannes, Minister of the Republic at Lisbon, was wrong in leaving that city. He has broken every rule, every form, failed in the first duty of a public official, which is not to leave his post without the positive order of his Government. The French Minister has been rude to the Court of Lisbon by employing dictatorial manners, and by going away without leave. He must be recalled.

October 18th, Saint Cloud:
Secret instructions for the Ambassador at Constantinople: The intentions of the Government are that the Ambassador at Constantinople should regain, by all possible means, the supremacy that France enjoyed in that capital during 200 years. The Ambassador has the finest Embassy. He must constantly keep on a higher level than the ambassadors of other nations, be surrounded by a numerous suite, and be seen in public only with great display.

Our trade must be protected in every way. Whenever public attention is drawn to the French Ambassador, care must be taken never to shock local customs and manners, but it must be shown, on the contrary, that we respect them.

Lastly, the Ambassador is expected to secure precise information for the ministers on the various pashaliks. We must even get posted about Persia.

22d. The vicar of St. Roch, in a moment of bad judgment, has declined to hold a service for Mlle. Chameroi, or even to open his church for her (funeral). The Archbishop of Paris has ordered the vicar of St. Roch into retirement for three months so that he may be reminded that Jesus Christ commanded that we should pray even for our enemies, and so that meditation may recall him to a sense of his duties and that he may realize that all the superstitious practices that degraded religion by their stupidity have been proscribed by the Concordat and by the law of the 18th of Germinal.

The priests are no longer to be feared in our time; they lost all their power on the day when their supremacy in science passed to the layman.

Every two years there shall be executed for and at the expense of the Government four historical pictures and two statues. The pictures shall measure five metres by four, and shall be purchased for 10,000 francs. The statues shall be two metres high, and shall be purchased for 15,000 francs. The Government will supply the marble.

28th. The relations between France and England are the treaty of Amiens, all the treaty of Amiens, nothing but the treaty of Amiens!

All the evils, all the plagues that afflict mankind come from London.

31st, Rouen:
(To the Consul Cambacérès.) It is five in the afternoon. I got on horseback at eight this morning to inspect the heights about Rouen. The Archbishop, who is much loved and esteemed, was obliging enough to say mass for us; but he gave us neither holy water nor a sermon. We shall make up to-morrow, which is All Saints' day. I have just received the officials, and have had to talk much and long. I am very pleased with the sentiments of the country.

November 2d, Rouen:
I was present yesterday at a fête given me by the city. There was a very large and fine company. To-morrow night I shall be at a fête given by the Commerce of Rouen. Thursday there will be a parade. I shall see the market Friday, market day. I shall start for Havre immediately, reaching there Saturday or Sunday. I shall return by Dieppe and by Beauvais, where I will stop the night.

(To Joseph Bonaparte.) My compliments to Madame Joseph. She gets such handsome daughters that we must be consoled at her not presenting you with a fine boy.

I am as pleased with Rouen as I was with Lyons. The city's demonstrations have touched me. Everything one sees here is fine and does one good. I really love this beautiful, excellent Normandy; it is the real France.

(To Cardinal Fesch.) You must delay no longer and proceed to your archbishopric. Do not forget that in the station to which you are called you will be the focus of all eyes. Be strict in your morals and hold yourself as you should, and devote yourself exclusively to the duties of your office.

3d, Elbeuf:
This morning at eight o'clock I started for a visit to Elbeuf, which is nothing but one great factory. I found everything in good shape. Its prosperity has increased by a third since 1788.

4th. I have held a parade which was very good. I was delighted with the appearance of the troops.

6th. I arrived at Havre at six o'clock this evening. I was surrounded by throngs of people all the way and had to make frequent stops. It would be difficult to realize the manner in which I am received. In every village, at the church doors, the priests under their canopies, surrounded by many people, sing hymns and throw incense. The illumination of Havre was very striking. I am several days behind on my journey, but it is not easy to do otherwise.

10th, Dieppe:
I arrived at Dieppe last night. The city was very tastefully illuminated, but owing to petty municipal pride I am lodged in a wretched house in which all the chimneys smoke.

I passed through Fécamp and St. Valéry. As the road from Havre to Dieppe is only a crossroad, our carriages were often brought to a walk, which enabled the inhabitants of the neighbouring villages to follow me all the way; so we held frequent conversations.

26th, Saint Cloud:
(To Laplace.) I thank you for your dedication, which I accept with great pleasure, and I hope that when future generations are reading *La Mécanique Céleste,* they will not forget the esteem and friendship I felt for the author.

December 4th. Citoyen Duroc may inform citoyen Beauvoisin that he may send me all the numbers he has of the *Ambigu,* and also the pamphlet of Ivernois. He may instruct him to make up a sheet on all he has seen in England, in which he can state what he knows about Pichegru and Willot, and about the obscure life of the royal princes. As I intend having it printed, he can aim at Pitt, Grenville, Wyndham, and the Court. Let him know that when this is done he is to return to

England. He must find pretexts for inspecting the coast from the Thames to beyond Plymouth, the bay of Bristol, Edinburgh, and the coasts of Scotland.

28th. (To Talleyrand.) Please inform Lord Whitworth how surprised and annoyed I am to learn that the Count d'Artois, wearing the star of the Order of a monarchy that England no longer recognises, should have reviewed a regiment; that we have long kept silence; but that it touches our dignity, and we venture to say the honour of the British Government; that the princes should be expelled from England, or at all events, if hospitality is to be extended to them, that they should not be permitted to wear the Orders of a monarchy England no longer recognises. It is a perpetual insult to the French people, and the time has come for quiet in Europe. It really looks as though there were not a peace between the two countries, but only a truce, and the English Government is entirely to blame.

30th. My power proceeds from my reputation, and my reputation from the victories I have won. My power would fall if I were not to support it with more glory and more victories. Conquest has made me what I am; only conquest can maintain me.

Friendship is only a word; I love nobody; no, not even my brothers. Perhaps Joseph a little; even then it's a matter of habit, it's because he is my elder.—Duroc? Ah, yes, I love him; but why? His character attracts me: he is cool, dry, severe; and Duroc never sheds tears. As for me, you don't suppose I care; I know perfectly well I have no real friends. As long as I remain what I am, I shall have as many as I need so far as the appearance goes. Let the women whimper, that's their business, but for me, give me no sentiment. A man must be firm, have a stout heart, or else leave on one side war and government.

1803

January 12th, Paris:
Until I was sixteen I would have fought for Rousseau against all the supporters of Voltaire. Now it's the other way about.

25th. Josephine is always afraid I may fall seriously in love; she doesn't realize that love was not made for me. For what is love? A passion that leaves the universe on one side, to place the loved one on the other. And, surely, such an exclusion is not in my character!

I have always enjoyed the analytic process, and if I fell seriously in love I would analyze my feelings step by step.

February 10th. (To Régnier.) Notwithstanding the prohibition, Mme. de Staël will arrive at Melun on the 15th. Please order a police agent there to make her return to the frontier at once, and to take her to the country either of her late husband or of her father. The intention of the Government is that this intriguing foreigner should not stay in France, where her family is already responsible for enough evils.

20th. British troops continue to occupy Alexandria and Malta; this gave the Government good ground for complaint; but it appears the transports that are to bring them back to Europe are now in the Mediterranean.

March 11th. Are all the efforts I have made for liberating Italy to remain unfruitful? Is that country irrevocably fated to remain nothing? The feebleness of the Government at Milan surpasses all that can be imagined.

(To Chef de brigade Colbert.) You will proceed to Russia. You will hand the inclosed letter to the Emperor. In conversation you will emphasize the esteem in which Russians are held in Paris. Dwell on liberal and philosophic ideas when talking with the Emperor. In case war with England should be mentioned, you can say that in view of the existing antipathy the French nation is perfectly ready for a conflict. Be civil to the diplomatic corps, to the English minister just like the others. You will speak of the First Consul as very busy planning canals, starting manufactories, and working at matters of public education.

Go, sir, gallop, and don't forget that the world was made in six days. You can ask me for anything you like, except time.

(To the Emperor of Russia.) A more serious contest has arisen with England. Under the provisions of the treaty of Amiens she was held to evacuate Malta within three months, and France on her side to evacuate Taranto within the same period. I have faithfully evacuated Taranto. On inquiring why Malta was not evacuated, I received the reply that there was as yet no Grand Master: that was adding a clause to the treaty. The Grand Master is appointed: I am told it was necessary to await the accession of Your Majesty, to which I agreed, and which is now accomplished; I notified the British Cabinet to this effect. Then England raised the mask and informed me that she wished to hold Malta for seven years.

13th. *Diplomatic reception at Madame Bonaparte's at the Tuileries:*
So it's war you want?

(Lord Whitworth: No, First Consul; we appreciate too deeply the benefits of peace.)

We have already been at war for fifteen years!

(Whitworth: That is already too much.)

But you want to continue for another fifteen years,—you force me to it. The English want war, but if they are first to draw the sword, I shall be last to place it in the scabbard. They don't observe treaties; we shall have to veil them in crape. If you want to arm, I will arm too; if you want to fight, I too will fight. Woe betide those who do not respect treaties! The French people can be killed, but cannot be intimidated!

16th. (To General Hédouville.) The First Consul is distressed to see that, in the face of all Europe, aspersions have been cast on his good faith, and that the English Ministry, in a public document, have suggested that at a time of peace the First Consul was meditating a military operation. This attack on his good faith has wounded him deeply, and Sunday last, at Madame Bonaparte's reception, he seized the opportunity of expressing his sentiments on an occasion that was likely to lend emphasis to what he said.

May 1st. So the English Ambassador is not here to-day?—He is probably packing up!

(To Talleyrand.) Your letter was handed to me at Malmaison. If the note contains the word ultimatum, make him understand that that word means war; if the note does not contain it, get him to put it in, on the ground that we must know where we are.

13th. The British Ambassador has just left Paris.

23d. The intention of the Government is that General St. Cyr should march immediately from Rimini, with his corps, to enter the states of the King of Naple. On reaching Taranto General St. Cyr will start throwing up fortifications at once.

I have just given orders to General Mortier to enter the Electorate of Hanover with a corps of 25,000 men.

26th. If the English want to make us jump the ditch, we will jump. They may capture a few frigates or a few colonies, but I will strike terror in London, and I prophesy that before the war is over they will weep tears of blood.

June 20th. From the date of these presents no colonial produce coming from English colonies shall be admitted to French ports, nor shall any merchandise coming directly or indirectly from England.

26th, Amitns:
I arrived here Saturday at seven in the evening. I am sending to Paris the four swans presented to me by the city of Amiens according to an ancient custom; I expect to have them placed in the ponds at the Tuileries.

July 1st, Calais:
I went to Boulogne, which I reached at ten o'clock at night. I employed the day, starting on horseback at three in the morning, in inspecting the port. I had the

gun-boats out, and they had a brisk engagement with two English frigates which finally bore off, one having lost an anchor.

To-day I breakfasted at Ambleteuse, and thence rode along the coast. In a marsh I discovered a very favourable spot for my plans, at the point that is nearest to England. I returned to Calais on horseback; it is nine o'clock, and I am going to dine.

I saw all the merchant and the Government ships; I took a boat to inspect Fort Rouge; so I am free to start to-morrow for Dunkirk, where I shall find my wife and the Ministers of the Interior and of Foreign Affairs. I shall stay there three days to catch up current business, and to give my suite some rest.

5th, Dunkirk:
I have spent the last two days in the saddle or at sea. To-day I have done no riding, which has rested us all.

7th, Lille:
I reached Lille at six in the evening.

(To Régnier.) I think it would be well for the prefect of police to draft a circular to the booksellers to prevent their selling books until seven days after sending you a copy, so that in the case of pernicious works, like the book of citoyen Salis, *The Correspondence of Louis XVI*, and the poem *Pity*, they can be stopped.

11th, Ostend:
I have crossed parts of Belgium and am pleased with the attitude of the people. Yesterday I visited Ostend, and viewed several points that are of importance to the town and its inhabitants. I am just starting on my way along the coast to Blankenberghe. To-night I shall reach Bruges, where my wife has preceded me.

17th, Ghent:
I was present yesterday at a splendid fête given by the Commerce of Ghent in the market-place. To-day I proceeded in full state to the cathedral to attend mass.

23d, Brussels:
I have been here two days, but have not gone out.

Fête given by the municipality, that seemed to me badly managed. Five or six times more people than the place could hold.

Oh! what an ugly headdress!

Who fiddled your hair like that?

No children? Perhaps it's not your fault. See that you get some!

26th. All the Belgian ladies were presented to my wife to-day. Illuminations are blazing in the *Allée Verte*. Having spent the day in the saddle, I prefer attending to my letters while the ladies have gone off.

The way in which the troops are placed near Boulogne, Etaples, and Ambleteuse is very important, and an essential feature of the operations; for the troops will have to embark and disembark frequently: their embarkation must be very prompt. From the giving of the order to its execution there must be only an hour or two.

August 4th, Namur:
Mortier has just sent me a Latin MS. by Leibnitz addressed to Louis XIV proposing the conquest of Egypt. It is a very curious work.

23d, Saint Cloud:
England will never get other terms from me than those of Amiens; I will face everything, but I will never consent to her holding anything in the Mediterranean. From Malta, Nelson holds all Italy blockaded. By the help of God and a good cause, the war, however unfortunate it may be, will never make the French people bow before this proud nation that makes its sport of all that is sacred on earth, and that has, especially these last twenty years, assumed a predominance and arrogance in Europe that menace the very existence of all nations in their industry and commerce, those mainsprings of national existence.

September 6th. The winter will be a severe one; meat very high. There must be plenty of employment in Paris.

Push on the construction of the Oureq canal.

Start work on the quais Desaix and d'Orsay.

Have the new streets paved.

Get other work for the masses.

October 1, Paris:

There shall be erected in Paris, in the centre of the *place Vendôme,* a column on the same lines as that erected at Rome in honour of Trajan. The column shall be surmounted by a pedestal adorned with an olive wreath on which there shall be a statue of Charlemagne.

3d. (To Régnier.). I am informed that Madame de Staël has arrived at Maffliers. Have her informed by one of her friends, and without any fuss, that if she is still there on the 7th she will be taken to the frontier by the gendarmerie. The appearance of this woman has always been like that of a bird of ill omen, a symptom of trouble. My intention is that she should remain out of France.

29th. (To Admiral Bruix.) I am glad to see that your port at Boulogne is beginning to fill up. Havre, Cherbourg, Granville, St. Malo, have large flotillas ready that may reach you at any moment. They will double your strength. In the meanwhile I have much satisfaction in hearing of the good spirit of the troops and of the zeal with which they work at their naval tactics.

30th. (To Rear-Admiral Decrès.) Please collect at Rochefort and Brest the transports for the expedition to Ireland.

November 5th, Boulogne:
I arrived unexpectedly at Boulogne on Friday at one o'clock. I set to inspecting with the liveliest interest the preparations for our great expedition; at midnight I was still at it. I am in barracks in the centre of the camp on the seashore, where the eye can measure the space that separates us from England.

9th. I spent Sunday visiting our new ports at Ambleteuse and Wimereux, and in manceuvring the troops.

I inspected to-day, in the closest detail, the naval workshops;—their condition is as bad as it well could be. I have just converted some barracks into a naval arsenal. I have to look after the smallest details in person.

I have spent some hours in inspecting the troops man by man.

Our fleet, which already numbers one hundred men-of-war, remains at anchor in the bay, and the English don't dare to close in to short range. Lord Keith is apparently in command and has several 64's; he has suffered some damage even at long range.

I passed some part of last night in making the troops perform night evolutions; these manœuvres may often be profitably undertaken by well-trained and disciplined troops against a militia.

Things are taking on a formidable appearance.

11th. The sea is heavy, and the rain is unceasing. I spent yesterday in the port inspecting,—there is always something to see.

12th. Rain in torrents. I spent all day yesterday in boats or on horseback. it seems to agree with me. I have never had such good health.

I hope I shall soon reach the goal that Europe is watching. We have the insults of six centuries to avenge.

16th. From the cliff at Ambleteuse I had a sight of the English coast. I could make out houses and movement. The thing is a ditch, and with a pinch of courage it can be jumped.

December 7th, Paris:
The combined fleets will start (in March), and reach Boulogne (in April).

At the end of February I shall be at Boulogne with 130,000 men. With a good wind we need the fleet for only twelve hours.

29th. I start to-morrow at six in the morning for Boulogne. I shall be back for the opening session of the Legislative Body.

1804

January 1st, Boulogne:
To-morrow at eight I shall inspect the whole flotilla. As I go on board the first cutter, the Admiral's ship will fire a salute of 60 guns.

2d, Etaples:
This country resembles that of Æolus!

4th, Boulogne:
(To the Consul Cambacérès.) There is no objection to a sword being presented to General Junot, and it is not unseemly that a plain statement of the fact should be made public. Beyond that the thing would be absurd. One might well ask: What would the city of Paris do at that rate for the general who first set foot in England? The City of London gave Nelson a sword after the battle of the Nile. I say this not in the sense that General Junot does not deserve a sword, but that he has done nothing noteworthy since becoming governor of Paris.

12th, Paris:
The land tax must be cut down by 10 millions of francs in the budget of 1804. This reduction will act as a passport for the new tax on alcohol. One must know where to give, and where to take.

16th. Lyceums and secondary schools are going up everywhere.

February 13th, Malmaison:
(To General Soult.) These last eight days we have been hunting a band of 40 ruffians, headed by Georges, who landed in three batches between Tréport and Dieppe. That scoundrel Pichegru has followed Georges and the rest to Paris; we know where they slept Sunday. The depositions of some whom we have arrested implicate generals of the highest rank. If we can verify this, justice shall be done. I thought it best to notify you at once so that you can get on the track of any intrigues there may be in your army. From the veiled character of part of my dispatch, you must see that I do not care to speak out for the moment. The police hold out hopes that they will catch Pichegru and Georges to-day.

16th. (To Régnier.) Please issue a writ to arrest General Souham and General Liébert, charged with conspiracy against the state with Generals Moreau, Pichegru, and the outlaw Georges.

Guess what I've just done! I have ordered the arrest of Moreau; it will make a fine scandal, won't it? People will not omit to say that I am jealous of Moreau, that it's a revenge, and a thousand silly things of the same kind. I, jealous of Moreau!

18th. (To the Senate.) Since the day on which I attained the Chief Magistracy numerous plots have been formed to kill me; they were really conspiracies against the glory, the liberty, the destinies of the French nation. Our citizens must allay their fears; my life will last as long as it is necessary to the nation.

19th. (To General Soult.) Moreau has been arrested; and fifteen or sixteen of the ruffians; the rest have taken to flight. Fifteen horses and some uniforms have been found that were to have been used in attacking me on the road between Malmaison and Paris.

March 1st. Pichegru was arrested yesterday. He was not able to use either his pistols or his dagger. He fought with his fists for half an hour against three or four picked policemen.

8th, Malmaison:
We are making arrests every day. I think it is certain that Georges and a few of his men are still in Paris.

9th, Paris:
The case against Moreau and Pichegru is being worked up by the Criminal Tribunal of the Seine.

10th. (To General Berthier.) Please give orders to General Ordener, whom I place at your disposal, to start to-night for Strassburg. He is to proceed to Ettenheim, to surround the city, and to seize the Duke d'Enghien, Dumouriez, an English colonel, and any other persons in the party.

12th, Malmaison:
(To General Soult.) Paris is still held closed by the police, and will be kept so until these ruffians are all under arrest. I may tell you, in the strictest confidence, that I hope to get Dumouriez. The rascal is near our frontiers.

(To General Marmont.) As soon as you reach the camp, form a line of battalions, and spend eight hours in reviewing the men one by one; listen to their complaints, inspect their arms, and see that nothing is missing. These reviews of seven or eight hours are very profitable; they accustom the men to remain under arms, and show them that their officers are not dissipating, but are concerned for their welfare, a thing that inspires the soldier with much confidence.

14th. In the present situation of Europe my policy aims straight at England. I have at Boulogne 1000 gun-boats and flatboats that will carry 100,000 men and 10,000 horses.

19th. Citoyen General Murat: I have received your letter. If the Duke de Berry were in Paris at the house of M. de Cobenzl, and if M. d'Orléans were staying with the Marquis di Gallo, not only would I have them arrested this very night and shot, but I would also have these ambassadors arrested and make them suffer the same fate; the law of nations would not be seriously affected.

There is no other prince in Paris than the Duke d'Enghien, who will arrive at Vincennes to-morrow. Get that well into your head, and don't listen to anything you may hear to the contrary.

20th. The *ci-devant* Duke d'Enghien, accused of having carried arms against the Republic, of having been and still being in the pay of England, of plotting with that Power against the security, internal and external, of the Republic, shall be tried by a court-martial of seven members appointed by the governor of Paris, assembled at Vincennes.

4 P.M.
(To General Murat.) The Duke d'Enghien is to be taken to the fort of Vincennes, where arrangements have been made to receive him. He is travelling under the name of Plessis.

4.30 P. M.
(To citoyen Harel.) A person whose name is to remain unknown to you is to be
sent to the fort which you command; place him in the room that is vacant, taking
proper precautions against his escape. The intention of the Government is that
everything relating to him should be kept very secret, and that no questions
should be addressed to him as to his identity, or the reason for his arrest.

(To citoyen Réal.) Apparently the Duke d'Enghien started at midnight on the
17th. He will therefore soon be here. I have just issued the decree of which I
enclose you a copy. Proceed to Vincennes at once to examine the prisoner. Here
are the questions to put to him:

Have you borne arms against your country?

Have you accepted the pay of England?

What knowledge have you of the plot formed by England for overturning the
Government of the Republic? On that plot meeting with success, were you not to
enter Alsace, and even march on Paris, in given circumstances?

You must take with you the public prosecutor, who is to be the major of the special gendarmerie, and you must instruct him to put things through quickly.

21st. *Execution of the Duke d'Enghien.*
I will respect the judgment of public opinion when it is well founded; but when
capricious it must be met with contempt. I have behind me the will of the nation
and an army of 500,000 men. With that I can command respect for the Republic. I could have had the Duke d'Enghien shot publicly; and if I have not done so,
I held back not from fear, but to prevent the secret adherents of his House from
breaking out and ruining themselves. They have kept quiet; it is all I ask of them.

I will not consent to a peace with England unless she expels the Bourbons, just as
Louis XIV expelled the Stuarts, because their presence in England will always be
dangerous for France. Russia, Sweden, Prussia have driven them out.

22d. These people wanted an upheaval in France, and by killing me to kill the
Revolution; it has been for me to defend and to avenge it. I have shown what it
can do. The Duke d'Enghien was a conspirator just like any other, and it was

necessary to treat him as any other might be treated. The Bourbons will always look at things through the *Œil de Bœuf*, and are fated to live under an eternal delusion. Ah! it would have been a different matter had they appeared like Henry IV on a battlefield, all covered with dust and with blood. Kingdoms are not won by letters dated "London" and signed "Louis." I have shed blood, I shall perhaps shed more, but never in anger, and merely because bloodletting enters into the practice of political medicine.

April 5th. Mr. Edward Livingston, President of the Academy of Arts of New York: I have learned with interest of the formation of a literary society in New York; and as your Academy has been so kind as to elect me a member, pray inform it that I accept with pleasure, and that I am grateful for its good opinion of me.

6th. (To Pauline Borghese.) Madam and dear sister: I learn with regret that you have not enough good sense to conform with the customs and habits of the city of Rome; that you show contempt for the inhabitants, and that Paris is your constant model. Although busy with matters of grave importance, yet I have thought it best to inform you of my views, hoping that you will conform with them.

Love your husband and your family; be obliging; accustom yourself to the habits of the city of Rome; and be persuaded that if at the age you have now reached you give way to bad advice, you can no longer count on me.

14th. The General Councils of Departments, the Electoral Colleges, and all the great Bodies of the State, demand that an end should be made of the hopes of the Bourbons by securing the Republic from the upheavals of elections and the uncertainty attending the life of an individual.

15th. It is not as a general that I rule, but because the nation believes I have the civilian qualifications for governing. My system is quite simple. It has seemed to me that under the circumstances the thing to do was to centralize power and increase the authority of the Government, so as to constitute the Nation. I am the constituent power.

I can best compare a constitution to a ship; if you allow the wind to fill your sails, you go you know not whither, according to the wind that drives you; but if you make use of the rudder, you can go to Martinique with a wind that is driving you to San Domingo. No constitution has remained fixed. Change is governed by men and by circumstances. If an overstrong government is undesirable, a weak one is much worse.

25th. Senators: I have constantly kept in mind your address of the 6th of Germinal; I have carefully meditated on it. You have decided that the heredity of the supreme magistracy was necessary to protect the French people from the plots of our enemies and from the dissensions of conflicting factions. I therefore invite you to disclose your intentions fully.

May 18th. *Proclamation of the Empire.*
(To the Consul Cambacérès.) Citoyen Consul: your title is about to change; your functions and my confidence in you remain unchanged. You will continue to display in the high dignity of Arch Chancellor of the Empire, as you did in that of Consul, the wisdom in counsel and the distinguished talent that have made your share so large in all that I may have accomplished.

Settle the titles to be given to the Senators and high dignitaries of the Empire.

Call the high dignitaries *Highness*, the Senators *Excellency.*

The Senate as a body is to be known as *Sénat Conservateur.* In private, use *Monsieur,* and to the Ministers as well.

Everything that can increase the happiness of the country is completely bound up with my own. I accept a title that you believe will be of service to the nation. I will submit to the people the law concerning the hereditary power. I hope that France will never regret the honours she has showered on my family.

The members of the Senate, of the Council of State, and of the Tribunate, the presidents and secretaries of the Legislative Body, and the president of the Court of Appeal will take the oath to the Emperor in person.

20th. For the moment I shall exclude two of my brothers from the succession, one of them because, despite his intelligence, he has contracted a masquerade marriage; the other because he has had the impudence, without my consent, to marry an American. I will reinstate them if they give up their wives.

29th. You Frenchmen love monarchy. It is the only government you really like. I will bet that you, Monsieur Rémusat, are a hundred times more comfortable now that you address me as *Sire.*

June 3d, Saint Cloud:
Russia, which has assumed mourning for the Duke d'Enghien, has thereby reminded Europe of the assassination of Paul I, which was nearly forgotten.

18th. The trial of the conspirators has started much gossip in Paris. The more than merciful judgment of the weak Tribunal of the Seine will be carried out as soon as the lawful period for entering an appeal has expired. Although I have pardoned several persons, there will still he a dozen ruffians who cannot be pardoned and who must meet their fate. As to General Moreau, although he was not condemned to death, he has been dishonoured by the verdict.

July 1st. Imagine the effect of the Emperor and his family decked in their imperial robes and exposed to the effects of the weather, the mud, the dust, or the rain! What a joke for the Parisians, who are so keen to ridicule everything, and who are used to seeing Chéron at the Opéra and Talma at the Théâtre Français play the Emperor a good deal better than I can. It has been suggested that the ceremony should take place at the Church of the Invalides because of its military associations, but Notre Dame will be better; it is larger, and also has associations that appeal more strongly to the imagination. It will lend dignity to the ceremony.

2d, Malmaison:
All this will last as long as I do; when I am gone, my son may think himself lucky if he has 40,000 francs a year!

(To Vice-Admiral Latouche-Tréville.) Let me know by return what day you can weigh anchor, weather permitting. Inform me also as to the position of the enemy,—where Nelson is. Think over carefully the great enterprise you are about to carry out; and let me know, before I sign your final orders, your own views as to the best way of carrying it out.

We have 1800 gunboats and cutters carrying 120,000 men and 10,000 horses between Etaples, Boulogne, Wimereux, and Ambleteuse. If we are masters of the Channel for six hours, we are masters of the world!

If you take Nelson in he will sail for Sicily, Egypt, or Ferrol. It would seem better, therefore, to sail very wide, to appear before Rochefort, which would give you a fleet of 16 of the line and 11 frigates, and then without delay, without touching, whether by circling around Ireland, or by carrying out the first plan, proceed to Boulogne. Our Brest fleet, 23 of the line, will have troops on board, and will remain constantly under sail, so that Cornwallis must keep close in to the coast of Brittany to prevent its getting out. But before my ideas are quite settled about these operations, which offer great risks but of which the success would mean so much, I shall wait for the plan you are to send me.

21st, Pont-de-Briques:
(To Josephine.) Madam and dear wife: It is now four days since I left you. I have spent them in the saddle and otherwise active, without any ill effect on my health.

The wind freshened to-night, and one of our gunboats dragged its anchor and struck on the rocks about one league from Boulogne; I thought all would be lost, the ship and the crew, but we were able to save them. The sight was a grand one; alarm guns were being fired; the shore seemed to blaze with fire; the sea roared furiously; all through the night we anxiously awaited the destruction or the safety of the unhappy men. My soul was in communion with Eternity, the Ocean, and Night! At five in the morning the weather cleared; all were saved; and I went tobed under the impression of a romantic and epic dream; a state that might have suggested to me my own solitude, were it not that fatigue and my soaked condition had left me with no other desire than sleep.

27th. Yesterday I reviewed the whole flotilla. Compared with that of England, our situation is most favourable. The war has no ill effect on France, because of its weighing so heavily on England, and I have here around me 120,000 men, and 3000 cutters and gunboats, that only await a favourable breeze to carry the Imperial eagle to the Tower of London. Time and Fate alone can tell what will come of it all.

30th. Order for the return to England of Lord Tweeddale, an English prisoner at Verdun, as a tribute to the talents and character of Mr. Fox.

August 3d. There are signs of a coalition forming; I shall not give them time to complete it; it is not right that Austria, by such equivocal conduct, should hold

300,000 men at attention on the shores of the Channel. The court of Vienna will have to come out of its ambiguous attitude, and if Vienna is so mad as to attempt the fortune of war again, and listen to the suggestions of London, woe betide the Austrian monarchy!

6th. The police commissioner at Boulogne is an excellent young man, but very young; at his age it is not possible to realize the depth of human perversity.

17th. The ceremony went off splendidly yesterday, except for a high wind. The spectacle was novel and imposing. Rarely have so many bayonets been seen together.

September 3d, Aix-la-Chapelle:
I must have a talk with Villeneuve about the great plan his fleet is to carry out.

6th. (To Vice-Admiral Ganteaume.) If you could carry 16,000 men and 1000 horses to Ireland in November, it would be fatal to our enemies. Tell me if you could be ready, and what are the probabilities of success. Have a talk with the Irish general O'Connor about the points where we might disembark.

I have no naval commanders. I would like to create a few rear-admirals, but I would prefer to select the men who showed most promise, regardless of seniority.

12th. Castle of La Haye, near Guelders:
I am here to-day in a little castle on the border of the Empire. I visited Crevelt yesterday, and am going to Venloo this morning. It was time this country was looked up both from the point of view of military fortification and of administration.

(To Decrès.) The navy must be tuned up by making a few examples. It's the only way to get a navy. Every naval expedition we have attempted since I have been at the head of the Government has failed, because the admirals see double and have picked up the idea, I don't know where, that you can make war without running risks.

I have sent you some reports on St. Helena.

15th, Cologne:
(To the Pope.) Holy Father: The excellent influence which the reëstablishment of the Christian religion has had on the habits and character of my people leads me to beg Your Holiness to give me a new proof of your interest in me and in this great nation, in one of the most important events recorded in the annals of humanity. I ask you to give the sanction of religion to the ceremony attending the consecration and coronation of the first Emperor of the French.

Treat the Pope as though he had 200,000 men.

27th. (To Marshal Berthier.) My Cousin: The expedition to Ireland will take place. You must confer with Marshal Augereau on the matter. We have at Brest transports for 18,000 men. General Marmont is ready on his side with 25,000. He will attempt to land in Ireland and will be under the orders of Marshal Augereau. At the same time the Grand Army will embark at Boulogne, and will make every effort to effect a landing in Kent. The navy holds out hopes of being ready on the 22d of October.

November 4th. It is from a sense of justice that I will not divorce her! It may be that my personal interests, or even the interests of my system call for my marrying again. But I said to myself: How can I put away this excellent woman, just because I am becoming great? No, that is beyond me. I have the heart of a man; it was not a tigress gave me birth. When she dies I will marry again, and perhaps I shall have children. But I will not make her unhappy.

Joseph is not marked out for my succession; he is older than I am; I shall probably outlive him, my health is good; and then he was not born in a high enough rank to maintain the illusion. I was born in poverty; he also was born in the most mediocre of surroundings; I have risen by my deeds; he has remained where his birth placed him. To reign in France, one must be born great, have been seen in childhood in a palace, surrounded with guards, or else be a man capable of raising himself above all others.

My mistress is power; I have done too much to conquer her to let her be snatched away from me. Although it may be said that power came to me of its own accord, yet I know what labour, what sleepless nights, what scheming, it has involved.

They are jealous of my wife, of Eugène, of Hortense, of all that is near me. What does it amount to? My wife has diamonds,—and debts! Eugène has an income of 20,000 francs a year! I love those children, because they are always trying to please me. If the cannon is fired, it is Eugène who runs out to see what it's about. If I have to cross a ditch, his hand is ready to help me. I love Hortense, yes, I love her; she and her brother always take my side, even against their mother, when she gets angry about some girl or such trivial matters. If Hortense should ask to see me while I was in the Council of State, I would go out to receive her. If Madame Murat (Caroline Bonaparte) asked for me, I would not go out. With her it's always a pitched battle; to bring a chit of a woman of my own family to reason, I must needs deliver harangues as long as if she were the Senate and the Council of State together. They say my wife is unfaithful, and that the attentions of her children are forced. Well! so be it! They treat me like an old uncle, and it makes the pleasant side of my life; I am getting old,—I'm thirty-six, I need rest.

They say I am going to give Italy to Eugène: so help me, I am not mad enough for that! I think myself capable of governing Italy, and even the Venetian state! My wife is a good wife, who does them no harm. She merely plays the Empress a little, has diamonds, fine dresses, the trifles of her age. I have never loved her blindly. If I have created her Empress, it was but bare justice. Yes, she shall be crowned! She shall be crowned if it costs me 200,000 men!

And then you are always talking to me about my death! My death! Always, my death! A very unpleasant idea to have constantly thrust under one's nose! If I could not find a little happiness in my family life, I should be a very unfortunate being. My death! My death! Always my death! Eh! may the universe break up after I've gone, if I am always to have the thought of death before me.

I speak to you as a friend, as the president of the Committee of the Interior. I know you, but I don't know the other persons who revolve about Joseph. How on earth could he have gone to Fouché, a little while ago, to complain that Madame Joseph would have to carry the train of the Empress at the Coronation? Well, if the restiveness of Joseph comes from the acrid blood that flows in his veins, he must retire to the country. He enjoys the rustic life and pastoral poetry; let him go off and compose idylls.

5th, Saint Cloud:
(To Cardinal Fesch.) It is absolutely necessary for the Pope to accelerate his journey. I am willing to postpone things till the 2d of December, which is my latest possible date. If the Pope is not here by then, the Coronation will take place, and the Consecration will be deferred. It is not possible to detain in Paris the troops and the departmental deputations, amounting to 50,000 persons.

December 1st, Paris:
I ascend the throne to which the unanimous votes of the Senate, the People, and the Army have called me, my heart full of the destinies of a Nation which I, from the midst of camps, first proclaimed great.

My descendants will long fill this throne.

2d, Notre Dame. The Coronation.

I swear that I will govern with the sole purpose of securing the interests, the happiness, and the glory of the French people.

5th, Paris.

Soldiers, here are your standards; these eagles must always be your rallying points.

27th. Deputies of the Departments to the Legislative Body, Tribunes, and Members of the Council of State, I have come among you to preside over your opening session. I have sought to lend a more imposing dignity to your labours. Prince, magistrates, soldiers, citizens, each in his own sphere, will have but one aim,—the interests of the country. If this throne, to which Providence and the will of the people have called me, is precious in my eyes, it is for the sole reason that by it alone can the most precious rights of the French nation be preserved. Without a strong and paternal government, France would have to fear a return of the evils from which she once suffered. Weakness in the executive power is the greatest calamity of nations. As soldier, or First Consul, I had but one purpose; as Emperor, I have none other: the prosperity of France.

If death does not surprise me in the midst of my labours, I hope to leave to posterity a renown that may always serve as an example, or as a reproach, to my successors.

1805

January 1st, Paris:
Ah! Good God! What red arms you've got! What a dirty dress! Don't you ever change your dress? I've seen that one at least twenty times!

Why don't you put on rouge? You're too pale. What? A woman who forgets her rouge? That wouldn't happen to you, would it, Josephine?

February 1st. We appoint our brother-in-law, Marshal Murat, Grand Admiral of the Empire.

27th. The time is drawing near when we can begin operations.

March 15th, Malmaison:
(To Vice-Admiral Ganteaume.) We have reached the 15th of March; there is not a day to spare. Be mindful of the greatness of the results that depend on you. If you show plenty of boldness, success is certain. In the Mediterranean Nelson has been damaged by the storms; he has only twelve of the line.

17th, Paris:
The Emperor of the French, Napoleon I, is King of Italy. The crown of Italy is hereditary by direct descent.

20th, Malmaison:

(To Marshal Berthier.) My Cousin: I would like you to write to Marshal Berna-dotte to have him send out people travelling under various pretexts in the provinces of Polish Russia, so that we may be well posted as to any movements of the Russian troops.

21st. (To Marshal Berthier.) I regret to find every day proposals placed before me for the quick promotion of staff officers, lieutenants of not more than two, three, or four years' service. They think themselves veterans if they date back to 1799. And yet there is no regiment that does not average eight captains dating from

1792, wounded, and who have fought in every campaign. I count seven of them in the 1st regiment, eight in the 3d, fourteen in the 4th, fourteen in the 5th, fifteen in the 6th, and so on.

22d. (To Vice-Admiral Villeneuve.) I am awaiting the news of your departure with impatience.

(To General Lauriston.) It is intended that the Toulon fleet shall combine with two other fleets. It is essential that it should weigh anchor by the 26th; hasten its departure by every possible means; let nothing delay you. Encourage the admiral to keep steadily on towards his objective, and to avoid hesitation in an operation of which the result is so vital to the future of France. My admirals lack boldness; they mistake frigates for line of battle ships, and merchant vessels for hostile fleets. Decision must be shown, and once the fleet is out it must fly straight to its mark and not go into port or turn back.

April 3d, Troyes:
Word has just come from Toulon stating that the fleet has sailed.

7th, Châlons-sur-Saône:
I reckon that with the weather we are having and with the wind prevailing when the fleet, started, Nelson has probably returned to Maddalena or some port of Sardinia.

11th, Lyons:
(To Ganteaume.) A message from Cadiz of the 29th states that Admiral Gravina is ready to sail with 8 ships and 2 frigates, which will bring the fleet of Admiral Villeneuve up to 20 of the line. You will find 8 Spanish and 4 French ships at Ferrol: I expect, therefore, that you can start from the point of concentration with 50 line of battle ships. The destinies of the world are in your hands.

(To Vice-Admiral Ver Huell.) I intend to concentrate the Dutch flotilla at Ambleteuse. The hour of glory is perhaps on the point of striking; it is all a matter of a few chances, of a few incidents.

20th, Stupinigi:
(To Decrès.) Admiral Nelson has once more been taken in about our fleet. I am beginning to feel a little easier about it. You will see that Admiral Villeneuve is

not under instructions to return immediately, but to wait thirty-five days so that the Brest fleet may have time enough to join him. By Heaven! stir them up!

22d. (To *Madame Mère*.) Mr. Jerome Bonaparte has arrived at Lisbon with the woman with whom he is living. I have ordered this prodigal son to Milan. Miss Patterson, who is with him, has prudently got her brother with her as an escort. I have ordered her sent back to America. I shall treat the boy harshly if, in the one interview I give him, he shows himself unworthy of his family and wishes to continue his liaison. Unless he is disposed to wipe out the dishonour he has attached to my name in abandoning his flag and his nationality for an unworthy woman, I shall wash my hands of him, and perhaps I shall strike an example to show young soldiers how sacred are their duties and how serious is the crime of abandoning their flag for a woman.

23d. Villeneuve joined Gravina off Cadiz on the l0th.

(To Decrès.) Keep the event at Cadiz, and the departure of the fleets secret. See that the Dutch gazettes publish that a French fleet has landed 10,000 men in Egypt; that the Admiral manœuvred very skilfully so as to throw Nelson off the track; that he made a show of passing the straits (of Gibraltar), but that at night he turned back and sailed along the African coast.

24th. (To Cambacérès.) My Cousin: I think the Council of State is not attending sufficiently to our manufactures; it is not idealism makes countries prosperous.

(To Fouché.) Have some well written articles published deriding the military movements of the Russians, the interview of the Emperor of Russia with the Emperor of Austria, and the absurd reports, phantoms born of the fogs and the spleen of England. Get active, and keep public opinion up. Tell the editors that although I am far away, I still read the papers, and that if they continue on the present tack I shall close their accounts.

(To Marshal Soult.) Let me know whether the horses, the supplies, the men, will all be ready for embarkation in two weeks. Don't reply in terms of metaphysics, but inspect your magazines and depots.

26th. (To Marshal Davout.) Don't let appearances send you to sleep. It may take me two months to travel down to Milan, but only a very few days to get back from Milan to Boulogne.

May 2d, Alessandria:
(To Talleyrand.) As the wording of the letters signed by me, when I have not drafted them in person, is often the work of Durand and his crew, it is not at all remarkable that, after the letter I was made to write to the Equestrian Order, the Emperor of Germany should have been encouraged to attack the princes. There are people in existence who imagine I have no teeth and no claws. By God, write to them not to trust to it! The habit of the Ministry of Foreign Affairs is always to write dispatches according to the protocol; there should be a special office for this duty; I am made to play too silly a part signing such letters.

Word reaches me from Naples that Nelson was at Maritimo on the 22d, and had only just learnt that the Toulon fleet had passed the straits.

4th. If Spain will send her six ships from Carthagena to Toulon, I will frighten the English so that they will keep an imposing force there; for I shall threaten Egypt in so many ways, and so obviously, that they will expect a big stroke; they believe my fleets are bound for the East Indies, and so it would appear as though I were carrying out a concerted scheme.

8th, Pavia:
On the 14th of July I shall be on the coast, and I expect the return of the fleets on the 29th.

22d, Milan:
(To Fouché.) Have some articles written against Princess Dolgorouki, who is spreading scandalous and ridiculous reports in Rome. You probably know that she long lived with an actor, and that the diamonds she displays so ostentatiously were given her by Potemkin and are the price of her dishonour. You can get information about her, and make her a laughingstock. She poses for a clever woman; she is on friendly terms with the Queen of Naples, and, which is equally surprising, with Mme. de Staël.

26th. *Assumption of the Iron Crown as King of Italy.*
Dio mi la donna, guai a chi la tocca!

27th. The coronation took place yesterday with much pomp. The cathedral was splendidly decorated. The ceremony went off just as well as in Paris, with this difference, that the weather was splendid. When I took the Iron Crown and placed it on my head, I added these words: "God gave it me, touch it who dares!" I hope I was prophesying!

30th. (To Decrès.) Why are you so anxious I should come back. to Paris? Nothing is better adapted to conceal my plans and deceive the enemy than my absence. It will give them confidence, and they will allow a few more ships to get away to distant seas.

(To Fouché.) Have some caricatures made: an Englishman, his purse in his hand, begging the various Powers to accept his money, etc. That is the note to strike. Have printed in Holland that advices from Madeira state that Villeneuve met a convoy of 100 English merchantmen bound for India, and captured it.

June 1st. I shall unite the territory of Genoa to my Empire.

(To Fouché.) I read in a paper that a tragedy on Henry IV is to be played. The epoch is recent enough to excite political passions. The theatre must dip more into antiquity. Why not commission Raynouard to write a tragedy on the transition from primitive to less primitive man? A tyrant would be followed by the saviour of his country. The oratorio "Saul" is on precisely that text,—a great man succeeding a degenerate king.

7th. Anxious to confer on our stepson, Prince Eugène, an emphatic testimonial of our confidence in his devotion to ourselves, and also to provide during our absence for the government of our kingdom of Italy, we hereby designate and appoint him by these presents Viceroy of our said kingdom.

(Instructions for Prince Eugène.) My Cousin: In entrusting you with the government of our kingdom of Italy, we cannot too strongly recommend that you should use circumspection and prudence. Our Italian subjects are of a more dissembling character than are French citizens. There is but one sure way of keeping their esteem and of helping them, which is to give your complete trust to no one, and to let none know what you think of the ministers and high officials about you.

Make show of a good opinion of the people you govern, and all the more when you discover motives to the contrary. A time will come when you will realize that there is little enough difference between one nation and another.

Speak as little as possible; you have not sufficient knowledge, and your education has been too much neglected for you to plunge into impromptu debate. Learn how to listen, and remember that silence often produces as much effect as knowledge. Don't blush to ask questions. Though a viceroy, you are but twenty-three years old, and whatever flattery may tell you, people are perfectly aware of just how much you know, and think better of you for what you may become, than for what they know you to be.

Don't preside over your Council of State frequently; you have too little knowledge to do so with success.

9th. Lucien prefers a dishonoured woman, who bore him a child before they were married, to the honour of his name and of his family. I can only lament such an aberration in a man whom nature endowed with talents. An unexampled egotism has drawn him away from a splendid career, away from the path of duty and honour.

28th, Piacenza:
Nelson has sailed for America; Villeneuve's objective is so hard to guess that even Nelson, after victualling at Barbadoes, will not think himself at fault letting three or four days slip by, as Villeneuve cannot be attacked in the bay of Martinique. I calculate that Villeneuve should start for Ferrol between the 9th and the 29th of June,—before Nelson could sight him. I shall hasten my return by a few days, because I think that possibly Nelson's arrival in America might decide Villeneuve to start for Ferrol.

July 13th, Fontainebleau:
I arrived at Fontainebleau 85 hours after leaving Turin. I lost three hours at the Mont Cenis, and I frequently stopped one or two hours for breakfast, and one or two hours for dinner, on account of the Empress, which cost me another eight or nine hours.

14th. Our papers are publishing a genealogy of the House of Bonaparte which is both flat and ridiculous. Such performances are childish, and when people ask for the origin of the House of Bonaparte, the answer is easy: it dates from the 18th of Brumaire.

18th, Saint Cloud:

I had foreseen in my instructions that the enemy might withdraw from in front of Brest; for four days they are reported to have been out of sight. This, together with the disappearance of the squadron blockading Rochefort, leaves little doubt as to Villeneuve's return. Admiral Gardner has sailed to meet Villeneuve, who will probably need several days to effect the concentration at Ferrol.

20th. (To Vice-Admiral Ganteaume, at Brest.) You have already received the order to proceed to sea; chase the enemy's frigates, and ascertain their movements. If the enemy are out of sight and have sailed for Ferrol, or are well out to sea heading for Villeneuve, our orders are that you should proceed to Boulogne where all is ready, and where, if we are masters of the sea three days, you will enable us to ring the knell of England.

When you receive this letter we shall already be at Boulogne in person, and everything will be packed on board. Great events are happening, or will shortly happen; don't let your fleet remain useless. If the enemy weaken their numbers in your front, it will be because they suppose that it is Villeneuve who is to make the offensive move. Counter their move by taking the initiative yourself. Be prudent; but know when to be bold.

31st. The news from Italy all points to war, and really Austria is barely keeping up appearances.

August 3d, Boulogne:
Without question, Austria is getting ready for war.

6th. (To Daru.) My intention is to turn Art specially in the direction of subjects that would tend to perpetuate the memory of the events of the last fifteen years. It is astonishing, for instance, that I have not been able to get the Gobelins to give up Sacred History and to employ their artists on those numerous actions of all sorts that have won glory for the army and for the nation, the events that have created our throne.

8th. The combined fleet has been in action near Ferrol; it has accomplished its object by effecting its junction with the Ferrol squadron. The fleet gave chase to the enemy, and for four days remained in possession of the field of battle.

9th. (To Barbé Marbois.) Reassure the financiers; explain to them that no imprudent risk will be run; that matters are going too favourably at present for foolishly hazarding the happiness and prosperity of my people. Undoubtedly I shall land at the head of my army. Everybody must see that this is necessary; but neither I nor my army will disembark unless we have every chance in our favour.

11th. The fleets have come to anchor at Corunna. Lauriston writes that they will keep on, that the captains and crews are all right, that Villeneuve, who is not without talent, is too slow in making up his mind.

13th. (To Cambacérès.) You will read in the *Moniteur* some articles that will make you think war with Austria is coming. The fact is that this Power is arming. I want her to disarm; if she won't, I shall pay her a little visit with 200,000 men which she will not soon forget. However, if any one asks you, and in your speeches, say that you don't believe in it, because I have had ample warning. For it would obviously be sheer folly to make war on me. There is certainly not in all Europe a finer army than the one I command to-day.

Pont-de-Briques:
I have made up my mind: I will either attack Austria and reach Vienna before November—to face the Russians, should they put in an appearance; or else my will, and that is the word, is that there should be but one Austrian regiment in the Tyrol. I want to be left to conduct my war against England in quiet.

Boulogne:

(To Decrès.) Send a special messenger to Ferrol. Inform Admiral Villeneuve of my dissatisfaction at his losing precious time.

(To Villeneuve.) Inform Admiral Ganteaume of your departure by a special courier. Never will a fleet have faced risks for a more important object, and never will my soldiers and sailors have an opportunity of shedding their blood for a greater and more noble result. We might all of us well die content for the sake of helping on the invasion of the Power that has for six centuries oppressed France. Such are the sentiments that should animate you, that should animate all my soldiers. England has not more than four line of battle ships in the Downs.

(To Josephine.) It is not often one hears from you. You forget your friends, which is wrong. I did not know that the waters of Plombières had the same effect as those of Lethe. It seems to me that it was drinking these same Plombières waters once made you say, "Ah, Bonaparte, if ever I die, who will there be to love you?" That was a very long time ago, wasn't it? Everything passes, beauty, wit, sentiment, even the sun, all but one thing that is endless: the good I wish you, your happiness. I cannot be more loving even if you laugh at me for my pains. Good-bye, dear friend. I had the English cruisers attacked yesterday; everything passed off well.

20th. The weather is very unsettled; there is much rain. The combined fleets left Ferrol with 34 sail of the line.

At this moment a division of the flotilla is working around Cape Grisnez in action with the English.

On the 2d Nelson was still off Cape St. Vincent; he was apparently short of provisions.

22d. I believe that Villeneuve hasn't enough in him to command a frigate. He has no decision and no moral courage. Two Spanish ships have been in collision, a few men are sick on his own ships, add to that two days of unfavourable winds, an enemy's ship reconnoitring, a report that Nelson has joined Calder: and his plans are changed, when, taking these facts one by one, they amount to nothing. He has not the experience of war, nor the instinct for it.

(To Villeneuve.) I hope you have reached Brest. Start; lose not a minute, and, with my combined fleets, sail up the Channel. England is ours. We are all ready, everything is embarked. Appear here for twenty-four hours, and all is over.

23d. I perceive the urgency of coming to a decision. In reality there is no point in demanding an explanation of Austria. My mind is made up.

My fleet sailed from Ferrol on the 17th with 34 ships of the line; there was no enemy in sight. If my instructions are followed, if it joins the Brest fleet and enters the Channel, there is still time; I am master of England. If, on the contrary, my admirals hesitate, manœuvre badly, and don't carry out my plans, all I can do is to await winter and then cross with the flotilla; it's a risky operation. Such being the state of things, I must attend to the more urgent matter. I can place 200,000 men in Germany, and 25,000 in the kingdom of Naples. I march on Vienna, and do not lay down my arms until Naples and Venice are mine, and I have so increased the electorate of Bavaria that I have nothing further to fear from Austria. I can certainly pacify Austria after this fashion during the course of the winter. I shall not return to Paris until I have touched my goal.

My plan is to gain two weeks. I want to get into the heart of Germany with 300,000 men before any one suspects it.

24th. No more news of the fleets. I continue reviewing the various divisions of my army.

25th. (To Talleyrand.) My movement is begun. You can say that, as my frontiers are exposed, I am moving 25,000 men to protect them. Don't show boldness, but absolute cowardice. It's a matter of gaining twenty days and of preventing the Austrians from crossing the Inn while I am marching on the Rhine. I did not suppose the Austrians would be so active, but I have made so many mistakes in my life, that I am past blushing for them.

Marshal Murat will start to-morrow under the name of Colonel Beaumont; he will proceed directly to Mainz, where he will change horses only. He will pass through Frankfort, reconnoitring Offenbach on the way; will go to Würzburg, reconnoitre it, staying a day and a half and having a look at the roads between that place, Mainz, and the Danube, getting some notions of the débouchés on Ulm, Ingolstadt, and Ratisbon. He will proceed from there to Bamberg, and must plan to reach Strassburg on the 11th of September.

26th. Prince Murat is appointed lieutenant of the Emperor, commander-in-chief of the army in the absence of His Majesty.

29th. How small England will become when France gets two or three admirals who are willing to face death!

31st. Everything has gone; I shall be ready on the 27th of September. I have given the army of Italy to Masséna. Austria is very insolent, and is redoubling her efforts. My fleet has gone into Cadiz.

September 2d. I start in one hour for Paris.

4th, Malmaison:
(To Vice-Admiral Decrès.) Admiral Villeneuve has touched the limit! The thing is unthinkable! Send me a report covering the whole expedition. Villeneuve is a low rascal who must be ignominiously cashiered. Without plans, without courage, he would sacrifice everything to save his skin!

13th, Saint Cloud:
The Austrians crossed the Inn on the 10th. The Elector of Bavaria retired to Würzburg.

My plan was to concentrate 40 or 50 battleships at Martinique by movements concerted from Toulon, Cadiz, Ferrol, and Brest; then have them return suddenly to Boulogne; get control of the straits for fifteen days; have 150,000 men and 10,000 horses ready; disembark in England, seize London and the Thames. This plan almost succeeded. Had Admiral Villeneuve, instead of going into Ferrol, merely effected his junction with the Spanish squadron, and made sail for Brest to join Admiral Ganteaume, my army was over, and there was an end to England. To carry out this plan, it was necessary to collect 150,000 men at Boulogne, a flotilla of 4000 boats, and immense stores; get all this on board ship, and yet prevent the enemy from guessing my intentions: this seemed impossible. If I was to succeed it was by doing the reverse of what seemed obvious. If 50 ships of the line were going to cover the passage of the army to England, all that we needed at Boulogne were transports; and the immense display of gunboats and floating batteries of various kinds was absolutely useless. Collecting 4000 vessels of this sort was opposing cannon to cannon, ship of war to ship of war; and the enemy were taken in. They believed I intended to force the passage by means of the flotilla, and never realized my actual plan. When, after my fleet had failed to carry out its manœuvre, they perceived the danger they had run, fear seized on the Cabinet of London, and every thinking man admitted that England had never been so near disaster.

18th. (To Marshal Masséna, commanding in chief the army of Italy, at Valeggio.) You have nearly 60,000 men under your orders; that is one third more than ever I had. I have full confidence in your courage and ability. Win me some victories.

23d. I leave for Strassburg to-morrow at half-past four in the morning.

26th, Strassburg:
The whole army is across the Rhine. We shall soon be manoeuvring.

27th. Events are moving rapidly. The Austrians are at the débouchés of the Black Forest. Heaven keep them there! My only anxiety is lest we frighten them away. If I am lucky enough, and the Austrians remain asleep three or four days more on the Iller, I shall be around them, and I hope that only débris will escape me.

29th. The King of Prussia has called up his reservists.

The weather is glorious; I hope I shall have a fine autumn.

(To Marshal Ney.) I assume you have reached Stuttgardt. Marshal Lannes is marching on Ludwigsburg; he can move rapidly to support you if it should be necessary. Prince Murat is marching on Rastadt. Keep him informed of everything.

30th. Soldiers! The war of the Third Coalition has begun. The Austrian army has crossed the Inn, has broken all treaties, has attacked our ally and driven him from his capital. You have been compelled to rush to the defence of our frontiers by forced marches. But you are already across the Rhine. We will not stay our march until we have secured the independence of the Germanic body, succoured our allies, and confounded the pride of our unjust aggressors!

I shall start to-night to back up Marshal Soult and outflank Ulm. Woe betide the Austrians if they let me gain a few more marches! I hope to concentrate my whole army between the Lech and the Isar.

October 2d, Imperial Headquarters, Ettlingen:
The enemy are marching forward and backward and appear to be completely puzzled.

(To Josephine.) I am starting for Stuttgardt, which I shall reach to-night. Our grand manœuvres are in full swing. The armies of Würtemberg and Baden are joining mine. I am in good position, and I love you.

3d, Ludwigsburg:
I am with the Elector (of Würtemberg), who has definitely joined our side.

4th. No new developments. The whole army is marching. The weather is splendid. I have effected my junction with the Bavarians.

(To Champagny.) I am at the Court of Würtemberg, and, though conducting war, I am hearing some very good music. The German style of singing, however, strikes me as rather queer. Are the reservists coming in? How goes the conscription of 1806?

5th. Between the 15th and 16th the whole army will be between Donauwerth and Ingolstadt; there never will have been so many troops packed into so small a space.

8th, Donauwerth:

Yesterday I crossed the Danube and the Lech. I ordered Augsburg and Aichach to be attacked. Twelve battalions of grenadiers have been surrounded at Wertingen between the Lech and the Danube; and the greater part of them, with their standards and artillery, has been captured.

I am marching to get behind Ulm. Each day becomes more critical, and if the enemy make a few mistakes, the consequences may be disastrous.

(To Marshal Soult.) Lannes' grenadiers will not stop till they reach Zusmarshausen, and to-night I shall move Suchet's division according to the reports that reach me before two o'clock. Allow no halts, and make up your mind to move night and day until you have captured their main body. The least you can send me is 3000 or 4000 prisoners.

4th. (To Prince Murat.) I have ordered d'Hautpoul to Wertingen. I shall sleep at Augsburg with the Guard, where I expect Marshal Soult has already arrived. Cut the main road from Augsburg to Ulm; push General Walther between Augsburg and Landsberg, and place Marshal Lannes so that if Augsburg is attacked at day-break his three divisions could get there.

10th, Zusmarshausen:
The weather has broken, there is much rain. The fight at Wertingen is very cred-itable to the dragoons and the cavalry. It's a minor success, and very gratifying to Murat, who was in command. I hold the enemy surrounded at Ulm; they were defeated last night by Ney's corps.

No army has ever marched with greater good will, dash, and confidence.

The Emperor reviewed the dragoons at Zusmarshausen. He ordered Marcate, of the 4th dragoons, who is one of the bravest men in the army, to be brought before him. At the passage of the Lech he saved the life of his captain, who, a few days previously, had reduced him to the ranks. His Majesty gave him the Legion of Honour.

11th, Augsburg:
The army of Prince Ferdinand is outflanked, and Prince Murat with the dra-goons and the corps of Marshal Lannes and Marshal Ney is pursuing him. Mar-shal Bernadotte should reach Munich to-day.

12th. The Austrian army is completely demoralized. Our worst regiments of chasseurs attack, with odds against them, heavy cuirassier regiments and rout them; the infantry make no stand at all.

(To Josephine.) My army holds Munich. On one side the enemy are beyond the Inn; I have the other army of 60,000 men penned on the Iller. The enemy are beaten and don't know what they are about. It all looks like the most successful, the shortest, and the most brilliant campaign ever fought. I start in one hour for Burgau.

(To Marshal Soult.) To-night, if my information from Munich warrants it, I shall move one of Davout's divisions to Landberg, where it will be at your disposal. See that your aide-de-camps and adjutants kill their horses. It is not a question of defeating the enemy, but of not a single man escaping. When you reach Memmingen assemble your generals and tell them that I expect, in such important circumstances, that nothing will be left undone that can make our success more complete and more absolute; that the event must be ten times more glorious than Marengo, and that in the most remote ages posterity must relate what each one of them accomplished; that if I had intended merely to defeat the enemy we need not have undertaken such marches and such fatigues, but that I must capture them.

10.30 P. M.:
I have just received a dispatch from Prince Murat. The enemy hold Ulm with 40,000 men.

The Emperor was at the bridge over the Lech when General Marmont's corps passed. He ordered each regiment to form circle, spoke to the men about the position of the enemy, told them a great battle would soon be fought, and that he had complete confidence in them. He delivered these harangues under awful weather conditions. A heavy snow was falling, and the men were in mud up to their knees; but the words of the Emperor were so vivid that the men, as they listened, forgot their fatigues and hardships, and only showed impatience to get into battle.

15th, Elchingen:
The weather is dreadful. The Emperor has not taken his boots off these last eight days.

19th. (To Josephine.) I have been rather overdone, my good Josephine. Eight days spent in the soaking rain and with cold feet have told on me a little; but I have stayed indoors the whole of to-day and am rested.

I have accomplished my object; I have destroyed the Austrian army by simple marching. I have made 60,000 prisoners, taken 120 guns, more than 90 flags, and more than 30 generals.

I am on the point of marching against the Russians; they are ruined. I am satisfied with my army. I have lost only 1500 men, of whom two thirds are slightly wounded. Good-bye, my Josephine, a thousand friendly sentiments.

Werneck's corps has just capitulated to Prince Murat at Noerdlingen. The garrison of Ulm will lay down their arms to-morrow at 3 in the afternoon. There are 27,000 men, including 3000 cavalry, with 60 guns fully horsed.

21st, Elchingen. (*Battle of Trafalgar.*)
Soldiers of the Grand Army! In fifteen days we have fought a campaign; we have accomplished our purpose! We have driven the troops of the House of Austria from Bavaria, and reëstablished our ally in the possession of his states. This army, that had with equal impudence and ostentation placed itself on our frontiers, has been annihilated. But what cares England for that? Her object is gained, we are no longer at Boulogne.

Of the one hundred thousand men who made up this army, 60,000 are prisoners; they will fill the places of our conscripts in the labours of the field. Two hundred guns, the whole train, ninety colours, all their generals are ours.

Soldiers! you owe this success to your boundless confidence in your Emperor, to your patience in supporting all kinds of fatigues and privations, to your splendid valour.

But we cannot rest yet. You are impatient for a second campaign. The Russian army, drawn by the gold of England from the furthest limits of the earth, must suffer the same fate. In this contest the honour of the French infantry is more especially at stake; for the second time the question must be decided, whether the French infantry is the first or the second in Europe.

There are no generals to lead them from whom I have any glory to win. My whole anxiety shall be to obtain the victory with the least possible effusion of blood: my soldiers are my children!

22d, Augsburg:
The march of Prince Murat from Albeck to Nuremberg amazes us all. Fighting every inch of the way, he has outmarched and overtaken the enemy, who had two days start of him. The result of this marvellous activity has been the capture of 1500 wagons, 50 guns, and 16,000 men, including those who surrendered with General Werneck, together with a great number of flags, and 18 generals, of whom 3 were killed.

23d. I am thoroughly rested after these last two nights, and am starting for Munich to-morrow.

27th, Munich:
I am manœuvring against the Russian army, which is in considerable strength behind the Inn. In another two weeks I shall have 100,000 Russians, and 60,000 Austrians in front of me. I shall beat them, but probably not without some loss.

30th, Braunau:
It is snowing heavily.

November 2, Ried:
It has turned cold, there is a sharp frost. This dry weather has the advantage of being healthier and better for marching.

3d, Haag:
We are in full march. All is going well; my enemies are probably more worried than I am.

5th, Linz:
My advance guard, is within six days' march of Vienna. Murat keeps in touch with the enemy.

6th. (To Prince Murat.) The officer you have sent me is such a fool that he could explain nothing, and your letter gives no details, so that I can't tell whether the enemy are retreating or are in position, the number of guns, and what part of Oudinot's division was engaged.

13th, Burkersdorf:
I entered Vienna this morning.

14th, Schoenbrunn:
Marshal Soult's corps passed through Vienna at nine o'clock this morning; Marshal Davout's is passing through now.

15th. All our columns are in Moravia at several days' march from the Danube.

(To Prince Joseph Napoleon.) I am now manœuvring against the Russian army, and have not had occasion to be very satisfied with Bernadotte. He has lost me a day, and the fate of the world may depend on a day. I should much like to see Junot, for I am each day more firmly convinced that the men I have trained myself are fair and away the best. I am still very pleased with Murat, Lannes, Davout, Soult, Ney, and Marmont. I intend to make the generals and officers who have served me well so rich that there can be no excuse for their dishonouring the most noble of professions by their greed, while drawing down on themselves the contempt of the soldiers.

16th. (To Josephine.) I am writing to M. d'Harville that you can proceed to Baden, from there to Stuttgardt, and from there to Munich. Be gracious, but accept all the honours: it is to you they are due, while from you there is nothing due save what pleases you. I am off to join my advance guard. The weather is horrible, with much snow; all is going well, however.

20th. Marshal Soult will move to Austerlitz.

23, Brünn:
(To Talleyrand.) I think the Austrians have more important matters on hand than the abduction of the Electress. Supposing they did abduct her, what the devil do you suppose they could do with her? I shall soon be at Vienna, as I have decided to give my troops a much needed rest.

25th. (To the Emperor of Russia.) Sire: I am sending my aide-de-camp, General Savary, to convey my compliments on the occasion of your joining your army. I have commissioned him to express all the esteem I have for you, and my anxiety to find opportunities for proving how high I value your friendship. I hope you will receive him with that graciousness which is peculiarly your own, and will hold me as one who desires to do what may be agreeable to you.

26th. The Emperors of Germany and of Russia are at Olmütz. The Russian army is receiving reinforcements.

28th. General Caffarelli will see that all arms are cleaned in his division, that the men have their cartridges; there will be a pitched battle. He must speak to his brigadiers and colonels, and he is to start with his division at one o'clock in the morning.

Well, Marbot, how many mounted chasseurs are there in my Guard? Are there 1200?

(No, sire, I could count only 1120.)

I was sure there were a lot missing!

December 1st, bivouac near Austerlitz:
Soldiers! The Russian army is marching on you to avenge the Austrians. Our position is strong, and while they march to turn our right, they will expose their own flank.

Soldiers! I will command your battalions in person, and I shall not expose myself if, with your usual courage, you throw the enemy's ranks into disorder and confusion. But should victory be for one moment uncertain, you would see your Emperor expose himself in the front rank, for there must be no question of victory on an occasion when the honour of the French infantry is at stake.

Before to-morrow night that army will be destroyed!

8.30 P.M.
The marshals will join the Emperor at his bivouac at seven thirty, so that fresh instructions may he given should the enemy have developed any new movements during the night.

9 P. M.
(The Emperor) decided to go the round of the bivouacs on foot and incognito; he was nearly at once recognised. It would be impossible to describe the enthusiasm of the soldiers when they saw him. In an instant blazing torches of straw were raised on a thousand poles, and 80,000 men were standing and acclaiming their Emperor, some for the anniversary of his coronation, others saying that the army would present the Emperor with a bouquet on the following day. An old grenadier came up to him and said: "Sire, keep out of the firing, I promise you in the name of the grenadiers, that you need not fight otherwise than as a spectator, for we will bring you the standards and the guns of the Russian army to celebrate the anniversary of your coronation." When the Emperor returned to his own bivouac a straw shanty without a roof that the grenadiers had built for him, he said: "This

is the most glorious night of my life; but I regret that so many of these brave fellows will be lost. They really are my children."

2d, Austerlitz:
As the sun rose the plateau of Pratzen could be distinguished, and the enemy moving down from it, like a torrent rushing to the plain.

How long will it take you to occupy the plateau of Pratzen?

(Soult: Less than twenty minutes.)

If that is so, we will wait fifteen minutes more.

Prince Murat, Marshals Lannes and Soult start off at a gallop. Each marshal rejoined his corps. The Emperor said, as he passed along the front of several regiments: "Soldiers, we must finish this campaign with a thunderbolt that will shatter the pride of our enemies." At once the shakos were hoisted on the men's bayonets, and acclamations of Vive l'Empereur were the real signal for opening the battle.

3d. Well done, soldiers! In the battle of Austerlitz you have accomplished all I expected of your valour; you have crowned your eagles with immortal glory. An army of 100,000 men commanded by the Emperors of Russia and of Austria has been dispersed or captured in less than four hours. What escaped your arms was drowned in the lakes. Forty flags, the standards of the Russian Imperial Guard, 120 guns, 20 generals, more than 30,000 prisoners are the result of this eternally glorious battle. This famous infantry, that outnumbered you, was unable to resist your attack, and henceforth you have no rivals to fear.

Soldiers! When we have completed all that is necessary to secure the happiness and prosperity of our country, I will lead you back to France; there you will be the constant objects of my loving care. My people will hail your return with joy, and you will have but to say, "I was at the battle of Austerlitz," to hear the reply, "He is one of the brave!"

The battle of Austerlitz is the most splendid of all I have fought. I have fought thirty battles of the same sort, but none in which the victory was so decisive, and so little in doubt. The infantry of the Guard was not sent into action,—the men were weeping with rage.

To-night I am lying in a bed, in the beautiful castle of Count Kaunitz, and I have changed my shirt, which I hadn't done for a week past. I shall get two or three hours' sleep.

The Emperor of Germany sent Prince Liechtenstein to me this morning to ask for an interview. We may possibly get peace before long.

4th. (To Talleyrand.) The Emperor of Germany has asked me for an interview, which I have granted; it lasted from two till four o'clock. I will tell you what I think of him when I see you. He wanted to make peace on the spot; he attacked me with fine sentiments; I defended myself, a manner of fighting which, I can assure you, I did not find very difficult. He asked me for an armistice, which I granted; the conditions are to be drawn up tonight.

10th, Brünn:

(To the Empress Josephine.) It is a long time since I heard from you. Do the festivities of Baden, of Stuttgardt, and of Munich make you forget the poor soldiers who live splashed with mud, blood, and rain?

I am starting very soon for Vienna. The peace is being negotiated. Good-bye, dear friend.

19th. (To Josephine.) Mighty Empress, I have had not one single line from you since you left Strassburg. You have passed through Baden, Stuttgardt, and Munich without writing me one word. That is not very nice, not very loving.

I am still at Brünn. The Russians have gone. There is an armistice. In a few days I shall be able to see how I am coming out. Deign from the height of your splendours to take a little notice of your slaves.

20th, Schoenbrunn:
The weather is very cold; winter is coming on, but it is still fine. It is curing our wounded, and setting up the army. We are resting, and getting into shape again.

We have already moved a part of the arsenal of Vienna to Braunau, and many valuable objects. Peace will undoubtedly be concluded.

23d. (To Talleyrand.) I have received your letter of to-day, and see with pleasure that you expect to conclude. But I expressly instruct you not to mention Naples. The insults of the rascally Queen increase with each courier. Her reign has got to come to an end. I will therefore absolutely not have her name mentioned. Whatever happens, my instructions are positive, do not mention her.

25th. The Emperor and Prince Charles have written to me. I will have an interview with Prince Charles on the 27th at two in the afternoon at a hunting box of the Emperor's, three leagues from Vienna. I wouldn't agree to meet Prince Charles here, because I am disinclined to talk business with him. At the rendezvous I have fixed, we can spend two hours together; one of them will go in dining, the other in talking war and in compliments.

In any event, get (the treaty) signed to-morrow if you can.

27th. Peace was signed at Presburg this morning at four o'clock between M. de Talleyrand and Prince Liechtenstein and General Gyulai.

The city and mainland of Venice, as ceded by the treaty of Campo Formio, are incorporated with my kingdom of Italy.

(To the army.) Soldiers! for ten years I have left nothing undone to save the King of Naples; he has left nothing undone for his ruin. After the battles of Dego, of Mondego, of Lodi, he could have offered but the feeblest resistance. I listened to the promises of this Prince, and I treated him with generosity.

When the Second Coalition was destroyed at Marengo, the King of Naples, first to wage an unjust war, remained isolated and defenceless; he implored me, and for the second time I pardoned him.

But a few months have passed since you were at the gates of Naples. I had good grounds for suspecting the treason hatching there, and for avenging the insults we had already suffered. Again I was generous. I allowed the neutrality of Naples; I ordered you to evacuate that kingdom; and for the third time the House of Naples was saved.

Shall we pardon for the fourth time? Shall we trust for the fourth time a Court without faith, without honour, without judgment? No! No! The dynasty of Naples has ceased to reign; its continued existence is incompatible with the repose of Europe and the honour of my Crown.

Forward, soldiers! Hurl into the waves, if they should await you, the feeble battalions of the tyrants of the seas; show the world how we chastise perjury. Send me word promptly that all Italy is subject to my laws, that the most lovely land on earth is freed from the yoke of the most perfidious of nations, that the sanctity of treaties is vindicated, and that the spirits of my brave soldiers, slaughtered in the ports of Sicily on their return from Egypt after escaping the dangers of shipwreck, of the desert, and of battle, are at last appeased.

Soldiers! my brother will lead you; he knows my plans; he carries my authority; he has my complete confidence; encircle him with yours.

31st, Munich:
(To Prince Joseph.) I have reached Munich. I propose seizing the kingdom of Naples. Start for Rome forty hours after receiving this letter; and let your first dispatch inform me that you have entered Naples.

I have asked for the hand of Princess Augusta. daughter of the Elector of Bavaria, a very pretty girl, for Prince Eugène. The marriage is settled. I have asked for another princess for Jerome.

(To Prince Eugène.) My Cousin: I have arrived at Munich. I have arranged a marriage for you with Princess Augusta. The matter is public. The Princess called on me this morning, and we had a long talk. She is very pretty. I am sending you her portrait on a cup, but it doesn't do her justice.

1806

January 2d, Munich:
Yesterday the Elector was proclaimed King.

3d, *2 P. M.*
(To Prince Eugène.) My Cousin: Not later than twelve hours after the receipt of this letter you must start for Munich, travelling posthaste.

7th. (To Cardinal Fesch.) On the 13th of November the Pope wrote me a letter of the most ridiculous, most insane, character: those people think I am dead! I am a religious man, but I am not a bigoted idiot.

For the Pope I am Charlemagne, because like Charlemagne I unite the Crowns of France and of the Lombards, and my Empire touches the East. I will reduce the Pope to be the mere bishop of Rome.

9th. I had long ago decided on a marriage between my son Prince Eugène, and the Princess Augusta, daughter of the King of Bavaria. The Elector of Ratisbon will marry them on the 15th of January. Princess Augusta is one of the most lovely and accomplished persons of her sex.

14th. The betrothal and marriage of Prince Eugène took place yesterday.

19th, Stuttgardt:
I am very impatient to be back in Paris. I arrived in Stuttgardt last night at six o'clock.

27th, Paris:
I arrived in Paris yesterday at midnight and incognito.

February 4th. The English Cabinet has been completely changed since the death of Mr. Pitt. If it is true that Mr. Fox is Secretary for Foreign Affairs, we could hand over Hanover to Prussia only as part of a general arrangement.

(To Prince Eugène.) My Son: I am surprised that you have not written me one word about your journey. Your wife has been more polite than you. I must insist on your writing me enough to inform me as to where you are, where you are going, and what you are doing;—how do you get on with her, and how much do you care for her?

6th. The Emperor incloses an extract from the *Bayreuth Gazette* for M. Talleyrand. We are threatened with the advance of 200,000 Russians. The Prussians must really be mad. M. Talleyrand must tell M. de Haugwitz that this sort of thing must be put a stop to.

14th. (To Marshal Berthier.) Stick closely to your orders; carry out instructions promptly; have every one on his guard and at his post; I alone know what I have to do. If the Prussian Minister at Munich should call on you and speak of the occupation of Anspach, reply that it is done by my orders. Have not the Prussians occupied Hanover? For the rest give Prussia plenty of fine speeches.

28th. I have 510,000 men with the colours; I have ordered heavy expenditures for the ports and the increase of the navy; I am going to increase the army by 100,000 men, and I am going to impose additional taxation on France.

March 1st. I want to create in France a lay state. Up till now the world has only known two forms of government, the ecclesiastic and the military. Constantine was the first to establish, by means of the priests, a sort of civilian state; Clovis succeeded in founding the French monarchy only with this same support. Monks are the natural enemies of soldiers, and have more than once served to check them. The lay order will be strengthened by the creation of a teaching body, and even more strengthened by the creation of a great corporation of magistrates.

I think it is unnecessary to take into consideration a system of education for girls, they can get no better teaching than that of their mothers. A public education does not suit them, for the reason that they are not called on, to live in public; for them habit is everything, and marriage is the goal.

If we are to establish the nation, we must hasten to regulate by means of codes the principal fields of legislation. The Civil Code, though imperfect, has done much good. Every one is familiar now with the first principles of conduct, and governs his property and business accordingly.

4th. In the report on burials I see that in the average year there are 14,000 deaths in Paris; that is enough for a splendid battle.

I have declined to commit myself to issuing tickets for the service in my chapel; I think the seats should go to the first comers.

At Cairo, and in the desert, the mosques are inns as well; as many as 6000 persons may shelter and eat in them; or even use the fountains and water for bathing. Our ceremony of baptism comes from this; it could not have arisen in our climate, in which water is not precious enough,—this year we are deluged. When water fails the Egyptians baptize with sand. As for me, it is not the mystery of the Incarnation that I see in religion, but the mystery of social order. Heaven suggests an idea of equality which saves the rich from being massacred by the poor. To look at it another way, religion is a sort of inoculation or vaccine which, while satisfying our sense of the supernatural, guarantees us from the charlatans and the magicians: the priests are better than the Cagliostros, the Kants, and all the dreamers of Germany.

I need a special Tribunal to judge public functionaries for certain infractions of the laws. There must be some arbitrary exercise of power in such a matter, and this should not be left in the hands of the Sovereign, because he will either abuse it or neglect to use it. I complain every day of the number of arbitrary acts I am made to commit; they would come with more propriety from such a tribunal. I want the State to be governed according to law, and that the things that have to be done despite the law should be legalized by the operation of a duly constituted body.

Forty-eight hours after peace with England is signed, I will shut out foreign produce and manufactures, and issue a Navigation Act that will exclude all but French ships from our ports. There will be a tremendous outcry, but in six years' time we shall be in the fullest prosperity.

6th. (To Joseph.) Shoot without pity any lazzaroni who indulge in dagger play. You can keep an Italian population down only by holy fear. Impose a war contribution of 30 millions on the kingdom. Your policy is too hesitating.

8th. I shall grant the duchies of Cleves and Berg to Prince Murat.

9th. (To Prince Eugène.) Instruct your engineers to reconnoitre the roads from Zara and from Ragusa to Constantinople.

11th. In the teaching body we must imitate the classifications of military rank. I hold strongly to the idea of a corporation, because a corporation never dies. There need be no fear that I want to bring back the monks; even if I wanted to I couldn't. The vices and scandal that arose among the monks are well known; I had opportunities for forming my own opinion in that matter, having been in part educated by them.

I respect what religion holds in respect; but as a statesman I dislike the fanaticism of celibacy; it was one of the means whereby the Court of Rome attempted to rivet the chains of Europe by preventing the cleric from being a citizen. Military fanaticism is the only sort that is of any use to me; a man must have it to get himself killed. My principal object in instituting a teaching body is to have some means of directing political and moral opinion.

14th. Holland is without an executive head; she should have one; I shall give her Prince Louis. Instead of a Grand Pensionary there will be a king.

20th. I think the teaching body should include about 10,000 persons. The essential thing is that the members of the University, for that is what we will call it, should hold the exclusive privilege of teaching, and that they should be under an oath.

We must succeed in making our young men neither too bigoted nor too sceptical; they should be in harmony with the conditions of the nation and of civilization.

My usual reading after going to bed is in the old Chronicles of the 3d, 4th, 5th, and 6th centuries; I either read them or have them translated to me. Nothing is more curious, and so little known, as the transition from the ancient states to the new ones that arose on their ruins. The Governments had little to do with education in Western Europe, especially under Christianity, because the clergy were intrusted with it. The Governments of the East, however, were much concerned with the matter, especially before the advent of Christianity.

If the kings of France have neglected education, is that a reason for following their example, in view of our ambition of doing better than they did? Emerging from the fog of ignorance hand in hand with the clergy, they found the rudiments of public instruction in existence, and were obliged to leave things to the Power at their side.

I want the members of the teaching body to take, not a religious vow as was the case formerly, but to enter into a civil contract before a notary or justice of the peace. They will embrace Public Instruction as their predecessors embraced the Church, with the difference that their engagement will be less sacred, and less binding; I wish, however, that some ceremonial may be put into the matter, even if it takes another name.

27th. I am willing that the head of the Bank should be called Governor if that pleases him, because titles cost nothing. I am also willing that his salary should be as high as you want it, because it is the Bank that will pay.

April 1st, Malmaison:
(To Marshal Berthier.) I inclose you the *Moniteur;* you will see what I am doing for you. I make only one condition, which is that you get married, and that is a condition that goes with my friendship. Your liaison has lasted too long; it has become ridiculous; and I am entitled to hope that he whom I have named my companion in arms, whom posterity will always place at my side, will not continue to show such an extraordinary example of weakness. I insist, therefore, that you should marry; otherwise I shall refuse to receive you. You are fifty years old, but you belong to a family that reaches eighty, and it is during these next thirty years that the comforts of marriage will be of most service to you.

You know that you have no warmer friend than I am, but you also know that the first condition of my friendship is that it should be based on my esteem. Until now you have deserved it. Continue to do so by concurring in my plans, and by becoming the stem of a good and great family.

14th, Saint Cloud:
(To Prince Eugène.) My son, you are working too hard; your life is too monotonous. It is all right for you, because work should be your pleasure; but you have a young wife, who will soon be a mother. I think you ought to arrange things so as to spend the evenings with her and so as to have a small social circle. Why don't

you go to the theatre once a week in the State box? You must have a little more gaiety about you; it is necessary for the happiness of your wife, and your own health. One can get through a lot of work in very little time. I lead the life you lead, but my wife is old and doesn't need me for her amusement; and yet it is quite true to say that I have more pleasures and dissipation than you. A young woman needs amusement, especially when in that condition.

18th, Paris:
The Opera costs the Government 800,000 francs a year; we must keep up an institution that flatters the national vanity.

May 31st, Saint Cloud:
(To the King of Naples.) You trust the Neapolitans too much, especially in the matter of your kitchen and your personal guards, which means that you are taking chances of being poisoned or assassinated. You have not known enough of my domestic arrangements to realize that, even in France, I have always been guarded by my most faithful and my oldest soldiers.

No one should enter your room at night except your aide-de-camp, who should sleep in the room next to your bedroom; your door should be locked on the inside, and you should not let your aide-de-camp in before having recognised his voice, and he should not knock at your door until after closing the door of his room, so as to be sure no one can follow him. These precautions are important; they are not troublesome, and they inspire confidence, quite apart from the fact that actually they may save your life. You should regulate your way of living this way once and for all. Don't be obliged to adopt it in an emergency, which would be humiliating both for you and for those about you. Trust my experience.

June 3d.
(To the King of Naples.) I have read your speech, and you must permit me to say that I find some of its sentences bad. You compare the attachment of the Neapolitans to you with that of the French to me; it sounds like an epigram! What affection do you expect from a people for whom you have done nothing, among whom you are by right of conquest, at the head of 40,000 or 50,000 foreigners? As a general rule the less you speak, directly or indirectly, of me and of France in your documents, the better.

5th. (To Joseph.) You will understand that if I have given the titles of Duke and Prince to Bernadotte, it was out of consideration for your wife; for I have generals in my army who have served me better, and in whom I place more reliance.

7th. (To Joseph.) I can send you no reinforcements. I can't coop up my whole army in Naples.

(To Talleyrand.) I have asked you for a report on the Prussian forces. I have no use for the information you have sent me. I need a complete statement as to the army of the King of Prussia.

July 4th. Up to the present the negotiations with England have made no headway. By acquiring the Cape of Good Hope England will forever insure her control of India. But if England held Malta and Sicily, she would erect an insurmountable barrier between the Adriatic and Constantinople. It would be difficult ever to accede to such a condition.

13th. (To the Princess Stéphanie of Baden.) I have received your letter. I see with pleasure that you are well. Love your husband, who deserves it for the affection he bears you.

Treat your people kindly, for sovereigns are made for the happiness of their people. Accustom yourself to the country, and think well of everything, for nothing would be more impertinent than constantly to speak of Paris and of the splendours which you know perfectly well you can't enjoy; it's a French fault, don't fall into it. Carlsruhe is an agreeable spot. You will be loved and well thought of in the same degree as you love and think well of the country in which you are placed: it is the most sensitive point men have.

19th. The English landed 5000 men in the bay of Saint Euphemia on the 3d of July. General Régnier marched on them; I don't know what resulted. It is probable that they had cause to repent.

21st. (To Joseph.) I have received your letters of the 11th and 12th of July; you then had no news of Régnier, and had made no movement from Naples. The art of war, which is so much talked about, is a difficult art; you have not one man among your ministers who has any knowledge of its elements. But, by Heaven! with 36,000 men, don't allow one of your divisions to be crushed! Since you have no news from Régnier, you may infer that communications are cut, and that an insurrection has broken out.

26th. (To Joseph.) The enemy would have to be quite mad to make any attempt against Naples. What! with 36,000 men you are placed on the defensive by 8000 English, and you give up two thirds of your kingdom to them! There are not two soldierlike ideas in your whole Council of Ministers. It would cause you useless pain if I were to tell you all I think.

26th. (To Joseph.) What is the meaning of this national guard of Naples? It is leaning on a reed, perhaps even placing a weapon in the enemy's hands. Oh! how little you know men! Come, take some vigorous decision. The whole art of war consists in a well thought out and prudent defensive, and in an offensive that is bold and rapid.

30th. (To Prince Joachim Murat.) Wesel can belong to none other than a great Power. As to the guarantee for your children, your arguments are pitiful and made me shrug my shoulders; I blush for you. I hope that you are a Frenchman; so will your children be; any other idea would be so dishonouring that I must ask you never to mention such a thing again. It would be a very extraordinary thing, if after all the benefits the French nation has showered on you, you thought of placing your children in such a way that they might injure France. Once more, never speak on that subject again, it's too ridiculous!

August 1st. (To the King of Holland.) Circumstances may make it necessary for you to form a camp of Dutch troops at Utrecht.

2d. (To Prince Joachim.) Your public utterances must be reassuring. I can hardly express the pain your letters cause me; your heedlessness is enough to drive me to despair.

Dupont's division is moving to the Inn; you must give it no orders of any sort. You don't know what I am doing. Keep quiet. With a Power like Prussia we cannot proceed too gently.

5th. The English are getting more accommodating. Lord Lauderdale and Lord Yarmouth are the negotiators. The first arrived this morning.

12th. The illness of Mr. Fox makes the negotiations with England drag.

17th, Rambouillet:
(To the King of Naples.) It would be a good thing if the Neapolitan rabble attempted a revolt. So long as you have not made an example you will not be their master. Every conquered nation should revolt at least once, and I would view an insurrection at Naples as the father of a family views measles in his children, providing the patient is not too much weakened. It marks a healthy crisis.

19th. (To Fouché.) If you know where General Dumoulin is, send for him and question him about a lady named Keilenfels, whom he married two months before abducting Mlle. d'Eckhardt. I have no power over the judges, and there must be an exemplary punishment for so detestable an offence. Does this general realize that the Criminal Court will condemn him to the galleys? How can he have been so unmindful of the laws of honour? The whole business is very humiliating for the French army.

23d. (To the King of Naples.) I have received your letter of the 13th. I regret that you anticipate never meeting your brother again, save in the Elysian Fields. It is a simple enough matter that I should not have the same sentiments for you at forty as I had at twelve!

29th, Saint Cloud:
The negotiations drag. The outcome is very doubtful.

31st. (To the Princess Augusta.) My Daughter: I have read your letter of the 10th of August with great pleasure. I thank you for all your compliments. Take great care of yourself in your present state, and try not to give us a daughter. I could give you the recipe, but you wouldn't believe me: it is to drink a little pure wine every day.

September 5th. The altered conditions in Europe make it necessary that I should seriously consider the situation of my armies.

(To Marshal Berthier.) Send engineer officers to reconnoitre carefully and in all directions the débouchés of the roads leading from Bamberg to Berlin.

8th. (To Lucchesini.) I always carry my heart in my head. I shall undertake a war against Prussia only for the honour of my country and the security of my allies. If your young officers and women at Berlin want war, they shall have it; I am preparing to satisfy them. But all my ambitions turn on Italy; there is a mistress whose favours I will divide with none.

10th. The attitude of Prussia is still provocative. They are dying to be taught a good lesson.

(To Caulaincourt.) Have all my field glasses overhauled. Send off sixty horses from my stables to-morrow, including eight of my saddlehorses. Do this as secretly as possible. To-morrow have my baggage carts got ready. One of them must carry a tent and an iron bed. The tent must be stout, and not a grand opera tent. You can add a few thick carpets. You will send off with the horses to-morrow my little campaigning chaise.

Marshal Bessières and Prince Borghese will also send their horses off. When you mention the matter to these officers, you will say that they are accompanying me to the Diet at Frankfort.

12th, Saint Cloud:
(To the King of Prussia.) *Monsieur mon Frère:* I have received your Majesty's letter. The friendly sentiments you express are all the more agreeable to me in that everything that has occurred these last two weeks gave me ground for supposing the contrary. If I am compelled to take up arms to defend myself, it will be with the greatest regret that I shall use them against Your Majesty's troops.

(To the King of Naples.) Prussia is arming in ridiculous fashion: she will, however, soon disarm, or pay dear for it. Nothing could be more foolish and more hesitating than the conduct of the (Prussian) cabinet. The Court of Vienna makes great protestations of friendship, which its extreme weakness makes me believe in. Whatever happens, I can and will face it out. The conscription which I have just levied is coming in on all sides; I shall call up the reserves; I am thoroughly supplied, and lack nothing. I may possibly take command of the Grand Army in a few days. It numbers about 150,000 men, enough to put down Vienna, Berlin, and St. Petersburg.

The negotiations with England still continue; whether it is peace or war will be decided within a week. Fox is altogether out of it, owing to an illness that will probably carry him down to the grave. If I really have to strike once more, Europe will know that I have left Paris only by hearing of the complete destruction of my enemies. It would be as well to have your newspapers speak of me as at Paris, occupied in amusements, in hunting, and in negotiating.

17th. I have just got the news of the death of Mr. Fox. In the present state of things, it is the death of a man who is regretted by two nations.

19th. The situation is becoming more critical daily. My Guard has started by stage, to travel from Paris to Mainz in six days.

24th. (To Joachim Murat, Grand Duke of Berg.) Send your horses to Bamberg rapidly. Wait for me at Mainz, which you can leave one hour after my arrival, so that you can reach Bamberg on the 1st of October at noon.

28th, Mainz:
I arrived this morning.

29th. There is no declaration of war yet.

Midnight:
(To Marshal Augereau.) Do not unmask your movement.

30th. (To the King of Würtemberg.) I should like to see Your Majesty. I shall be at Würzburg on the 2d of October, at Bamberg on the 5th. I should much like, under existing circumstances, to have an hour's conversation. I would have been glad to await Your Majesty's visit at Mainz, if I were not the most complete slave, compelled to obey a heartless master: the calculation of events and the nature of things.

As for myself, Your Majesty must see that no man is less able than I to make precise arrangements at this moment. Not that war is declared yet; I have not heard that M. Laforest has left Berlin; I am told that a Prussian officer has been sent to me by the King of Prussia with a letter; for three days past I have been hearing about him, but I have not yet seen him.

October 1st. I start to-night at nine.

3d, Würzburg:
I reached Würzburg yesterday.

5th. The armies are in touch. We shall soon have fighting. The King of Würtemberg came here two days ago. He can't make heads or tails of what is going on. The Duke of Brunswick has written him a very pernicious letter, to the tune of the German nationalistic excitement. All my columns are marching. I start to-night for Bamberg.

(To Marshal Soult.) I am debouching in Saxony with my whole army in three columns. You lead the right; half a day's march behind you is the corps of Marshal Ney, and one day's march behind you are 10,000 Bavarians; all of which totals more than 50,000 men. Marshal Bernadotte leads the centre; behind him Marshal Davout's corps is marching, with the greater part of the Reserve Cavalry and my Guard; which totals over 70,000 men. (Bernadotte) will debouch through Kronach. The 5th corps leads my left, and is followed by the corps of Marshal Augereau. They will come through Coburg and Saalfeld, and will make upwards of 40,000 men. The day you reach Hof, the rest of the army will be in line with you. I shall hold myself in general at the centre. With so great a preponderance in numbers, and so closely concentrated, you will realize that my purpose is not to jump at chances but to attack the enemy, wherever they choose to make a stand, with double their numbers.

My information to-day seems to show that if the enemy are manœuvring, it is against my left; their principal forces appear to be at Erfurt. I cannot urge you too strongly to communicate with me very frequently, and to inform me of all you can hear from the Dresden road. You can see what a splendid manœuvre it would be to move towards that city in a battalion square of 200,000 men. All this demands some skill, however, and some happenings.

10 P.M.:
I am leaving for Bamberg. All our corps are marching. I am in excellent health, and in great hopes of soon bringing this business to a good end.

6th. Soldiers! The orders were already issued for your return to France. Triumphal festivities awaited you. But just as we were lulled by a sense of false security, new plots were brewing under the mask of friendship and of alliance. Cries of war have been raised in Berlin. These two months past we are daily more loudly challenged.

The same faction, the same vertigo, that carried Prussia to the plains of Champagne fourteen years ago, dominate their councils. They want us to evacuate Germany at the sight of their arms. Fools! Let them learn that it would be a thousand times more easy to destroy the great capital than to smirch the honour of the children of the great nation and its allies! Then their schemes were dashed to pieces; in the plains of Champagne they found only death, defeat, and shame. But the lessons of experience fade away, and with some men hatred and jealousy never die.

Soldiers! Not one of you would wish to regain France by any other path than that of honour; we must return only under triumphal arches. Forward, then! Let the Prussian army meet with the same fate as it did fourteen years ago.

It is really quite amusing that the Prussians should have handed me their ultimatum on the 8th; and that I, without knowing this, should have entered Bayreuth and begun my movements on the 7th.

(To the King of Bavaria.) I have at last received the King of Prussia's letter. I cannot send you his actual text; it is a rhapsody copied from the English newspapers and twenty pages long. But I send you the note which M. de Knobelsdorf has this very moment handed me. My answer you will find in my proclamation to the army. It is therefore the King of Prussia who has declared war! I am truly thankful for his forethought in thus proving mine to be the right cause in the face of all Europe.

8th. The Queen of Prussia is with the army, dressed as an amazon, wearing the uniform of her dragoon regiment, writing twenty letters a day to feed the fire. Next to her is Prince Louis of Prussia, a young prince full of courage, who expects to win great glory from the incidents of war. Following the example of these two high personages all the Court clamours: War! war!

Kronach:
I have reached Kronach, which I shall leave to-night. The army is marching rapidly.

3.30 P. M.:
(To Marshal Soult.) Let me hear from you more frequently; in a combined manœuvre like this it is only by very frequent communication that we can achieve the best results. We are at the crisis of the campaign; they did not anticipate what we are attempting to do; woe betide them if they hesitate and if they lose a single day.

4 P. M.:
(To Marshal Lannes.) My Cousin: I am displeased at your having entered Coburg yesterday: your instructions were to occupy it this morning, and in force.

March as rapidly as you can on Grafenthal. Marshal Augereau will follow you at half a day's march. I myself shall reach Lobenstein at 2 A. M.

10th, Ebersdorf, 5 A. M.:
On the 9th the Prussian general Tauenzien, with 6000 Prussians and 3000 Saxons, was attacked by the advance guard of the army commanded by the Grand Duke of Berg, and was routed.

(To the Grand Duke of Berg.) General Rapp has brought me your good news of last night. Marshal Lannes will attack Saalfeld to-morrow.

Your chief task to-day is to make use of yesterday's success for picking up all the prisoners and information you can; then to reconnoitre Auma and Saalfeld, so as to learn the movements of the enemy positively.

(To Marshal Soult.) Here is what I can make out: that the Prussians intended to attack, and that their left was to debouch by Jena, Saalfeld, and Coburg. Whatever the enemy may do, I shall be delighted if they attack me; if they let me attack them, I shall not miss them; if they turn off towards Magdeburg, you will be at Dresden before them. I hope very much for a battle. After a battle I can get to Dresden or Berlin before them.

Schleiz, *5.30 P. M.:*
The sound of the guns can no longer be heard.

6 P. M.:
(To Marshal Soult.) My Cousin: I believe that Marshal Lannes attacked Saalfeld to-day. There has been a brisk cannonade, but it lasted only two hours; I don't know the result. As soon as I am secure on my left things will get lively.

12th, Auma, *4 A. M.:*
Order for Marshal Davout to march on Naumburg as rapidly as he can.

Marshal Lannes is marching on Jena.

(To Marshal Lannes.) I have received, with great pleasure, the news of your action on the 10th. I had heard the sound of the guns and moved a division in your direction, to support you. The death of Prince Louis of Prussia seems like a punishment of Heaven, for he is the real author of the war.

All the intercepted correspondence we get shows that the enemy have lost their heads. They are debating night and day, and don't know what decision to come to. You perceive that my army is massed, and that I am on their road to Dresden and Berlin. Our skill now will consist in attacking everything we meet, so as to beat the enemy in detail and while they are concentrating. When I say that we must attack all we meet, I mean that we must attack everything that is on the march and not in an advantageous position.

8.30 A. M.:
I am getting into the saddle *en route* for Gera. The Prussians have hardly a chance left. Their generals are perfect idiots. It is inconceivable how the Duke of Brunswick, who has a reputation, can direct the operations of his army in so ridiculous a fashion.

13th, Gera, *2 A. M.:*
(To the Empress.) I am to-day at Gera, my dear friend; my affairs go on prosperously, and as I had hoped. With the aid of God, things will assume a terrible complexion, within a few days, for the poor King of Prussia, whom I pity personally because he is a good man. The Queen is at Erfurt with the King. If she wants to see a battle, she can indulge that cruel whim. I am wonderfully well, fatter than when I started, and yet I get over twenty or twenty-five leagues each day, on horseback, in carriages, in every sort of a way. I go to bed at eight, I am up again at midnight; sometimes it occurs to me that you have not yet gone to bed!

Within three or four days we shall fight a battle which I shall win. It will take me to the Elbe, perhaps to the Vistula. There I will engage a second battle, which I shall also win. Then...then...but that's enough, and we must not romance. Clarke, in one month you will be governor of Berlin, and you will be quoted as having been in one year and in two different wars, governor of, Vienna and of Berlin.

(Bulletin.) Consternation reigns at Erfurt where the King, the Queen, and the Duke of Brunswick still are. But while they deliberate the French army is marching. Ever since the campaign opened the weather has been splendid, the country full of supplies, the soldiers healthy and strong. The men cover ten leagues in a day's march, without a straggler; the army has never been so fit.

9 A. M.:
(To Murat.) At last the veil is torn; the enemy have begun their retreat towards Magdeburg. March as rapidly as possible with Bernadotte's corps on Dornburg, a big village between Jena and Naumburg. Above all, get your dragoons and cavalry there.

All the heavy cavalry and General Klein's command are marching on Jena. I think that the enemy will either attempt to attack Lannes at Jena or else slip away. If they should attack Lannes, you can support him from Dornburg. I shall reach Jena at two in the afternoon.

10 A. M.:
We have caught the Prussian army in the act, and have turned its flank.

At night, bivouac near Jena:
(To Marshal Ney.) The enemy are between Weimar and Jena; push your corps on as far as you can get, so as to reach Jena early to-morrow.

14th, Jena:
Marshal Augereau commands the left.

At dawn Marshal Lannes will have his artillery in the intervals and in the order of battle in which he passed the night.

The Guard will be behind the plateau, in five lines.

The Emperor will give the signal; every one must be ready at dawn.

Marshal Ney will be placed at the edge of the plateau, so as to move on Marshal Lannes' right as soon as the village is carried, and we get enough space to deploy.

Marshal Soult will debouch on the right.

15th, *3 A. M.:* (To Josephine.) Dear friend: I have carried out some splendid manœuvres against the Prussians. I won a great victory yesterday. They numbered 150,000 men; I made 20,000 prisoners, captured 100 guns and some flags. I was faced by the King of Prussia; I nearly captured him and the Queen as well. I have bivouacked these last two days, and am in splendid health.

The Duke of Brunswick, General Ruchel are killed; Prince Henry of Prussia is severely wounded; many generals and officers of rank are wounded. The losses of the French army are comparatively slight. Marshal Davout, at Naumburg, prevented the enemy from passing. He fought there all day and routed over 60,000 men. His army corps covered itself with glory. The Queen of Prussia was pursued by a squadron of hussars; she had to seek refuge in Weimar, and left only three hours before our advance reached the place.

16th, Weimar, *7 A. M.:*
(To Marshal Davout.) My Cousin: I congratulate you with all my heart on your splendid conduct. I regret the brave men you have lost; but they are dead on the field of honour. Inform your corps and your generals of my satisfaction. They have forever acquired a claim on my esteem and my gratitude.

Erfurt has capitulated; there are 14,000 prisoners, among them the Prince of Orange and Field Marshal Moellendorf.

17th. The Emperor is quartered in the palace of Weimar, occupied but a few days previously by the Queen of Prussia. It appears that what was said of her is true: she was here to fan the flames of war. She is a pretty woman, but lacking sense, and incapable of foreseeing the consequences of what she is doing.

19th. The first object of the campaign is accomplished; Saxony, Westphalia, and all the country on the left bank of the Elbe, are freed from the presence of the Prussian army. That army, defeated and relentlessly pursued for more than fifty leagues, is now without guns, without transport, without generals, reduced to less than a third of what it was a week ago; and, which is even worse, it has lost its morale and self-confidence.

20th. The Grand Duke of Berg, with Marshals Soult and Ney, has invested Magdeburg.

(To Marshal Soult.) Don't let yourself be blinded by good fortune, and keep on your guard.

21st. (To Marshal Bernadotte.) The Emperor is extremely dissatisfied at your not carrying out the order you received yesterday to march on Kalbe. His Majesty reminds you in this connection that you took no part in the battle of Jena. The Emperor has made up his mind to let you know his views on the matter, because he is not accustomed to have his manœuvres spoiled by empty disputes of etiquette.

22d, Dessau:
I am across the Elbe; all is going well.

Immediately after the battle the King of Prussia sent me an aide-de-camp with a letter. To-day he has sent me Marquis Lucchesini. I had him stopped at the outposts, and sent Duroc to find out what be wanted. I am awaiting his return. The King seems to have made up his mind to make peace. I am willing; but that will not hinder my going to Berlin, which I expect to reach in four or five days.

23d, Wittenberg:
(To Marshal Davout.) Order your march so as to enter Berlin on the 25th at noon.

(To Marshal Bernadotte.) I have your letter. It is not my habit to recriminate over the past, since it cannot be altered. Your corps was not in the battle, and that might have proved disastrous.

25th, Potsdam:
(Bulletin.) The Emperor reached Potsdam yesterday, and took up his quarters in the Palace; in the evening he visited the new palace of Sans Souci, and all the positions around Potsdam. He remained some time in the room of the great Frederick, which is still furnished and hung as it was when he died.

26th. (To the army.) We have reached Potsdam and Berlin even before the renown of your victories. We have captured 60,000 prisoners, 65 flags, including those of the Prussian Royal Guard, 6000 cannon, 3 fortresses, more than 20 generals. And yet more than half of you can complain of having had no opportunity of firing a shot.

Soldiers! The Russians boast that they are marching against us, we will move to meet them, we will spare them half the journey!

The Emperor has visited the tomb of Frederick the Great. He has presented to the Invalides at Paris, Frederick's sword, his ribbon of the Black Eagle, his General's sash, and the standards carried by his Guard in the Seven Years' War.

29th, Berlin:
Prince Hohenlohe has surrendered with 16,000 infantry, 4000 cavalry, 45 colours, 84 guns; Prince Augustus of Prussia, the Prince of Schwerin are prisoners, with other Prussian generals and the Royal Guard.

30th. Up to the present we have 150 flags, among them those embroidered by the hands of the lovely Queen, a beauty as fatal to the Prussians as Helen was to the Trojans.

31st. (To the Grand Duke of Berg.) My Brother: I congratulate you on the capture of Stettin; if your light horse can capture fortresses in this fashion, I shall have to disband my engineers and melt down my siege guns. But you have done nothing yet. You still have General Blücher and the Duke of Weimar to capture; they have over 25,000 men.

November 1st. (To Lannes.) Do you suppose that I don't know that your corps has made forced marches, and that you have commanded it with the greatest skill? You are big babies, all of you. At the right time and place I will give you and your corps the proofs of my satisfaction with your conduct.

2d. Küstrin surrendered yesterday. We captured 80 guns and 4000 prisoners.

3d. (To Fouché.) Send for Koseziusko; tell him to start posthaste to join me, but secretly and under an assumed name. Give him what money he needs. Send me all the Poles you can.

Our outposts have reached the Polish border. I therefore need troops; but unless reinforcements reach me quickly they will be too late. The Russians are still far away, but an encounter is possible.

6th, *9 P. M.:* (To the Empress.) I have received the letter in which you appear vexed about what I say of women. It is true that I hate intriguing women above all things. I am accustomed to kind, soft, amiable women; they are those I am fond of. If they have spoiled me it is not my fault but yours. But you will see that I have been kind to one who has shown herself good and kind-hearted, Mme. de Hatzfeld. When I showed her her husband's letter, she sobbed and, with the greatest emotion and naïveté, said: "Yes, that is his writing." To hear her reading it was pitiful. It was most painful, and I said to her: "Well, Madam, throw the letter in the fire; then it will no longer be in my power to harm your husband." She burned the letter and seemed very happy. Her husband has not been troubled since; two hours later it would have been all up with him. So you see that I do like women who are good, kind, and naïve; but then they are the only ones who are like you.

9th. (To the Empress.) Good news! Magdeburg has surrendered; and at Lübeck, on the 7th, 20,000 men, who for a week had escaped, were taken prisoners. So the whole army is captured; Prussia has not 20,000 men left beyond the Vistula.

Lübeck was stormed by the Grand Duke of Berg, the Prince of Ponte Corvo, and Marshal Soult. The slaughter was awful. On the following day what was left of Blücher's corps, 18,000 men, surrendered.

11th. (To Sultan Selim.) Most High, Most Excellent, Most Powerful, Most Magnanimous and Invincible Prince, great Emperor of the Mussulmans, Sultan Selim, my very dear and perfect friend, may God increase your glory and power!

On the very day when our enemies summoned you to give up Moldavia and Wallachia, on the plea of my disasters, I was gaining a memorable victory at Jena, and marching to further triumphs. The troops of Prussia are either destroyed or captured. The whole country is mine. With 300,000 men I am pursuing my successes and I will not make peace until you are once more in possession of the Principalities. Take courage. Fate has declared that your Empire is to stand; it is my mission to save it; and I divide with you the fruits of my victories. The moment has come when the Sublime Porte must recover its energy and send forth its armies. I know that the Russians are withdrawing their forces; they are marching on me; I will seek them out forthwith.

Given in our Imperial Palace of Berlin, this 11th day of November, 1806.

21st. The British Isles are declared in a state of blockade. All commerce and correspondence with the British isles are hereby forbidden.

(To Champagny.) I have read some extremely bad stanzas that are being sung at the Opera. Is there a deliberate intention, then, in France, to degrade literature? Convey my displeasure to M. de Lucay, and forbid anything being sung at the Opera that is unworthy of that great theatre. An obvious thing to have done was to have ordered a fine cantata to celebrate the 2d of December. As literature belongs to your department, I think you had better look after it, for really what they are singing at the Opera only degrades it.

23d. The Emperor spent the day in reviewing the infantry of the 4th Corps. He made promotions and distributed rewards in all the regiments.

I assembled the officers and men; I asked them who had done well; and I promoted those who could read and write.

25th, Küstrin:
I hope to get news from the outposts to-day.

27th, Miseritz, *2 A. M.*:
(To Josephine.) I am entering Poland; this is its first city; to-night I shall be at Posen. After that I will send to have you come to Berlin, so that you may reach there the very day I return. My health is good; the weather is rather bad, we have had rain for three days.

Yesterday the Grand Duke of Berg was following hard on the Russians, and was one day's march from Warsaw.

29th, Posen:
The Poles are exceedingly well disposed. They are forming corps of horse and foot with great activity. They show eagerness to recover their independence: the nobility, clergy and peasants are all of the same mind.

December 1st. To-morrow I go to a ball given me by the nobility. All the ladies have been presented to me; it is the first time since the destruction of Poland that they have attended an official function. All the educated people speak French, and the peasants love France.

The Grand Duke of Berg holds Warsaw with 100,000 men.

2d. (To the Grand. Duke of Berg.) The Poles who show so much prudence, who ask for so many conditions before declaring themselves, are egotists who cannot be kindled to enthusiasm for love of their country. I am old in my knowledge of men. My greatness does not depend on the help of a few thousand Poles. It is for them to take advantage of the present circumstances with enthusiasm; it is not for me to take the first step.

I know Poniatowski better than you do, because I have followed Polish affairs these last ten years. He is even more flighty than the average Pole, which is saying a good deal. He is not much trusted at Warsaw. All the same he is a man with whom to keep on good terms. As for what he has said about making Czartorivski king, that is merely to give himself importance. Russia, let me assure you, has never dreamed of giving up Poland.

For the rest I approve your measures. Put patriots in office, men who are willing to act, and do not dwell on the mathematical calculation of the reëstablishment of Poland. Have it clearly understood that I have not come to beg for a throne for one of my own people; I have plenty of thrones to distribute among my family.

(Decree.) Every year on the anniversaries of the battle of Austerlitz and of Jena there shall be held a concert, preceded by a speech on the qualities necessary to a soldier, and by a eulogy of those who died. A competition shall be held to determine the best ode and the best and most fitting composition. In the speeches and in the ode it is expressly forbidden to mention the Emperor.

(To Josephine.) This is the anniversary of Austerlitz. I have been to a ball; it is raining; I am well. I love you and want you. The weather has not yet turned cold. All these Polish women are French. There is only one woman in the world for me; do you know her by any chance? I could draw her portrait; but I should have to flatter too much before you would recognise her; however, truth be told, my heart could only find nice things to say to you. These solitary nights are very long.

5th. (To the King of Naples.) Send me all the Polish officers you have. Poland is in full insurrection. Troops are being raised on all sides.

9th. (To the Grand Duke of Berg.) Have proclamations printed urging the soldiers of Prussian and Russian Poland to desert and to range themselves under their own national flag, and have them distributed everywhere by our outposts.

10th. Boots! Boots! Give your most prompt attention to the matter.

(To Josephine.) I am pretty well. The weather is very changeable. I love you, and want you badly. Good-bye, dear friend; I shall write to you tocome with at least as much pleasure as you will come.

12th. (To Champagny.) Literature needs encouragement. You are its official head. Propose some means of shaking up the various branches of literature that have so long distinguished our country.

7 P. M.: Paër, the famous musician, is here with his wife and Brizzi; they perform a little music for me every evening.

14th. (To the Grand Duke of Berg.) With such a large force of cavalry you should be able to cut the road from Pultusk to Koenigsberg, and inflict some damage on the enemy's rearguard. Your cavalry should crush them, and throw them into utter confusion, and give them the idea that you have 100,000 mounted men, which is what you had better say openly. Always speak of the cavalry as 100,000 men, and of the infantry as 500,000. If the enemy retire, my infantry will be useless; we can only get at them with cavalry,and that is your business.

15th. (To Cambacérès.) My Cousin: I have received your letter of the 4th of December. I have also the pamphlet on Poland, which appears to be fairly good. See if M. d'Hauterive couldn't write a little book under the title: *The three partitions of Poland?* You need not give away 700 copies; that is unnecessary; better sell them.

(To Louis, King of Holland.) Send me all English reports that are circulating in your trading centres. The blockade will ruin many commercial cities, Lyons, Amsterdam, Rotterdam; but we must get past this stage of uncertainty; we must be done with the thing. Keep your warships fully equipped, as that keeps the English at work. All my efforts are on land; it is with my armies that I expect to reconquer the Cape and Surinam. Come, show energy! Energy! It is only by defying the opinions of the weak and the ignorant that one can achieve the happiness of a nation.

19th, Warsaw:
I arrived at Warsaw at midnight.

23d, near Okunin:
Order for Marshal Lannes' light cavalry to cross the bridge over the Narew tonight.

29th, Golymin:
(To Josephine.) Only one line, dear friend; I am in a wretched barn. I have defeated the Russians; I have captured their baggage, 30 guns, and 6000 prisoners. But the weather is awful; it is raining and the mud is up to our knees. In a couple of days I shall be (back) at Warsaw and will write.

(To Cambacérès.) You will see from the bulletins the brilliant successes we have obtained over the Russian army. Had it not been for inclement weather they would have been even greater. I think the campaign is over. The enemy have retired behind swamps and deserts. I am going into winter quarters.

31st, Pultusk:

(To Josephine.) I laughed heartily over your last letter. You exaggerate the attractions of the beauties of Poland.

(To Fouché.) Raynouard might easily produce good work if only he could get well into the spirit of the tragedy of the Ancients: Fate pursued the family of the Atridæ, and the heroes were guilty yet not criminal; they shared the crimes of the gods. In Modern narrative this idea could not be employed., but only the force of circumstances in its stead; a policy may lead to a catastrophe without any real crime being committed.

If Chénier indulges in the least sally I shall order him sent to the island of Sainte Marguerite. The time for joking has passed. Let him behave; that's the only privilege he's got.

1807

January 2d, Warsaw:
(To the Countess Walewska.) I saw only you, I admired only you, I desire only you. A quick answer will calm the impatient ardour of N.

3d. (To Josephine.) I have received your letter, dear friend. Your disappointment touches me, but one must submit to circumstances. It is a very great distance from Mainz to Warsaw; so that events must allow of my returning to Berlin before I write to you to come there. I am inclined to think you had better go back to Paris, where your presence is necessary. I am well; the weather is wretched.

4th. (To Countess Walewska.) Was I mistaken? You have deprived me of sleep! Oh, grant a little joy, a little happiness, to a poor heart that is ready to adore you. Is it so difficult to obtain an answer? You owe me two. N.

6th. (To the Princess Augusta.) I have received your letter. For your sake I have given orders that the House of Strelitz is to be treated considerately. Your grand-mother will not be disturbed, and yet your aunt, the Queen of Prussia, has behaved so badly! But she is so unfortunate to-day, that I mustn't speak of her any more. Write to me soon that we have got a big boy, and if you should give us a daughter, let us hope she will be as lovable and as good as you are. Your affec-tionate father.

12th. (To the Countess Walewska.) Oh come! come!

All your wishes shall be complied with. Your country will become more dear to me if you take compassion on my poor heart. N.

14th. Until the affairs of Poland are definitely regulated by a treaty of peace, the administration shall be entrusted to a Provisional Government.

15th. (To the Countess Walewska.) Marie, my sweet Marie, my first thought is for you, my first wish is to see you again. You will come again, will you not? You have promised that you would. If not, the eagle would wing its way to you!

23d. (To Josephine.) It is out of the question that I should allow women to undertake such a journey: bad roads, unsafe, and quagmires. Go back to Paris; be gay and happy; perhaps I shall soon be back myself. I laughed over your saying that you had taken a husband to live with him; in my ignorance I supposed that the wife was made for the husband, the husband for his country, his family, and fame; excuse my ignorance, one is always learning at the hands of our pretty women.

Good-bye, dear friend; pray believe that I regret not being able to send for you; say to yourself: Here is a proof of how precious I am to him.

27th. (To Baron La Bouillerie.) I wish you to buy 6 per cents when they fall below 78, and that no one should know it is you buying.

The enemy seem to be manœuvring with a view to holding Elbing. Such being the case, I am raising my camps to make a countermarch. It appears that General Bennigsen commands the army now.

28th. (To the King of Naples.) *Monsieur mon Frère:* It was not without keen emotion that I received the letter of Your Majesty and your good wishes for my happiness. Your destiny, my successes, have placed vast countries between us: you in the south touch the Mediterranean; I touch the Baltic; but by the combination of our efforts we tend towards the same result. Your kingdom is rich and popu-lated; by the grace of God it will become powerful and happy. Accept my most sincere wishes for the prosperity of your reign, and always rely on my fraternal affection.

30th. I am starting, in the saddle, at 5 A. M.

Orders for headquarters to move immediately, to reach Makow to-night.

Przasnysz:
As the enemy are pushing the Prince of Ponte Corvo's corps, we must keep close to the wind so that they can't get away again. We shall have news to-night.

31st, Willenberg:
The whole army is marching.

February 1st. (To the Empress.) Your letter of the 20th of January has pained me; it is altogether too depressed. The mischief is that you've got no religion! You say that happiness makes your joy: that is not generous; you should say the happiness of others makes my joy: that is not conjugal; you should say, the happiness of my husband makes my joy: that is not maternal; you should say the happiness of my children makes my joy; and since the nations, your husband, your children cannot be happy without a little glory, you must not say fie to it. Josephine, your heart is excellent, but your mind is weak; your instinct is sure, but your reasoning not altogether so.

Come, no more quarrelling; I want you gay and contented with your lot, and obeying not with tears and scolding, but with a joyous heart, and not unhappily. Good-bye, dear friend, I am off to my outposts to-night.

I am manœvring against the enemy; unless they retreat promptly I may possibly cut them off.

2d. I have just finished reading Lacretelle's *History of the Directoire.*

3d, Passenheim:
Up to the present we keep pushing the enemy back. One can see that our movement has alarmed them; and that they are trying to meet it. The country reports from all sides are to the effect that they are in full retreat.

5th, Schlitt:
I am pursuing the Russian army. I have driven it from every position. I shall throw it back beyond the Niemen.

7th, Eylau:
Parts of the two armies passed the night of the 6th to the 7th in each other's presence. The enemy retreated during the night.

At dawn the French advance guard started and got into contact with the enemy's rearguard between the wood and the little town of Eylau. Several regiments of the enemy's light infantry that held it were attacked and in part captured. We soon reached Eylau and found the enemy in position.

9th. We had a great battle yesterday; victory is mine, but my losses are very heavy; the enemy's losses, which were heavier, do not console me. The great distance at which I find myself makes my losses even more acutely felt.

(Bulletin.) A mile or two from the little town ofPreussich-Eylau is a plateau that commands the débouché from the plain. Marshal Soult ordered the 46th and 18th of the line to carry it. The troops penetrated the town of Eylau. The enemy had placed several regiments in the church and cemetery. They made a desperate resistance at this point, and, after a struggle most destructive for both sides, at ten o'clock at night we remained masters of the position. We passed the night where we were.

At daybreak the enemy opened their attack with a brisk cannonade of the town of Eylau and of St. Hilaire's division. The Emperor took up his station at the church which the enemy had so long defended the day before. He ordered up Augereau's corps, and cannonaded the hill (opposite) with forty guns of the Imperial Guard.

Just as the corps of Marshal Augereau and St. Hilaire's division were going into action, snow so dense that one could not see at two paces blotted out the two armies. In the darkness our columns lost their direction, inclining too much to the left, and became unsteady. This distressing darkness lasted half an hour. Then, the sky having cleared, the Grand Duke of Berg at the head of the cavalry, supported by Marshal Bessières, commanding the (cavalry of the) Guard, passed in front of St. Hilaire's division, and charged the enemy's army; this manœuvre, as daring in its execution as was ever seen and that covered our cavalry with glory, had become necessary because of the state of our (infantry) columns. Meanwhile Marshal Davout's corps was debouching on the enemy's flank. The snow, which fell at intervals through the day, had also retarded his advance and the formation of his attack.

The victory, long uncertain, was won when Marshal Davout gained the plateau and outflanked the enemy, who, after desperate efforts to regain their ground, fell back in retreat.

The army will return to its cantonments and take up winter quarters again.

14th. The country is covered with dead and wounded.

18th, Landsberg:
The army is going into quarters. I am anxious it should have a month or six weeks' rest.

The battle of Eylau was at first claimed as a victory by several of the enemy's generals. At Koenigsberg this was believed during the whole of the morning of the 9th.

March 1st, Osterode:
(To the King of Naples.) The staff, colonels, officers, have not undressed in two months, some not in four; I myself have gone two weeks without getting out of my boots; we are in the midst of snow and mud, without wine, without brandy, without bread, eating potatoes and meat, making long marches and countermarches, without any kind of luxury, and fighting with bayonets and grapeshot; the wounded often compelled to go fifty leagues in open sleighs. Therefore it is a pretty poor joke to compare us with the army of Naples, making war in a lovely country, where one can get wine, oil, bread, cloth, sheets, social life, and even women. After having destroyed the Prussian monarchy, we are fighting against what is left of the Prussians, against the Russians, the Kalmucks, the Cossacks, the northern tribes that long ago invaded the Roman Empire. We are making war in the strictest sense of that term. In the midst of these great fatigues we have all been more or less sick. As for myself I have never been stronger, and have become fatter.

5th. I am displeased with the absurd notes inserted in the *Moniteur*. Berthier wrote from the battlefield, in a state of fatigue, and with no idea that his message would get into print.

11th. (To General Clarke.) Colonel Aubert's report makes me laugh. We may conclude that that officer, finding himself in a fire that was too hot for him, lost his head; that is the thing to say to M. de Bray. The battle was won by four o'clock in the afternoon, when Marshal Davout was fully engaged. I was rather exposed to artillery fire, but it was necessary. It is possible that to a person who did not realize what was happening the battle appeared doubtful; but I, knowing that my columns were arriving, could be anxious only about the half hour's snow we got. As for 15,000 French having been routed, that is a horrible calumny; a few laggards and wagons took to flight because the cry was raised that the Cossacks were on them; it resulted in the stampede of 800 or 900 led horses. The colonel has magnified this into the flight of 15,000 men. Had he been at Marengo, at Rivoli, and at twenty other battles I have fought, he would understand that to go under fire and to encourage the troops in person is not of necessity to consider that a battle is lost. In any case, it's all a pack of lies; this officer was presumably not there, for I was not on foot for one moment of the battle.

12th. (To Talleyrand.) I have 300,000 rations of biscuit at Warsaw; it takes eight days to get from Warsaw to Osterode; perform miracles and be sure to send us 50,000 rations a day. To defeat the Russians is child's play, provided I can get bread. The importance of the duty I set you is greater than all the negotiations in the world.

13th. The weather is cold again. There is nothing new,—small outpost affairs of no importance. We are resting, a little. I am making use of this to secure supplies, to blockade Dantzig, and to make ready for its siege.

14th. An alliance with Russia would be very valuable. Only women and children are capable of supposing that (I) would go and lose myself in the deserts of Russia.

15th. The Munich Gazette states that the Russians won the battle of Eylau.

20th. (To Daru.) I have received your letter of the 18th of March. I do not share your views in any particular. Order all the employés to rejoin. I have been making war for a good long time. Carry out my orders without discussion. Your arguments are bad; I have been telling you so for three months; you persist in your opinion. You say that we can withdraw one or two employés from Erfurt; my purpose is to withdraw every one. Repeat your orders. If I accepted all your arguments I would not have 6000 men with the army; and if I accepted the arguments of every governor of a fortress my whole army would not suffice to hold the country. The question for you is not, therefore, is such and such an employé useful in such a place? but rather: is he more useful there than at headquarters? This is a commonplace for any one who has any experience of warfare. In any case, even if every one disagrees with my views, it is my will.

26th. I have written to the Minister of Police to send Mme. de Staël back to Geneva, while leaving her at liberty to go abroad if she should prefer it. This woman continues her intrigues. She came back near Paris against my orders. She is a perfect pest.

27th. (To the Empress.) Dear friend; Your letter has caused me pain. There is no occasion for you to die; you are well, and have no reasonable cause for worry. You must give up all idea of a journey this summer; it is not possible. I am as anxious to see you as you are to see me, and even to lead a quiet life. I know how to do other things than wage war, but duty must come first. All my life I have sacrificed everything, my repose, my interests, my happiness, to my destiny.

(To Prince Eugène.) I congratulate you on the happy delivery of the Princess. Is Augusta disappointed at not getting a boy? Tell her that when one begins with a daughter one always has at least twelve children. Have your daughter called Josephine.

29th. (To General Savary.) Proceed to Dantzig. Your mission has (two) objects: the first is to post me as to the real state of things, after you have made careful inquiries; the second, to encourage poor Marshal Lefebvre, who is getting worried and excited beyond reason, and showing very little for it in results.

31st. (To Cambacérès.) Junot is always writing to me on heavy mourning paper, which produces the most sinister effect on me when I read his letters. Tell him that it is contrary to etiquette, and that one never writes to a superior displaying the tokens of a personal grief.

April 2d, Finkenstein:
I have placed my headquarters here, in a country where forage is plentiful, and where my cavalry can be maintained. I am in a splendid castle with chimneys in all the rooms, which is a very pleasant thing.

4th. I am off to-night at a gallop for Warsaw, which I shall reach tomorrow. I shall stay two days to give audiences to the Persian and Turkish ambassadors, and to make some administrative arrangements.

(To the King of Holland.) A prince who in the first year of his reign gets so great a reputation for benevolence is a prince who in the second year is despised. The affection inspired by kings must be a virile one, a blend of respectful fear and of high esteem. When it is said of a king that he is a good man, the reign is a failure.

Your quarrels with the Queen are known to the public. Show in your private life the paternal and soft character that you display in your administration, and in your administration the rigour you display in your family life. You treat your young wife as though she were a regiment. Let her dance as much as she likes, she is just of the age. I have a wife of forty, and from the battlefield I write to her to go and dance, but you expect a young woman of twenty to live in a cloister, to be like a nurse, always washing the baby! You put too much of yourself in your private, and not enough in your public, life. It is only the interest I feel in you makes me tell you all this. You ought to have been given a wife like some of those I have known in Paris. She would have fooled you when your back was turned, and kept you at her knees. It is not my fault, for I have told her so.

As for the rest, you may do foolish things in your own kingdom; that is all right: but I have no intention that you should do the same in mine. You offer your Orders to everybody; many individuals who have not the least claim have written to me about them. I am annoyed that you do not perceive how this transgresses what is due from you to me. My intention is that none of my subjects shall wear your Orders, as I myself am resolved not to wear them. If you ask for my reasons, my answer must be that you have as yet accomplished nothing to deserve that men should wear your portrait on their breasts.

6th. (To Cambacérès.) I have received your letter of the 27th of March, and regret to see that your health is not good. If you would stop drugging yourself you would be a great deal better; but it's the inveterate habit of the inveterate bachelor!

12th. (To M. Talleyrand, Prince of Benevento.) General Gardanne wishes to proceed to Persia. Maret will draw up his credentials and instructions. They turn on (the following) points:
Investigate the resources of Persia from the military point of view, studying particularly the obstacles that would have to be overcome by a French army of 40,000 men marching to India with the help of the Persian and Turkish governments. Deal with Persia in regard to England by urging her to prevent the passage of English dispatches and messages, and to hamper the trade of the East India Company in every way possible.

13th. The trenches have been opened against Dantzig. I hope to have the city in a month, if our gunpowder holds out.

14th. (To Joseph.) Since you ask for my views on Neapolitan affairs, I must tell you that I do not like the preamble (to the decree) for the suppression of the monasteries. In matters that touch religion, the wording should be in terms of religion and not of philosophy. That is the great art of the ruler, one which the man of letters does not possess. The secret of it lies in giving to each edict the style and the character of the special craftsman it involves. Now a learned monk, who should be in favour of the suppression of the monasteries, would not have expressed himself in that manner. Men will accept misfortune if insult be not added.

19th. (Notes.) There have been historiographers of France, but it is true to say that they have accomplished nothing. And yet an institution of this sort might serve a purpose; but it would be best to avoid the word historiographer. It is accepted that the historian is a judge who is to be the organ of posterity, and so many qualities, so many perfections, are expected of him that it is difficult to believe that a good history can be made to order. What can be obtained to order from men of well-regulated talent are historical monographs, the results of laborious research, setting out authentic documents, with critical observations that tend to clear up our view of events. If these researches and these documents are framed in a good narrative, a piece of work of this sort will bear some sort of resemblance to history, and yet its author would not be a historian in the sense in which we use the word.

(To Fouché.) Among the thousand and one products of Mme. de Staël's pen that fall into my hands, you may judge from the inclosed letter how excellent a French patriot she is. One day an aristocratic toady and the next a nationalizing democrat, in truth one can hardly restrain one's indignation in seeing all the shapes that this...takes. I shall not tell you the plans this ridiculous clique have made in the happy event of my death, as a Minister of Police may be supposed to know all about that.

24th. (To Prince Jerome.) Make war seriously. You must be up at one in the morning. Your troops must be under arms at two, and you must be on the spot to receive reports from the reconnaissances sent out in all directions. You must not turn in again until eight, when you are sure there is nothing new. I am watching your operations; success does not alter the case, and I cannot as yet see that you are waging war.

Our batteries opened on Dantzig this morning; they are within 80 yards of the walls.

The Emperor of Russia has joined his army.

26th. I covered over thirty leagues on horseback to-day.

May 4th. (To Joseph.) Prince Jerome is doing well; I am very pleased with him, and unless I am mistaken there is the stuff of a first-rate man in him. However, you may rest assured that he does not suspect it, as I drop on him in all my letters.

I am fairly satisfied with Louis; but he is too much given to benevolence, and this goes badly with the dignity of the crown. He takes very little heed of the advice that I give him, but I continue offering it to him, and in time experience will show him that he has made many mistakes. I am very well. We are at last getting signs of summer.

10th. (To Josephine.) I have your letter. I don't know what you mean by ladies who correspond with me. I love only my little Josephine, good, sulky, capricious, who can quarrel gracefully, as she does everything else, for she is always fascinating except when she is jealous, and then she becomes a little devil.

21st. There should be at Toulon better frigates than the *Muiron*. I want that ship, which brought me back from Egypt, to be kept as a monument, and placed so that it may be preserved, if possible, for several centuries. I would feel a superstitious foreboding if any misfortune happened to the frigate.

26th. Dantzig has fallen: our troops entered the city this morning.

June 5th. Marshal Ney sends me word that he was attacked this morning at six. Is it a real attack? I shall know in a few hours. I have ordered my cavalry to concentrate. We shall soon be on the move.

It would suit me if the enemy are sparing me the trouble of seeking them out. I had intended to open operations on the 10th.

6th. The armies are manœuvring. It looks as though the enemy did not know what they are about, since after having allowed us to capture Dantzig they are now jamming themselves up against our fortified positions.

8 P.M.:
What will the enemy do? Will they continue marching on Allenstein, while we still occupy Liebstadt? All this may result in some curious events. I shall reach Saalfeld in an hour.

7th, Saalfeld:
I am still guessing as to what the enemy really intended. To-day I am bringing together at Mohrungen my infantry and cavalry reserves; I shall try to get at the enemy and fight a general action to finish the business.

(To Bernadotte.) You will find Talleyrand at Dantzig. You had better reassure him, as he is fairly frightened.

8th, Alt Reichau:
I made a feint against the enemy this morning at eight. They showed about 20 guns, 10,000 infantry, and 7000 or 8000 cavalry.

13th, Eylau:
(To the Grand Duke of Berg.) If the enemy should show up at Domnau to-day you might still push Marshal Soult out towards Koenigsberg, placing Marshal Davout between Domnau and Koenigsberg, to oppose the march of the enemy's army.

The enemy's movements are quite undecided.

3 P. M.:
(To Marshal Lannes.) I want your whole corps in position at Domnau, with outposts towards Friedland.

9 P. M.:
(To Lannes.) My staff officer has just come in. He does not give me sufficient information to judge if it is the enemy's army that is debouching at Friedland, or only a detachment. Marshal Mortier is moving his cavalry to support yours, and is starting with his corps. Subject to the information I may receive, I shall send Marshal Nek to your support at one in the morning.

14th, bivouac near Posthenen:
At three we heard the cannon. The enemy was debouching by the bridge at Friedland.

(Orders.) Marshal Ney will command on the right, supporting the position of General Oudinot. Marshal Lannes will be in the centre, from Heinrichsdorf to about opposite Posthenen. The grenadiers of Oudinot will bear a little to the left, to draw the enemy in that direction. Marshal Lannes will deploy on as great a depth as he can, and may therefore form two lines. Marshal Mortier will be on the left. General Victor and the Imperial Guard will be in reserve and will form behind Posthenen. I will be with the reserve. The advance must always be right wing forward, and it must be left to Marshal Ney to begin the movement; he will wait for my orders before advancing.

As soon as the right goes forward, the artillery must redouble its fire along the whole line in the proper direction for protecting this wing.

Have you a good memory?

(Marbot: Pretty fair, sire.)

Well, what anniversary is this to-day, the 14th of June?

(That of Marengo.)

Yes, yes, that of Marengo; and I am going to drub the Russians, just as I drubbed the Austrians!

15th, Friedland:
(To the Empress.) I write only a line, as I am very tired; I have been bivouacking a good many days on end. My children have worthily celebrated the anniversary

of Marengo; the battle of Friedland will be equally famous and glorious for my people. The whole Russian army is routed; 80 guns, 30,000 men captured or killed; 25 Russian generals killed, wounded, or prisoners; the Russian Guard smashed;—it is a worthy sister of Marengo, Austerlitz, Jena. The bulletin will tell you the rest. My losses are not heavy; I outmanœuvred the enemy. Good-bye, dear friend, I am just getting into the saddle.

18th, Skaisgirren:
My headquarters are here. I intend to march on Tilsit, and to engage the enemy should they have the impudence to stand their ground.

19th, Tilsit:
My health is good; the army is superb.

A curious incident which made the soldiers laugh, occurred for the first time near Tilsit; we met a horde of Kalmucks, who fought with bows and arrows.

20th. I control the Niemen. I shall probably conclude an armistice this evening.

22d. An armistice has been signed.

(To the Grand Army.) Soldiers! On the 5th of June the Russian army attacked us in our cantonments. The enemy had mistaken the reason for our inactivity. They discovered too late that our slumber was that of the lion.

In the actions of Guttstadt, of Heilsberg, and in the ever-memorable one of Friedland, in a ten days' campaign, we have captured 120 guns, 7 flags, killed, wounded, or captured 60,000 Russians, taken the enemy's magazines, ambulances, and hospitals, the fortress of Koenigsberg, 300 ships that were in its port laden with military supplies, 160,000 muskets that England had sent to arm our enemies.

From the banks of the Vistula we have darted to those of the Niemen with the swiftness of the eagle. At Austerlitz you celebrated the anniversary of the coronation; this year you have worthily commemorated the battle of Marengo which brought the war of the Second Coalition to an end.

Frenchmen, you have been worthy of yourselves and of me. You will return to France covered with laurels, and after having secured a glorious peace containing guarantees for its permanence. The end must come, and our country must be able to live quietly, freed from the malign influence of England. The rewards I will grant will prove all my gratitude and my affection for you.

24th. The Emperor of Russia is within a league, and, I am told, desires an interview. I do not much care about it, and yet I shall not refuse. Things are quite different now.

Duroc went off at three in the afternoon to present my compliments to the Emperor Alexander.

25th. I have just seen the Emperor Alexander in the midst of the Niemen on a raft on which was erected a splendid pavilion. I am very pleased with him; he is a handsome and excellent young Emperor, and has more intelligence than is generally supposed. He is coming to stay in the town of Tilsit.

30th. The Emperor of Russia and the King of Prussia are both staying here, and dine with me every day.

July 3d. (To Fouché.) See to it that no more abuse of Russia takes place, directly or indirectly. Everything points to our policy being brought into line with that of this Power on a permanent basis.

5th. The Queen of Prussia had decided ability, a good education and fine manners; it was she, really, had reigned for more than fifteen years; and, in spite of all my efforts and skill, she retained command of our conversation, and always got back to her subject, perhaps even too much so, and yet with perfect propriety and in a manner that aroused no antagonism. In truth, the matter was an important one for her, and time was short and precious.

I proceeded to call on her, but she received me on the tragic note, like Chimène:—Sire, Justice! Justice! Magdeburg!—She continued after this fashion, which embarrassed me very much; at last, to shift the ground, I asked her to sit down,—there is nothing that cuts into a tragic scene better, for when people are seated, it becomes a comedy. She had on a superb collar of pearls; so I complimented her on them:—Ah! what lovely pearls!—

6th. The beautiful Queen of Prussia dines with me to-night.

(To the Emperor of Russia.) I am sending a summary to your Majesty of the difficulties our negotiators have met with, and a *mezzotermine* that disposes of them. I hope Your Majesty will approve, for I should be glad to hear that the treaty of peace can be signed this very day.

7th. (To Josephine.) The Queen of Prussia dined with me yesterday. I had to defend myself from making some concessions she wanted to obtain for her husband. I was merely gallant, and stuck to my policy. She is very agreeable.

She was tormenting me for Magdeburg; she wanted to obtain a promise from me. I kept refusing politely. There was a rose on the chimney; I took it, and offered it to her. She drew her hand back, saying:—If it is with Magdeburg!—I answered at once:—But, Madam, it is I am offering the rose!—After this conversation I conducted her to her carriage; she asked for Duroc, whom she liked, and began to cry, saying:—I have been deceived!

I have just concluded peace. People tell me I am wrong and that I shall be taken in; but, faith, we have made enough war, and must give the world repose.

9th. The Emperor Alexander and I parted to-day after spending twenty days together here. We gave one another tokens of the greatest friendship.

10th, Koenigsberg:
I am staying in the old castle, cradle of the Prussian monarchy.

18th, Dresden:
(To Josephine.) I reached Dresden yesterday at five in the evening. I was one hundred hours in my carriage without getting out. Here, I am the guest of the King of Saxony, with whom I am very pleased. I am now halfway back to you. One of these fine nights I shall turn up at Saint Cloud like a jealous husband;—be warned!

It takes many years and skilful ministers to change the financial system of a country. I view men of science and clever men as I do coquettes; it pays to see them, to converse with them, but not to choose a wife or a minister from among them.

19th. (To Talleyrand.) We must immediately provide for the closing to England of the ports of Spain and Portugal. As soon as you reach Paris you will notify the Portuguese minister that on the 1st of September the ports of Portugal must be closed to England.

22d. (To Prince Eugène.) I have received the letter from the Pope which you forwarded. Answer His Holiness in some such terms:

"Holy Father: I have placed Your Holiness' letter before the Emperor, my revered Father and Sovereign, who has replied to me in a long letter from Dresden, from which I will quote an extract to Your Holiness to make you understand the views of His Majesty, and so as not to conceal the real state of affairs.—

My son, I perceive by his Holiness' letter, which he certainly never wrote himself, that I am threatened. I would not tolerate this from any other Pope. What does Pius VII wish to do when he denounces me to Christendom? Put an interdict on my throne? Excommunicate me? Does he imagine that their muskets will drop from my soldiers' fingers? Or is it to place a dagger in my people's hands to assassinate me? Frenzied Popes, born for the misfortune of men, have already preached this infamous doctrine. I shall doubtless hear that the Holy Father intends to apply the scissors to my head and to lock me up in a monastery! Does he suppose that the present century has reverted to the ignorance and the brutishness of the ninth century? Does he take me for Louis le Débonnaire?

The present Pope has too much power; priests are not made to rule; let them follow the example of St. Peter, St. Paul, and the holy Apostles, who were certainly worth any Julius, Boniface, Gregory, or Leo. Jesus Christ declared that his kingdom was not of this world. Why will not the Popes render unto Cæsar that which is Cæsar's? Is he something greater on earth than was Jesus Christ? But is there anything in common between the interests of religion and the prerogatives of the Court of Rome? Is religion to be based on anarchy, on civil war, on revolt? Is that preaching the doctrine of Jesus Christ? The Pope threatens me with an appeal to the people. In truth, I begin to blush and to feel ashamed at all the foolery that the Court of Rome makes me endure; and perhaps it will not be long, if they insist on creating disturbances in my States, before I refuse to recognise the Pope as anything more than bishop of Rome, the equal of, and on the same rank as the bishops of my States. I would not hesitate to convene the Gallican, Italian, German, and Polish churches in a Council, to settle affairs without the Pope, and to protect my people against the pretensions of the Court of Rome. My crown proceeds from God and from the will of my people; only to God and to my people am I answerable for it. For the Court of Rome I shall always be Charlemagne, and never Louis le Débonnaire.—

Holy Father, this letter was not intended to be seen by Your Holiness. I intreat you to put an end to this quarrel. The Emperor's complaint is justified."

Send this letter to the Pope, and inform me when M. Alquier presents it.

29th, Saint Cloud:
I have reached Paris in good health. A year ago I arranged the marriage of Prince Jerome with the Princess Catherine of Würtemberg; it is to take place some time this month.

August 2d. Unless England accepts the mediation of Russia, Denmark will have to declare war against her, or I shall declare war against Denmark.

12th. (To Champagny.) I would like you to write a confidential letter to M. de Metternich in some such terms as these: "What vertigo has seized people at Vienna? What enemy threatens you? You are calling the whole population to arms; your princes beat up the country like knights errant; what would you say if your neighbours did the same? Do you wish to bring on a crisis? Knowing as we do that you have no alliance with Russia, the help of England is clearly of no service to you. The Emperor cannot understand what you are about; up to the present he has taken no military steps. Can you inform me confidentially what it all means, and how we can prevent a crisis occurring?"

Make your letter pleasant, guarded in terms, confidential in form; but let them perceive clearly what will happen.

26th. The English disembarked near Copenhagen on the 16th. They are bombarding the city.

September 7th, Rambouillet:
(To Eugène.) Your aide-de-camp Bataille has lost his dispatches; he deserves to he punished; place him under arrest for a few days. It is allowable for an aide-de-camp to lose his breeches travelling, but never his dispatches nor his sword.

16th. (To the Emperor Alexander.) I thank Your Majesty for your splendid gift of furs. I have nothing so fine to offer in return. I hope, however, that some porcelain from Sèvres which I am sending may prove acceptable.

I have no news from England, and have no idea as to her policy. I am getting my fleet and my flotillas ready, and I think the moment is not far off when we shall be able to drive the English from the Continent.

28th, Fontainebleau:
(To General Savary, at St. Petersburg.) I have your letter of the 9th. M. de Champagny is replying to it in detail.

I had no notion you could be so gallant as now appears. However, the furbelows for your fair Russian ladies shall be sent. I wish to pay the account myself. When you present them, you can say that I happened to open the dispatch in which you asked for them, and that I insisted on choosing them myself. You know my taste in frills is pretty good. Talleyrand will send them some actors and actresses.

Herewith you will find two letters for the Empress. You will only present them after having first ascertained that they will be politely received, and answered.

October 1st. (To Prince Eugène.) My Son: The Empress is sending a wreath of Hortensias to the *Vicereine*. I would like you to have it valued, without the Princess' knowledge, by some good jewellers, and to let me know the valuation, so that I may judge at what sort of rate these gentlemen are accustomed to rob me.

12th. (To Champagny.) I consider that we are in a state of war with Portugal; I expect my troops to reach Burgos on the 1st of November; if Spain wants more troops, she has but to ask and I will send them. Junot's corps must amount to nearly 20,000 men.

As the English may possibly send troops to Lisbon, I would like to know what number of troops Spain is placing in the field. But make it clear that this must not be like the last war; we must push straight for Lisbon.

30th. I have hunted a great deal these last six weeks.

November 7th. (To Savary.) M. de Tolstoi presented his credentials to me yesterday at Fontainebleau. I wore the ribbon of St. Andrew all day. The manner in which he has been distinguished has already resulted in protests from some of the members of the diplomatic corps. M. de Tolstoi talked at great length about the evacuation of Prussia.

8th. (To General Junot.) I assume that as a result of my last dispatch you have quickened your march; it was too slow; ten days are precious; all the English troops and the Copenhagen expedition have returned to England.

13th. Order for the 1st division of the 2d corps to start from Bayonne on the 22d of November for Vittoria, there to act as a garrison to maintain communication with General Junot.

14th. There are many canals I must build: one from Dijon to Paris, one from the Rhine to the Saône, and another from the Rhine to the Scheldt. I have staked all the glory of my reign on changing the appearance of my Empire. The carrying out of these great works is as necessary to the prosperity of my people as it is to my own satisfaction.

I also attach the utmost importance and the greatest glory to stamping out pauperism. One must not live without leaving some evidence behind to commend one's memory to posterity.

15th. (To Jerome Napoleon, King of Westphalia.) My Brother: I inclose you herewith the Constitution of your kingdom. This Constitution embraces the conditions on which I abandon my rights, won by conquest, over your country. You must observe it strictly. Do not listen to those who will tell you that your people, accustomed to servitude, will accept your benefits with ingratitude. What the people of Germany impatiently expect is that men who are not born noble, but who have ability, should have an equal right to your regard and to employment; it is that all kinds of serfage, and the intermediate stages between the sovereign and the people, should be entirely abolished. The benefits of the Code Napoleon, the publicity of trials, the establishment of the jury, will distinguish your monarchy.

23d, Milan:
I have been at Milan these last two days.

24th. (To Joseph.) I saw Lucien for several hours at Mantua and talked with him. His manner of thinking and speaking are so far removed from mine that I could hardly tell what he wanted. If only he would divorce Mme. Joubersthon I would not interfere with his tastes or affections.

Here is what I propose: let him promise to send his daughter to Paris, and place her entirely at my disposal, for there is not a moment to lose, events are developing rapidly, and my destiny must be accomplished.

December 6th, Venice:
(To Marshal Victor.) I have received the letter in which you inform me that Prince Augustus is behaving badly in Berlin. I am not surprised, because he has no sense. He spent his time paying his attentions to Mme. de Staël at Coppet, and could only have got bad notions in that quarter. See that he is informed that the first time he chatters you will have him arrested and sent to a castle, and that you will send him Mme. de Staël for consolation. There is nothing so flat as these Prussian princes!

(To Maret.) I see by your reports that conversation still turns on subjects that must pain the Empress, and that are in every way improper.

17th, Milan:
The British Isles are declared to be in a state of blockade by sea as well as by land.

23d. (To General Clarke.) Order General Dupont to have his headquarters at Valladolid on the 10th of January, to concentrate his corps there, keeping an eye quietly on the bridge over the Douro, and placing a detachment at Salamanca as though he intended to move on Lisbon.

Order Marshal Moncey to organize the corps of observation of the Atlantic Coast, and to enter Spain at once, so that his leading division may reach Vittoria on the 15th of January.

1808

January 4th, Paris:
(To Jerome.) I see that you propose giving the Fürstenstein property, with 40,000 francs a year, to M. Lecamus. I cannot imagine a more absurd step. Since my reign began I have never ventured on a more arbitrary act. There are more than ten men who have saved my life and to whom I grant pensions of not more than 600 francs. I have Marshals who have won ten battles, who are covered with wounds, and whose reward has been less than what you are giving to M. Lecamus. If M. Lecamus has 40,000 francs a year, what must I give to Marshals Berthier, Lannes, Bernadotte, who have won the throne on which you sit at the price of countless wounds?

February 2d. (To the Emperor of Russia.) General Savary has just arrived, and I have spent many hours with him, talking about Your Majesty.

An army of 50,000 men, made up of Russians, of French, perhaps even with a few Austrians, marching by way of Constantinople on India, would no sooner reach the Euphrates than England would tremble and be on her knees to the Continent. I am all ready in Dalmatia, and so is Your Majesty on the Danube. One month after we had concluded an agreement our armies could be on the Bosphorus. The shock would reverberate to India, and England would be conquered.

(To Caulaincourt.) You will find herewith a letter for the Emperor Alexander. I have no doubt that Tolstoi writes home many foolish things. At a hunting party a few days ago at St. Germain, he was in the same carriage as Marshal Ney; a quarrel arose, and they went so far as to challenge one another. Three things that Tolstoi said on this occasion were noted: the first, that we would soon have war; the second, that the Emperor Alexander was too weak; and lastly, that if Europe was to be divided the Russian right must reach Hamburg and the left Venice. You can imagine what might be said in reply by Marshal Ney, who knows nothing of what is going on, and is as ignorant of my plans as a drummer of the line! The fact is that Russia is poorly represented.

Tell Romanzoff and the Emperor that I am inclined to favour an expedition to India, that nothing could be easier. If the Emperor Alexander can come to Paris, I would be delighted. If he can come only halfway, put the compasses on the map and strike the middle point between St. Petersburg and Paris.

12th. My troops have entered Rome.

20th. (To the Grand Duke of Berg.) I have appointed you my lieutenant with the army in Spain. Write to the generals informing them of your arrival at Bayonne, and giving them your instructions.

Your relations with the Spanish commanders must be friendly, and your only explanation for occupying the fortresses must be that it is necessary to protect the rear of our army. If the Governor-general of Navarre should decline to surrender the fortress of Pamplona, you can use the troops of Moncey's corps to take it.

Murat is a hero, and an ass!

25th. (To de Tournon.) Proceed to Madrid by the quickest way, and hand my letter to the King. You will await the answer, spending five or six days in Madrid. When you write by the courier of M. de Beauharnais you will give only vague information and nothing that could raise the suspicion that you are informed as to my plans.

March 5th. I may possibly start for Spain in less than a week. I have 80,000 men within 30 leagues of Madrid. Junot with 30,000 men is in control of Lisbon and Portugal, and yet I have not brought a single man from the Grand Army back to France. I have nearly 300,000 men in Poland and on the Oder. This year's conscription is being levied. But my expenses are enormous!

16th. (To the Grand Duke of Berg.) Continue to talk smoothly. Reassure the King, the Prince of Peace, the Prince of the Asturias, the Queen. The great thing is to reach Madrid, to rest your troops, and to collect supplies. Say that I shall soon be there to arrange and conciliate everything.

25th. We have reached the fifth act of the play, and shall soon get to the climax.

27th. (To Louis Napoleon, King of Holland.) My brother, the King of Spain has just abdicated; the Prince of Peace has been put into prison; an insurrection has broken out in Madrid. The Grand Duke of Berg presumably entered the city on the 23d at the head of 40,000 men. This being the state of things, I have thought of placing you on the throne of Spain. Reply categorically what you have to say to this proposal.

30th. (To the Grand Duke of Berg.) I have received your letter, and those of the King of Spain. Get the Prince of Peace out of the clutches of those people. I don't want any harm to happen to him. The King says he is going to your camp. I am waiting to hear that he is safely there before giving you instructions. You did right in not recognizing the Prince of the Asturias. Get King Charles IV into the Escurial if you can, treat him with the highest respect, and declare that he continues to govern Spain until I recognise the revolution. I highly approve all you have done.

April 5th, Bordeaux:
I arrived here just when no one was expecting me.

9th. (To the Grand Duke of Berg.) I perceive that, as a rule, you attach too much importance to the opinion of the city of Madrid. It is not for the sake of complying with the whims of the population of Madrid that I have brought together such large armies in Spain.

It is desirable that the Prince of the Asturias should come to meet me,—in which case I would await him at Bayonne.

12th. I am just starting for Bayonne. When I judge the moment has come, I shall arrive in Madrid, like a cannon-ball.

15th, Bayonne:
I reached Bayonne yesterday. I am expecting the Prince of the Asturias, who now styles himself Ferdinand VII; he is near the frontier. I am also expecting the unfortunate Charles IV and the Queen.

17th. King Charles IV left the Escurial on the 14th; he will therefore reach Burgos to-day or to-morrow. I hope to see him here.

(To Prince Murat.) If there should be any excitement, you can give out in the newspapers that the French armies have moved into Spain for an expedition to Africa, and that I am to direct their movements in person from Madrid; that the Prince of Peace, thinking I would influence the King, and influence him unfavourably to himself, became alarmed, and that all the trouble has come from this.

(To Marshal Bessières.) If the Prince of the Asturias should attempt to turn back at Burgos, have him placed under arrest, and send him to Bayonne.

18th. I have nearly 100,000 men here in provisional regiments. What with drill and exercise they are improving daily. They are all fine big boys of twenty, and I am very pleased with them.

19th. The interests of my House and of my Empire demand that the Bourbons should cease to reign in Spain! Countries where monks (rule) are easy to conquer!

It might cost me 200,000 men!

25th. The Prince of the Asturias is here; I am treating him well. I receive him at the head of the stairs, but do not accompany him (to the door).

The King and Queen will be here in a couple of days. The Prince of Peace arrives to-night. The unfortunate man excites pity. For a month he was between life and death, under constant threats. He never changed his shirt during all that time, and had grown a beard seven inches long.

26th. (To Murat.) It is time to show energy. I assume you will not spare the Madrid mob if it budges. A man at the head of 50,000 soldiers should not write such a letter as you wrote to the Infant Don Antonio, nor have recourse to intriguing methods. Your order of the day to the soldiers on the Burgos affair is wretched. Good God! where should we be if I were given to writing four pages to the soldiers to tell them not to allow themselves to be disarmed, and to extol as a heroic deed the fact that a detachment of fifteen men fired on a mob? Frenchmen are too acute not to laugh at such proclamations, and mine is not the school at which you learned to write them. What will you do in a crisis if you lavish your proclamations now? Three orders of the day like yours would demoralize an army.

(To Marshal Bessières.) There occurred at Santander, on the 22d, a demonstration against the French. Send an officer there, and declare to the inhabitants that if a single Frenchman is touched they will pay for it dear; my intention is, on the news of the least disorder, to send a brigade there, with cannon, and to burn the whole place down.

May 1st. I have just met the King and Queen, who are very glad to be here. The King received his sons with displeasure. All the Spaniards have kissed bands; but the old King appears to be very angry with them.

The Prince of the Asturias is very stupid, very surly, very hostile to, France; with my knowledge of how to handle men, his twenty-four years' experience makes no impression.

King Charles is a good soul. Whether it comes from his position, or from his circumstances, he gives the impression of an honest and kindly patriarch. The Queen's heart and history are revealed in her face; that is saying everything. It surpasses all one could imagine. They are both of them dining with me. The Prince of Peace looks like a bull; he is rather like Daru.

(To Charles IV., *offering his arm.*) Lean on my arm, I am strong.

(To the Queen.) Perhaps Your Majesty thinks I am going too fast?

(The Queen: Well, sire, that is rather your habit!)

If this thing were going to cost me 80,000 men I wouldn't do it; but it won't take 12,000; it's mere child's play. I don't want to hurt anybody, but when my great political chariot is rolling, it's as well to stand from under the wheels.

2d. As the Prince of the Asturias is not accommodating, it must all end in a crisis and an act of mediation.

(To Murat.) I am pleased with King Charles and the Queen. I shall send them to Compiègne. I intend to place the King of Naples on the Spanish throne. I propose giving you the throne of Naples or of Portugal. Let me know what you think of it immediately, for the whole business must be finished in one day.

5th. (To the Prince of the Asturias.) If you have not recognised your father as your rightful sovereign before midnight, and notified Madrid to that effect, you will be treated as a rebel.

6th. King Charles is an honest and good man. By the treaty he transfers all his rights over the Spanish Crown to me.

The worst of the job is done.

An insurrection broke out in Madrid on the 2d. Thirty or forty thousand people collected in the streets, and in the houses, firing from the windows. Two battalions of the fusiliers of the Guard, with 400 or 500 horse, restored order. More than two thousand of the mob were killed.

18th. Order for the Grand Duke of Berg to move General Dupont with his first division towards Cadiz.

21st. All the talk about a divorce does a great deal of harm; it is as improper as it is hurtful.

28th. (To Decrès.) If we have 19 of the line in the Mediterranean; 3 in the Adriatic, at Ancona; 20 at Flushing; 25 at Brest, Lorient, and Rochefort; 2 at Bordeaux; 8 at Cadiz and Lisbon; total 77 French ships, to which add 10 that the King of Holland has in his port; 1 for Denmark; 12 of the Emperor of Russia in the Baltic; 11 which the Emperor of Russia has at Lisbon and Toulon; 20 of the Spaniards: total 54; this would form a mass of 131 ships; and if we were to deduct the 12 Russians in the Baltic, it would leave 119 under my direct control, and backed up by camps of 7000 men at the Texel, of 25,000 men at Antwerp, of 80,000 men at Boulogne, of 30,000 at Brest, of 10,000 at Lorient and at Rochefort, of 6000 Spaniards at Ferrol, of 30,000 men at Lisbon, of 20,000 men at Carthagena, of 25,000 at Toulon, of 15,000 at Reggio, and of 15,000 at Taranto. That looks to me like a chess board on which, without asking much of Fortune, or demanding extraordinary skill from our seamen, we should get very good results.

31st. The bottom of the great question is: who shall have Constantinople?

June 3d. I have dictated orders for energetic steps to be taken at Santander. That city apparently needs an example. As the insurrection looks serious, we must act with large numbers.

7th. Dupont should have reached Cordova to-day.

9th. The King of Naples arrived here yesterday. He is recognised as King of Spain, and will start for Madrid. He has already accepted the oaths of allegiance of several grandees of Spain who are here, of the deputation from the Council of Castille, of the Council of the Indies, and of the Inquisition.

Saragossa has raised the standard of revolt.

13th. (To Murat.) I am sending General Savary to help you. I regret your illness from every point of view.

16th. General Lefebvre found the army of the rebels of Saragossa, commanded by Palafox, on some heights. General Lefebvre marched straight on the enemy, struck them in flank, and did great execution.

17th. (To Cambacérès.) My Cousin: I hear that extravagant reports are circulated at Fouché's. Since the rumours of a divorce were first started, I am told that it is a constant topic at his receptions, although I have expressed my opinion on the matter to him ten times. Have a talk with Fouché and tell him it is time people stopped speaking in this way, and that the thing is scandalous.

30th, Marracq:
It is very desirable that Saragossa should surrender promptly; it appears that such an event would greatly influence the submission of Spain.

July 1st. If it is true that (the troops from) the camp of Gibraltar have marched on Cordova, it may be that General Vedel will not be strong enough to unblock General Dupont.

9th. (To King Joseph.) Be gay and happy; never doubt your complete success.

The King started this morning. I escorted him as far as the frontier. H was followed by the whole Junta in nearly one hundred carriages; but they were carriages that had been rather hurriedly equipped.

13th. Dupont has more troops than he needs. Any reverse with which he might meet would not amount to much.

17th. The Emperor wishes to form a portable library of about one thousand books. The Emperor also wishes M. Barbier to take in hand the following piece of work: To draw up accounts of the campaigns that have been fought in the valley of the Euphrates from that of Crassus down to the eighth century; to indicate on suitable maps the line followed by each army, with the names, ancient and modern, of the chief cities, geographical details, and historical narratives of each expedition, drawn from the original sources.

(To Joachim Napoleon, King of the Two Sicilies.) My brother I have received your letter. I note with pleasure that the baths are beneficial to your health.

I have good news for you. On the 14th of July General Cuesta was encountered at the head of 35,000 men at Medina de Rio Seco. At six in the morning Marshal Bessières attacked them with 15,000 men, carried their positions, completely routed them, made several thousand prisoners, killed 5000 or 6000, took all their artillery, and dispersed their army. The army charged to the shout of *Vive l'Empereur,* and *No more Bourbons in Europe.*

19th, Bayonne:
(To Joseph Napoleon, King of Spain.) My Brother: You should not be surprised at having to conquer your kingdom. Philip V and Henry IV had to conquer theirs. Keep your spirits up, don't allow yourself to be depressed, and never for one moment doubt but that matters will finish better and more quickly than you imagine.

25th, Toulouse:
Austria is arming, but denies it; she is therefore arming against us. She is spreading the report that I demand some of her provinces: she is therefore trying to cloak as a rightful defence an unprovoked and hopeless attack. Since Austria is arming, we too must arm. I am therefore ordering the Grand Army to be reinforced. My troops are concentrating at Strassburg, Mainz, Wesel.

31st, Bordeaux:
(To Joseph.) I don't like the tone of your letter of the 24th. There is no question of dying, but of fighting, and of being victorious. I shall find in Spain the pillars of Hercules, not the bounds of my power. In all my military career I have seen nothing more cowardly than these mobs of Spanish soldiers.

You must support Dupont. Don't be uneasy as to the outcome of all this business.

August 1st. I can see from the report of the cuirassier officer that Dupont's corps will have to retreat. The whole thing is inconceivable.

2d. Brute! Fool! Coward! Dupont has lost Spain to save his baggage!

It's a spot on my uniform!

3d. (To General Clarke.) The inclosed documents are for you alone; read them with a map, and you will be able to judge whether there was ever anything since the world was created so senseless, so stupid, and so dastardly! Here are the Macks and the Hohenlohes justified! One can see clearly enough, by General Dupont's own report, that all that happened resulted from his inconceivable folly. This loss of 20,000 picked men, with the moral effect which it is bound to have, has made the King take the grave decision of falling back towards France. The influence which it will have on the general situation prevents my going to Spain in person; I am sending Marshal Ney there.

(To Joseph.) The knowledge that you have been thrown into the midst of events that are beyond your range of experience and of character grieves me, my dear friend. Dupont has covered our standards with infamy. An event like this makes my presence in Paris necessary. I feel the sharpest pang at the thought that at such a moment I cannot be at your side and in the midst of my soldiers. Let me know that you are keeping your spirits up, that you are well, and getting used to soldiering,—here is a splendid opportunity for studying the business.

5th, Rochefort:
I have ordered the 1st corps of the Grand Army, the 6th corps and two divisions of dragoons back to Mainz.

6th. Lisbon is threatened by an English expedition and by an insurrection. Part of the Spanish army has gone over to the English, and the situation looks very grave.

16th, Saint Cloud:
What is going on in Spain is lamentable. My army is not commanded by generals who have made war, but by postal inspectors.

21st. *Defeat of Junot at Vimiero.*

22d. (To Pauline.) And how are you feeling, lovely princess; are you very tired? What are you doing to-day?

(To Marshal Davout.) As the English have landed large forces in Spain, I have recalled the 1st and 6th corps and three divisions of dragoons from the Grand Army, so as to complete the conquest of that country this winter. Dupont has dishonoured our arms; his stupidity is only equalled by his cowardice. When you (get the details) it will raise the hair of your head. I will do them good justice, and if they have stained our uniform they will have to wash it out.

29th. Russia and Austria have recognised the King of Spain. It is clear that nothing will happen in October; but as to what may be hatched this winter to explode in the spring, that is another matter.—And so life goes, making and unmaking.

30th. (Note on Spanish affairs.) It needs a long experience of war to perceive its principles; one must have undertaken many offensive operations to realize how the slightest incident means encouragement or discouragement, brings about one result or another. In warfare men are nothing, a man is everything.

September 3d. (To M. Cretet.) Give orders for the city of Metz to entertain the troops when they pass. As the city cannot afford it, I will grant three francs per man, but it must all be done in the name of the city. I wish you to instruct the prefects who are on the line of march to look after the troops well, and to maintain in every way possible their loyalty and their love of glory. Speeches, songs, free theatre performances, dinners,—that is what I expect from our citizens for our soldiers.

14th. The Emperor of Russia has given me a rendezvous at Erfurt to confer on European affairs and on the means of putting an end to the unrest of the world and restoring a general peace.

17th. (To Cretet.) Have songs composed in Paris and sent to the chief cities; these songs are to proclaim the glory the army has already won, that which it still has to acquire, and the liberty of the seas that will result from its victories. These songs shall be sung at the dinners (given to the troops). You will have three sets of songs composed, so that the soldiers shall not hear the same song repeated.

18th. (Proclamation.) Soldiers, after your triumphs on the banks of the Danube and of the Vistula, you have crossed Germany by forced marches. I now order you through France without allowing you one moment's repose.

Soldiers, I need you! The Leopard's hideous apparition has sullied the continent of Spain and Portugal; he must flee in terror at your approach. We will carry our triumphant Eagles to the columns of Hercules: there also we have insults to wipe out.

Soldiers, you have surpassed the fame of all armies of modern times, but have you as yet equalled the glory of the armies of Rome, which in the same campaign triumphed on the Rhine and on the Euphrates, in Illyria and on the Tagus?

27th Erfurt:
I arrived this morning at nine.

29th. Your Emperor Alexander is as obstinate as a clam!—That infernal Spanish business is costing me dear!

October 1st. (To Alexander.) What you are suggesting I should do really represents a policy of concessions; if I adopted it, Europe would treat me like a little boy. Is it the act of a friend, of an ally, to propose that I should abandon the only position from which I can threaten Austria in flank if she should attack me while my troops are in the south of Europe? If you absolutely insist on my evacuating (Prussia), I shall consent; but if I do, instead of going into Spain I shall settle Austria's business first.

3d. Erfurt is very brilliant.

5th. (To the Empress.) Conversations lasting whole days are not doing my cold much good. However, all is going well. I am pleased with Alexander, and he ought to be pleased with me: if he were a woman I think I could have him at my feet. I shall soon be back; take good care of yourself; I shall expect to find you plump and in good colour.

9th. I am just back from hunting over the battlefield of Jena. We breakfasted on the spot where I bivouacked.

I went to the ball at Weimar. The Emperor Alexander danced, but I didn't. Forty years of age are forty years!

12th. (Treaty of alliance.) His Majesty the Emperor of the French, King of Italy, and His Majesty the Emperor of all the Russias, desirous of binding more closely and of making more durable the alliance between them, confirm and renew the treaty of alliance concluded at Tilsit.

13th. (To Joseph.) You need me there.

19th, Saint Cloud:
(To General Junot, Duke of Abrantes.) The Minister of War has shown me all your reports, and in particular your letter of the 15th of October. You have done nothing that is dishonourable. You have brought me back my soldiers, my standards, and my guns. I had hoped, however, that you would do better. You secured the convention, not so much by your foresight as by your courage, and the English are right in blaming the general who signed it. I have now made public my approval of your conduct; what I write confidentially is for you alone. Before the end of the year, I intend myself to place you once more at Lisbon.

21st. Berthier started for Bayonne to-day; I shall be there in a few days.

22d. The Civil and Commercial Codes, and the Code of Procedure, have met with success. The Criminal Code will come before the Legislative Body this session. The Civil Code is the code of the century; its provisions not only preach toleration, but organize it,—toleration the greatest privilege of man.

Liberty is the need of only a small class, endowed by nature with higher faculties than common men. Equality, on the contrary, is what appeals to the mass.

November 3d, Bayonne:
I have just arrived. As I rode at a gallop through some considerable part of the Landes I am a little tired.

4th, Tolosa:
I shall start to-morrow at five, and shall reach Vittoria in the night. I want to cover not more than four or five leagues on the same horse. I intend to enter Vittoria incognito; that is why I shall get there at night. The news will not be out till morning. At nine a salute of sixty guns may be fired.

7th, Vittoria:
Troops are coming in daily. The Guard arrived to-day. I am very busy.

10th, Cubo, *8 P. M. :*
(To Joseph Napoleon, King of Spain.) My Brother: I shall start at one in the morning so as to reach Burgos before dawn; there I will make my arrangements for the day, for a victory is nothing, it must be turned to account.

While I think it unnecessary that there should be any ceremony made for me, I think it necessary that there should be for you. As to me, it does not fit my business of soldiering; in any case I don't want any. It seems to me that deputations from Burgos should wait on you and give you a good reception.

16th, Burgos:
Marshal Ney attacks Aranda to-day, and Marshal Bessières, who is marching for the same point, will immediately cover the plain with cavalry up to the mountains of Madrid.

Blake's army of 45,000 men has been defeated at Espinosa and Reinosa.

18th. (To M. de Champagny.) I have read Miss Patterson's letter. I will see her child with pleasure, and will take charge of him, if she will send him to France; as for herself, she can have all she wants. At the time I refused to recognise her I was influenced by political considerations; apart from that, I wish to provide for her son to her satisfaction. For the rest, deal with this matter secretly and tactfully.

23d, Aranda:
I got here at four. Apparently there are serious disturbances at Madrid.

26th. The battle of Tudela completes that of Espinosa. The army of Andalusia commanded by Castaflos, that of Aragon commanded by Palafox, those of Valencia and of New Castille, are destroyed and scattered. We have captured many guns and prisoners and much baggage.

27th. In six days I shall be in Madrid.

30th, at the foot of the Somosierra:
(Colonel Piré: Impossible, sire!)

That is a word I don't know!

(To the Polish lancers.) Carry that position, in a gallop!

(Kozietulski: Forward, trot! Vive l'Empereur!)

On the summit of the Somosierra:
(The last surviving Polish officer, to Berthier: I am dying, there are the guns; tell the Emperor!)

You are worthy of my Old Guard! I proclaim you my bravest cavalry!

(The Polish lancers: Ave Cæsar!)

Buitrago:
(To Joseph.) We have had an engagement. A corps of 9000 men was in position at the Somosierra, and 4000 at Sepulveda. We defeated those at Somosierra, captured their guns, 50 transport wagons, and a great number of prisoners.

December 4th, Madrid:
Madrid has capitulated, and we occupied it at noon.

From the date of the publication of the present decree, feudal dues are at an end in Spain. The tribunal of the Inquisition is abolished as infringing on the sovereign power and civil authority. From the 1st of January next, the custom houses between province and province shall be suppressed and carried to the frontiers.

11th, Chamartin:
(To Alexander, Prince of Neuchâtel.) My Cousin: Send one of your staff officers to Talavera so as to get news of what the English are doing.

22d, Madrid:
I am starting immediately to operate against the English, who appear to have received reinforcements and to be making a show of boldness.

The English move is extraordinary. It is clear that they have left Salamanca. It is probable that they have sent their transports to Ferrol, with the idea that a retreat on Lisbon would be dangerous.

The whole of the Guard is on the march. We shall probably reach Valladolid on the 24th or 25th.

Afternoon, Pass of the Guadarrama:
(Napoleon passes astride on a gun in the midst of a terrific snowstorm. The soldiers: Convicts suffer less than we do! Shoot him down, damn him!)

Espinas, *evening:*
I have crossed the Guadarrama with a part of the Guard in rather disagreeable weather.

23d, Villacastin:
(To Joseph.) The English appear to be at Valladolid. Put in the Madrid newspapers that 20,000 English are surrounded and lost.

26th, near the Douro, floods, mud, rain:
If the English remained in their positions to-day it is all up with them.

(Sir John Moore, near Valladolid: I am in a hornet's nest, and God knows how I shall get out of it.)

31st, Benavente:
My advance guard is near Astorga. The English are flying as fast as they can, and are abandoning their supplies and baggage.

1809

January 1st, near Astorga, *arrival of the courier from Paris.*

2d, Astorga:
We have found 800 dead horses along the road and much baggage, with supplies. The Guard is returning to Benavente, and I am coming back closer to the centre of my armies.

6th, Benavente:
(To Joseph.) I thank you for your good wishes for the new year. I have no hope as yet that Europe will be pacified this year. I have so little hope of it that I signed a decree yesterday to raise 100,000 men.

Happiness? Ah! of course! There's little enough question of happiness these days!

7th, Valladolid:
I have left the Duke of Dalmatia with 30,000 men to pursue the English.

8th, Morning parade:
Ah, yes. I know, you all want to get back to Paris, to your bad habits, and your mistresses! Well, I mean to keep you with the colours till you're eighty!

9th. (To Josephine.) Moustache has brought me your letter of the 31st of December. I perceive, dear friend, that you are worried, that you are in a state of black anxiety. Austria will not make war on me. If she does, I have 150,000 men in Germany, and as many on the Rhine, and 400,000 Germans with whom to reply. Russia will not leave my side. People are mad in Paris; all is going perfectly well.

I shall be in Paris the moment I think it necessary. I warn you to beware of ghosts: one of these fine days, at two o'clock in the morning—But, good-bye.

11th. I have to stay at Valladolid, where dispatches from Paris can reach me in five days. The events of Constantinople, the present situation of Europe, the reorganization of my armies of Italy, of Turkey, and of the Rhine prevent my moving away from here. It was with great reluctance that I turned back at Astorga.

On the parade ground:
(To General Legendre, Dupont's chief of staff.) You have the impudence to appear before me! Your dishonour is written on the face of every brave soldier. Men have blushed for you in the most remote parts of Russia. On the field of battle a man fights, sir, he does not surrender, and if he surrenders he deserves to be shot. A soldier should know how to die. Your surrender was a crime!

15th. (To Joseph.) The condition of Europe compels me to go to Paris for three weeks. I expect to be there on the 21st of January. I shall travel most of the way in the saddle, rapidly. If you think it advisable you can keep my absence secret for a fortnight by saying that I have gone to Saragossa.

24th, Paris:
I arrived here in good health on the 23d at 8 in the morning.

28th. (To Talleyrand.) You are a thief, a coward, a man without honour, you disbelieve in God, you have betrayed everyone, to you nothing is sacred, you would sell your own father! You suppose, without rhyme or reason, that my Spanish affairs are going wrong. You deserve that I should smash you like a glass, but I despise you too profoundly to put myself to that trouble!

(Talleyrand: What a pity that so great a man should be so ill-bred!)

29th. (To Metternich.) Well! this is something new at Vienna! What does it mean? Has a spider stung you? Who is threatening you? Whom are you aiming at? Do you want to set the world aflame again?

Metternich has almost become a statesman, he lies very well.

(Austria) wants to get slapped; she shall have it, on both cheeks. If the Emperor Francis attempts any hostile move, he will soon have ceased to reign. That is clear. Before another ten years mine will be the most ancient dynasty of Europe.

February 11th. My memory will not store a single alexandrine verse; but I do not forget one syllable of the regimental returns. I always know where my troops are.

I am fond of tragedy; but were all the dramas of the world there, on one side of me, and the regimental returns on the other, I would not so much as glance at the dramas, while every line of my regimental returns would be read with the closest attention.

March 9th. I am leaving my best troops with Joseph, and am starting alone for Vienna with my little conscripts, my name, and my long boots.

14th, Rambouillet:
(To Maximilian Joseph, King of Bavaria.) My Brother: If war should break out, your troops must be employed vigorously. The Prince Royal, however distinguished he may be by his natural gifts, has never conducted military operations, and is therefore not competent to command. I should be depriving myself of the services of your 40,000 men if I had not a firm and able commander at their head. I have selected an old soldier, the Duke of Dantzig, for this duty. At this day the Bavarian army is too large, and the circumstances too serious, for me to speak less than frankly to Your Majesty. After the Prince Royal has won his promotions through six or seven campaigns, he will be fit to command.

23d, Paris:
A French officer has been stopped at Braunau, and his dispatches, though sealed with the arms of France, have been forcibly taken by the Austrians.

24th. All the infantry of the Guard coming from Spain will proceed to Paris by coach.

30th. My intention is to carry my headquarters to Ratisbon and to concentrate my whole army there.

April 10th. Intercepted dispatches addressed to M. de Metternich, and his demand for passports, show clearly enough that Austria is on the point of beginning hostilities, if she has not already done so; if she attacks before the 15th everything must fall back on the Lech.

12th. (To the Prince of Neuchâtel.) The semaphore is just giving me, at 8 P. M., the first half of your dispatch, from which it would appear, according to a letter of M. Otto, that the Austrians have crossed the Inn and declared war. I shall start in two hours.

15th, Strassburg:
In an hour 1 shall cross the Rhine.

16th, Ludwigsburg.
(To Alexander, Prince of Neuchâtel.) I have received your dispatch stating that you are moving Oudinot's corps to Ratisbon. You state no reasons for so extraordinary a move that weakens and disperses my forces.

17th, Donauwerth, 4 *A. M.:*
I have absolutely no knowledge of the whereabouts of the Duke of Auerstadt.

It appears that the Duke of Dantzig is retreating on Eisenfeld.

8 A. M.:
(To the Duke of Dantzig.) Let me know your personal view as to where the mass of the enemy's forces is situated.

10 A. M.:
(To the Duke of Auerstadt.) I have just reached Donauwerth. I hear that you are at Ratisbon. My intention had always been to concentrate behind the Lech. Fall back with all your troops on Ingolstadt.

(To the Duke of Rivoli.) You will receive in the night orders to march to-morrow at two in the morning with your whole corps and that of General Oudinot. The object of your march will be to get contact with the rest of the army, to catch the enemy in a false manœuvre, and to destroy his columns.

6 P. M.:
(To Davout.) Since arriving here this morning I have sent you General Savary, my aide-de-camp Vence, an artillery officer, a Bavarian major, and have ordered General von Wrede and the Duke of Dantzig, to both of whom I have sent several dispatches, to send on my views to you. It is now 6 P. M. and I am sending off your aide-de-camp, with a duplicate copy of my orders, and he has promised me that he will reach you by six in the morning. We have heard the sound of guns from between Pfaffenhofen and Freising. We are moving towards one another.

18th, *4 A. M.:*
It appears as though the Archduke Charles were moving on the line Landshut
Ratisbon.

(To Masséna, Duke of Rivoli.) In a word you will see the whole situation. Prince
Charles debouched yesterday from Landshut on Ratisbon with his whole army;
he had three corps, estimated at 80,000 men. You therefore perceive that there
never was a stroke that demanded more energy and swiftness than this.

Rapidity! Activity! activity! All lies with you!

20th, Vohburg:
I am in the saddle to get to the outposts and see things for myself. I shall attack
the enemy if they are still in position, and pursue them rapidly if they are retreating.

21st, Rohr:
Yesterday and day before are a second Jena. The Duke of Rivoli should have
reached Landshut (yesterday) at three in the afternoon.

22d, Landshut:
I shall be at Ergoltsbach before noon. If I hear the guns, that will be a sufficient
signal for me to attack. I am determined to destroy the army of Prince Charles to-
day, or at latest to-morrow.

(Order.) The Duke of Rivoli will move on Eckmühl with his three divisions, and
cut off the enemy. The Emperor will be with him.

24th, Imperial headquarters, Ratisbon:
Soldiers, you have done all that I expected! You have balanced numbers by cour-
age. You have gloriously marked the difference that lies between the soldiers of
Cæsar and the armed hordes of Xerxes.

In a few days we have triumphed in three pitched battles, at Thann, at Abensberg
and at Eckmühl, and in the actions of Freising, of Landshut, and of Ratisbon.
Before another month has elapsed we shall be in Vienna.

27th, Mühldorf:
We are now in Austria and covering long days' marches.

30th, Burghausen:
(To Prince Eugène, commanding the army of Italy.) I regret to see that you have abandoned the line of the Piave. In warfare one sees one's own deficiencies, but not those of the enemy. You should have held on until the enemy actually attempted to force the passage of the Piave.

War is a serious business in which one risks one's own reputation and that of one's country; a reasonable man should examine himself and decide whether or no he is fitted for it. I know that in Italy you affect a great contempt of Masséna; had I sent him there things would not have happened as they have. Masséna has military talents to which we may well doff our hats; we must forget his foibles; every man has some. I made a mistake in giving you the command of the army; I should have placed you under Masséna in command of the cavalry. Kings of France, even reigning Emperors, have often enough commanded a regiment or a division under the orders of an old Marshal. I think that if you are hard pressed you should write asking the King of Naples to join the army; he could leave his government to the Queen. You could hand the command over to him, and place yourself under his orders; that would be highly proper, and would have a good effect. It is a simple enough matter that you should know less of warfare than a man who has been waging it for sixteen years. I am not vexed at your mistakes, but I am at your not writing and posting me, so that I can advise you, and direct your movements from here. If you only knew history you would also know that quips serve no good purpose, and that the greatest battles of which we know were lost through following the opinions of the armies.

May 4th, Enns:
I crossed the Traun yesterday. There has been an engagement at Ebelsberg in which we took 6000 prisoners.

6th. (To Josephine.) Dear friend: I have received your letter. The bullet that struck me did not wound me; it just grazed the tendon of Achilles. My health is excellent and there is no cause for worry. My affairs are going well.

9th, S. Poelten:
I shall be in sight of Vienna to-morrow at noon. The inhabitants are armed, and appear inclined to defend themselves. We shall see if we are to have a repetition of the Madrid business.

12th, Schoenbrunn:
We took possession of the suburbs on the 10th, and of the city to-day, after a bombardment.

(Decree.) Napoleon, Emperor of the French, King of Italy, protector of the Confederation of the Rhine, etc.

Whereas Charlemagne, Emperor of the French, our illustrious predecessor, when donating various counties to the bishops of Rome, granted them by way of fiefs and for the greater benefit of his states; and whereas Rome did not cease, by the said donations, from being a part of his Empire; and whereas nothing that we have put forward for the purpose of conciliating the safety of our armies, the tranquillity and prosperity of our people, the dignity and integrity of our Empire with the temporal claims of the Popes, has been of any effect; we hereby decree: The States of the Pope are annexed to the French Empire.

17th. The immense quantity of material necessary for throwing a bridge over the Danube is already assembled. I hope to cross on the 18th and 19th, and to disperse the armies between the Danube and Moravia.

19th, Ebersdorf:
The Emperor hopes the bridge will be ready to-morrow forenoon, and that the whole army will reach the left bank in the course of the day.

22d, bivouac, island of Lobau:
The nearest villages are Aspern, Essling, and Enzersdorf. To cross a river like the Danube in the presence of an enemy knowing the ground thoroughly, and having the sympathies of the inhabitants is one of the most difficult military operations conceivable.

It was all over with the Austrian army when at 7 A. M. a staff officer reached the Emperor and informed him that, owing to a sudden flood of the Danube which had carried down many trees and rafts, the bridges between the right bank and the island of Lobau had been broken. This deplorable mishap caused the Emperor to stop the advance of the troops.

The enemy made desperate efforts, backed by the fire of 200 guns, to drive the French army away. Their efforts ended ingloriously. Three times they attacked the villages of Aspern and Essling, and three times they filled them with their dead. Towards six o'clock in the evening the Duke of Montebello had a leg carried away by a cannon-ball; for a moment it was thought, he was killed.

23d, Ebersdorf:
(To Count Daru.) A great part of the army will be in the island to-night, and will need provisions. In the present situation of affairs there is nothing more pressing than to get us supplies.

28th. On the night of the 26th to the 27th our bridges over the Danube were carried away by the flood and by mill wheels that had been thrown in (and floated down). To-day one of the bridges is repaired.

31st. (To the Empress Josephine.) I am in great grief for the loss of the Duke of Montebello, who died this morning. And so all things come to their end! Good-bye, dear friend; do anything you can to console the Marshal's poor wife.

There are some wounds to which death itself is preferable. It is at the moment of leaving life that a man clings to it with all his might. Lannes, the bravest of men, Lannes, deprived of his two legs, did not want to die, and said to me that the two surgeons who had treated a Marshal so brutally and with such scant respect ought to be hanged. With his remnant of life he clung to me; he wanted only me, thought only of me. A sort of instinct! For surely he loved his young wife and his children more than he did me; yet he never spoke of them, which was because he expected no help from them. But I was his protector; for him I was some vague and superior power; I was his Providence, and he was imploring....

(To Mme. Lannes, Duchess of Montebello.) My Cousin: The Marshal died this morning of wounds received on the field of honour. My sorrow is as deep as yours. I lose the most distinguished general in my armies, my comrade in arms during sixteen years, he whom I considered my best friend. His family and his children will always have a special claim to my protection. It is to assure you of this that I have written you this letter, for I am convinced that nothing could lighten the grief that you must feel.

June 5th, Schoenbrunn.
I am here to review the Guard, which is superb. There are 60 guns, 4000 sabres, and 12,000 of the finest infantry in Europe.

9th. (To Jerome Napoleon, King of Westphalia.) Experience will teach you the difference between reports spread by the enemy and reality. I have never, in the whole of the sixteen years during which I have exercised command, given counter-orders to a regiment, because I always wait until matters are ripe and understood before I begin operations. Don't be so nervous; there is nothing to be alarmed about; it is all empty noise.

11th. (To General Clarke.) It seems to me that the Spanish operations are being poorly conducted, and so poorly conducted that I foresee a catastrophe unless more vigour is imparted to the movements of the columns. The English have been given enough respite to form another army at Lisbon. It is the English we have to fear; they alone, unless the army is managed differently, will bring it to a catastrophe before many months.

12th. I believe that in German Schoenbrunn means the beautiful fountain; the spring in the park produces delicious water which I drink every morning. Do you also like fresh water?

(Colonel Sainte Croix: Faith, no, Sire; I prefer a good glass of Bordeaux or of Champagne.)

Send the Colonel 100 bottles of Bordeaux and as many of Champagne.

14th. (To Count Fouché.) I have received a wretched scrawl from that black-guard Palafox. I am displeased that you should have accepted it, had it translated, and thereby allowed it to become known that he was at Vincennes, instead of leaving that fact unpublished. This blackguard is stained with the blood of 4000 Frenchmen whom he barbarously slaughtered it Saragossa. Let him remain at Vincennes, forgotten, without pen or paper, and unable to secure the intervention in his favour of the most bitter enemies of France.

16th. (To Josephine.) On the 14th, anniversary of Marengo, Eugène won a battle at Raab in Hungary against the Archduke John; he captured 3000 prisoners, several guns, four flags, and has pursued the enemy far on the road to Baden.

17th. (To Joachim Napoleon.) I received Your Majesty's letter of the 8th of June. I would much like to have you here. But in the present state of things it is better that you should not be too far away from Naples. In another campaign, when things are quite settled in your direction, it will be possible to call you to the army.

20th. (To Eugène.) The art of questioning prisoners comes with experience and the practice of war. What he said appears uninteresting to you; had I questioned him I would have obtained much information about the enemy.

Be ready to start, as soon as my orders reach you, to take part in the great battle.

30th. (To Fouché.) Find out who influences the Prussian Minister. The stupid and infamous reports he sends to his Court are inconceivable. Is he a fool, or is he malicious, or is he taken in by some intriguing person at Paris? He writes to Berlin that my position is desperate, that the discontent in France is at the highest pitch, and the refrain of the whole is that Prussia should pay no more money. The man must be very silly or very ill-intentioned.

July 2d, Island of Lobau:
The army of Prince Charles is ranged in battle opposite; I shall cross on the night of the 4th.

4th. Notwithstanding his redoubts and intrenchments, I hope, with the help of God, to crush the army of Prince Charles.

9 P. M.:
I am delighted with this storm. What a splendid night for us. The Austrians can't see our preparations.

6th. *Battle of Wagram :*
(To Bernadotte.) I relieve you, sir, from the command of a corps which you handle so badly!

7th, Ebersdorf:
(To the Empress Josephine.) I am sending you a page with the good news of the victories of Enzersdorf and of Wagram which I won on the 5th and 6th of July. The enemy's army is retreating in disorder, and all is going as well as possible. My losses are rather heavy, but the victory is complete and decisive. We have over a hundred guns, twelve flags, many prisoners.

I am sunburnt. Good-bye, dear friend. I embrace you. Many compliments to Hortense.

8th, Wolkersdorf:
I have my headquarters in the house that the weakling Francis I occupied; he was content to watch the battle from an observatory twelve miles away from the field.

I reckon that the enemy played on us with from 700 to 800 guns. I had 550, and fired 100,000 rounds of shot and grape.

13th, Znaym:
There shall be an armistice between the armies of H. M. the Emperor of the French and King of Italy, and of H. M the Emperor of Austria.

15th, Schoenbrunn:
The bull of excommunication is so ridiculous a document that one may as well take no notice of it.

17th. (To Jerome.) I have seen an order of the day signed by you that makes you the laughing stock of Germany, Austria and France. Have you no friend who will tell you the truth? You are a King and a brother of the Emperor,—ridiculous title in warfare! You must be a soldier, and again a soldier, and always a soldier! You must bivouac with your outposts, spend night and day in the saddle, march with your advance guard so as to get information, or else remain in your seraglio. You wage war like a satrap. By Heaven! is it from me you have learned that?—from me, who with an army of 200,000 men live with my skirmishers?

You have much ambition, some intelligence, a few good qualities,—but spoiled by silliness, by great presumption,—and have no real knowledge. In God's name keep enough wits about you to write and speak with propriety.

18th. After matters are settled here, I hope that Spain will not hold us up very long. But it is to be feared that the English will attempt something, and I can see very little brains to take care of things there.

August 3d. (To the Polish deputation.) One does what one can. Poland is a question on which all negotiations, with Russia fail. Russia sees quite well that she is vulnerable only through Poland. If I were Emperor of Russia I would never consent to the least increase of the Duchy of Warsaw; just as I would meet death, and ten armies behind me, in defence of Belgium; and more than that I would raise an eleventh army of women and children to fight and to defend the interests of France.

I know that the reëstablishment of Poland would balance Europe, but you must see that Russia would never consent unless her armies were totally destroyed. The reëtablishment of Poland is not, at this moment, within the power of France. I will not make war on Russia.

15th. (Message to the Senate.) Senators, we have thought proper to acknowledge in the most marked manner the special services rendered to us in the campaign just concluded by our cousins, the Prince of Neuchâtel and the Dukes of Auerstadt and of Rivoli. We have therefore erected the castle of Chambord into a principality, under the style of principality of Wagram, to be Possessed by our cousin the Prince of Neuchâtel, and by his descendants. We have erected the castle of Brühl into a principality, under the style of principality of Eckmühl, to be possessed by our cousin the Duke of Auerstadt and his descendants. And we have erected the castle of Thouars into a principality, under the style of principality of Essling, to be possessed by our cousin the Duke of Rivoli and his descendants.

(To General Clarke.) I have your letter of the 8th. I don't exactly understand the event in Spain (Talavera), or what took place. The King says that for a month past he has manœuvred with 40,000 men against 100,000. Write to him that it is his own fault; they don't understand the art of war at Madrid.

27th. The conferences at Altenburg still continue, but it appears that the English raid on Zeeland has given the Austrian negotiators new hopes, or makes them delay.

September 6th. (To Fouché.) Maret will send you a collection of all the banknotes. You will find herewith a decree on the subject. I want you to start manufacturing these notes in all denominations, to total not more than 100 millions. It is by means of this paper money that Austria was able to make war on me; and it is by the same means that she may be able to renew it. That being the case, my policy, in time of peace as in time of war, is to destroy this paper money and to force Austria to come back to a metallic currency, which would naturally compel her to reduce her army and the insane expenditure by means of which she has threatened the safety of my dominions. I wish this business to be carried through with the utmost secrecy. My object, however, is far more political than a matter of speculation or profit. There is no quiet to be looked for in Europe so long as the House of Austria can supply itself with loans of 300 or 400 millions by the credit of its paper money.

10th, Schoenbrunn:
(To Champagny.) I inclose the letter written to me by the Austrian Emperor. I do not exactly understand the object of his step, unless the letter is a passport to enable his aide-de-camp to reach Vienna and have a conversation with me. The aide-de-camp says that the Emperor has declared that he approves the proposed bases, and is disposed to make sacrifices. I replied that the Emperor of Austria is always of the opinion of the last speaker, and that in five or six years he would begin the war again and become once more the tool of England. After that the aide-de-camp made the usual Austrian speeches and spoke of an alliance. I told him that the House of Austria had always rejected it; that we were two bulls struggling for the love of Italy and of Germany; and that so long as Austrian sentiment remained what it was, there could be no possible understanding.

23d. (To Maret.) I do not propose giving the Emperor of Austria the title of "Apostolic." You will make believe that you understood this title to belong to the Emperor of Germany; as he is no longer that, he is no more apostolic than I am; I am as christian as he is.

30th. (To Joachim Napoleon.) I think you should give nothing to your minister Saliceti, because he has not been in your service long enough. As a rule give nothing to people who have not worked ten years for you. You are right in making the rule that no member of the diplomatic corps can see either you or the Queen. They are spies, and insatiable, and the better you treat them the worse they abuse you. Notwithstanding the Emperor of Russia's practice of inviting Caulaincourt to dinner twice a week, I have never invited Prince Kourakine. Base yourself on the principle that the less the diplomatic corps see you the better.

October 3d. (Note.) The Institute proposes conferring on the Emperor the title of Augustus and of Germanicus. Augustus gained one battle, at Actium. Germanicus won the sympathy of Rome by his misfortunes, but his life shows a decidedly moderate record. There is nothing to provoke emulation in the memory of the Roman Emperors. The only man, and he was not an Emperor, who was distinguished by his character and by his many illustrious achievements was Cæsar. If the Emperor could wish a new title it would be that of Cæsar: But so many puny princes have dishonoured that title,—if such a thing were possible,—that it no longer evokes the memory of the great Cæsar, but that of a mass of German sovereigns, as feeble as they were ignorant, of whom not one has left a reputation behind him.

The Emperor's title is Emperor of the French.

10th. In a battle even the most skilful soldiers find it difficult to estimate the enemy's numbers, and as a rule; one is apt instinctively to exaggerate the number. But if one is foolish enough to accept an inflated estimate of the enemy's forces, then every cavalry colonel on reconnaissance espies an army, and every captain of light infantry battalions. Again I repeat that in war morale and opinion are half the battle. The art of the great captain has always been to make his troops appear very numerous to the enemy, and the enemy's very few to his own. So that to-day, in spite of the long time we have spent in Germany, the enemy do not know my real strength. We are constantly striving to magnify our numbers. Far from confessing that I had only 100,000 men at Wagram, I am constantly suggesting that I had 220,000. In my Italian campaigns, in which I had only a handful of troops, I always exaggerated my numbers. It served my purpose, and has not lessened my glory. My generals and practised soldiers could always perceive, after the event, all the skilfulness of my operations, even that of having exaggerated the numbers of my troops.

12th. At parade to-day a young man of seventeen, the son of a Lutheran pastor of Erfurt, tried to get near me. Some officers stopped him, and as the boy showed confusion, suspicion was aroused, he was searched, and a dagger was found on him. I have ordered him to be brought before me.

What did you want of me?

(Staps: To kill you).

What have I done to you? Who made you my judge?

(I wanted to bring the war to an end.)

Why didn't you go to the Emperor Francis?

(He? What for? He doesn't count. And if he died another would succeed him; but after you the French would disappear from Germany.)

Do you repent?

(No!)

Would you do it again?

(Yes!)

What, even if I spared you?

(To Fouché.) The wretched boy, who seems to be pretty well educated, told me that he wanted to assassinate me to rid Austria of the presence of the French. I could find in him no traces of religious or of political fanaticism. He see med to have no clear idea of who Brutus was. His excitement prevented my finding out more. He will be questioned after he has cooled down and fasted. Possibly it all amounts to nothing.

I have sent you the news of this incident to prevent its importance being exaggerated. I hope nothing will be said about it; if there should be talk, make out that the fellow is insane. If there is none, keep the matter a close secret. There was no scene at the parade. I. myself had no notion that anything had happened.

14th. Peace was signed at two o'clock by Champagny and Prince Liechtenstein.

15th. The individual named Staps, arrested in the courtyard of Schoenbrunn with a dagger in his possession, shall be tried by court-martial.

21st, Munich:
(To the Empress.) I arrived here yesterday, and in good health. I shall stop one day in Stuttgardt. You shall have twenty-four hours' notice of my arrival at Fontainebleau. I am impatient to see you again.

22d. (To the Empress.) Dear friend: I start in one hour; I shall reach Fontainebleau on the 26th or 27th; you may go there with a few of your ladies.

26th, Fontainebleau:
I have arrived; it is ten o'clock in the morning. The weather is lovely.

November 23d, Paris:
(To General Clarke.) Summon a council of the Guard to go over the accounts and get it into shape for the Spanish campaign. I propose going to Spain with nearly 25,000 men. I want the Guard all ready to start about the 15th of January.

30th. *The divorce question.*
(To Josephine.) Will you do it of your own free will, or won't you? My mind is made up!

December 1st. Josephine sent me word that she consented. As we were sitting down to dinner she suddenly uttered a cry and fainted.

3d. I have annexed Tuscany to the Empire. Its people are worthy of it because of their good character and of the attachment their forefathers have always shown us, and of the services they have rendered to European civilization.

(To the Empress.) I am going to Paris, dear friend. I want to hear that you are happy. I shall see you some time this week. I have received your letters which I shall read in the carriage.

15th. (To Prince Cambacérès.) My Cousin: We have ordered the convocation of a privy council to be held) to-day at nine in the evening at our palace of the Tuileries.

We have deemed it proper not to assist in person at this Council, and we have written the present letter to inform you that it is our will that you should place before it the following proposed Senatus Consultum:

The Senate, in view of the decree of the 15th of the present month drawn up by the Archchancellor, decrees as follows:

The marriage contracted between the Emperor Napoleon and the Empress Josephine is dissolved.

The ceremony took place in the state apartments of the Tuileries and was very touching; all those present wept.

The policy of my Empire, the interests, the needs of my people, which have guided all my actions, demand that I should leave after me, to my children,—the heirs of my affection for my people,—the throne on which Providence has placed me. I have, however, for some years past, lost hope of having children from my marriage with my beloved wife the Empress Josephine: and it is this has brought me to sacrifice my dearest affections, to consider only the good of the State, and to wish the dissolution of our marriage. At the age of forty I may yet hold the hope of living long enough to bring up in my own way of thinking the children which it may please Providence to grant me. God knows how much my present resolve has cost me, but no sacrifice goes beyond my courage when it can be shown to be for the interests of France.

17th, Trianon:
(To the Empress Josephine.) I think, dear friend, that you were weaker than you should have been to-day. You have shown courage; you must keep it up; you must not give way to a dangerous melancholy; you must be happy, and look after your health, which is so precious to me. If you are attached to me, if you love me, you must show strength. You cannot doubt my constant and loving friendship, and you would only show how little you know me if you thought that I could be happy unless you are. Good-bye, dear friend, sleep well,—remember that I want you to.

18th. My expenses are enormous and I really must consider reforms. My army, on its present basis, would eat up three times the actual revenue of France.

19th. (To the Empress.) I have just received your letter. Savary tells me that you do nothing but cry; it's very wrong of you. I hope that you were able to get out to-day. I have sent you some game from my bag. I will come and see you when you let me know that you are more reasonable, and that your courage has returned. Good-bye, dear friend, I also am sad to-day; I want to hear that you are contented, and are regaining your balance. Sleep well.

(To Marshal Augereau.) I have received your letter of the 11th of December, with the capitulation of Gerona, which your aide-de-camp has handed me. Your news gives me a double pleasure, because of the importance of the fortress, and because it is you have captured it.

22d. (To the Empress Josephine.) I would have come to see you to-day had it not been necessary for me to call on the King of Bavaria, who has just arrived in Paris. I hope to see you to-morrow.

27th. (To Josephine.) Eugène tells me you were quite sad yesterday; it is very wrong of you, dear friend, and contrary to what you had promised. I am very bored at seeing the Tuileries again; this great palace seems empty and I feel isolated.

31st. To-day there is a grand parade; I shall see all my Old Guard with sixty artillery trains.

(To Alexander I, Emperor of Russia.) My Brother: I have received a second note from your Chancellor Romanzoff; it grieves me. Why turn back to matters that were disposed of by my letter from Vienna? After all this, I don't know what people want; I cannot destroy chimeras or tilt against clouds. I leave it to Your Majesty to decide which of us holds closer to the language of alliance and friendship. A beginning of suspicion means that. Erfurt and Tilsit are already forgotten.

1810

January 1st, Paris:
Hereafter the Popes shall swear allegiance to me, as they did to Charlemagne and his predecessors. They will not be inducted until after my consent, as the use was for the Emperors of Constantinople to confirm them. But from the present Pope I demand nothing; I ask him for no oath, not even to recognise the annexation of Rome to France; I have no need for it.

17th, Trianon:
(To Josephine.) D'Audenarde, whom I sent to you this morning, tells me that since you reached Malmaison all your courage has gone. And yet the place is full of our love, which must and can never change, at least on my side. I want to see you very much; but I must be sure that you will be strong and not weak; I feel the same way, a little, myself, and it makes me suffer horribly. Good-bye, Josephine, good-night; you would be ingrate to doubt me.

February 6th, Paris:
A council was held a few days back at which opinions were divided as to the Russian and Austrian princesses.

(To Champagny.) I must ask you to get the courier off to Russia, according to my instructions, before going to bed. Do not mention to-night's session. To-morrow night, after you have concluded with Prince Schwarzenberg, you will send off a second one, announcing that I have decided for the Austrian. Come to my levee tomorrow, and bring me the contract of Louis XVI with the documents.

7th. So people are pleased that I am marrying, are they?

(Decrès: Yes, sire, very much so.)

I understand!—they think the lion is going to sleep. Well, they are mistaken. He might perhaps enjoy sleep as much as any one. But can't you see that although I always appear to be attacking, yet what I am doing is defending myself all the time?

(To Champagny.) Kindly transmit the following instructions to M. Otto. As the courier carrying the marriage contract may reach Vienna on the 13th, he can send one back on the 14th to confirm the ratification; we shall get this in Paris on the 21st. The Prince of Neuchâtel, who has been designated as Ambassador Extraordinary for requesting the hand of the Princess, could start on the 22d; he would reach Vienna on the 28th or 29th, and present his request on the following day. Before his arrival M. Otto must have settled all the questions of ceremonial for celebrating the marriage by procuration. The marriage might be fixed for the 2d of March. The Princess could finish the Carnival in Vienna, and start on Ash Wednesday.

23d, Rambouillet:
The convention for the contract of marriage between me and the Archduchess Maria Louisa was ratified at Vienna on the 16th.

(To the Archduchess Maria Louisa of Austria.) My Cousin: the brilliant qualities that mark you have made me wish to serve and honour you. May I hope that you will look favourably on the step I have taken in begging the Emperor your father to intrust your happiness to me? May I flatter myself that your approval will not be wholly determined by duty and obedience to your parents? If only your Imperial Highness will manifest some little partiality for me I am determined, by making it my constant effort to please you in all things, to succeed in making myself agreeable to you sooner or later; that is my object, one for which I beg the favour of Your Imperial Highness.

March 4th. (To the Deputation of the Senate.) Senators, I am touched by the sentiments you have expressed. The Empress Maria Louisa will be a tender mother for the French Nation, and in so doing will make my happiness. I rejoice that Providence has called me to reign over this loving and responsive Nation that I have ever found so faithful and so good to me through the events of my life.

11th. (ToFouché.) I had told you to prevent the news-papers from writing about the Empress Josephine, yet, they do almost nothing else: to-day again the *Publiciste* is full of it. See to it that the papers to-morrow don't republish the *Publiciist's* news.

16th. (To Champagny.) Make up the courier's bag for St. Petersburg. Inform the Duke of Vicenza that the grievances of Russia appear ridiculous to me; that he must talk to the Emperor straight; that the Emperor does me an injustice in believing that there was a double negotiation; that I know enough not to have done such a thing; that it was only when it became clear that the Emperor was not master in his own family, and that he was not acting up to our agreement of Erfurt, that we opened a negotiation with Austria, a negotiation begun and concluded in twenty-four hours, because Austria had sent her Ambassador full powers that covered the case.

20th. I am starting for Compiègne.

28th, Compiegne:
(To Francis I, Emperor of Austria.) *Monsieur mon Frère et Beau Père:* Your Majesty's daughter arrived here two days ago. She fulfils all my expectations and during these two days I have not ceased to give and to receive from her the proofs of the tender sentiments that unite us. We suit one another perfectly. I shall make her happiness, and shall owe mine to Your Majesty.

To morrow we start for Saint Cloud, and on the 2d of April we will celebrate the ceremony of our marriage at the Tuileries.

(To the Archduke Charles.) My Cousin: I owe many thanks to Your Imperial Highness for having consented to act as my representative at my marriage with the Archduchess Maria Louisa. She arrived here two days ago, and I have very sincerely renewed to her the promises that you made in my name.

Your Highness knows that my high regard for you dates back many years, and is founded on your high qualities and actions. I am anxious to mark it by some substantial token, and so beg you to accept the Grand Eagle of the Legion of Honour. I also beg you to accept the medal of the Legion of Honour, which I myself wear, and which is worn by twenty thousand soldiers who have been mutilated or distinguished on the field of battle. The one is a tribute to your talent as a general, and the other to your rare courage as a soldier.

April 21st, Compiègne:
(To the Empress Josephine.) Dear friend: I have received your letter of the 19th of April; it is in bad taste. I am always the same; men like me never change. It

pleases me to hear that you propose going to Malmaison, and that you are happy; it would make me so to hear from you and to reply. I leave you to judge who is the better and inore friendly, you or I. Good-bye, dear friend; keep well, and be fair to yourself and to me.

28th. (To the Empress Josephine.) Don't listen to the gossips of Paris; they are good-for-nothings who are far from knowing the real facts. My sentiments for you are unchangeable and I am anxious to hear that you are happy and contented.

May 20th, Bruges:
(To Josephine.) I want to see you. If you are at Malmaison at the end of the month I shall come to see you. I expect to reach Saint Cloud on the 30th. My health is excellent, all I need is to have you happy and well.

23d, Lille:
(To Louis, King of Holland.) It is time I should know whether you really intend being an affliction for Holland, and by your folly bringing that country to ruin. I will not permit you to send a minister to Austria. I will not allow you to dismiss the Frenchmen who are in your service. I shall not maintain an ambassador in Holland any longer, but leave only a chargé d'affaires. Don't write me any more of your platitudes; I have been listening to them for three years past. This is the last time in my life I shall ever write to you.

July 1st, Paris:
What does Russia want? Is it war? Why these continuous complaints? Why these insulting doubts? Had I wished to restore Poland I would have said so, and I would not have withdrawn my troops from Germany. Does Russia wish to prepare me for her defection? I shall be at war with her the very day she makes peace with England.

I do not wish to regtore Poland. I do not wish to accomplish my destiny in the sands and the desert. But I will not dishonour myself by declaring that the kingdom of Poland will never be restored. No, I cannot undertake to arm against people who have always shown me the greatest good-will and constant devotion. For their own sake and for Russia's I exhort them to be quiet and to submit, but I will not declare myself their enemy, and I will not say to the French: your blood must flow to place Poland under the yoke of Russia.

September 6th, Saint Cloud:
(To Charles XIII, King of Sweden.) My Brother: Count Rosen has handed me your letter of the 21st of August. Your Majesty informs me that the Diet has chosen the Prince of Ponte Corvo as Prince Royal of Sweden, and asks me for my permission for him to accept. I was quite unprepared for this intelligence. Yet I appreciate the sentiments that have led the Swedish nation to give to my people and my army this proof of its esteem. I authorise the Prince of Ponte Corvo to accept the throne to which he is called by Your Majesty and the Swedish people.

November 4th, Fontainebleau:
The colonial produce placed on the market at the Leipzig fair was conveyed in 700 carts from Russia; which means that to-day the whole trade in colonial produce goes through Russia, and that the 1200 merchantmen that were masked by the Swedish, Portugese, Spanish, and American flags, and that were escorted by twenty English men-of-war, have in part discharged their cargoes in Russia.

23d, Paris:
(To General Savary.) In to-day's number the *Journal de l'Empire* states that I was having a statue of the Emperor of Austria made in Vienna, doubtless with a view to placing it in some public square of Paris. Don't fail to tell M. Etienne that the next time he allows such stuff to get into print I shall discharge him from the editorship of the paper.

The Germans are so notoriously silly that I am surprised that Etienne, who ought to know better, should be taken in. Why not repeat, on the authority of the German papers, that I kiss the slipper of the Princess Louisa, whom I don't even know? There is a thing with extreme absurdity to recommend it. It is the newspapers of Paris that should state what I am doing, not the gazettes of Vienna.

December 5th. The Russians are throwing up many earthworks on the Dwina and even on the Dniester.

(To Champagny.) Let me have on the 15th of December a statement showing the strength of the troops of the Confederation of the Rhine, including the Duchy of Warsaw, another for the Russian army, and another for the Austrian.

26th. We have news from London up to the 22d, showing that Masséna still occupied Santarem; there had been a few skirmishes in which the English had been repulsed, and Lord Wellington had fallen back on his positions at Lisbon.

1811

January 5th. The Emperor desires that M. Barbier should send him as soon as possible the results of his investigations as to whether there are instances of Emperors having suspended or deposed Popes.

Yesterday, at the Council of State, I took occasion to ask Count Portalis whether he had seen a libel by the Pope now circulating here inciting to rebellion. After hesitating, this Councillor of State admitted that he had, whereupon I dismissed him from my Council, deprived him of is offices, and exiled him forty leagues from Paris.

February 28th. (To Alexander, Emperor of Russia.) I have commissioned Prince Tschernitchef to present my compliments to Your Majesty. My sentiments have not changed, although I realize that Your Majesty is no longer my friend, our alliance is already broken in the eyes of England and of Europe; even if it still subsisted in Your Majesty's mind, as it does in mine, this widespread opinion would do the greatest harm. I remain in my old position, but I am struck by these obvious facts, and by the opinion that as soon as an opportunity presents itself Your Majesty is ready to come to an understanding with England, which is equivalent to beginning war between our two Empires.

March 9th. (To the Prince of Neuchâtel.) Please write a personal letter to General Suchet expressing my satisfaction with his conduct in the recent campaign, and stating that I expect much from him in pushing the siege of Tarragona briskly. It is in Tarragona he will find his baton of Marshal of France.

19th. At seven in the afternoon the Empress sent for me. I found her on the sofa, feeling the first pains. She went to bed at eight, and from that moment felt rather acute pains, but that brought the event no nearer. The doctors thought it might be another twenty-four hours, so I dismissed the Court and informed the members of the Senate, the municipality, and the Chapter of Paris, who were all assembled, that they could retire.

20th. This morning at eight Dubois ran in, he was pale as death and very agitated; I shouted to him:—Well, is she dead? If she is dead, we will have a funeral!—because I am accustomed to great events, and it is not when I am brought face to face with them that they affect me; it's only afterwards. Whatever news might be brought to me I should show nothing. It is only an hour later that I feel any bad effects.

Dubois answered no, but that the child presented itself sideways. It was most unfortunate, because that's a thing that doesn't happen once in two thousand times. I ran down quickly to the Empress' apartments. She was screaming horribly. I am not soft-hearted, and yet to see her suffering as she was moved me. Dubois, who had lost his head, decided to wait for Corvisart, who put new courage into him.. The Duchess of Montebello stood around like a fool. Ivan and Corvisart held the Empress....

The King of Rome was at least a minute before he uttered a sound; as I came in he was lying on the carpet as though dead. Mme. de Montebello wanted to adhere to etiquette. Corvisart sent her about her business. At last, after considerable friction, the child came to; he had only been scratched on the head by the irons. The Empress had thought it was all over with her; she was convinced that she would be sacrificed for the child; and yet I had said that the opposite should be done.

21st. The child is perfectly well; the Empress as well as can be expected; she has already slept a little and taken, a little nourishment.

22d. Monge, Berthollet, Laplace, are thoroughgoing atheists. My belief is that man sprang from earth heated by the sun and combined with electric fluids.

April 2d. The Emperor Alexander is already far from the ideas of Tilsit; every suggestion of war has its origin in Russia. Unless the Emperor turns the current back very promptly, it will certainly carry him away next year in spite of himself, in spite of the interests of France, and of those of Russia; I have so often watched the process that my experience of the past unfolds the future to me. It is all an opera setting with the English pulling the wires.

13th. I have appointed the 2d of June next for the baptism of the King of Rome, which will be celebrated at Notre Dame, where the Empress and I will proceed in state to render thanks to God for his birth. After the ceremony I shall dine at the Hôtel de Ville of my good city of Paris, and will attend the illuminations. On the same day a Te Deum will be sung throughout the Empire.

May 27th, Caen:
I cannot appoint a commander-in-chief for all my armies in Spain, because I can find no one fit for the job.

June 23d, Saint Cloud:
So many horses have been bought up for Spain and for army remounts, that France has been drained of horses.

July 5th. (To Marshal Davout.) Colonial produce coming from Sweden and from Prussia must be confiscated, because it comes from England; all colonial produce must be confiscated, wherever it comes from, because it all comes from England. Issue orders and see to it that all colonial produce is confiscated wherever it comes from.

15th, Trianon:
(To Maret.) There are no American ships; all the socalled American ships are English, or chartered on English account; if the American minister maintains the contrary, he doesn't know what he is talking about.

August 18th, Paris:
Gentlemen, deputies of the department of the Lippe. the city of Münster belonged to an ecclesiastical prince: deplorable result of ignorance, and superstition! You had no fatherland. Providence, that has enabled me to restore the throne of Charlemagne, has by a natural course brought you back, together with Holland and the Hanseatic cities, within the fold of the Empire. From the moment when you became Frenchmen, my heart made no difference between you and the other parts of my dominions. As soon as circumstances permit I shall feel a keen satisfaction in visiting your country.

September 25th, on board the *Charlemagne* off Flushing:
We have been thirty-six hours without communication with the land because a storm sprang up. It did not prevent my eating and sleeping well. The sea was rough, but the anchorage is a good one. As the weather is moderating, I expect to put the fleet through evolutions to-morrow.

30th, Antwerp:
I arrived to-day at one in the morning, very pleased with my fleet, with its appearance, its morale, and its manœuvring power.

November 1st, Wesel:
The Empress Maria Louisa has only 500,000 francs; she settles her accounts every week; she goes without dresses and accepts all sorts of deprivations so as not to get into debt.

3d, Dusseldorf:
To-morrow I shall review several regiments of cuirassiers at Cologne. After that I go straight to Paris.

6th, Cologne:
If Russia will disarm I am perfectly willing to do the same; it would quiet Prussia and reassure the world; but she must not show us displeasure, a thing which, as between great Powers, always implies war.

December 2d, Paris:
(To Davout.) I reply to one of your last letters. The Germans complain that at Rostock you declared that you would know how to prevent Germany becoming a second Spain; that so long as you were in command, no one would venture to stir. There is no parallel between Spain and the provinces of Germany. Spain would long since have been conquered without her 60,000 English and her 1000 leagues of coastline, and without the 100 millions she has drawn from America. But as in Germany we have no America, no sea, no great number of fortresses, no 60,000 English, there is nothing to fear.

I don't know why Rapp interferes in what does not concern him. Why does he talk about what is going on in Hungary, of the state of opinion in the Confederation, when he is at a distance from those countries? Let him look after his own government and attend to his own business, and confine his reports to Dantzig and its neighbourhood. I must ask you not to place such rhapsodies before me again; my time is too valuable to spend it over such rubbish. Do you propose to post me on affairs in Hungary and Austria by reports from Dantzig, especially coming from Rapp, a weak man of whom I have little enough opinion, save when he is actually on the battlefield? It all results merely in wasting my time and fouling my imagination with absurd pictures and suppositions.

13th. (To Count Decrès.) I have received your letter, and I do not agree with your views. I think too much of your services to grant your request. Remain in the position in which Providence and my will have placed you; you are in strong enough health to serve me another ten years.

16th. The Princes of the Confederation must be notified as to the necessity for remounting their cavalry and preparing their contingents.

The Guard must be got ready for active service.

17th. (To General Savary.) The Tuscan newspapers give in great detail all the doings of the Grand Duchess. The Paris newspapers, as might be expected, reproduce them too frequently. I read in one article that some French crews shouted "Vive Eliza! Vive l'Empereur!" The thing is too ridiculous!

19th. His Majesty wants the most detailed accounts we have in French of the campaign of Charles XII in Poland and in Russia.

1812

January 16th, Paris:
(To the Prince of Neuchâtel and of Wagram.) My Cousin: Everything that belongs to your staff and to general headquarters must be assembled at Mainz between the 15th of February and the 1st of March.

24th. I propose having 2016 carts, 4 battalions totalling 2424 carriages, 4 battalions of ox teams making 1224 carts, one battalion of ox teams for the kingdom of Italy with 306 carts; grand total 17 battalions with close on 6000 vehicles, and carrying 5500 to 6000 tons, equal to one million rations of flour, or enough to supply an army of 200,000 men for two months.

February 18th. (To Marshal Marmont.) You are superior to the enemy, and yet instead of taking the initiative you accept the defensive. You are constantly moving your troops and fatiguing them. That is not the art of war. The capture of Ciudad Rodrigo is a check for you.

19th. (To Marshal Bessières.) Start the 3d regiment of the grenadiers of the Guard to-morrow, the 20th, for Metz, without going through Paris. The regiment will take its guns and wagons with it. Order the Polish light horse to Compiègne to-morrow. Keep the secret, so that the Poles shall not know where they are going. Take good care to make these movements at night and that the troops do not know their destination.

21st. Order for the Prince of Eckmühl to begin his movement immediately.

24th. (To the Emperor Alexander.) After the arrival of the courier sent off by Count Lauriston on the 6th of this month, I decided to have a talk with Colonel Tschernitchef on the unfortunate events of the last fifteen months. It lies entirely with Your Majesty to settle everything. I hope Your Majesty will never doubt my anxiety to display every proof of my highest regard.

March 28th. (To Prince Eugène, Viceroy of Italy.) Get everything ready for a start, as in three or four days I will send for you to come to Paris, and it may be that from Paris you will proceed directly to Glogau, and from Glogau to your army corps. I must not leave you in ignorance of the fact that I concluded an alliance with Austria several months ago, and that she will make common cause with me, and furnish me with a contingent of 40,000 men.

April 23d. (To the Prince of Neuchâtel.) We are getting closer to war, and must increase in firmness and vigilance. Here are my instructions: It is in conformity with the spirit of the treaty that no Prussian general or officer should command in Berlin; there must be no Prussian troops in the city; it must be under the control of a French general. The best way of insuring the tranquillity of Prussia is to leave her incapable of making a single movement.

The Duke of Belluno must always show the greatest respect for the King and the Prussian government; this may be carried to the point of affectation on all ceremonial and similar occasions.

May 4th. (To Berthier.) On Tuesday you may hand over to the Minister of War all business relating to the armies in Spain, so that you can be ready to start on the night of Tuesday to Wednesday.

21st, Dresden:
I arrived here day before yesterday with the Empress, and the Emperor and Empress of Austria. I expect to remain several days. My whole army is on the Vistula. As yet there are no new developments. Hostilities have not yet begun.

26th. I may possibly open war operations on the 6th of June, without being at war, however, as I shall have six or eight days' marching in the territory of Prussia and the Grand Duchy.

June 5th, Thorn:
(To General Clarke.) It would seem that people in Paris view the army as the end of all things, and try to find excuses for not joining. Recall all officers on leave and send them to the front.

The fortress of Thorn appears to be in a state of anarchy.

The Guard is concentrating here. I expect to parade it to-morrow, to settle some questions of administration, and to push on to Marienberg and Dantzig.

6th. (To Jerome.) I believe I have already told you how best to open the campaign: first, make a show of entering Volhynia, and hold the enemy there as much as possible while I outmarch them on their extreme right, and gain twelve or fifteen days' march in the direction of St. Petersburg. I shall cross the Niemen and take Vilna, which is the first objective of the campaign.

When our manœuvre is unmasked, the enemy will decide on one of the two following alternatives: they will either retreat into the interior so as to concentrate for battle, or they will take the offensive.

8th, Dantzig:
(To Josephine.) It will always be with the greatest interest that I hear from you, dear friend. I hope the waters will do you good, and I look forward with pleasure to seeing you on your return. I will attend to all the matters you refer to.

10th, Dantzig:
To-morrow I start for Koenigsberg, which I shall reach at 2 A. M. on the 12th.

13th, Koenigsberg:
(To Berthier.) I send you a letter of to-day's date from Commissary Deschamps which reveals the had situation of the 2d corps for provisions. It is entirely the fault at the Duke of Reggio and of the commissary. Tell the Marshal that it is most important he should have his supplies assured.

15th. I am inclined to think the first shot will be fired on the 22d or 23d. To-morrow I shall carry my headquarters to Wehlau.

16th. (To Berthier.) Write to the Duke of Elchingen that his corps should not leave the route marked out for it, and that it is carrying devastation everywhere.

17th, Insterburg:
(To Eugène.) Stop your advance until further orders for above all things you must have provisions. Let know what amount of bread you had on the evening of the 19th. I shall decide then whether to order you forward. In this country bread is the chief thing.

(To Davout.) I assume you have supplies for twenty-five days.

22d, Imperial headquarters, Wilkowyski:
(Proclamation to the Grand Army.) Soldiers! The second Polish war has begun; the first ended at Friedland and Tilsit. At Tilsit Russia pledged an eternal alliance with France, and war on England! To-day her oath is broken. She refuses all explanations of her strange conduct unless the French eagles recross the Rhine. Fate draws Russia on; her destiny must be accomplished! Does she then think us degenerate? Are we no longer the soldiers of Austerlitz? She places us between dishonour and war; can our choice be in doubt? Forward, then, across the Niemen, and let us carry the war on to her own soil!

The Emperor orders the marshals and generals in command of army corps, of divisions and of brigades, and colonels, to take all measures for maintaining the strictest discipline and for preventing the disorders that are beginning to ravage the country.

24th, Kovno:
(To the Prince of Neuchâtel.) Tell the King of Naples that until he reaches the steppes he had better not encumber himself with too much cavalry; he must use the cuirassiers as little as possible; he only has to brush aside the enemy's light troops, and to try for news in the direction of Vilna.

29th, Vilna:
We entered Vilna yesterday; the enemy had evacuated the town after burning the bridge and immense quantities of stores.

30th. We are still anxiously awaiting the arrival of our transport trains from Tilsit.

(To Marshal Davout.) Herewith is a report of General Bordesoulle, which shows the movement of Doktourof's corps on Ochmiana; try to discover the direction of the Russians.

July 1st. (To the Emperor Alexander.) After having for eighteen months constantly refused to give me an explanation, Your Majesty has at last, through your Minister, placed a summons before me to evacuate Prussia as a preliminary to an understanding. A few days later this Minister asked for his passports, and three times repeated that demand. From that moment I was in a state of war with Your

Majesty, and by that step Your Majesty was taking from Prussia that very independence which it appeared that Your Majesty wished to guarantee, while pointing out to me the Caudine Forks. I pity the wickedness of those who could give Your Majesty such advice. But however it may be, never shall Russia use such language to France; it might possibly be accepted in the mouth of the Empress Catherine and addressed to the last of the Kings of Poland.

War has therefore begun between us. God himself cannot undo what is done; but I shall always be ready to listen to proposals for peace, and when Your Majesty really attempts to cut loose from the influence of men who are the enemies of your family, of your glory, and of that of your Empire, you will always find me of the same mind and of equal friendship.

3d. The whole of the Guard is at Vilna. The Viceroy's corps is here.

4th. (To Berthier.) Write to the Duke of Elchingen that the condition of his corps is alarming. Tell him to send out detachments of cavalry, commanded by staff officers, to bring the stragglers up; many of them are committing crimes, and will finish by getting picked up by the Cossacks.

7th. The Guard must march. But I shall not feel easy until the Guard and headquarters have secured twenty days' provisions, as they come last and must set an example of discipline.

8th. We lose so many horses in this country that with all the resources of France and Germany it will be very difficult to keep up the present strength of our mounted troops.

10th. (To Berthier.) Send a brigade of gendarmes to Voronovo. They will arrest the looters of the 33d, who are devastating that country horribly.

14th. Deputies of the Polish Confederation, I have listened to your address with interest. The love of country is the highest virtue of civilized man. My position entails the harmonizing of many interests and the carrying out of many duties. Had I lived in the days of the first, the second, or the third partition of Poland, I would have armed my whole people to support you. I feel affection for your nation; during sixteen years your soldiers have fought by my side on the fields of Italy as on those of Spain.

If your efforts are united you may hope to compel your enemies to recognise your rights.

15th. The enemy have attacked Sebastiani's cavalry. The King of Naples is taking position at Ikazni with the 2d, 3d, and part of the 1st corps, and all his cavalry.

19th, Gloubokoie:
I have just got fresh news from Drissa. The enemy have abandoned their fortified camp. Their movements seem very uncertain.

22d. The King of Naples is marching on Polotsk and has overrun the whole of the right bank of the Dwina with his cavalry.

(To the Prince of Neuchâtel.) Reply to General Jomini that it is absurd to say there is no bread when we have 25 tons of flour a day. Instead of complaining let him be up at four in the morning, proceed to the mills and to the baking ovens in person, and have 30,000 rations of bread baked every day; if he goes to sleep, or if he whines, he will get nothing.

We shall soon have a battle that will eat up an enormous amount of powder and supplies: how are we to replenish our stores? Must we send empty wagons back to Vilna? That would mean a month or six weeks before we could get them to the front again.

24th, Kamen:
The enemy appear to be at Vitebsk; we are marching there.

25th, Biechenkovitchi:
The Prince of Eckmühl was in action on the 23d at Mohilef; I have no details. Bagration attempted to force his way through but was thrown back.

26th. I am starting immediately. If the enemy hold their positions we shall have a battle day after to-morrow.

29th, Vitebsk:
The enemy are retreating on all sides; we cannot catch them up.

August 1st. General Guyon's light cavalry brigade has pushed as far as Nevel, and found nothing; the Viceroy has also pushed out detachments as far as Velije.

2d. Nothing new.

6th. I propose marching straight on the enemy, probably by the left bank of the Dnieper, capturing Smolensk and bringing the Russian army to battle if it chooses to remain in its present position.

7th. (To Barbier.) The Emperor would like a few amusing books. If there are any good new novels, or old ones he has not read, or some interesting memoirs, you might send them on, for we have spare time here that is not easy to kill.

10th. My information is that the enemy have completely withdrawn; we have pushed out parties for several leagues and have not seen them.

15th, bivouac at Boyarintsova:
I am marching on Smolensk. We may have a great battle to-morrow. The advance guard was engaged yesterday, and the 27th Russian division was smashed.

18th, Smolensk:
I am just in, the heat is oppressive and there is much dust, which is rather tiring. The whole of the enemy's army was here; it was under orders to fight, but didn't dare to. We had to force our way into Smolensk.

The Russian army, which is very discouraged and dissatisfied, is retreating in the direction of Moscow.

23d. (To the Countess de Montesquiou.) I have received the King (of Rome's) portrait, and think it a good likeness. I have pleasure in taking this opportunity to express all my satisfaction for the good care that you take of him.

(To Marshal Davout.) On hearing from you to-night, I shall move the Guard forward so that if the enemy will wait for us we can give battle.

26th, Dorogobouje:
After throwing up earthworks, batteries, and redoubts, and after announcing their intention of holding them, the enemy, as usual, have shown the white feather. We are now in this town, which is sizable, that is to say has eight or ten churches. The country is good, and people say it remains fertile all the way to Moscow. The heat is excessive, the weather splendid. Reports state the enemy are resolved to make a stand at Viazma.

29th, Viazma:
We have reached Viazma. The enemy continue their retreat on Moscow.

September 1st, Velitchevo.
The enemy are across the main road in front of the King of Naples and our advance guard.

2d, Ghjiatsk:
(To the Prince of Neuchâtel.) My Cousin: Order the King of Naples, the Prince of Eckmühl, the Viceroy, Prince Poniatowski, the Duke of Elchingen, to take a day's rest, to get in their stragglers, to have a roll-call at three in the afternoon, and to let me know precisely the number of men they can place in line.

The staff is useless; not one of the officers does his duty properly, not the provost-general, nor the quartermaster.

You have my order for the baggage. See to it that the first baggage wagons I order burnt are not those of the general staff.

3d. (To the Prince of Neuchâtel.) Write to officers commanding army corps that we lose many men daily because there is no system in the supply service; it is urgently necessary that they should take measures in concert with their colonels to put an end to a state of things that threatens the army with destruction. Every day the enemy pick up several hundred prisoners. During the twenty years in which I have commanded French armies, I have never seen the commissariat service so hopelessly bad; there is no one; the people sent out here have no ability and no experience.

7th, on the heights of Borodino:
Soldiers, here at last is the battle that you have so long expected! Victory now depends on your efforts, and is essential. It will give us abundance, good winter quarters, and a speedy return to our country. Do what you did at Austerlitz, at Friedland, at Vitebsk, at Smolensk, and let posterity point with pride to your conduct on this day: let people say of you: "He was at that great battle fought under the walls of Moscow!"

8th. *Battle of Borodino.*
The battle of Borodino is the most glorious, most difficult, and most creditable operation of war carried out by the Gauls, of which either ancient or modern history makes mention. Dauntless heroes,—Murat, Ney, Poniatowski,—it is to you the glory is due! What great, what splendid deeds History might place on record! How our intrepid cuirassiers charged and sabred the gunners, on their guns; the heroic devotion of Montbrun, of Caulaincourt, who found death in the midst of their glory; our gunners, in the open and without cover, firing against a heavier artillery protected by earthworks; and our brave infantry, at the most critical moment, not in need of their general's steadying voice, but calling out to him.: "It's all right! your soldiers have sworn they will conquer, and they will!"

The Russian army of Austerlitz would not have been driven from the field of Borodino.

9th, Mojaisk:
(To Francis I, Emperor of Austria.) I take the earliest opportunity of informing Your Majesty of the fortunate result of the battle fought on the 7th of September at the village of Borodino. Knowing the personal interest Your Majesty is good enough to take in me, I wished to announce the event myself; and to add that my health is perfect. I estimate the enemy's loss at 40,000 or 50,000; they had 120,000 to 130,000 men in line. I lost 8000 or 10,000 killed and wounded. I captured 60 guns and a large number of prisoners.

10th. We are in great need of French muskets; we want them at Vilna, at Minsk, at Smolensk, and at the abbey near the battlefield, to arm the stragglers and the wounded who have lost theirs.

18th, Borisovka:
We had marched but a few miles from Mojaisk when we were astonished to find ourselves, notwithstanding our proximity to one of the great capitals of the world, in the midst of a sandy and absolutely desert waste.

The army crossed the place with difficulty. Our horses were harassed and worn out with hunger and thirst, for water was as scarce as forage. The men suffered very much.

14th, Moscow:
We arrived at Moscow in the evening.

15th. *The fire of Moscow begins.*

18th. We are following the enemy, who have withdrawn beyond the Volga. We have found immense quantities of valuables in Moscow, which was a beautiful city. Russia will not recover from her loss in two hundred years. Without exaggeration it must amount to a thousand millions of francs.

20th. (To the Emperor Alexander.) *Monsieur mon Frère:* The beautiful and splendid city of Moscow no longer exists. Rostopchin has burnt it down. Four hundred incendiaries have been caught in the act; all declared they were starting fires by order of the Governor and of the Chief of Police: they were shot. The fire seems to have died out at last; three quarters of the houses have gone, a quarter remains. Such conduct is atrocious and aimless. Was the object to deprive us of a few resources? Well, those resources were in cellars that the fire did not reach. Even then the destruction of one of the most beautiful cities in the world, the work of centuries, for so slight an object, is inconceivable. If I supposed that such things were being done under the orders of Your Majesty, I should not write this letter; but I hold it impossible that any one with the high principles of Your Majesty, such heart, such right feelings, could have authorized these excesses, unworthy as they are of a great sovereign and a great nation.

I have conducted the war against Your Majesty with no animosity. A line written to me before or after the last battle would have stopped my march, and I would gladly have foregone the advantage of entering Moscow, If anything of our old friendship remains, Your Majesty will take this letter in good part. In any case I shall deserve thanks for rendering this account of what is happening in Moscow.

Despite the poet's art, all the imaginary details of the burning of Troy can never equal the reality of that of Moscow. The city was built of wood, the wind was very strong, all the fire engines had been removed. It was literally an ocean of fire!

23d. I have just levied a conscription of 140,000 men in France, and of 30,000 in Italy. The result of the battle of Borodino and our entry into Moscow must not reduce our energy.

October 4th. The enemy's movement towards Kief shows clearly that they are expecting reinforcements from the army of Moldavia. To march against them would be to operate in the line of their reserves, and without any supporting positions. Moscow, now that it is burned down and deserted by its inhabitants, is of no use to us; it cannot even accommodate our sick and wounded.

If the army is to fall back on Smolensk, is it wise to follow up the enemy and to run the risk, while executing a movement that would look like a retreat, of losing several thousand men in the face of an army that knows the country, that has many spies, and a large force of light cavalry?

If we should decide to fall back so as to take up winter quarters in Poland, is it the best course to retire directly by the same road by which we came?

5th. (To Berthier.) I find it hard to believe that we need forty-five days to evacuate the wounded from Mojaisk; for I calculate that, even if we do nothing, in those forty-five days part of them will die, part of them will get well; we should therefore only have to evacuate those that remained, and experience shows that three months after a battle only one-sixth of the wounded remain. Reckoning on 6000, there would therefore be at the end of three months only 1000 to move. My purpose is to keep control of my line of operations and to evacuate the wounded.

6th. The Russian army of Moldavia, amounting to three divisions, crossed the Dnieper early in September. General Koutousoff's army, which was beaten at Borodino, is now near Kaluga, which suggests that it is to be reinforced from Moldavia by way of Kief.

14th. (To Berthier.) Send orders to the Duke of Abrantes not to let through any artillery convoys for Moscow after to-morrow the 15th, and to turn them all back to Smolensk.

15th. (Decree.) There shall be at our Imperial Conservatory eighteen pupils preparing for the Théâtre Français, nine of each sex. They may attend courses in music, but they are more especially to study the art of declamation, and shall diligently follow the courses of the professors, according to the branch they intend to pursue.

For this purpose there shall be, in addition to the professors, two instructors in the dramatic art, who shall teach the students every day at such hours as may be appointed. There shall also be a professor of grammar, and of history and mythology applied to the dramatic art, who shall instruct especially those pupils who are intended for the Théâtre Français.

18th. (To Berthier.) Inform the King of Naples that the whole army is moving. The Duke of Istria with the cavalry of the Guard will march four leagues before camping; I shall start in person to-night.

The Guard will bivouac in square around the Emperor's quarters.

19th. General Sebastiani, placed about one league to the left of the King of Naples, was caught napping by a horde of Cossacks, at five in the morning of the 18th. He lost six guns at his bivouac. The enemy's infantry then marched on the rear of the King of Naples, to cut him off. The King of Naples, at the head of the carabiniers and cuirassiers, broke them and cut them up.

The army is in motion; to-morrow we shall decide to blow up the Kremlin and to march by Kaluga or by Viazma, so as to arrive before severe weather sets in, and get into winter quarters. All is going well.

Well, Rapp, we are retiring on Poland; I shall find good winter quarters; I hope Alexander will make peace.

(Rapp: The natives say we shall have a severe winter.)

Bah! bah! with your natives! Look! See how fine it is!

20th, Troitzkoie:
(To Berthier.) Order the Duke of Treviso to start the invalids of the corps of the Prince of Eckmühl, of the Viceroy, of the dismounted cavalry, and of the Young Guard at daybreak to-morrow. At two in the morning he will set fire to the Kremlin. When the Kremlin is well alight in several places the Duke of Treviso will move by the Mojaisk road. At four o'clock the artillery officer detailed for this service will blow up the Kremlin. On his way he will set fire to all abandoned wagons, will have as many bodies as possible buried, and will smash all the muskets he may find.

11st, Krasnoie:
The Duke of Elchingen will command the rearguard.

23d, Borovsk:
The natives are amazed at the weather of the last three weeks. We are having the sunshine and lovely days of the trip to Fontainebleau. The army is in a very rich country that is comparable with the finest of France and Germany.

26th. (To Berthier.) Write to the Duke of Abrantes to inform him that the Russian army had marched on Malo-Yaroslavetz; that its advance guard reached it on one bank at the same moment as ours did on the other; that the city lay on the enemy's side and on a considerable height, so that an engagement followed which lasted the whole of the 24th; that while our advance guard was engaged the whole Russian army came up; that on our side the Prince of Eckmühl's troops reinforced those of the Viceroy; that we remained in possession of the battlefield. Write further that on the 25th the army was deployed; the Russian army faced us about one league behind Malo-Yaroslavetz, but the necessity of moving the wounded who are with the army made the Emperor decide to march towards Mojaisk.

30th, Ghjatsk:
The general headquarters train will move forward as far as it can go. The division of the Old Guard will remain here all day to rally its stragglers.

November 1st, Viazma:
The 8th corps will reach Dorogobouje to-morrow, where it will find headquarters. We shall be in great need of provisions at Dorogobouje.

3d, Sembvo:
The weather continues very fine, which is most fortunate.

(To Maret.) You must buy all the horses you can get, and above all buy them at once.

5th, Dorogobouje:
Order for the 5th corps to march to-morrow behind the Viceroy, and to press on for Smolensk.

6th. (To Berthier.) Write to the Prince of Eckmühl that if, as I fear, at nine o'clock this morning his corps has no supplies, he must move ten or twelve leagues from Smolensk on the Yelvia road. The country is said to be good and full of provisions. This move will be all the more useful as there is no forage at Smolensk.

7th, Mikhailovka:

(To Berthier.) Write the following letter to the Duke of Belluno, not ciphered:
I have shown the Emperor your letter of the 2d. His Majesty's orders are that you should concentrate your six divisions, attack the enemy at once, drive them beyond the Dwina and reoccupy Polotsk!

Ciphered:
This movement is of urgent importance. In a few days your line of communication may be flooded with Cossacks: the army and the Emperor will reach Smolensk to-morrow, but worn out by a continuous march of 120 leagues. Take the offensive; the safety of the army depends on it; every day lost is a disaster. The cavalry is dismounted, the cold has killed our horses. March, that is the order of the Emperor, and of necessity.

9th, Smolensk:
We must employ to-morrow in getting the troops together, so that on the following day the corps can be formed up to start on their march.

11th. Order for the corps of General Baraguey d'Hilliers to be disbanded.

14th. I am having the fortifications of Smolensk blown up, and shall then start for Orcha.

(To Berthier.) Write to the Duke of Elchingen that it is necessary for him to continue in command of the rearguard.

18th, Doubrovna:
I shall reach Orcha to-morrow.

(To Maret.) Since my last letter to you our situation has become worse. Ice and frost of near zero (Fahr.) have killed off nearly all our horses, say 30,000. We have been compelled to burn nearly 300 pieces of artillery, and an immense quantity of transport wagons. The cold has greatly increased the number of stragglers. The Cossacks have turned to account our absolute want of cavalry and of artillery to harass us and cut our communications so that I am most anxious about Marshal Ney, who stayed behind with 3000 men to blow up Smolensk.

19th. My intention is to move on Minsk, and, after getting possession of that point, to make for the Berezina.

20th, Orcha:
We have found here about 60 guns that are quite useless to us. My health is excellent. I have no news from Marshal Ney; I have given him up.

I have two hundred millions in my cellars; I would give all of it for Ney!

Baran:
My anxiety about Ney has passed; he has just joined us.

21st. We have no maps.

23d, Bobr:
(To Berthier.) Send an aide-de-camp to the Duke of Reggio to tell him that I am impatient to hear from him in the course of to-night that he controls a passage over the Berezina and that he is throwing bridges.

24th. (To Berthier.) Order General Zayonchek to transfer 200 horses, and more if he can, to General Sorbier. If this draft is not made, when I pass to-morrow I shall order every carriage and transport wagon of his corps to be burnt.

General Dombrowski, who held the bridge of Borisof, allowed his position to be forced on the 21st. The Duke of Reggio arrived on the 23d, recaptured the city, and defeated the two Russian divisions that were there. But the bridge is burnt; we hope to build another to-day. The weather is cold. I am anxious to get news from Vilna and from Paris.

25th, Lochnitsa:
The Duke of Belluno will reach Kostritsa about noon, and will be ready to cross the river to-night.

General Eblé has arrived with a number of engineers.

27th, Studienka:
I have just crossed the Berezina; but the river is full of floating ice and our bridges are therefore very insecure. The army that had been facing Schwarzenberg tried to prevent our passage, and is to-night concentrated on the right bank opposite Borisof. The cold is very severe; the army is excessively fatigued.

29th, Zanivki:
(To Maret.) I have received your letter of the 25th in which there is not a word of French news, nor of Spanish. This makes two weeks during which I have heard nothing and am in the dark about everything.

Yesterday we were sharply engaged with Admiral Tchichagof and Wittgenstein. We defeated the first-named, who attacked us on the right bank on the Borisof road. The latter, who attempted to carry our bridges over the Berezina, was contained. The Duke of Reggio was wounded, and many other generals.

The army is numerous but in a frightful state of disbandment. We need two weeks to reform the men into regiments, and where can we get two weeks? Cold and privation have broken up the army. We shall soon reach Vilna; can we stay there? Yes, if we can hold on for eight days; but if we are attacked during the first eight days, it is doubtful whether we can stay there. Food! food! food! Otherwise there are no horrors which this undisciplined mob is not capable of wreaking on the city.

Possibly the army cannot be rallied short of the Niemen.

In this state of things I may decide that my presence in Paris is necessary for the safety of France, of the Empire, of the army itself. Give me your opinion. I am anxious that there should be no agents of foreign powers at Vilna. The army is not good to look at now. As to those who are in the city, they must be got out of the way; you might say to them that you are going to Warsaw, and that I am too, and convey them there, starting at a fixed hour.

30th Plechtchennisky:
If 100,000 rations of bread are not awaiting us at Vilna, I am sorry for the city. An abundance of supplies is the only thing that can bring back discipline. The Governor can meet me to let me know the position of things. The army is horribly worn out. This is the 45th day's march.

December 2d, Selitché:
M. de Montesquiou will start immediately for Paris, and will hand the inclosed letter to the Empress. He will announce everywhere the arrival of 10,000 Russian prisoners and the victory at the Berezina, where we captured 6000 Russian prisoners, 8 flags, and 19 guns.

3d, Molodetchna:
(Bulletin.) Until the 6th of November the weather was perfect and the movement of the army was carried out with complete success. On the 7th the cold set in; from that moment we lost several hundred horses at each night's bivouac. On reaching Smolensk we had already lost an immense quantity of cavalry and artillery horses. The cold became more intense, and between the 14th and 16th the thermometer fell to zero (Fahr.) The roads were covered with ice, the horses were dying every night, not in hundreds but in thousands, especially the French and German horses. More than 30,000 horses died in a few days; our cavalry was dismounted, our artillery and transport had no teams. Without cavalry we could not risk a battle; we were compelled to march so as not to be forced into a battle, which we wished to avoid because of our shortness of ammunition.

The enemy, marching in the footsteps of the frightful calamity that had over-taken the French army, tried to profit by it. All our columns were surrounded by Cossacks who, like the Arabs in the desert, picked up every cart or wagon that lagged behind. This contemptible cavalry, which only knows how to shout and couldn't ride down so much as a company of light infantry, became formidable from the force of circumstances!

But the enemy held the passage of the Berezina, a river 80 yards wide; the water was full of floating ice, and the banks are marshy for a distance of 600 yards, which made it a difficult obstacle to overcome. The enemy had placed four divisions at four points where they supposed the French army would attempt to pass. After having deceived the enemy by various manœuvres on the 25th, the Emperor marched on the village of Studienka at break of day on the 26th, and, in the face of a division of the enemy, had two bridges thrown across the river. The army was crossing all through the 26th and the 27th.

It may be concluded from what has been said that the army needs to reëstablish its discipline, to be reëquipped, to remount its cavalry, its artillery, and its transport.

During all these events the Emperor constantly marched in the midst of the Guard, the cavalry commanded by the Duke of Istria, the infantry by the Duke of Dantzig. Our cavalry was so reduced that it became necessary to form all the officers who were still mounted into four companies of 150 men each. Generals acted as captains; and colonels as corporals. This Sacred Squadron, commanded by General Grouchy, and under the orders of the King of Naples, kept the closest watch over the Emperor.

His Majesty's health has never been better.

4th. There seems to be nothing of much importance about Spain in the *Moniteur*. The defence of the citadel of Burgos is a fine feat of arms. Lord Wellington has drawn back to operate against the army of Andalusia. If we lose a battle there, affairs in that country would become critical.

(To Maret.) If you cannot make the necessary commissariat arrangements at Vilna, we must prepare to evacuate everything, and first and foremost the military chest. We have three or four millions here. I am informed that there is twice as much at Vilna; have all removed to Dantzig.

5th, Binitsa:
(To the Prince of Neuchâtel.) The inclosed decree is to be published in orders two or three days after my departure. Circulate the report that I am proceeding to Warsaw with the 7th and the Austrian corps. Five or six days later, as circumstances may dictate, the King of Naples can issue an order informing the army that I have had to proceed to Paris and have left him in command.

Smorgoni:
(To Prince Eugène.) I have received your letter. Do your duty and trust me. I am always the same, and know best what is good for you. Never doubt my paternal affection.

44th, Dresden:
(To Francis I, Emperor of Austria.) I am stopping for a moment at Dresden to write to Your Majesty and to give you my news. In spite of severe hardships my health has never been better. I started on the 4th from Lithuania, after the battle of the Berezina, leaving the Grand Army under the command of the King of Naples, the Prince of Neuchâtel still acting as chief of staff. In four days I shall be in Paris; I shall stay there through the winter to attend to my most pressing affairs.

I have every confidence in the sentiments of Your Majesty. Our alliance is a permanent arrangement so advantageous to our countries that I feel certain Your Majesty will carry out all the engagements entered into at Dresden to assure the triumph of the common cause and to lead us promptly to a suitable peace.

18th, Paris:
(To the Prince of Neuchâtel.) I note with regret that you did not stop seven or eight days at Vilna, so as to take advantage of the clothing stores and rally the army a little.

19th. I am working incessantly at reorganising all my resources. I have already got an army of 40,000 men in the neighbourhood of Berlin and the Oder.

26th. (To General Clarke.) We must assume that the whole of the artillery belonging to the cavalry and to the 1st, 2d, 3d, 4th, and 6th corps is lost. If necessary I will set the naval arsenals at work on artillery material; that would be better than requisitions. One or two ships more or less are of no weight one way or the other, but the slightest deficiency of artillery might be a very serious matter.

29th. (To Pope Pius VII.) Holy Father: I hasten to send one of the officers of my household to express press all my gratification at what the bishop of Nantes has told me of the satisfactory condition of Your Holiness' health; for I had been for a moment alarmed this summer on hearing that Your Holiness had been seriously indisposed. The new residence of Your Holiness will give us an opportunity for meeting, and I have it much at heart to declare that, notwithstanding all that has passed, I have always maintained the same sentiments of friendship for Your Holiness. Perhaps we can now reach a settlement of all those questions that divide State and Church. I, on my side, am altogether disposed that way, so that it will depend entirely on Your Holiness.

30th. (To Berthier.) I have received your dispatch of the 21st, also your memorandum: *actual losses;* I shall consider it most anxiously. This year's conscription is splendid: I had about 25,000 or 30,000 men on parade Sunday.

1813

January 3d, Paris:
(To General Clarke.) As the King of Spain asks to have the Duke of Dalmatia recalled to Paris, and as that marshal demands the same thing, send him leave of absence by special courier.

Tell the King, writing in cipher, that in the present state of things he should place his headquarters at Valladolid.

7th. (To Francis I.) Every time I met the Russian army I defeated it. My Guard was not once engaged, never fired a shot, nor did it lose a man in the presence of the enemy. It is true that between the 7th and the 16th of November 30,000 of my cavalry and artillery horses died; I abandoned several thousand wagons for lack of horses. In that frightful storm of frost, our men could not stand bivouacking; many wandered off to seek houses for shelter; there was no cavalry left to protect them. Cossacks picked up several thousands.

As for France, I could not be more satisfied with her: men, horses, money, everything is offered me. My finances are in good order. I shall therefore make no advances looking to peace.

Your Majesty can now judge my situation and my views as well as I can, I assume that this letter and its contents will remain a matter between Your Majesty and myself; but, knowing my views, Your Majesty may take any step that appears desirable with a view to peace.

9th. (To Berthier.) On hearing of the treachery of General York I immediately decided to issue an address to the nation, which will be out to-morrow, and to raise an extraordinary levy. I have formed a corps of observation of the Elbe which is concentrating at Hamburg, and will have a strength of 60 battalions; I have given the command to General Lauriston. I have formed a corps of observation in Italy, which is concentrating at Verona, and that will have a strength of 40 battalions; I have given the command to General Bertrand. I have formed a first corps of observation of the army of the Rhine, of 60 battalions, commanded by the Duke of Ragusa, whose headquarters will be at Mainz. I shall form a 2d corps of observation of the Rhine, which will also have 60 battalions. I am calling to the colours 100,000 conscripts left over from 1810, so that we shall have men of over 21 years of age. The conscription of 1814 will give us 150,000 men, and will be levied some time in February.

18th. The Emperor of Russia has just appointed Baron von Stein Minister of State; he admits him to his inmost councils, together with all the men who want to revolutionize Germany.

22d. (To Prince Eugène.) My son: Assume the command of the Grand Army. I regret I did not give it you when I left. I am persuaded that your retirement would have been less rapid, and that I should not have suffered such heavy losses. Past evils are without remedy.

23d. (To Vice-Admiral Count Decrès.) I cannot bring myself to a reduction of my naval armaments; I am not so situated as to weigh 12 or 15 millions against the moral effect that such a retrenchment would product on my navy and on our enemies.

24th. (To Caroline Murat, Queen of Naples.) The King left the army on the 16th. Your husband is very brave on the battlefield, but weaker than a woman or a monk when out of sight of the enemy. He has no moral courage. He has been frightened; he has never for one moment been in danger of losing what he can only hold from me and with me. Show him the absurdity of his conduct. I can still forgive him the harm he has done me.

29th. I have a superb corps of 20,000 marines on the march, in which not one soldier has less than a year's service.

In the coming campaign I shall sweep the enemy back beyond the Niemen.

February 8th. (To Marshal Kellermann.) I approve the steps you have taken for putting down the insurrection in the Grand Duchy of Berg.

10th. (To Maret, Duke of Bassano.) Write to M. de Saint Marsan that the levying of troops now proceeding in Prussia gives us just cause for uneasiness, and that I desire that all should remain quiet.

(To Prince Eugène.) Make the Prussians stop recruiting.

14th. Gentlemen, deputies of the departments to the Legislative Body: The war rekindled in northern Europe proved a favourable opportunity for the English to act in the Peninsula. They have made great efforts; but all their hopes have been deceived. I penetrated into Russia. The French arms were constantly victorious, in the battles of Ostrovno, of Polotsk, of Mohilef, of Smolensk, of the Moskova, of Malo-Yaroslavetz. The Russian armies were not once able to hold their ground against our eagles. Moscow fell into our hands. After the frontiers of Russia had been pierced and the weakness of her armies had been proved, hordes of Tartars turned their parricide hands against the most fertile provinces of the vast Empire to the defence of which they were summoned. In the space of a few weeks, notwithstanding the tears and the despair of the unfortunate Muscovites, they burned down more than 4000 of their most prosperous villages, more than fifty of their finest cities, thus satisfying an old standing hatred on the plea of retarding our march and of surrounding us with a desert. We triumphed over these obstacles; even the fire of Moscow, which in four days ingulfed the fruit of the labour and accumulations of forty generations, did not affect the security of our position. But the excessive and premature severity of winter bore down our army in a frightful calamity. In the space of a few nights all was changed, I suffered great losses; my spirit would have been broken, if, in such circumstances, I could have allowed myself to think of anything but the interests, the glory, and the future of my people.

The misfortunes brought on us by the severity of winter have served to reveal to their fullest extent the grandeur and solidity of this Empire. It is with the most lively sense of satisfaction that we have seen our subjects of the kingdom of Italy, of what was formerly Holland, of the new departments, rivalling the French in showing that their hope, their future, and their interest lie in the consolidation and triumph of the Great Empire.

I need great resources to face all the demands imposed on me by the present circumstances; but by means of the measures that will be laid before you by my Minister of Finance, I shall not have to impose any fresh burdens on my people.

21st. The Duke of Valmy writes that there are no scabbards at Mainz, and no fry-ing-pans, no water-bottles, no boots, and no shirts; and that the few boots left in store at Wesel are very poor.

23d. I propose having my equipment on a smaller footing than in the last cam-paign. I want a much reduced staff, fewer cooks, less crockery, a smaller outfit, and all this not only to simplify matters but also by way of example. In the field each mess, even my own table, shall be served with one soup, one boiled dish, one roast and vegetables; no dessert. In the large cities each mess can do as it pleases.

26th. Patrols of Cossacks have appeared near Berlin; I am anxious as to what to-morrow's courier may bring; I suppose the Viceroy and Marshal Saint Cyr will have driven them off.

March 2d: The Duke of Treviso will reach Mainz on the 12th, and Gotha on the 14th, where he will find the Imperial Guard. The Prince of the Moskowa will reach Frankfort on the 10th of March with the 1st corps of 60 battalions. The Bavarians are concentrating at Bamberg, Bayreuth, and Kronach; the Würtem-bergers, Hessians, and Badeners at Würzburg. The Viceroy is at Berlin.

(To Prince Eugène.) The corps of observation are on the move, 300,000 strong; the scene will soon change.

5th. (To Prince Eugène.) Hold Berlin as long as you can. Make examples to pre-serve order. At the least insult from a Prussian village or city, have it burned down; even Berlin, if it does not behave well. The cavalry is being rapidly trained in France, but we need the whole of April yet.

9th. (To Prince Eugène.) I can't see why you gave up Berlin. Your movements are so hasty that you have not been able to take up the line of march assigned to you. You might have gained us three weeks, which would have been of the greatest advantage in both the political and the military sense.

10th. This is a most alarming state of things! What are 150,000 muskets? Almost nothing; we need 300,000 to arm the levy of 1815, and to have a reserve of 150,000 in store.

11th. (To Prince Eugène.) It is time we began to make war. Our military operations are ridiculed by our allies at Vienna and by our enemies in London and St. Petersburg, because our army consistently retreats a week before the approach of the enemy's infantry, at the sight of their light-horse, or even on mere rumours.

17th. (To Prince Eugène.) My Son: I inclose you a Hamburg bulletin of the 12th from which you will see that 200 Cossacks are going to take possession of the whole of the 32d military district. A number of gunboats have been sunk; it means a loss of many millions; it will mean insurrection in all that lies at the back of the Elbe. It all comes from the fact that from the left bank of the river you have no longer any hold on the enemy.

20th. I have news from Breslau the 12th. The Prussians were arming but still kept up appearances, and Minister was being treated with all due regard.

23d. (To Prince Eugène.) I see in the Prince of Eckmühl's reports that General Régnier's corps numbers only 2000 men; I had always supposed it totalled 12,000. I also see that Dombrowski's corps is reduced to 300 men; I had always supposed, from your reports, that it numbered 3000.

28th. (To Marshal Ney.) The Prince of Eckmühl has blown up the bridge at Dresden, which has had the double effect of angering the inhabitants and of drawing the enemy in that direction. The Viceroy has concentrated on Wittenberg, Magdeburg, and the lower Elbe. Prussia has raised the standard and declared war.

April 8th, Saint Cloud:
(To General Clarke.) Continue the inquiry into General Loison's conduct. The time has come for making examples; the generals show the greatest insubordination; this affects the glory of my arms and the lives of my soldiers. See that the small newspapers state that General Loison, who left the army without leave, is under arrest, and that General Lacroix, who abandoned his post, has been arrested and will be tried by strict martial law.

11th. (To Prince Eugène.) I shall probably reach Erfurt at the head of 200,000 men between the 20th and 22d. I cannot judge what your movements should be. Manœuvre on that assumption, and see that our communications remain open.

12th. I intend to refuse my right and to let the enemy reach Bayreuth, making the converse movement to that of Jena, so that if the enemy should reach Bayreuth I would be at Dresden before them and cut them off from Prussia.

18th. If to-morrow's news confirms the fact that the enemy are executing an important movement, I Shall start instantly.

17th, Mainz:
I travelled to Mainz in 40 hours, in good health and without accidents. I shall stay several days in Mainz to look after matters that require my attention.

20th. (To Frederick Augustus, King of Saxony.) Your Majesty's letter pains me. Your Majesty's friendship for me is gone; for which I hold the enemies of our cause in your cabinet responsible. I need all the cavalry and all the officers. I have stated my views with the frankness Your Majesty knows, to your aide-de-camp. Whatever the event, Your Majesty may rest assured of my esteem.

24th. If I had another 15,000 cavalry I could settle matters very quickly.

26th, Erfurt:
The Guard is in column between Erfurt and Weimar. For the moment the great thing is to effect my junction with the Viceroy. To-night I shall move headquarters to Auerstadt.

(To Prince Cambacérès.) I think the Minister of Police should send his reports to you, and that you should show the Empress only such matters as she may well know: it is useless to place before her things that would only alarm her, and put wrong ideas in her head. The same holds good with the other ministers: they should not speak to the Empress of things that would give her anxiety or pain.

27th. I hope the Viceroy will be at Querfurt to-day, and our junction effected.

(To General Clarke.) I have just inspected the 37th light infantry; I can't wish to see a finer body of soldiers, but I don't expect to see a worse one of officers. If your office had laid itself out to appoint the most incapable officers of France, it couldn't have succeeded better; the soldiers laugh at them. They are drawn from colonial, from Dutch battalions, or from the national guards of the Pyrenees or of the Scheldt; most of the captains have never been under fire. I shall have to dismiss these officers or reduce them in rank.

28th. I shall be at Weimar at noon. I shall stop only a quarter of an hour to see the Duchess. I shall then get into the saddle and place myself at the head of the Guard.

29th, Naumburg:
(To Prince Eugène.) Shift towards Merseburg with your whole army. The Prince of the Moskowa will probably push out an advance guard to-morrow as far as Lützen.

May 1st, Weissenfels:
(To Marshal Marmont.) This morning, May the 1st, the Viceroy, with 60,000 men, is halfway between Merseburg and Leipzig. Get your divisions as near Weissenfels as you can so that you could support Marshal Ney it that should become necessary.

(To Prince Eugène.) It is eight o'clock. At nine we shall move on Lützen. I assume that at ten you will have your whole army with its left at Moeritzch, and its right at Schladebach. If you hear firing in the direction of Lützen, move on the enemy's right.

Lützen:
(To Cambacérès.) To-day I have moved my headquarters to Lützen. The enemy tried to prevent our debouching on the plains of Lützen, and had assembled a large force of cavalry there. Our infantry, supported by many batteries, drove it back some four leagues. The enemy, who had few guns, did us little damage.

The first cannon-shot of the day inflicted a heavy loss on us. The Duke of Istria was struck in the body by a cannon-shot, and fell stone dead. I write this in haste so that you may inform the Empress and also his wife, to prevent the news reaching her through the newspapers. Make it quite clear to the Empress that the Duke of Istria was nowhere near me when he was struck.

2d. *Battle of Lützen.*
(To Marshal Marmont.) Headquarters are at Lützen, and the Guard also. The Viceroy is at Markrannstadt; General Lauriston is marching on Leipzig, which he

will probably reach in a couple of hours. All our information points to the enemy retiring towards Levenkau.

At 9 A. M., the sound of firing being heard in the direction of Leipzig, the Emperor started at a gallop. The enemy were defending the bridges in front of Leipzig. But at 10, the enemy debouched in the direction of Kaja in several dense, black columns; they covered the horizon. The enemy were showing very large numbers; the Emperor promptlyprepared to meet them. The Viceroy received orders to come into line on the left of the Prince of the Moskowa; but he needed three hours to carry out his movement. The Prince of the Moskows formed his five divisions in line, and sustained the shock; in half an hour the struggle became terrific. His Majesty moved in person with the Guard behind the army to support the Prince of the Moskowa's right. The village of Kaja was several times taken and lost. The battle stretched over a line of two leagues covered with smoke, and fire, and clouds of dust. The Prince of the Moskowa, General Souham, General Girard, were everywhere, meeting every emergency.

We could now see in the distance the first flashes and the dust of the advance of General Bertrand's corps. At the same moment the Viceroy was coming into line on our left, and the Duke of Taranto was attacking the village on which the enemy's right rested. The enemy now redoubled their efforts on our centre; once more they carried the village of Kaja; our centre was beginning to give way.

It's nothing, my lads, keep steady!

A few battalions were disbanded, but our brave boys rallied at the sight of the Emperor, shouting: Vive l'Empereur!

There was not a moment to lose. The Emperor ordered the Duke of Treviso to march on the village of Kaja with 16 battalions of the Young Guard, to charge straight in, to recapture the village, and to clear out all its defenders. At the same moment His Majesty ordered his aide-de-camp, General Drouot, to concentrate a battery of 80 guns on the front of the Old Guard, which was formed in echelons like four redoubts, to support our centre, with all the cavalry massed behind. The fire became tremendous. The enemy gave way on all sides. The Duke of Treviso carried Kaja, broke the enemy, and continued his advance, his drums beating the charge. Cavalry, infantry, artillery, all the enemy began to retreat.

His Majesty cannot praise too highly the spirit and courage of the army.

3d. (From our Imperial Camp at Lützen.) Well done, soldiers! You have achieved all that I expected of you! Your high spirit and your courage have stood in the stead of all we lacked. You have shed new lustre on the glory of my eagles; you have shown all that the French race can do. The battle of Lützen will rank higher than the battles of Austerlitz, of Jena, of Friedland, and of the Moskowa!

We will hurl these Tartars back into that frightful clime whence they must never more depart. Let them remain in their frozen steppes, the abode of slavery, of barbarism,and of corruption, where man is reduced to the level of the brute! You have deserved well of civilized Europe. Soldiers! Italy, France, and Germany tender you their thanks!

4th. The Prussian and Russian armies are in flight in the direction of Roehlitz. I am moving the army on Dresden.

Nothing could equal the courage, the good-will, the devotion that all these young soldiers show me; they are full of enthusiasm.

6th, Colditz:
The Viceroy defeated the corps of Miloradovitch yesterday at Gersdorf, but we have got very few prisoners.

7th, Waldheim:
We shall probably reach Dresden to-morrow; the Prince of the Moskowa will cross the Elbe and, march on Berlin.

Nossen:
The peasants declare that firing was heard in the direction of Meissen this morning at ten o'clock.

The enemy have burnt all the bridges, and done an they could to delay my advance.

8th, Dresden:
Order for sending out pickets on all the roads leading into Bohemia to get information.

9th. We are hard at work on a bridge so as to get over to the right bank.

10th. The Duke of Ragusa will pass through the city to-morrow at noon, his troops in parade uniforms, taking his guns, and marching in the strictest order. He will send his baggage with everything that doesn't look well around by the floating bridge.

To-morrow noon the whole army will be on the right bank.

12th. (To Prince Eugène.) My Son: You must start to-night for Italy. I am ordering the Minister of War to place under your command the troops that are in the Kingdom of Italy and the Illyrian provinces.

13th. (To Ney.) I am beginning to get some cavalry.

My three principal aims, to be accomplished before the end of the month, are to unblock Glogau, to occupy Berlin, thereby enabling the Prince of Eckmühl to reoccupy Hamburg, and to seize Breslau.

The King of Saxony made a triumphant entry into Dresden yesterday; he is dining with me to-day.

14th. I have precise information as to Blücher's movements; he is marching on Bautzen by the Breslau road. The Russians and Prussians are said to be together. Their rearguard shows 30,000 men with many guns, and is covering the little city of Bautzen.

15th. The Prince of the Moskowa and General Lauriston started two days ago from Torgau to turn Bautzen.

17th. Information from every quarter shows conclusively that the enemy is resolved to fight.

(To Francis I, Emperor of Austria.) I am deeply touched by the sentiments of personal interest in me expressed by Your Majesty, which I reciprocate and (therefore) deserve. If Your Majesty is interested in my happiness, let Your Majesty promote it. If it be necessary I am resolved to die at the head of all generous

Frenchmen rather than become the laughing-stock of the English, and help my enemies triumph. Your Majesty should consider the future and not destroy the results of three years' friendship, nor sacrifice the happiness of the present generation to petty considerations,—why should I not say the happiness of a most sincerely attached part of Your Majesty's own family. I hope Your Majesty will never doubt my entire devotion.

(Instructions for General Caulaincourt.) Let me know, from headquarters, what is said. By finding out the views of the Emperor Alexander we will end by coming to an arrangement. In any case, my intention is to build him a golden bridge to escape from the intrigues of Metternich. If I am to make sacrifices I prefer they should be for the benefit of the Emperor Alexander, who is meeting me in fair fight, and of the King of Prussia, who has the support of Russia, than that they should profit Austria, that has played false, and that under the guise of mediation wants to arrogate to herself the right of disposing of everything after first taking what suits her.

You must try and establish a direct negotiation on this basis.

18th. I am leaving Dresden with all the Guard to attack the enemy, who have concentrated all their forces, and who have been reinforced on the Breslau road by Barclay de Tolly's corps. They have left nothing to cover Berlin.

24th, Goerlitz:
(Bulletin.) The Emperor left Dresden on the 18th, and arrived in front of Bautzen on the 19th at 10 A. M. He spent the day reconnoitring the enemy's position.

On the 20th at 8, the Emperor took up his station on the height behind Bautzen. At noon the artillery opened fire.

General Bonet occupied the village of Nieder Kayna, and by a charge carried a plateau that gave him control of the centre of the enemy's position; the Duke of Reggio carried the hills, and at seven o'clock in the evening the enemy had been driven back to their second position. At eight o'clock in the evening the Emperor entered Bautzen, and, was received by the, inhabitants and by the authorities with such sentiments as might be expected from allies happy at being delivered from Stein, from Kotzebue, and from the Cossacks. This engagement, which, were it not for its sequel, might well be called the battle of Bautzen, was only the prelude to the battle of Wurschen.

At five o'clock in the morning of the 21st the Emperor took up his station on a hill three quarters of a league beyond Bautzen. At eleven o'clock the Duke of Ragusa advanced some 2000 yards and opened a terrific cannonade. The Guard and the reserves, infantry and cavalry, were masked and had convenient débouchés for advancing to the right or to the left as events might develop. The enemy was by this means kept in doubt as to the real point of attack.

In the meanwhile the Prince of the Moskowa had driven the enemy from the village of Klix, and pushed everything in his front steadily back to Preilitz. At ten o'clock he carried that village; but, on the enemy's reserves being thrown in, the Prince of the Moskowa was driven back.

The Duke of Dalmatia got into action at one in the afternoon. The enemy, who had discovered all the danger with which they were threatened by the turn the battle had taken, attempted to check the Duke of Dalmatia's attack. The crisis of the battle was clearly at hand. By facing left the Emperor, in the space of twenty minutes, with the Guard, the four divisions of Latour Maubourg and a great number of guns, reached the flank of the enemy, which was the centre of the Russian army.

The enemy were obliged to weaken their right to repel this new attack. The Prince of the Moskowa seized this instant to resume his forward movement. Turning the allied army, he pressed on towards Wurschen. It was now three in the afternoon, and with the army still quite uncertain as to whether it had been successful, and while a terrific fire raged along a line of three leagues, the Emperor announced that the battle was won.

The enemy, seeing that their right was turned, beat a retreat, and soon that retreat turned to flight. At seven in the evening the Prince of the Moskowa and General Lauriston reached Wurschen. The Emperor slept by the roadside, surrounded by his Guard.

At seven o'clock the Grand Marshal, Duke of Friuli, was standing on a hillside in conversation with the Duke of Treviso and General Kirgener; they were all three on foot and at some distance from the firing line. One of the last cannon-shots fired by the enemy grazed the Duke of Treviso, tore open the lower part of the body of the Grand Marshal, and killed General Kirgener outright. The Duke of Friuli realized at once that his wound was mortal; he died twelve hours later.

As soon as our outposts were placed, and the army had bivouacked, the Emperor went to see the Duke of Friuli. He found him fully conscious and calm. The Duke grasped the Emperor's hand and kissed it. The Emperor, putting his right arm around the Grand Marshal, remained a quarter of an hour with his head resting on his left hand and in complete silence. The Grand Marshal was the first to break it:—Ah, sire, leave me; such a sight as, this must pain you!—The Emperor, leaning on the Duke of Dalmatia and on the Grand Equerry, left the Duke of Friuli, unable to say more than these words:—Good-bye, my friend!—His Majesty returned to his tent, and admitted no one that night.

25th. (To Maret.) As the Swedes have reached Hamburg, it is proper that you should immediately draw up a declaration of war against Sweden for my approval.

The Duke of Reggio will reach Hoyerswerda to-night, on the march to Berlin.

June 1st, Neumarkt:
(To Caulaincourt.) I have no dispatch from you later than the one sent at 3 A. M. As I am getting into the saddle to advance along the Einsdorf road, I hope to hear from you there. I want to be informed the instant that the orders go out, on both sides, for suspending hostilities. You must see how important it is for me to get this information, as if there should not be a suspension of hostilities, military dispositions must be made for to-morrow. I still urge you to try for a direct negotiation. I want peace, a solid peace, but on honourable terms.

Bubna has reached Liegnitz; he has conferred with the Duke of Bassano. The House of Austria appears somewhat exacting; we must be ready to face her in the field.

2d. (To General Clarke.) This armistice arrests the tide of my victories. I decided to accept it for two reasons: my lack of cavalry, which prevents my dealing heavy blows, and the hostile attitude of Austria. That Court, in the most friendly, tender, I might almost say sentimental terms, actually presumes to force me, for fear of the army it has concentrated at Prague, to give up Dalmatia and Istria, and even what lies beyond the Isonzo. It demands, further, the left bank of the Inn, and Salzburg, and even one half of the Grand Duchy of Warsaw, leaving the other half to Prussia and Russia. And these benefits are to be secured by the mere display of 100,000 men and without actual hostilities.

If possible I shall delay till September, and then strike hard.

(To Maret.) We must gain time. To gain time without making Austria hostile we must stick to our text of the last six months, that we can do anything provided Austria is our ally.

4th. The armistice was signed to-day at two in the afternoon.

6th, Liegnitz:
(To General Count Bertrazid.) I have received your letter. It is true that I was not, satisfied with the way in which you drew up your troops, nor with the way in which you evacuated the plateau in front of Jauer, when you had not more than 22 battalions in your front, while you had Pegri's and Morand's divisions still intact. On more than one occasion you have shown conspicuous talent, but war can be conducted only with energy, decision, and constant resolution; there must be no experimenting, no hesitation. Maintain strict discipline, and when you go into action show confidence in your men.

7th, Hagenau:
(To the Empress Maria Louisa.) *Madame et chère Amie*: I have received the letter in which you inform me that you received the Archchancellor while still in bed: my will is that, in no circumstance, for no reason whatever, should you receive any one whomsoever while still in bed. It is not permissible until past the age of thirty.

(To the Countess of Montesquiou.) I am pleased to hear that my son is growing and continues to give bright promise. I can only express my satisfaction for all the care you bestow upon him.

The death of the Duke of Friuli has grieved me. In twenty years it was the only occasion on which he had failed to guess what would please me.

8th, Bunzlau:
(To Cambacérès.) My Cousin: The Grand Equerry has presumably written to Count Rémusat to get us some actors for Dresden. I would like this to be talked about in Paris, as it would have a good effect in London and in Spain, by making them think we are amusing ourselves in Dresden. The season is not well suited for the theatre, so that you need not send us more than six or seven actors.

13th, Dresden:
(To General Savary.) The tone of your correspondence displeases me: you are always worrying me about the need for peace. I know more about the situation of my Empire than you do, and your manner of writing produces a disagreeable effect on me. I want peace, and am more concerned to get it than any one else: your discourses on that topic are therefore wasted; but I shall never conclude a dishonourable peace, nor one that would mean another even more bitter war in six months. Don't reply; these matters don't concern you; don't interfere in them.

15th. (To Cambacérès.) It would appear that the Minister of Police wants to make me pacific. No good can come of it, and it hurts my feelings, because it suggests that I am not pacific. I am not a rodomont; I do not make of war my occupation, and nobody is more pacific than I am.

26th, Dresden:
Ah! there you are, Metternich! Welcome! But if you wanted peace why didn't you come to see me sooner? We have already lost a month, and your mediation is so tardy that it looks hostile.

So it's war you want! You shall have it; I give you rendezvous in Vienna!

I win two victories, my defeated enemies are just realizing their situation, and all of a sudden you slip into our midst, offering me an armistice, mediation, offering them your alliance, complicating everything. Without your pernicious intervention peace would have been signed by now between me and the allies. You must admit that from the moment Austria assumed the position of mediator you were no longer on my side, no longer impartial, but my enemy.

To-day your 200,000 men are ready, over there, behind the screen of the Bohemian mountains. And because you think you are in a position to dictate terms, you now approach me. Very well, let us negotiate, I consent. What is it you want?

(Metternich: It rests with Your Majesty to give the world peace.)

My honour first, and then peace. You cannot know what passes through a soldier's mind. A man like me does not count the lives of a million of men. I have offered you Illyria for your neutrality, does that suit you? Your neutrality is all I ask for.

(Metternich: Ah, sire, we cannot remain neutral any longer; we must be for you, or against you.)

If it costs me my throne, I will bury the world under its ruins!

Well, what do you mean by peace? What are your conditions? Do you want to strip me? Do you want Italy, Brabant, Lorraine? I will not surrender one inch of territory; I make peace on the basis of in statu quo ante bellum. I will give you nothing because you have not defeated me; I will give Prussia nothing, because she has betrayed me. Illyria has cost me 300,000 men; if you want it, you must spend an equal amount.

Do you know what is going to happen? You will not make war against me.

(Metternich: You are lost, sire; that was my presentiment when I came here; now, I am certain of it.)

And it's my father-in-law concocts this scheme! It is my father-in-law has sent you here! Ah! Metternich, how much has England paid you to play such a part against me?

30th. I have at this date, 15,000 men without muskets.

July 1st. The armistice may be prolonged till the 15th of August.

(To Marshal Soult.) Start before ten o'clock to-night. Travel incognito, using the name of one of your aides-de-camp. You can get to Paris on the 4th, where you can stay with the Minister of War; go with him to see the Arch-chancellor, who will post you. Stop not more than 12 hours in Paris, and proceed thence to take up the command of my armies in Spain. You will take all measures necessary for reëtablishing our affairs in Spain.

3d. I cannot yet understand the Spanish business. I don't know whether we have really lost a battle (Vittoria), what corps were engaged, nor what has become of the King and the army. It is difficult to imagine anything so extraordinary as what is happening in Spain.

15th. The armistice is prolonged until the 15th of August through the mediation of Austria.

20th. Our disasters in Spain are as ridiculous as they are great, even the English think so. But the army has not lost its prestige. The army of Spain had no general, and was burdened with a King. I am bound to admit that the fundamental mistakes lie at my own door.

22d. I am just back from a journey of fifty leagues through lower Lusatia.

I suppose the Empress has started and will sleep tonight at Châlons. She will probably not reach Mainz before the 25th, when I expect to be already there.

25th. The Emperor will start for Mainz in his carriage at 9. A. M. with the Prince of Neuchâtel,—Roustan on the box.

27th, Mainz:
I covered the distance in 42 hours. The Empress is in good health.

There must be from 60,000 to 80,000 conscript deserters in France.

28th. There is nothing left to do in Europe these last two hundred years; it is only in the Orient a man can accomplish great things.

29th. (To the Prince of Neuchâtel.) Tell the Duke of Castiglione that I shall leave here on the night of the 1st, arriving at Würzburg on the morning of the 2d; that I shall inspect the two divisions, all I can see of his corps at Würzburg, as well as the citadel, and then proceed to Bamberg, where, on the evening of the 2d, I shall inspect the other two divisions; that on the 3d I will see the division at Bayreuth, the one at Hof, and General Milhaud's cavalry, so that on the night of the 3d to the 4th I can be back at Dresden. Notify General Pajol so that I may find escorts everywhere, but care must be taken to keep it secret. It must be given out that it is the Prince of Neuchâtel travelling.

The Duke of Dalmatia entered Spain on the 24th at the head of his army numbering nearly 100,000 men with a numerous artillery. He was marching on Pamplona to raise the siege.

31st. (To General Clarke.) Give orders that all the wives of generals, officers, and administrators, all the loose women, including those who go dressed as men, who are at Bayonne or in the departments of the Landes and of the Lower Pyrenees coming from Spain, be removed beyond the Garonne immediately. Specifically, the wives of Generals G—, F—, and V—are to be sent not only beyond the Garonne but to their homes.

August 4th, Dresden:
There is nothing doing at the Congress of Prague. An English agent is intervening. There can be no result, and the Allies intend to denounce the armistice on the 10th.

9th. (To General Savary.) It is probable that Austria will declare war on the 11th or 12th. That Power has had a beautiful dream in which she saw herself recovering all she has lost in twenty years! She wants everything, even Venice!

Keep this secret till the last moment.

11th. Order for the Duke of Reggio to concentrate his three army corps with the 3d cavalry corps and to march on Berlin.

12th. The armistice is denounced. I am not informed that Austria has declared war, but expect to get the news in the course of the day.

Apart from the 110,000 men I have marching on Berlin, and from there on Stettin, I shall have nearly 300,000 men near Goerlitz. With these 300,000 men I shall occupy a position between Goerlitz and Bautzen, so as to see what the Russians and Austrians propose doing, and to act according to circumstances.

14th. The King of Naples joined the army to-day.

15th. The unfortunate and unexpected turn taken by Spanish affairs makes it necessary to provide for the defence of the frontier. A levy of men must therefore be made in the south.

General Moreau has arrived in Berlin. He left America before the news of the battle of Lützen had reached there, and when these gentlemen thought they were coming back to France.

16th, Bautzen:
We are manœuvring. I am very hopeful of the result of the campaign. Jomini, chief of staff of the Prince of the Moskowa, has deserted. He is a poor soldier, but a writer who has shown some understanding of warfare.

18th, Reichenbach:
I have here 365,000 rounds for my artillery, all horsed, which is the equivalent of four battles like Wagram, and 18 million cartridges.

Goerlitz:
The Austrians have crossed the Elbe and are marching I know not where. I may possibly move straight into Bohemia to catch the Russians napping.

20th, Zittau:
I crossed the mountains yesterday and reached Gabel.

(To General Corbineau.). Push your cavalry out as far as you can on the road to Lauben. We are manœuvring, and must close up for giving battle.

I am afraid a dispatch I sent to the Duke of Taranto has been intercepted, and that the enemy's eyes will be opened.

22d, Loewenberg:
People will be anxious in Paris, and the Allies will not fail to spread bad reports. I am far from having given up my Bohemian enterprise. The worst feature of the situation is the lack of confidence of the generals: whenever I am absent they imagine the enemy are in large numbers.

23d, Goerlitz:
The troops that are here can reach Dresden on the 25th, or, if there is less urgency, on the 26th.

24th. I am now marching on Dresden to attack the forces of the enemy that have moved in that direction. The army that I sent towards Berlin should have reached that city to-day. It appears that two regiments of Westphalian hussars have gone over to the enemy bag and baggage.

Bautzen, *3 P. M.:*
I have reached this place with the Guard. To-morrow by two o'clock in the afternoon I can throw forty thousand men into Dresden; day after to-morrow 100,000 more.

25th, Stolpen:
I have just arrived at Stolpen. Vandamme's troops are already nearing Dresden. I want as little show made as possible so that the enemy may not suspect the arrival of these troops, and the operations we are undertaking. The Old Guard will arrive at eleven.

(To Marshal Saint Cyr.) You must hang on. I shall reach you early in the morning.

The reports about the Duke of Reggio are so confused that I can form no opinion as to what they mean. The letter says that on the 21st and 22d we had some minor successes; but it is clear from the official dispatches that only a few shots were fired on the 20th and 21st.

26th, *4 A. M.:*
Yesterday at midnight the whole of the enemy's army was in sight of Dresden, and Marshal Saint Cyr feared an attack for this morning.

On the Dresden road, *9 A. M.:*
We are just arriving at Dresden, the enemy face the city.

27th, Dresden:
I won a great victory at Dresden yesterday over the Austrian, Russian, and Prussian armies commanded by the Emperor of Austria, the Emperor of Russia, and the King of Prussia. Many prisoners, flags, and guns are being brought in.

The enemy are not retreating. If they remain in position, my intention is to turn their left, and the King of Naples will carry out this operation with the 38 battalions of the Duke of Belluno.

29th. The news of the death of Moreau is coming in from every quarter; it is probably true.

30th. (To the Prince of Neuchâtel.) Write to the Duke of Treviso to support General Vandamme, if he is pressed. Send an officer to General Vandamme to find out what is going on, and give him orders to return at once.

September 1st. The Duke of Taranto is at Goerlitz to-day. If he continues his retreat, I shall have to move to his support; I cannot allow him to be driven back beyond Bautzen.

The misfortune that has overtaken the 1st corps could not well be foreseen. General Vandamme, who seems to have been killed, had left no posts in the mountains, and had no reserves anywhere; he ran into a corner without seeing what he was doing.

2d. (To Berthier.) Inform the Duke of Reggio that I learn with great displeasure that, making no use of his three corps, he has retired under the guns of Wittenberg; that perceiving his hesitation I had already sent the Prince of the Moskowa to take command of his army.

3d. I shall be at Bautzen to-morrow morning to join the Duke of Taranto and his army; the enemy are pursuing him briskly and appear very confident; I shall attack them in the course of the day and try to drive them back to Reichenbach, and after the battle I shall make a forced march on Berlin.

(To General Count Friant.) On your march towards Bautzen you will find many stragglers and plunderers belonging to the 3d, 5th, and 11th corps who have thrown their muskets away. Turn them back on Bautzen, where muskets will be served out to them.

(To General Durosnel.) Look after the bridges sharply; allow none but wounded men to cross, and arrest all the rabble that are deserting from the army.

6th, Bautzen:
I am at Bautzen. I pursued the enemy beyond the Niesse; at six o'clock we reached Goerlitz. As soon as the enemy discovered I was with the army, they promptly ran away in all directions. It proved impossible to catch them up; they did little more than fire a few cannon-shots. I immediately returned here, where I have the 6th corps and the Guard.

8th, Dresden:
The enemy show themselves along all the passes into Bohemia, and we may soon become engaged.

9th, Liebstadt:
The great thing now is to give the Guard a little rest.

10th. The Prince of the Moskowa, who with his three corps met with a check on the 6th, is rallying his troops at Torgau.

11th, Breitenau:
We hold all the passes into Bohemia. I could see the enemy's army yesterday retreating in haste to form in front of Teplitz. If I had been able to move artillery through Geyersberg we should have attacked the enemy in flank, and won a great success; but all our efforts were in vain, and the misfortune that has overtaken the Berlin army prevents my pressing on further.

19th, Pirna:
The weather is horrible. The Prince of Neuchâtel is ill; I don't know whether it is his gout or only an attack of fever.

(To the Duke of Bassano.) Tell the Count of Narbonne that his dispatches are ridiculous and only prove one thing, that he has no experience of warfare. Is it extraordinary that there should be some confusion in a fortress that has just served as the rallying point for a defeated array? Tell him to use more sensible language in his letters than, for instance, his formula about speaking the truth, as though it were not everybody's duty to speak the truth, and as though everybody did not actually speak it. Protestations of speaking the truth suggest that it is not always spoken. Try as politely as possible to make him see all this; but really he is writing to the chief of staff in a ridiculous manner. He should not go off into amazement at everything he sees, but state it simply, and all will be mended; the Prince of the Moskowa's army will presently move away; the enemy will be dislodged from the right bank; the general in command of the artillery will send guns; Count Daru will send equipment; clothes will come in from all sides; the depots will be armed and equipped; the thing is only momentary.

20th. (To Marshal Marmont.) The weather has been so awful yesterday and through the night that we can't possibly move. It is unlikely that the enemy's infantry will attempt to advance. It they should, I will support you and we will give them battle, which would suit us well, but appears not to be what they want.

22d, Hartau:
I am sleeping at Hartau. I attacked and pushed back the enemy, who are now retreating on Bautzen.

23d. (To Count Daru.) The army is not properly fed, it would be a delusion to think it is. Twenty-four ounces of bread, one ounce of rice, and eight of meat are not enough for a soldier. Now we are getting only eight ounces of bread, three of rice, and eight of meat.

24th. The enemy will probably retreat to-night and cross the Spree. If they don't cross to-night, they certainly will to-morrow when they see large forces being deployed against them. I should lose several days to no purpose.

30th, Dresden:
At noon on the 28th the Swedes attempted to recapture Dessau; the Swedish Guard lost 1500 men, and failed completely.

October 2d. It would be the beat possible news to hear that the enemy are running their heads into Leipzig with 80,000 men; the war would soon be over then; but I imagine they know my methods too well to take any such risks.

3d. (To Berthier.) Write to the Prince of the Moskowa that the reports are false, that Bavaria has not abandoned our alliance, on the contrary.

(To Marmont.) The current rumours are false. You must act with the greatest prudence. Above all, you must support the Prince of the Moskowa. The King of Naples with the 2d, 5th, and 8th corps will oppose everything that comes out of Bohemia.

I repeat that to cover Leipzig,—7 since you are there,—to prevent the Elbe being crossed between Wittenberg and Torgau, to support the Prince of the Moskowa, those are your chief objects. The rest will come after.

(To Savary.) I have received your ciphered letter of the 27th. It's very good of you to look after the Bourse; what concern of yours is it if prices are falling? People who sell Government bonds at 60 will have to buy them back at 80. The less you interfere in such matters the better. It is natural that there should be more or less of a fall in prices under such circumstances as these; let them go on their own way. Who is hurt by it? Only those who are soft enough to sell. What does it matter if Government bonds drop to 6 francs, provided the interest is regularly paid. The one thing needed to make things worse is for you to mix yourself up with them, and to act as though you attributed some importance to the matter. As for me, I don't.

6th. Order for the Duke of Castiglione to march on Leipzig.

The whole of the army of Silesia, commanded by General Blücher, has slipped away towards Wittenberg. He threw a bridge in the night at Wartenberg. General Bertrand fought for twelve hours; the enemy attacked him seven times without dislodging him. At night, seeing that the enemy were being reinforced, General Bertrand retreated.

I shall reach Meissen to-night at the head of 80,000 men, with my advance guard at the fork of the Leipzig and Torgau roads.

7th. (To Berthier.) Write to the King of Naples that his principal object must be to retard the enemy's advance towards Leipzig, so that we may all close in on Leipzig together, hold the enemy at a distance from it, or, if necessary, fight a pitched battle.

Marshal Saint Cyr must distribute the Westphalians in his different divisions, one regiment per division.

Headquarters will start at ten o'clock this morning for Meissen, as I mean to defeat Blücher and the Swedes before they can effect their junction with Schwarzenberg.

Seerhausen:
We are here, with headquarters in an old castle. We are expecting news every moment.

9th, Würzen:
I think it important we should hold Düben, and if the enemy have not more than 30,000 men there I propose attacking this very evening. General Blücher is said to be at Düben. Unfortunately the weather is very bad.

10th, Eilenburg:
We got to Düben yesterday. General Langeron had left there at three in the afternoon.

I am anxious to get news from Leipzig as to the movements of the enemy, and to know whether they are advancing or otherwise.

Düben, *3 P. M.:*
The Austrian army is debouching through Penig. At daybreak the King of Naples was at Frohburg. It seems probable that he will retreat towards Leipzig in the course of the day.

This will all finish with a thunderclap!

11th. (To General Count Régnier.) General Latour Maubourg is arriving; clear the bridge for him. With the cavalry we shall be able to get some information as to what the enemy is doing at Dessau. Do they intend to cross back and give us battle on the right bank, or do they mean to take up their bridge and stay on the left bank?

12th. All my information points to General Blücher's having moved on Halle during the 10th. Wittgenstein has been engaged with the King of Naples at Borna.

3 P. M.:
We have seized the enemy's bridges over the Elbe, and it appears that the Berlin army crossed back to the right bank. In the other direction the King of Naples occupied the position of Croebern this morning, and is holding it; I have instructed him to hold it the whole of to-morrow the 13th. To-morrow at noon we shall have 70,000 men concentrated within reach of Leipzig.

4 P. M.:
The King of Naples estimates the enemy in his front at 60,000 men. If he can hold out through the 13th without reinforcements, I shall march on Leipzig and bring the enemy to battle.

(To Marshal Marmont.) March so that you can send help to Leipzig, and take your orders from the King as to coming into action. We seem to have reached the crisis; now all depends on fighting hard.

13th, *5 A. M.:*
The Bavarian army has joined the Austrian, and they are threatening the Rhine.

(To Ney.) I have drawn back all the Guard so as to march on Leipzig to-morrow; the King of Naples is covering the city. I have moved the Duke of Ragusa there, which will give the King of Naples 90,000 men. I think we must concentrate as quickly as we can. There will certainly be a great battle at Leipzig.

10 A. M.:
(To Marmont.) It is to be feared that Blücher may debouch at Halle, or at some other point. It is important that the army of Silesia should not approach Leipzig nearer than two leagues.

You are to dispose your troops in two ranks instead of three. The enemy, who are used to seeing us in three ranks, will think our battalions one third larger. Issue precise orders for carrying out these instructions.

(To Joachim Napoleon, King of Naples.) I have received your letter. The Duke of Ragusa will reach Hohenleina this morning at eight. It is very important that you should not make use of this marshal, for if you do, you would have to weaken your line at a very critical moment in the event of Blücher's debouching through Halle. That is the sort of movement that brings about the loss of battles; they are won only by strengthening the line at the critical moment. Take good care not to use the 6th corps except as a last resource, for all the indications are that the army of Silesia is in the neighbourhood of Halle.

14th. I shall start for Leipzig at seven.

7 A. M.:
(To Macdonald.) I hope you will arrive early. We shall undoubtedly be attacked to-morrow by the army of Bohemia and the army of Silesia. March rapidly therefore, and if you should hear them, move towards the sound of the guns. The army of Silesia is debouching through Halle.

Reudnitz:
(To Marmont.) Headquarters are at Reudnitz. I am sending you an account of the battle fought by Gustavus Adolphus that deals with the positions you occupy.

15th. The enemy engaged the King of Naples yesterday with 80,000 men; they delivered six attacks and were driven back each time. The 5th cavalry corps, in part made up of cavalry from Spain, made some splendid charges. Not only did the King of Naples maintain his positions, but he even recovered some ground he had evacuated in the night in order to concentrate.

16th, 7 A. M.:
(To Marmont.) As I am on the point of attacking the Austrians, I think you should come up in reserve about half a league from the city, with your divisions in echelons; you can move from there on Lindenau, if the enemy should make a serious attack on that side, which appears highly improbable. I shall draw you into line as soon as I have estimated the enemy's numbers and seen that we can bring them to action. Or, again, you could move to support General Bertrand if, which is unlikely, the enemy appeared on the Halle road.

At nine in the morning the grand army of the Allies advanced against us. Its movement tended constantly to extend towards the right. At noon the enemy's sixth attack had been thrown back.

The Emperor ordered the Duke of Reggio to move on Wachau with two divisions of the Young Guard; ordering the Duke of Treviso at the same time to move on Liebertwolkvitz with two other divisions of the Young Guard, and to seize the wood on the left of the village. He also pushed forward in the centre a battery of 150 guns under the command of General Drouot.

This combined movement resulted as was hoped. The enemy retired, and left us the whole of the field of battle.

It was now three o'clock in the afternoon. All the enemy's forces had been engaged; they had recourse to their reserves. Count Merveldt, who was in command of the whole Austrian reserve, relieved with his six divisions every column of their troops; while the Russian Imperial Guard, which formed the Russian reserve, relieved them in the centre.

The King of Naples placed himself at the head of the cuirassiers and marched on the enemy's cavalry to the left of Wachau, while the Polish horse and the dragoons of the Guard charged to the right. The enemy's cavalry was routed. Matters being thus reëstablished on our right, the enemy fell back, and did not dispute possession of the battlefield any longer.

It is impossible to praise too highly the conduct of Count Lauriston and Prince Poniatowski in this battle. As a proof of his satisfaction the Emperor promoted the latter on the battlefield to be a Marshal of France.

The Duke of Ragusa was engaged on the right of the Partha about one league from Leipzig, and four from the battlefield where the Emperor commanded. The Duke of Ragusa, with no supports, defended Leipzig and maintained his position during the whole day; but be suffered losses that were not compensated by those, however great, he inflicted on the enemy. At night the Duke of Ragusa, who was slightly wounded, was compelled to draw in his lines towards the Partha.

18th. Having discovered that the enemy had been reinforced and held a very strong position, the Emperor decided to draw them on to another battleground.

At two o'clock in the morning of the 18th he fell back two leagues towards Leipzig and there firmly awaited the onset of the enemy.

At nine o'clock our pickets reported them advancing at every point. At ten o'clock the artillery opened fire.

Throughout the day the repeated efforts of the enemy to carry Connewitz and Probstheyda failed. The Duke of Taranto was outflanked at Holzhausen.

At five in the afternoon the Emperor threw in the reserve artillery and developed all our fire against the enemy who were pushed back the distance of one league.

While this was happening the army of Silesia had fought its way into the suburbs of Halle, and the Saxon army, horse, foot, and guns, with the Würtemberg cavalry, passed over to the enemy. This treachery not only opened a gap in our line, but placed the enemy in possession of the important passage intrusted to the Saxon army, which carried its infamy to the point of immediately turning its forty guns against Durutte's division. A momentary disorder ensued; the enemy crossed the Partha and pushed on to Reudnitz, which they occupied; they were only half a league from Leipzig.

At six the Emperor issued his orders for the next day. But at seven General Sorbier and General Dulanloy, commanding the artillery of the army and of the Guard, reported at his bivouac with an account of the expenditure of ammunition during the day. They stated that the reserve supplies were exhausted, and that there remained not over 16,000 rounds. This state of things made a movement towards one of our two great magazines necessary; the Emperor decided for Erfurt.

By this decision the French army was compelled to abandon the fruits of two victories, in which it had acquired such glory in defeating the far more numerous armies of the whole Continent.

19th, Lindenau:
The Emperor had ordered the engineers to mine the great bridge between Leipzig and Lindenau so as to blow it up at the last moment; part of the army was still on the further side with 80 guns and a train of several hundred wagons.

The head of column of this part of the army, on seeing the bridge blow up, supposed it had fallen into the power of the enemy. A cry of dismay went up from the ranks: "The enemy are in our rear; the bridge is cut!" The unfortunate men broke their ranks and sought all means of escape. The Duke of Taranto swam across; Count Lauriston, less lucky, was drowned; Prince Poniatowski, on a spirited horse, plunged in and was never seen again.

It is impossible as yet to estimate the loss involved by this unfortunate accident, but the disorder it has caused in the army has completely altered the appearance of things. The victorious French army will reach Erfurt with all the appearance of a defeated army. The enemy, shaken by the battles of the 16th and 18th, have taken heart owing to the disaster of the 19th and have assumed a victorious attitude.

I could see clearly enough the fatal hour coming! My star was growing paler; I felt the reins slipping from my fingers; and I could do nothing. Only a thunderstroke could save us. I had, therefore, to fight it out; and day by day, by this or that fatality, our chances were becoming more slender!

20th, on the road to Weissenfels:
A dispatch must be sent to the Duke of Valmy, who will send a semaphore message stating that after much fighting, of which the honour remains with us, I am marching on the Saale; that the Emperor is in good health.

23d, Erfurt:
Order for General Sebastiani to start. He is to push back the Cossacks and reëstablish communications with Erfurt.

It seems to me highly improper that in the address of the Municipal body of Paris to the Empress the conduct of Maria Theresa should have been recalled: it shows lack of tact.

25th, Gotha:
I shall proceed to Mainz, and concentrate the army on the frontier. The treachery of Bavaria, which is as inconceivable as it was unexpected, has upset all my plans, and compels me to bring the war nearer to our frontiers.

I am writing to the Minister of War on the subject of a levy of 80,000 to 100,000 men which I need. With the whole of Europe under arms, when everywhere married as well as unmarried men are being raised and everybody is in arms against us, France is lost unless she does the same.

A great stream of stragglers is constantly coming in.

28th, on the road near Schluchterne:
(To the Polish officers.) Is it true that the Poles want to leave me?

I went too far. I have made mistakes. Fortune has turned her back on me these last two years; but she's a woman, and will change. Who can tell? Perhaps it is your evil star has drawn mine on? In any case have you lost confidence in me? Is there no...left in my...? Do I look thinner?

I only hope the Allies will burn down two or three of my good cities of France; it would give me a million of soldiers. I would offer them battle, I would beat them, and I would drive them at tap of drum all the way back to the Vistula.

I have been informed as to what you want. As Emperor, as general, I have nothing but gratitude for all you have done; I have nothing to reproach you with, you have acted loyally towards me; you have not been willing to abandon me without notice, and you have even undertaken to reconduct me to the Rhine, To-day, I want to give you good advice. If you abandon me I shall no longer have the right of speaking for you; and I imagine that in spite of our disasters I am still the most powerful monarch of Europe.

31st, Frankfort:
I have just reached Frankfort. The Bavarian army, together with the Austrian army that was opposed to it, with a total of 60,000 men, had taken position at Hanau so as to cut me off from France. I defeated them yesterday at sight, capturing guns, flags, and 6000 prisoners.

November 1st. (To Maria Louisa.) Madam and beloved wife: I am sending you twenty standards captured by my armies at the battles of Wachau, of Leipzig, and of Hanau; they are a tribute I delight to pay you. Pray see in them a mark of my satisfaction with your conduct during the regency which I intrusted to you.

2d, Mainz:
I have arrived at Mainz. I am trying to rally, to rest, and reorganize the army.

3d. (To Prince Cambacérès.) My Cousin: Talk with the Councillors of State and Senators who are nervous. I am told in many quarters that they are showing great lack of courage. I regret not being in Paris, so that people might see me more cool and more calm than in any event of my life.

(To Savary.) The alarms and apprehension at Paris amuse me; I thought you capable of facing the truth. I shall defeat the enemy quicker than you think.

My presence is too much needed with the army at this moment for me to leave it. When it is necessary I shall come to Paris.

7th. I leave to-night for Paris.

10th, Saint Cloud:
The Director of the conscription promises 150,000 men. As 150,000 are not enough, I must have 100,000 more.

The conscription of 1815 is estimated at 160,000 men; I shall be able to levy 200,000.

12th. I am working at present on raising 600,000 men.

14th, Palace of the Tuileries:
Senators, I thank you for your sentiments. One year ago all Europe was marching with us; now all Europe is marching against us. The reason is that the opinion of the world is governed either by France or by England. We should therefore have everything to fear were it not for the courage and power of the nation. Posterity will declare that the great and critical events that face us were not superior to France nor to me.

15th, Saint Cloud:
Order, in the event of the English reaching the château of Marracq, that the château and all the buildings belonging to me there be burnt down, so that they may not sleep in my bed. All the furniture may he removed and stored at Bayonne.

17th. I am informed by semaphore that the people of Amsterdam have risen in insurrection.

December 14th, Paris:
I regret to see that the epidemic continues; is there no hope that the cold weather will cheek it?

15th. We are badly off for muskets.

17th. (To Count Montalivet.) You will find herewith a schedule of 21,200 unemployed workmen drawn up by the Prefect of Police; I intend to provide them with work. It is difficult to believe that there can be in Paris 350 braid makers, 700 hatters, 1200 locksmiths, 500 carpenters, 2000 ironsmiths, 2000 carriage builders, 300 shoemakers, without employment, when complaints are constant that we cannot get any for the war administration or for the Guard. In any event, I intend doubling, tripling employment, rather than leave thern without any.

20th. (To Marshal Mortier.) Brussels is surrounded by Russian Cossacks, Dutch Cossacks, and, I suspect, a few local Cossacks; your mounted division must be quickly put in order so as to get after them.

21st. The chief of staff will inform the Duke of Belluno that he must form his corps into three divisions without fail on the 1st of January, even if he has no more than 3000 men in each division.

26th. The enemy have debouched by Bâle and are marching on Belfort, which their advance guard probably reached on the 24th. It is absolutely necessary to move the Guard, horse and foot, with the reserve artillery, to Reims. If the news should become more urgent, I will give orders for the infantry to travel by stage, but so far this does not appear to be necessary.

31st. The Legislative Body, instead of helping to save France, is helping on her ruin, and is false to its duties; I carry out mine and dissolve it.

This is my decree, and if I were assured that its consequence would be that the people of Paris would march to massacre me in the Palace of the Tuileries, still I would maintain it; for that is my duty. When the French people placed their fate in my hands, I considered the laws under which I was asked to govern; had I thought them insufficient I would not have accepted. Let no one imagine that I am a Louis XVI!

1814

January 1st, Paris:

Gentlemen, you might have done some good, and you have only done harm. You say that adversity has counselled me well. How can you turn my reverses into a reproach? I have supported them with honour, because Nature gave me a strong and proud character; were not this pride in my soul I could not have risen to the greatest throne of the Universe.

Yet I needed sympathy, and it was to you I looked for it. You have tried to spatter me with mud, but I am one of those men who must be killed and cannot be dishonoured. When it is a question of driving away the enemy, you ask me for institutions; as though we had none! Is not the constitution enough for you? You should have asked for another one four years ago, or else wait until two years after peace is made. Do you want to imitate the Constituent Assembly and start a Revolution?

(Orders to be issued by the chief of staff.) The army will comprise four corps.

The chief of staff will arrange with the Defence Committ ee to divide the frontier among these four commands.

Attached to each of these four armies there shall be an Insurrectional Committee.

4th. (To Caulaincourt.) I doubt whether the Allies are acting in good faith, and whether England wants peace; I do, but only solid and honourable.

You must listen, observe. It is not certain that they will let you reach headquarters; the Russians and English will want to prevent our coming to an explanation and understanding with the Emperor of Austria. You must try to get the views of the Allies, and to let me know what you find out daily, so that I may be able to draw up instructions for you, instructions for which I have no data at present. Do they want to reduce France to her old frontiers? Italy is untouched, and the Viceroy has a good army. In another week I shall have collected enough men to fight several battles, even before the arrival of my troops from Spain. The pillaging of the Cossacks will drive the inhabitants to arms and double our numbers. If the nation supports me the enemy are on the road to ruin. If Fortune betrays me my resolve is taken, I am not wedded to the throne. I shall abase neither the nation nor myself by accepting shameful terms.

The thing is to know what Metternich wants. It is not the interest of Austria to push things to extremes; one step more and the leading rôle will escape her.

I am starting for the army. We shall be so close that your first reports will reach me without loss of time. Send me frequent couriers.

7th. (To Joseph.) My Brother: I have received your letter. It is too full of subtleties to fit my present situation. Here is the question in two words. France is invaded, Europe is all in arms against France, but especially against me. You are no longer King of Spain. What will you do? Will you, as a French prince, support my throne? If so you must say so, write me a straightforward letter that I can publish, receive the officials, and display zeal for my cause and for that of the King of Rome, good-will towards the Regency of the Empress. Can you not bring yourself to this? Haven't you enough good sense to do this?

Otherwise you must retire quietly to a ch1teau forty leagues from Paris. If I survive, you can live there quietly. If I die, you will be assassinated or arrested. You will be useless to me, to the family, to your daughters, to France, but you will be doing no harm and will not embarrass me. Decide at once, choose your path.

8th. Communications with Mainz are cut.

10th. (To Marshal Macdonald.) You must see how important it is to delay the enemy's advance. Use the foresters, the game-keepers, the national guards, to harass the enemy as much as possible.

12th. General Bülow is concentrating at Breda. General Blücher, with the army of Silesia, has debouched by Coblentz, and is marching on Metz. A third body, commanded by Prince Schwarzenberg, has debouched by Bâle.

No preparations are to be made for abandoning Paris; if necessary we must be buried under its ruins.

17th. I am sending cavalry, infantry, and artillery to Châlons, where I expect to place my headquarters very soon.

(To Marshal Victor.) The Emperor disapproves your abandoning Nancy. His Majesty orders you not to leave the line of the Moselle without fighting. It is bringing the enemy down on us, and doing us the greatest harm.

18th. I continue receiving, through the police, the most alarming news from the north.

For 300 guns I need three or four hundred thousand rounds; I wonder if the artillery department has thought of this? If I had had 30,000 rounds at Leipzig on the night of the 18th I should to-day be master of the world.

21st. (To General Savary.) Start the Pope off before five in the morning. The adjutant can say that he is taking him to Rome, where he is to be dropped like a shell.

23d. (To General Count Belliard.) I shall take the offensive. Try to have information for me when I reach Châlons as to where the enemy's infantry is placed, so that I may fall on it. Keep the news of my arrival secret. Don't take any risk with dispatches so that nothing may be intercepted, and nothing known of my arrival.

24th. King Joseph is to command the National Guard of Paris as my lieutenant-general.

26th, Châlons:
(To Berthier.) You must get information as to what the enemy are doing at Saint Dizier: who is in command, and what are their numbers? If there are only 25,000 or 30,000 men, we can beat them, and if we succeed in this, the whole state of affairs would be changed. If, on the contrary, we give them long enough to concentrate, we should stand no chance at all. Get two or three hundred thousand bottles of wine and brandy at Vitry to serve out to the army to-day and to-morrow. If there should be nothing but champagne, take it just the same; better we should have it than the enemy.

Vitry-le-Français:
We can crush the enemy by our great superiority in artillery. I expect to get 300 guns into line to-morrow.

28th, St. Dizier:
On the 27th I advanced against St. Dizier, which the enemy occupied, and drove them out. We captured a few guns and made a few prisoners. I discovered that Blücher had marched on Brienne with 25,000 men; he will reach there to-day. I, have cut his line of operations and am marching to attack him in the rear. If he holds his position, we may possibly have an action at Brienne to-morrow.

29th, Montiérender:
There is a decided thaw; we can manage to get through to-day.

31st, Brienne:
We had a lively engagement on the 29th at Brienne. I attacked the whole army of Marshal Blücher and of General Sacken just at the end of a forced march. I fortunately got possession of the castle which dominates (the town) at the beginning of the action. As firing only began one hour before dark, we fought through the night. Blücher was defeated; we captured 500 or 600 prisoners, killed or wounded 3000 or 4000; and drove the enemy on Bar-sur-Aube. I pursued them for two leagues in that direction yesterday, firing salvos from forty guns. In our present circumstances, and with such troops as I have to handle, I count myself lucky that things have turned out as well as they have.

We have taken up a position two leagues in front of Brienne. Our prestige has gone up with the Allies since this engagement. They thought we had no army left.

February 1st. Battle of La Rothière. Retreat on Paris.

2d, Piney:
The enemy's soldiers are behaving horribly everywhere. All the inhabitants are fleeing to the woods. There are no peasants left in the villages. The enemy consume everything, take all the horses, all the cattle, all the clothing and rags of the peasants; they strike everybody, men and women, and commit a great number of rapes. I hope soon to draw my people from this miserable state and from this truly horrible suffering. The enemy should think of this twice, for Frenchmen are

not patient; they are courageous by nature, and I expect to see them forming themselves into free companies.

I shall be at Troyes to-morrow. Perhaps Blücher's army will operate between the Marne and the Aube.

3d, Troyes:
I expect to get 15,000 men from the army of Spain day after to-morrow.

4th. (To Caulaincourt.) Prince Schwarzenberg's report is moonshine. There was no battle. The Old Guard was not on the field; the Young Guard was not engaged. We lost a few guns that were taken in cavalry charges. It appears that the whole of the enemy's army was in line, and that they regard it as a battle; if they do, it is not much to their credit. They had not more than 15,000 of us in their front, and we held our positions all day.

6th. (To General Clarke.) You told me that the artillery had a great number of pikes: have them served out to the national guards who are collecting near Paris. They will serve for the third rank. Have regulations printed on how to handle them. Send pikes to the departments also; they are better than pitchforks, and in any case they are short even of pitchforks in the cities.

I shall be at Nogent early to-morrow; I can therefore cover Paris.

7th, Nogent:
(To Cambacérès.) I have your letter of the 6th. I see that instead of encouraging the Empress you are discouraging her. Why lose your head? What is the meaning of these *Misereres* and forty hour services in the Chapel? Are you getting insane in Paris?

Subject to the news I get, I expect to march at daybreak with the 6000 cavalry of the Guard and the 10,000 foot of the Old Guard. But as I cannot risk a false move, I must wait for precise information.

8th. (To Marmont.) Cut the Montmirail road and send news as quickly as you can. I cannot believe the enemy are marching on the Epinay road.

(To King Joseph.) If, owing to circumstances I cannot foresee, I should move to the Loire, I would not leave the Empress and my son far from me, because whatever happened they would be seized and taken to Vienna. It would be all the more certain to happen if I were no longer alive.

I confess that your letter of the 7th at 11 P. M. hurt me, because I can distinguish no reason in your ideas, and because you follow the chatter and the opinions of a lot of unreflecting people. If Talleyrand is in any way connected with the idea of leaving the Empress in Paris if our troops evacuate the city, it means that some treachery is being hatched. I repeat it, be on your guard against that man. I have had dealings with him during sixteen years. At one time I even held him in high regard; but now that Fortune has for a while abandoned our House, he is assuredly its greatest enemy. Stick to my advice. I know more than do all those people.

If news should come of a lost battle and of my death, you would receive it before my ministers. Send the Empress and King of Rome to Rambouillet; order the Senate, the Council of State, and all the troops to rally on the Loire; leave in Paris the Prefect, or an Imperial Commissioner, or a Mayor. Never let the Empress or the King of Rome fall into the hands of the enemy. I feel that I had rather my son were strangled than see him brought up at Vienna as an Austrian prince; and I have a high enough opinion of the Empress to believe that she thinks the same way, as much as a woman and a mother can. I have never seen *Andromaque* performed without grieving for the fate of Astyanax surviving his House, and without thinking it happiness for him not to survive his father. You don't know the French nation: the results of what might occur during these great events are incalculable.

(To Daure.) The army is dying of starvation, although we have marked our route in flames and in blood in order to get food. And yet if I were to credit your reports, the army is fed. The Duke of Belluno has nothing; General Gérard has nothing; the cavalry of the Guard is dying of hunger.

9th. (To Savary.) Send twenty picked gendarmes and twenty Paris gendarmes to arrest the stragglers and to decimate them, that is to shoot one in ten.

I had to work hard through the night and was unable to start for Sézanne. The Duke of Ragusa is at Champaubert. General Sacken is at Montmirail with 15,000 men. I will have him attacked to-morrow.

10th, Sézanne:
I am just getting into the saddle to move on Champaubert. I am rather delayed by the roads; they are awful; we have six feet of mud.

Champaubert, *10 P. M.:*
I attacked the enemy at Champaubert. They had twelve regiments and forty guns. The general-in-chief, Olsouvief, was captured, with all his generals, officers, guns, wagons, and baggage. We have counted so far 6000 prisoners, 40 guns, 200 wagons. The rest were driven into a pond, or killed on the field of battle. This corps is absolutely destroyed.

We are marching on Montmirail, which we should reach at ten o'clock to-night. I have the strongest hopes that Sacken is lost; and if luck is with us, as it has been to-day, the whole look of things will change in the twinkling of an eye, because Sacken's corps is the backbone of the Russian army, made up as it is of 10 divisions or 60 battalions. Blücher is cut off from Sacken: he has two divisions with him.

11th, near Montmirail:
My brother, it is eight o'clock and before turning in I send you these two lines to inform you that to-day's work has been decisive. The enemy's army of Silesia no longer exists; I have completely routed it. We have captured all its guns and baggage and taken thousands of prisoners, perhaps 7000; they are coming in every minute. There are 5000 or 6000 of the enemy left on the field. All this was effected with only one half of the Old Guard engaged. I am writing to the Empress to have a salute of 60 guns fired. Our loss is slight. The infantry of my Guard, my dragoons, my horse grenadiers, did wonders.

12th. The enemy have crossed the Marne at Château-Thierry and burned the bridge. The Old Guard surpassed by a great deal all that could be expected of a picked body. It really was the Head of Medusa!

13th. I cannot believe that Prince Schwarzenberg will run his head into Fontainebleau while we retain control of the bridge at Nogent; the Austrians are too well acquainted with my manner of operating, and have carried its marks for too many years; they must surely realise that if they leave us in possession of the bridge at Nogent I shall debouch on their rear, in the same way as I have at this point.

I am not yet clear as to my move for to-day. I tremble at the thought that these miserable Russians may set fire to Fontainebleau by way of reprisals.

Château-Thierry:
The conduct of the King of Naples is vile, and that of the Queen defies description. I hope to live long enough to avenge myself and to avenge France for such an outrage and such horrible ingratitude.

(To Caulaincourt.) As the King of Naples has declared war on me, you will kindly notify the Neapolitan Ambassador that he is to quit Paris within 24 hours, and the territory of the Empire as promptly as possible.

14th. It is three o'clock in the morning and I am starting for Montmirail, thence to attack Blücher, who has debouched.

Montmirail:
I left Château-Thierry at three this morning, and re ached Montmirail just as the enemy were arriving at its gates. I marched straight on the enemy, who formed line near the village of Vauchamps. I defeated them, took 8000 prisoners, 8 guns, and 10 flags, and drove them to Etoges. I did not lose 300 killed and wounded. This splendid result was due to the fact that the enemy had no cavalry, while I had 6000 or 8000 excellent horse, with which I constantly menaced them and outflanked them, while all the time I crushed them with grape from 100 guns.

15th, *3 A. M.*:
I shall start at the earliest dawn and shall reach La Ferté-sous-Jouarre with my Guard quite early.

4 A. M.:
I am moving on Meaux to operate against the Austrians who have crossed the Seine at Bray and Nogent.

La Ferté-sous-Jouarre:
We shall probably have a great battle with the Austrians on the 17th, 18th, or 19th in the neighbourhood of Guignes. I shall get to Meaux with the cavalry of

the Guard early this evening. I am not sure that the infantry of the Guard can get there, but I hope it will at all events get beyond La Ferté.

16th, Meaux, *8 A. M.:*
I am starting for Guignes and shall attack the enemy to-morrow.

Guignes:
I arrived here at three in the afternoon. We are going into camp this evening so as to reach Nangis to-morrow at dawn.

17th, Nangis, *3 P. M.:*
The whole of the enemy's Grand Army, Austrians and Russians, Bavarians and Würtembergers, are recrossing the Seine in all directions with the utmost haste. To-night there probably will not be a single man left on this side. But I shall have to lose precious time in repairing the bridge at Montereau.

(To Caulaincourt, Duke of Vicenza.) I had given you a free hand to save Paris, and to avoid us a battle which would be the nation's last hope. That battle has been fought; Providence blessed our arms. I have made 30,000 or 40,000 prisoners; I have captured 200 guns, many generals, and destroyed several armies. Yesterday I began to cut into the army of Prince Schwarzenberg, and I hope to destroy it before it recrosses our frontiers. Your attitude must correspond with all this; you must try your best for peace; but you are to sign nothing without my orders, because I alone know my real situation, I am certainly in a stronger position than when the Allies were at Frankfort. To-day all is changed; I have won tremendous successes over them, and such victories as are unmatched in a not undistinguished military career of twenty years.

18th. (To Berthier.) Convey my displeasure to the Duke of Belluno at his not having carried out the order that directed him to proceed to Montereau. He must explain the reasons why he did not carry out this order, a thing that puts in jeopardy the success of the whole campaign. Write him a stiff letter.

At last Prince Schwarzenberg shows signs of life. He has sent in an officer to ask for an armistice. It would not be easy to match such cowardice! He had constantly refused, in the most insulting terms, to discuss any suspension of hostilities. The hounds!—at the first reverse, they are on their knees! Happily the aide-de-camp of Prince Schwarzenberg was not allowed to pass (the outposts). I merely received his letter, which I shall answer at my convenience. I shall grant them no armistice till my soil is purged of their presence.

(To Count Tascher de la Pagerie.) Tascher, start back for Italy to-night; you may stay over in Paris long enough to see your wife but without communicating with anybody. You will tell Eugène that I defeated the best troops of the coalition at Champaubert and at Montmirail; that Schwarzenberg has sent me an aide-de-camp to-night asking for an armistice; which does not take me in, for it is only to trick me and gain time. You will tell him that had Marshal Victor carried out his orders precisely, by moving from Melun to Montereau yesterday, the Bavarian and Würtemberger corps would have been surprised and caught at a disadvantage, and then having only the Austrians, who are poor soldiers, in his front, he would have driven them before him by cracking a whip in their backs; but that as nothing of what was ordered was done we shall have to attempt something else.

Tell Eugène I am pleased with him, that he may announce to the army of Italy that I am satisfied with it; have him fire a salute of 100 guns in honour of the victories of Champaubert and of Montmirail.

10th, Surville:
Yesterday I routed two reserve divisions of the Austrian general Bianchi and the Würtembergers; they lost heavily. We took several flags and 3000 or 4000 prisoners. And, which is most important, I had the good luck to carry the bridge before they could destroy it. I have dismissed the Duke of Belluno, dissatisfied with his excessive slowness and negligence.

(To Caulaincourt.) I am so moved at the sight of the infamous proposal that you send me, that I feel dishonoured at merely being in such a position that such a proposal can be made. I will send you my instructions from Troyes or Châtillon; but I think I had almost sooner lose Paris than see such propositions made to the French people. You are always talking about the Bourbons,—I had sooner see the Bourbons back in France, with reasonable conditions, than such infamous proposals as you have transmitted!

(To Savary.) The newspapers are stupidly written. Is it sensible, at such a moment as this, to say that I had small numbers, that I won only because I surprised the enemy, and that we had three to one against us? You must have lost your heads in Paris to say such things, while I am saying everywhere that I have

300,000 men, while the enemy believes it, and it is essential to keep on repeating it continually.

It has taken us all day to get through this wretched defile of Montereau. It is snowing, and the weather is rather rough.

20th. Since their defeat at Montereau the enemy have evacuated Bray and Nogent, and are hastily retreating on Troyes. What are their intentions? Do they intend to call in Blücher and offer battle at Troyes?

Montereau:
(To General Clarke.) I send you four flags; two should have come in with the prisoners, which makes six. There are four more Russian ones which we can't find; but by fair count we had ten. You can present them to the Empress. We will try to find the four missing Russian ones, but if we can't find them in time, replace them by four other Russian flags. It would be a good thing to have a parade of the National Guard, and to carry the flags along their front, with the band.

Nogent:
I have just reached Nogent. The enemy are in great luck because the heavy frost has enabled them to cut across country; they would otherwise have lost half their baggage and artillery.

21st. (To Marshal Augereau, at Lyons.) My Cousin: The Minister of War has submitted your letter of the 16th to me. This letter grieves me profoundly. What! Were you not in the field six hours after being joined by the first troops coming from Spain? Six hours' rest was enough. I won the engagement at Nangis with a brigade of dragoons coming from Spain, which had not unbridled all the way from Bayonne. You say that the six battalions of the Nimes division are deficient in uniforms and equipment, and don't know their drill; what a poor reason is that, Augereau! I have destroyed 80,000 of the enemy with battalions made up of conscripts, with no cartridge-boxes and badly clothed! You say that the National Guards are wretched: I have 4000 of them here coming from Angers and Britt-any, in round hats, with no cartridge-boxes, with wooden shoes but with good muskets; and I have turned them to good use. You go on to say that you have no money: and where do you expect to draw money from? We shall get some only when we recapture our tax-collecting offices from the enemy. You have no teams:

seize them everywhere. You have no magazines: this is ridiculous. I order you to get into the field twelve hours after the receipt of this dispatch. If you are still the Augereau of Castiglione, keep your command; if your sixty years weigh too heavily on you, quit it, and hand it over to your senior general officer. The country is threatened and in danger; it can only be saved by boldness and zeal, and not by useless middle courses. You must have 6000 good troops as a starting-point: that is more than I have, and yet I have destroyed three armies, made 40,000 prisoners, captured 200 guns, and three times saved the capital. Get to the front with your firing-line. It is no longer a case for acting as in recent years, but you must again put on your boots and your resolution of '93! When the French see your cocked hat with the skirmishers, and see you exposing yourself foremost to the enemy's fire, you can do what you like with them.

(To Francis I, Emperor of Austria.) *Monsieur mon Frère et trés cher Beau-Père: I* did what I could to avoid the battle that has just been fought. Fortune has smiled on me: I have destroyed the Russian and Prussian army commanded by General Blücher, and later the Prussian one commanded by General Kleist. In this state of things, whatever prejudices may prevail at your headquarters, my army outnumbers that of Your Majesty, in foot, in horse, and in guns, and if the acceptance of this fact should be a prerequisite for Your Majesty's decision, I have no doubt but that I can demonstrate it to the satisfaction of men of such sound judgment as Prince Schwarzenberg, Count Bubna, or Prince Metternich. I think it my duty to write to Your Majesty because this struggle between a French army and an army that is principally Austrian appears contrary to the interests of both countries. Should Fortune deceive my hopes, the position of Your Majesty would be still more difficult.

I therefore propose to Your Majesty that we should sign a peace immediately, on the basis laid down by Your Majesty at Frankfort, which I and the French nation have accepted as our ultimatum. I say more, these bases alone can maintain the European equilibrium. Should Your Majesty persist in subordinating (Austrian) interests to those of England and to the rancour of Russia, and be unwilling to lay down arms on any terms but the disastrous ones proposed at the Congress, the genius of France and of Providence will be for us.

24th, Bourg des Nöes:
(To Montalivet.) I have your letter. If the French People were as contemptible as you imagine, I would blush with shame. You and the Minister of Police know no

more of France than I do of China. You discourage the King by evoking exaggerated pictures which his character is only too prone to accept.

25th, Troyes:
As soon as I can make out what Blücher is up to, I shall try to get in his rear and cut him off.

26th. If I had had a train of ten pontoons, the war would now be over, and the army of Prince Schwarzenberg would no longer exist; I would have captured eight to ten thousand wagons and beaten his army in detail. But I was unable to cross the Seine for lack of boats.

Blücher is moving towards Sézanne, a few cannon-shots were exchanged last night. The Prince of the Moskowa crossed the Aube at Arcis this morning to fall on Blucher's rear.

27th. I am starting for Arcis to manœuvre against the troops that are advancing towards La Ferté Gaucher.

(To the King of Naples.) I shall not speak of my displeasure at your conduct, which was precisely opposite to what it should have been. It all comes from your weak disposition. You are a good soldier on the battlefield, but otherwise you have no decision, no courage. Turn to advantage an act of treachery which I put down to fear, so as to serve me by a mutual understanding. I rely on you, on your repentance, on your promises. If you act otherwise, you may count on having to regret it. I imagine you are not one of those who believe the lion is dead.

Arcis-sur-Aube:
(To King Joseph.) I shall sleep at Herbisse. I shall be at Fère Champenoise tomorrow morning at nine.

I have received the engravings of the King of Rome. Please substitute for the legend: "God guard my father and France," this one: "I pray to God for my father and for France." It is more direct. I also wish you to have some copies made showing the King in the uniform of the National Guard.

March 1st, Jouarre:
The enemy have crossed back to the right bank of the Marne, but I got up in time to cannonade their rear-guard. To-morrow I must see what we can do. I have no information yet as to where they are moving.

2d. I have been held up here for many hours because of the difficulty of repairing the bridge.

7 P.M.:
Our bridge will be finished at nine. By midnight I shall have got 6000 cavalry over, and pushed them on after the enemy. The country people say that their transport is in difficulties in the marshes of Cocherel; that the enemy's army is in such a state that men weep and throw their muskets away in despair. I hope we may have a good day to-morrow.

4th, Bézu:
(To General Clarke.) I have crossed the Marne; I moved to Château-Thierry; I pushed my advance guard as far as Rocourt, and I have come (here) to sleep.

You forward me letters of Marmont that tell me nothing; the excessive vanity of this marshal stands out in all his dispatches; nobody values him highly enough; it is he has done everything, has advised everything; it is regrettable that with his talents he can't get rid of this foolish side, or at all events keep it sufficiently under control and out of sight.

Blücher appears to be extremely embarrassed and constantly changes direction. I hope this will lead to some good result.

5th, Fismes:
I supposed that the Duke of Ragusa had reached Soissons yesterday; but the commandant was vile enough to evacuate without firing a shot. He evacuated with all his men with the honours of war and four guns. I am sending orders to the Minister of War to have him arrested, tried by a court-martial, and shot. He must be shot in the middle of the *Place de Grève,* and the execution must he made a conspicuous event. Five generals can be appointed to try him. Without any doubt the enemy's army was lost and would have been destroyed. As it is, I shall have to manœuvre and lose much time throwing bridges.

Berry-au-bac, 4 P. M.:
Wintzingerode's corps tried to prevent our crossing, but, on our infantry appearing, only Cossacks and Baskirs remained to face us. We charged across the handsome bridge over the river Aisne.

6th. To-day I am marching on Laon to drive away the troops of the Crown Prince of Sweden and of Blücher, on which we are daily inflicting serious losses.

7th, Craonne:
I have defeated Wintzingerode, Langeron, Voronzof, together with the remains of Sacken. I have taken 2000 prisoners, some cannon, and driven them from Craonne to the *Ange Gardien.* Craonne is a glorious success. The Duke of Belluno and General Grouchy were wounded.

My advance guard is nearing Laon.

9th. *Battle of Laon. Retreat towards Soissons.*

10th, Chavignon:
(To King Joseph.) The army I defeated at Craonne was the Russian army commanded by Sacken, with that of Wintzingerode. They lost heavily and retired to Laon, where they joined the corps of Bülow, of York, and of Kleist, of the Prussian army. As their position at Laon was very strong, I confined myself yesterday to reconnoitring it. The Duke of Ragusa, who was marching on Laon from Berry-au-bac, got near to the city, his soldiers lost their heads, and he had to retire in some disorder for several leagues, abandoning a few of his guns. This is only an incident of warfare, but a very unfortunate one to occur at a moment when I needed a little luck. This event had made me decide not to attack to-day.

11th. I have decided to fall back on Soissons. The Young Guard is melting away like snow. The Old Guard keeps up. The cavalry of the Guard also melts away fast.

12th, Soissons:
(To the Prince of Neuchâtel.) Write to the Duke of Ragusa that I have no idea of what his corps represents at this moment.

(To King Joseph.) I regret to see that you have spoken to my wife about the Bourbons, and the difficulties the Emperor of Austria might raise. I must beg you to avoid such conversations. I do not wish to be protected by my wife. Such an idea would spoil her and lead to a quarrel. What is the good of talking to her that way? Never, in four years, have the words Bourbon or Austria issued from my lips. In any case, all this can only trouble her sleep and spoil her excellent temper.

You always write as though peace depended on me, and yet I have sent you the documents. If the Parisians want to see the Cossacks they will repent, and yet the truth must be told. I have never sought the applause of the Parisians; I am not an operatic performer.

(To Prince Eugène.) I inclose you a copy of a very extraordinary letter I have received from the King of Naples. Such sentiments are inconceivable at a moment when I, when France, are being assassinated. Send an agent to this extraordinary traitor and sign a treaty with him in my name. You can do what you think best for this purpose; nothing must be omitted in the actual situation that may bring the Neapolitans into line. Afterwards we can do as we please, for after such ingratitude and in such circumstances nothing is binding. To embarrass him I have given orders to have the Pope sent to his outposts, through Parma and Piacenza.

Midnight:
I am starting with the Old Guard.

14th, Reims:
I arrived at Reims yesterday. I recaptured the city, took twenty guns, much transport, and 5000 prisoners.

(To Savary.) You send me no news of what is going on in Paris. A Regency is being discussed, an address, and a thousand foolish and ridiculous intrigues that proceed at best from the brain of a fool like Miot. These people have forgotten that I cut Gordian knots after the fashion of Alexander. They had better remember that I am to-day the same man that I was at Wagram and at Austerlitz; that I will permit no intrigues in the State; that there is no authority but mine, and that in the case of urgent events it is the (Empress) Regent in whom my trust reposes.

(To Joseph.) I have received your letter of the 12th of March. The National Guard of Paris is a part of the people of France, and so long as I live I intend to be master everywhere in France. Your character and mine are opposite; you like to cajole people and to follow their opinions. I prefer to be cajoled and to have my views followed. To-day as at Austerlitz, I am the master. I imagine that they can perceive the difference between the time of Lafayette when the mob was sovereign and to-day when it is I.

16th. (To King Joseph.) I am going to manœuvre in such a way that you may be several days without news from me. Should the enemy advance on Paris with forces so large as to make resistance impossible, send the Regent (and) my son in the direction of the Loire. Don't leave my son's side, and remember that I would sooner know him in the Seine than in the hands of the enemies of France. The fate of Astyanax as prisoner of the Greeks has always seemed to me the most unhappy in history.

17th. There are three possible courses:

One is to march on Arcis, thirteen leagues; we could get there to-morrow, the 18th; this is the boldest and the result is incalculable.

To move on Sézanne;

The third would be to march straight on Meaux by the highroad. The third is the safest because it takes us rapidly towards Paris, but is also the one that has no moral effect, and leaves everything to the chance of a great battle. But, if the enemy have 70,000, or 80,000 men, such a battle would be a fearful risk, while if we move towards Troyes and strike in at their rear, while the Duke of Taranto retreats disputing every position, we may stand a much better chance.

Epernay:
To-morrow before dawn I shall start for Arcis-surAube; I shall be there day after to-morrow at noon, to strike the enemy's rear.

20th, Plancy:
I crossed the Aube yesterday. I then moved straight on Méry. I attacked the town and occupied it at 7 P. M. The Emperor Alexander was at Arcy on the 18th. He only staid an hour; we were nearly face to face.

(To Berthier.) Write at once to the Duke of Taranto to, move everything on Arcis, even General Gérard, even the National Guards.

During the fight at Arcis-sur-Aube I did all I could to meet with a glorious end defending the soil of our country inch by inch. I exposed myself continuously. Bullets rained all around me; my clothes were full of them; but not one touched me. I am condemned to live!

23d, Château du Plessis:
(To Berthier.) Send a gendarme in disguise to Metz, send another one to Nancy, and one to Bar, with letters for the mayors. Inform them that we are operating against the enemy's communications, that the moment has come for a levy *en masse*, to ring the tocsin, to arrest everywhere the enemy's officers and commissaries, to attack the convoys, to seize the magazines and reserves of the enemy; let them immediately publish this order in every parish of the 2d and 4th military divisions. Write to the governor of Metz to concentrate the garrisons and to march so as to meet us on the Meuse.

31st. *Capitulation of Paris.*

La Cour de France:
We order the Duke of Vicenza, our Grand Equerry and Minister of Foreign Affairs, to see the Allied Sovereigns and the Commander-in-chief of their armies, to recommend to them our good subjects in our capital.

We invest him by these presents with full powers to negotiate and conclude peace, pledging ourselves to ratify whatever he may effect for the good of our service.

(To Berthier.) The Duke of Ragusa will form the advance guard, and will concentrate his troops at Essonne, The Duke of Treviso's corps will take position between Essonne and Fontainebleau. Write to the Prefect of Orléans to give him the bad news of the occupation of Paris by the enemy, which my arrival would have prevented had they delayed another three hours.

Remind the Minister of the Interior to enforce the levy *en masse* everywhere so as to fill up our battalions.

April 1st. The Old Guard with its artillery and the reserve batteries will take position to-morrow at the débouché of the forest.

3d. Officers, non-commissioned officers, and men of the Old Guard: The enemy have stolen three marches on us, and have entered Paris. I offered the Emperor Alexander a peace that cost me great sacrifices. He not only refused, but he did more: at the perfidious suggestion of those *émigrés* whose lives I had spared and on whom I had showered favours, he has authorized them to wear the white cockade, and soon he will try to substitute it for our national cockade. In a few days I shall attack him in Paris. I count on you…

(A pause; silence.)

Am I right?

(Vive l'Empereur! Vive l'Empereur! To Paris! To Paris!)

We will go and prove to them that the French nation is mistress of her own soil; that if we have long been masters among others, we will always be so here, and that we are able to defend our colours, our independence, and the integrity of our country, Communicate what I have said to your men.

4th. (To Berthier.) Order the Dukes of Ragusa, of Treviso, of Reggio, of Conegliano, to report at the palace to-night at ten, and to arrange so as to be back at their posts before dawn.

(Declaration.) The allied Powers having announced that the Emperor Napoleon is the sole obstacle to the reëstablishment of peace in Europe, the Emperor Napoleon, mindful of his engagements, declares that he is ready to descend from the throne, to give up France and even life itself for the good of the country, inseparable from the rights of his son, those of the regency of the Empress, and the maintenance of the laws of the Empire.

Done in our palace of Fontainebleau the 4th of April, 1814.

5th. (To Berthier.) Order General Trelliard, who is near Nernours, to march to-morrow towards Pithiviers. Tell him that we shall move through Malesherbes on Pithiviers. He could join us if we had to fight.

Order General Friant to start to-morrow morning at six for Malesherbes with the division of the Old Guard.

The artillery will follow immediately after the Old Guard.

10th. I cast about for an uncomfortable corner of earth, where I might profit by the errors that would certainly be made. I pitched on the island of Elba. It was the choice of a soul of adamant. My character is certainly curious, but a man cannot be extraordinary without being unlike others; I am a fragment of rock hurled into space.

11th. The Emperor Napoleon renounces for himself, his heirs and successors, all right of sovereignty over the French Empire, the Kingdom of Italy, and all other countries.

The island of Elba, chosen as his abode by the Emperor Napoleon, shall, during his lifetime, be an independent principality.

The French Imperial Guard shall furnish a detachment of 1200 to 1500 men to serve as an escort. H. M. the Emperor Napoleon may keep for his own guard 400 men who shall volunteer for this service.

13th. Providence has decreed it,—I shall live! Who can fathom the future? In any case, my wife and my son will be enough for me.

16th. (To Countess Walewska.) Marie, I have received your letter of the 15th. I am profoundly touched by the sentiments you express, they are worthy of your noble spirit. If you go to the baths of Lucca I would be very glad indeed to see you and your son. Never doubt me.

19th. (To the Empress Maria Louisa.) My good Louise, I have received your letter; I understand all the grief there is in it, and it increases my own. I am glad to see that Corvisart encourages you. I am very grateful to him for it; his noble conduct justifies the high opinion I had of him. Please tell him so from me. Have him send me little bulletins about you at frequent intervals. Try to go at once to the baths of Aix, which I am told Corvisart recommends for you. Keep well; preserve your health for your son, who needs your care. I am starting for the island of Elba, and will write to you from there. I will get everything ready to receive you. Write to me frequently. Address your letters to the Viceroy and to your uncle, if, as it is said, he is to be Grand Duke of Tuscany.

20th. (Farewell to the Guard.) Soldiers of my Old Guard, I have come to say good-bye. During twenty years I have always met you on the path of honour and of glory. In these last as in prosperous days you have never ceased to be the pattern of courage and of loyalty. With men like you our cause was not lost. But the war was interminable; it would have meant civil war, and France would have been even more unhappy. I therefore sacrificed all our interests to those of the country I am leaving. You, my friends, must continue to serve France. Her happiness was my only thought; it will always be the object of my hopes! Do not pity my fate; if I have consented to survive it is still to work for your fame; I mean to write down those great things that we have done together! Good-bye, my children! I wish I could press you all to my heart; let me at all events embrace your standard!—Good-bye once more, old comrades! May this last embrace pass into your hearts!

21st, Briare:
Well! You heard my speech to the Old Guard yesterday, you saw the effect it produced? That is the way to talk to them!

24th, Valence:
(To Augereau.) Where are you off to like that? You are going to the Court? Your proclamation is stupid enough: why insult me?

27th, Fréjus:
(To General Dalesme.) Circumstances having brought me to renounce the French throne, I have reserved for myself the sovereignty and ownership of the island of Elba, to which all the Powers have consented. I am therefore sending you General Drouot so that you may immediately hand over to him the said island, the stores of food and ammunition, and the property appertaining to my Imperial domains. Please notify this new state of things to the inhabitants, and my selection of their island for my abode because of their good disposition and the excellence of their climate. They will be the constant object of my solicitude.

28th, on board H. M. S. *Undaunted:*
The Bourbons—poor devils—are glad to get back their palaces and their estates, but if the French people become dissatisfied and think that their manufactures are not being looked after, they will be driven out within six months.

May 3d, Porto Ferrajo, island of Elbe:
Well! this is a fine abode for me!

5th. It will be an island of rest!

7th. (Orders for General Count Drouot.) Find out from the sub-prefect what is the system of administration.

Have the flag of the island hoisted in every parish tomorrow, and turn this into some sort of a festival.

I think that the governor should communicate a note, stating that my flag has been hoisted, to the governments of Naples, Rome, Tuscany, and Genoa.

Convene the sub-prefect, the navy commissioner, the chief registrar, the war commissary, the collector of revenue, and other persons who can give me information on the administration of the island, to a council to-morrow.

Inform the intendant of my dissatisfaction at the dirty state of the streets.

9th. Eh! My island is none too big!

29th. *Death of Josephine at Malmaison.*

July 11th. (To Count Bertrand.) Ask Cardinal Fesch whom I could appoint consul at Civita-Vecchia. That port, Leghorn, and Genoa are the most important points.

17th. (Note for the Grand Marshal.) Write to my brother Lucien that I have his letter of the 11th of June; that I am touched by the sentiments he expresses; that he must not be surprised at my not answering, as I write to no one. I have not even written to Madame (Mère).

24th. (To Count Bertrand.) Order the *Abeille*, if the weather is fine, to start to-night for Civita-Vecchia. She will carry letters for the consul at Naples and for Cardinal Fesch. Instruct the *Abeille* not to remain more than two or three days at Civita-Vecchia and to get all the information possible about the journey of Madame and of Princess Pauline.

August 2. (Note for General Bertrand.) As I am not at present well enough established for entertaining I shall wait for the arrival of the Empress or of Princess Pauline, which should be early in September, for having the fireworks. I want the town to give a ball at its own expense on the public square in which a wooden booth can be erected, and to invite the officers of the Guard. Outside the booth there should be music for the soldiers to dance to, and there must be a few barrels of wine so that they may have something to drink. I also want the town to marry two young people and set them up. The Grand Marshal and officials will witness the marriage, which is to take place at High Mass.

9th. (To Bertrand.) Colonel Leczinski, who is leaving to-day, will carry a letter from me to the Empress at Aix. Write to Méneval to tell him that I expect the Empress at the end of August; that I want her to bring my son, and that it is curious I don't hear from her, which must arise from her letters being intercepted.

26th. (To Bertrand.) I believe I have told you to ask Princess Pauline not to bring the pianist, but only two good singers, as we have a good violinist and a good pianist here.

One of my mules has just been drowned, which is a considerable loss, and arises from there not being a small pump at the stable. Have one put in.

28th. I have news from the Empress to the 10th of August. She is to write care of M. Senno and will send her letters to Genoa under cover to M. Constantin Gatelli.

September 2d. (To Bertrand.) Write to Princess Pauline to say that I have received all the letters from Naples; tell her that I am annoyed at having had letters sent me through Stahremberg unsealed, as though I were a prisoner and he my gaoler; I think this way of doing things is offensive and absurd, and insulting both to me and to them.

9th. I have received a most sentimental letter from the King of Naples; he declares that he has already written several times, but I doubt it. It appears that the French and Italian questions are disturbing him, and making him amiable.

20th. My wife no longer writes to me. My son is snatched away from me. No such barbarous act is recorded in modern times.

30th. *The Congress of Vienna assembles.*

October 10th. (To Ferdinand, Grand Duke of Tuscany.) *Monsieur mon Frère et trés cher Oncle:* Having received no news from my wife since the 10th of August, nor from my son for six months, I have intrusted this letter to Cavaliere Colonna. I beg Your Royal Highness to let me know whether I may send a letter to the Empress once a week, and receive in return her news and a letter from the Countess of Montesquiou, the governess of my son. I flatter myself that in spite of events that have so changed many persons, Your Royal Highness still retains some degree of friendship for me.

November 14th. Any news of the Congress? Do you think they have it in mind to exile me? I will never permit them to carry me off.

December 11th. (To Count Drouot.) Take great care to have the discharges of the grenadiers who are leaving and who are good men, drawn up in their favour. You must state that the discharge is granted on the orders of General Drouot, because the situation of the families of these men demands their presence, and that it is with regret the battalion loses the services of such good soldiers. Their services, battles, and wounds shall be set out, in fact everything that can testify to my satisfaction with brave men who have given me so many marks of their devotion.

Have a proof of the discharge printed. Place my arms in the middle; strike out the expression *Sovereign of Elbe,* which is ridiculous, and see that the form is known in the Guard, so that it may realize how it is honoured when my grenadiers get leave of absence.

1815

January 1st, Elba:
Well, old grumbler, are you getting tired of it?

(No, sire, but it's not very exciting!)

You are wrong. You should take things as they come. It won't last forever!

2d. (To Drouot.) Order the *Abeille* to take in supplies for a week this evening. Eight sailors of the Guard are to go on board, so as to cruise to-morrow off Cape St. André and observe the movements of the French ships that appear to be cruising around the island. The captain in command of the *Abeille* will have an additional 100 francs a month until he can be given a larger ship. Get him a good glass if he hasn't one.

3d. (Note.) On Sunday there will be a ball in the large reception room. The invitations must cover the whole island, though they must not include more than 200 persons. There must be refreshments, but no ices because of the difficulty of getting them. The whole must not cost more than 1000 francs.

On Sunday the 15th the Academy might inaugurate its theatre and give a masked ball. On the 22d I may give another ball. On the 29th there might be a second masked ball at the theatre.

February 16th. (To General Drouot.) Order the brig into port to be careened and have its copper bottom overhauled, and its leaks stopped, and generally put into seaworthy condition. Have it painted like the English brigs. I want it in the bay and ready, as I have said, by the 24th or 25th of this month.

Order M. Pons to charter two large-sized vessels for a month, brigs or xebecs of more than 90 tons.

18th. Drouot, all France regrets me and wants me. In a few days I shall leave the island.

24th. Ali! France! France!

26th. I am leaving the island of Elba.

Twenty-four hours before weighing anchor only Bertrand and Drouot knew the secret.

28th, at sea:
I shall reach Paris without firing a shot.

March 1st, Golfe Jouan:
(To the army.) Soldiers! we were not defeated!

Soldiers! In my exile I have heard your voice. I have come to you through every obstacle, every danger. Your general, called to the throne by the voice of the people, and raised on your bucklers, is back among you; come to him! Pluck off the colours that the nation has proscribed, and that, for twenty-five years, were the rallying point of all the enemies of France. Put on the tricolour cockade; you wore it in our great days. Here are the eagles you had at Ulm, at Austerlitz, at Jena, at Eylau, at Friedland, at Tudela, at Eckmühl, at Essling, at Wagram, at Smolensk, at the Moskowa, at Lützen, at Wurschen, at Montmirail! Do you believe that the little handful of Frenchmen who are so arrogant to-day can support their sight? 'They will return whence they came; there let them reign as they pretend that they did reign these last nineteen years.

Soldiers, rally around the standard of your chief! Victory will advance at the double! The Eagle, with the national colours, will fly from steeple to steeple to the towers of Notre Dame. Then will you be able to display your honourable scars. Then will you be able to claim the credit of your deeds, as the liberators of your country. In your old age, surrounded and honoured by your fellow-citizens, all will respectfully listen while you narrate your great deeds; you will be able to say with pride: "And I also was one of that Grand Army that twice entered the walls of Vienna, of Rome, of Berlin, of Madrid, of Moscow, and that cleansed Paris from the stain left on it by treason and the presence of the enemy!"

6th, Gap:
Citizens, I am deeply touched by your demonstrations. Your hopes will be fulfilled; the nation's cause will triumph once more. You are right to call me your *Father*, I live only for the honour and for the happiness of France. My return dispels all your anxieties, guarantees your property. To-day equality among all classes, and the rights you enjoyed for twenty-five years and that our fathers so longed for, become once more a part of your existence.

9th, Grenoble:
Citizens, when in my exile I learned all the misfortunes that weighed on the nation, that the rights of the people were trampled on, and that I was reproached for my inactivity, I lost not a moment, I embarked on a frail vessel, I crossed the sea amid the warships of various nations, I landed on the soil of the fatherland, and I thought of nothing but of flashing with the rapidity of the eagle to this good city of Grenoble, of which I knew the strong patriotism and devotion to me.

Men of Dauphiné, you have fulfilled all my hopes!

11th, Lyons:
The old soldiers came at the head of the inhabitants of their villages and assured them that I really was Bonaparte. Peasants pulled from their pockets 5 franc pieces with my effigy, and said: "Yes, that's the man!"

(To Maria Louisa, Empress of the French, at Schoenbrunn.) *Madame et chère amie,* I have reascended my throne.

12th. (To Marshal Ney.) My Cousin: My chief of staff is sending you marching orders. I feel sure that on hearing I was in possession of Lyons you made your soldiers go back to the tricolour flag. Carry out Bertrand's orders and join me at Châlons. I shall receive you as I did the day after the battle of the Moskowa.

21st, Paris:
(To Fouché.) According to first information the King is in the neighbourhood of the Somme. Try to get news about this matter.

(To Marshal Davout.) Order the Count de Lobau to assume command of the 1st military division and of all the troops there. If there are bad colonels with the Paris troops, put proposals before me for replacing them.

Communicate by semaphore in the course of the morning my arrival in Paris, and your appointment as Minister of War.

26th. Princes are the first citizens of a State. Their power is more or less extensive as the nations they govern decide. Sovereignty is hereditary only because that is the interest of the people. Apart from this doctrine I do not recognise legitimity.

I have given up the idea of the Grand Empire, of which, in fifteen years, I had only laid the foundations. Henceforth the happiness and consolidation of the French Empire will be the object of all my thoughts.

I thank my good city of Paris for its sentiments. It gave me special pleasure to enter its walls on the anniversary of a day, four years ago, on which the people of this capital gave me such touching evidence of its interest in the affections nearest my heart. To be here I had to come on in advance of my army, and to trust myself unattended to that national guard which I myself created, and that has so fully attained the object of its creation. I am ambitious of retaining its command for myself.

27th. (To Davout.) Establish workshops in Paris for mounting 400 muskets a day, with spare parts. It will give the city employment.

29th. From the date of the present decree the slave trade is abolished.

30th. (To General Rapp.) At the time when you came back from Egypt, at the time that Desaix was killed, you were only a soldier; I have made a man of you. I shall never forget your conduct on the retreat from Moscow. Ney and you are among the few whose souls are as tempered steel. And at your siege of Dantzig you did more than the impossible.

April 1st. The work of fifteen years is undone, it cannot be begun afresh. It would take twenty years and the sacrifice of twenty millions of men. In any case, I need peace and can obtain it only by victories; I will not raise false hopes in you; I allow it to be said that there are negotiations, but there are none. I foresee a difficult struggle, a long war. To maintain it the nation must support me; but in return it will demand liberty,—it shall have it. The situation is a new one. I ask for nothing better than advice,—a man is not at forty-five what he was at thirty. The repose of a constitutional monarch may suit me. It would suit my son even better.

(To Francis I, Emperor of Austria.) At a moment when Providence has placed me once more in the capital of my State, my keenest wish is soon to see my wife and my son. My efforts will tend exclusively to consolidate the throne that the love of my people has restored to me, and some day to transmit it, settled on unshakeable foundations, to the child whom Your Majesty has guarded with paternal affection. As the maintenance of peace is essential to my object I have nothing more at heart than to maintain it with all the Powers, but I attach special importance to maintaining it with Your Majesty.

11th. We must assume that the enemy will declare war about the 1st to the 15th of May.

18th. A great number of Frenchmen have followed the Count de Lille: for instance, Marshal Victor, Generals Bordesoulle and Maison. A hint was thrown out to them that they might return; they answered that it would be at the head of 500,000 men.

(To Marshal Masséna.) I have read your proclamation with pleasure. I am very anxious to see you. If the state of your health unfits you for anything save to return to the south, I will send you back there from Paris.

22d. I propose presenting eagles to all the regiments at the Assembly of May, which will take place about the 25th of that month.

(*Constitutional Act.*) Napoleon by the grace of God and the Constitution Emperor of the French, to all present and to come greeting.

Since we were called, fifteen years ago, by the will of France to the government of the State, we have, at various times, attempted to improve its constitutional forms according to the necessities and desires of the nation, and by taking advantage of the lessons of experience. Our object then was to organize a great European federal system that we had adopted as conforming with the spirit of the age and as favouring the advance of civilization. From now on our object will be only to increase the prosperity of France so as to strengthen civil liberty. From this it follows that several modifications must be made in the constitutions and other laws that govern this Empire.

27th. (To Marshal Ney.) Order magazines to be formed at Avesnes for 100,000 men and for 20,000 horses for 10 days.

(To General Bertrand.) Send one of my campaigning outfits off to Compiègne.

May 9th. (To Count Mollien.) It is of the utmost importance that the funds due to the regiments for clothing expenses should be paid in within a week. I have 100,000 men that are useless because I have no money to clothe and equip them. The fate of France lies there; set to work night and day, and take measures so that we can raise this money immediately.

15th. (To Prince Lebrun.) I have received your letter; I shall not hide from you that I no longer viewed you as Arch Treasurer, because you had accepted a lower station in the Chamber of Peers from the Royal Government. But I recognised so much affection and heart in yesterday's address, and in the manner in which you delivered it, that I can refuse you nothing, and that I am very glad to forget anything that was not right which you did during my absence. I shall have the patent of Arch Treasurer sent to you; you are entitled to what you have reconquered.

17th. (To Drouot.) I have already told you that the officers of the Young Guard must advertise and get to work recruiting in Paris. Send officers to the various town halls, have a band and drummers, and do everything to stimulate the young men.

27th. The Guard will probably start soon; there will then be no troops left in Paris.

28th. (Note for the Duke of Vicenza.) It is probable that the Chamber will vote a resolution about the King of Rome to voice the indignation that Austria's conduct should provoke. This would have a good effect.

Méneval is to make a report dated the day after his arrival. He will set forth the conduct of Austria and the other Powers to the Empress from Orléans up to the time of his leaving Vienna: the violation of the treaty of Fontainebleau by, so to speak, snatching her and her son from the Emperor; in this connection he will emphasize the indignation which his grandmother the Queen of Sicily showed at Vienna. He will dwell particularly on the separation of the Prince Imperial from his mother, from Mme. de Montesquiou, on his tears as he left her, on the apprehensions of Mme. de Montesquiou for the safety, for the life of the young Prince. He will keep within bounds on this last point. He will mention the distress of the Empress at being separated from the Emperor. She was thirty days without sleep at the time of the Emperor's embarkation. He will insist on the fact that in reality the Empress is a prisoner, since she is not allowed to write to the Emperor.

June 1st. Gentlemen, Electors, Deputies of the army and navy to the *Champ de Mai:*

Emperor, Consul, soldier, I hold all from the people. In prosperity, in adversity, on the battlefield, in council, on the throne, in exile, France has been the one and only object of my thoughts and of my deeds.

Frenchmen, you are returning to your departments. Tell the citizens that we are at a great moment, that with union, energy, and perseverance we shall emerge victorious from this struggle of a great people against its oppressors. Tell them that the foreign kings whom I have placed on their thrones, or who owe me the preservation of their crowns, who, in the days of my prosperity, all begged my alliance and the protection of the French people, are to-day aiming their blows at me.

Frenchmen, my will and my duties are those of the French people; my honour, my glory, my happiness, can be none other than the honour, the glory, and the happiness of France.

3d. Prince Jerome is to serve with the rank of lieutenant-general. He must join the army at once.

(To Marshal Davout.) Herewith you will find a copy of my orders for the cavalry of the army. Marshal Grouchy will command it. All unemployed generals are at his disposal. Order Marshal Grouchy to be at Laon on the 5th so that we may open the campaign on the 10th.

(To Marshal Soult.) Draw up a plan for the movement of the corps of General Gérard from the Moselle to Phillippeville, masking it as much as possible from the enemy. We should be there on the 12th, by making long days' marches.

My Guard will all be at Soissons on the 21st.

7th. (To Soult.) Give positive orders for stopping an communications along the whole of the northern Rhine and Moselle frontiers; not a stage or carriage must pass.

I think you had better start to-morrow night. You will go straight to Lille, incognito so far as possible, and make all arrangements. You must get the latest information as to the enemy's positions.

My travelling carriage must be made ready, without any one's knowing it, so that I can start two hours after issuing my orders.

11th. I leave to-night to place myself at the head of my army.

(To Marshal Davout.) Send for Marshal Ney; if he wants to be in the first fighting, tell him to get to Avesnes, where my headquarters will be on the 14th.

12th, Laon:
Neither at Laon nor at Soissons have I found any of the stores that were promised me for the army.

Avesnes:
The infantry of the Imperial Guard will bivouac a quarter of a league in front of Beaumont and will be ranged in three lines. Each army corps will march with its sappers leading, and the bridging material collected by the generals. The corps must be well closed up and in good order. Moving on Charleroi every opportunity must be seized for getting forward and crushing any hostile bodies that may be manœuvring or attempting to attack the army.

14th. To-night I shall move headquarters to Beaumont. To-morrow, the 15th, I move on Charleroi, where the Prussian army is, which will result in a battle or the enemy's retreat. The army is splendid, and the weather pretty good; the country seems well disposed.

(To the army.) Soldiers! This is the anniversary of Marengo and of Friedland, that twice decided the fate of Europe. Then, as after Wagram, as after Austerlitz, we were too generous; we believed in the protestations and in the oaths of the princes whom we left on their thrones! And now, coalized against us, they are aiming at the independence and the most sacred rights of France. They have begun an unjust aggression. Forward! Let us march against them; are not they and we the same men?

Soldiers! You were one against three at Jena against these same arrogant Prussians; at Montmirail, you were one against six. Madmen! A moment's prosperity has blinded them. If they enter France they will find their graves. Soldiers, we have forced marches to make, battles to fight, dangers to encounter, but with constancy the victory will be ours; the rights, the honour, of our country will be reconquered. For every Frenchman who has courage the moment has come to conquer or to die.

15th, Charleroi, *11 A. M.:*
Good-morning, Ney, I am glad to see you. You can assume command of the 1st and 2d corps. Push the enemy back along the Brussels road and take position at Quatre Bras.

Evening:
The army has forced the passage of the Sambre near Charleroi and is throwing out pickets midway between Charleroi and Namur, and Charleroi and Brussels. We have captured 1500 prisoners and six guns. Four Prussian regiments have been routed. The Emperor, who has been in the saddle since 3 A. M., has come in very fatigued. He has thrown himself on a got to rest a few hours, and will be in the saddle again at midnight. We may have serious fighting to-morrow.

General Gérard reports that Lieutenant-General Bourmont, Colonel Clouet, and Captain Villoutreys have deserted to the enemy.

16th. (To Ney.) I am sending you my aide-de-camp, General Flahault, with this letter. The chief of staff should have sent you orders, but you will get mine more quickly because my officers ride faster than his.

I am moving the Guard to Fleurus, and shall be there myself before noon. I shall attack the enemy if they are there, and reconnoitre to Gembloux. There, according to events, I will come to a decision, perhaps at three this afternoon, perhaps at night.

(To Marshal Count Grouchy.) I shall reach Fleurus between ten and eleven; if the enemy hold Sombreffe I shall attack them, and even at Gembloux and take that position, as I intend to start to-night and operate with my left wing, commanded by Marshal Ney, against the English. All my information points to the Prussians not being able to oppose us with more than 40,000 men.

3 P. M.:
It may be that in three hours the result of the campaign will be decided. If Ney carries out his orders well, not a gun of their armies will escape me.

The right wing made up of the 3d and 4th infantry and 3d cavalry corps, commanded by Marshal Grouchy, was in position along the hills at the back of Fleurus. At three o'clock General Lefol's division of General Vandamme's corps got into action and carried Saint Amand, from which it drove the enemy at the point of the bayonet. On the extreme right Marshal Grouchy and General Pajol fought at the village of Sombreffe. The enemy had 80,000 or 90,000 men in line, with many guns.

At seven o'clock we had carried all the villages; the enemy still occupied the plateau of Bussy in force. The Emperor moved forward with the Guard to the village of Ligny. Eight battalions of the Guard advanced with the bayonet, with four squadrons of the body-guard, General Delort's and General Milhaud's cuirassiers and the horse grenadiers of the Guard in support. The Old Guard advanced with the bayonet against the enemy's columns on the heights of Bussy, and in an instant covered the field of battle with dead. At ten o'clock the battle was over and we were in possession of the field.

17th, near Ligny, *11 A. M.:*
(To Grouchy.) While I start after the English, you must pursue the Prussians.

On the road from Quatre Bras to Genappe, *4 P. M.:*
Fire! fire! they are the English!

6 P. M., Farm of the Belle Alliance:
The Emperor orders that the army be ready to attack at nine in the morning.

18th, Battlefield of Waterloo:
8.30 A. M.:
There are ninety chances in our favour.

I tell you Wellington is a had general, the English are bad soldiers; we will settle the matter by lunch time.

(Soult: I sincerely hope so!)

(Order.) As soon as the army is in position, about one o'clock, when the Emperor gives the order to Marshal Ney, the attack will commence for capturing the village of Mont Saint Jean, where the crossroads are. Count d'Erlon will open the attack.

At three in the afternoon the Emperor ordered the Guard forward to the plateau which the 1st corps had occupied at the beginning of the battle. The Prussian division, the advance of which was anticipated, opened fire on the skirmishers of Count de Lobau along all our right flank.

This morning we had ninety chances in our favour; we still have sixty. And if Grouchy moves quickly, Bülow's corps will be completely destroyed.

The Emperor intended to push home an attack on Mont Saint Jean which should have been decisive, but by one of those impatient movements so frequent in our military history and that have so often been fatal to us, the reserve cavalry, seeing the backward movement made by the English to avoid our artillery fire from which they had already suffered heavily, advanced to the plateau of Mont Saint Jean and charged the enemy. This movement, which, made at the right moment and supported by the reserves, would have decided the battle, made without supports and before matters were settled on the right became fatal. All our cavalry became engaged in mutual support. There, for three hours, many charges were delivered in which we broke several squares of British infantry and captured six flags, which, however, did not compensate the losses suffered by our cavalry from grape and musketry. We could not engage our reserves until we had disposed of the flank attack of the Prussian corps.

Troops! Where do you expect me to find them? Do you want me to make them?

This attack continued and developed perpendicularly to our right flank. The Emperor sent General Duhesme with the Young Guard and several reserve batteries. The enemy were checked and driven back; they were spent and no longer to be feared. That was the moment for attacking the enemy's centre. At half-past eight the four battalions of the Middle Guard that had been sent up to the plateau beyond Mont Saint Jean to support the cuirassiers and that were being annoyed by the enemy's grape, advanced with the bayonet to carry their batteries. The light was failing; a charge made in their flank by several English squadrons threw them into disorder; the fugitives recrossed the valley. Several regiments near by, seeing part of the Guard in flight, thought it was the Old Guard, and were shaken; shouts of: All is lost! The Guard is beaten! were raised. The soldiers even declare that at some points ill-disposed men shouted: Every man for himself! However that may be, a panic spread over the whole battlefield; a disorderly rush was made towards our line of retreat; soldiers, gunners, wagons all crowded in to reach it.

We must die here, we must die on the battlefield!

The Old Guard, which was in reserve, was struck and carried away.

June 19th, Philippeville:
Deep within me was the instinct that the result would be fatal!

(To King Joseph.) All is not lost. I estimate that collecting all my forces I shall have 150,000 men left. The national guards and a few plucky marching battalions will give me 100,000 men; the depot battalions 50,000. I therefore have 300,000 men to face the enemy with at once. I can drag my artillery with carriage horses; I can raise 100,000 conscripts; I can arm them with the muskets of royalists and ill-disposed national guards; I will raise a levy *en masse* in the Lyonnais, Dauphiné, Burgundy, Lorraine, Champagne; I will crush the enemy; but everybody must help me, and not deafen me. I am starting for Laon: I shall doubtless find troops there. I have not heard from Grouchy; unless he is captured, as I fear he is, I shall have 50,000 men in three days. Write and tell me what effect this horrible scrimmage has had on the Chamber. I think the deputies will realize that their duty, in this great crisis, is to join me in saving France. See that they support me as they should; above all courage and firmness.

21st, Paris:
I had had no food for three days! I was extremely tired. As soon as I arrived I jumped into my bath, and had something to eat.

(Lavalette: He came to me with a frightful, epileptic laugh!)

Ah! my God!

The army did wonders; it was seized with a panic. Ney behaved like a madman. I am exhausted. I must have two hours' rest. I am bursting, here!

Well, all is not lost. I shall inform the Chamber of what has occurred. I hope that this step will rally them around me. After that I shall go off again.

(Message to the Chamber of Representatives.) Mr. President: After the battles of Ligny and of Mont Saint Jean, and after having arranged for rallying the army at Avesnes and Philippeville, for the defence of the frontier fortresses, and of the cities of Laon and Soissons, I have come to Paris to concert measures for the national defence with my ministers, and to come to an understanding with the Chamber concerning all that the safety of the country demands.

I have appointed as a Committee the Minister of Foreign Affairs, Count Carnot, and the Duke of Otranto to renew and continue the negotiations with the Powers, so as to discover their real intentions and to put an end to the war, providing that is compatible with the independence and honour of the Nation.

My political existence is at an end.

22d, *morning:*
If they mean to use force with me, I shall not abdicate. I must be left to come to my decision in peace. Tell them to wait.

4 P. M.:
Lucien, write: When I began the war to maintain the national independence, I counted on the unanimous support of every individual, of every official. I had

good reason to anticipate success. Circumstances appeared to be changed. I offer myself as a sacrifice to the hatred of the enemies of France. I only hope that their declaration may prove sincere, and that their hostility is solely to my person. Let all unite for the public safety and to remain an independent nation. I proclaim my son, under the style of Napoleon II, Emperor of the French.

They have forced me to it!

(Vive l'Empereur! Vive l'Empereur!)

They have done so much for me! Will the people ever know how much this night of indecision and of agony has cost me? I had to give in, and once done, it is done; I am not for half measures.

I could not be, I would not be, a king of the mob!

23d. Ah, wretched man! What have you written there? Strike it out, sir, strike it out quickly! A battle of the spurs! What a mistake! What a calumny! A battle of the spurs! Ah! poor army! brave soldiers! You never fought better!

24th. They are debating, the hounds, with the enemy at our gates!

(To Hortense.) Malmaison is yours. Will you grant me hospitality there?

25th. (To Barbier.) The Grand Marshal requests M. Barbier to bring to Malmaison to-morrow:
some books on America;
a schedule of all that has been printed about the Emperor during his various campaigns.

The great library must be invoiced to an American firm that can ship it to America by way of Havre.

Malmaison:
(To the army.) Soldiers! Although absent, I shall follow your footsteps. Every regiment is known to me, and I shall render justice to its courage when it gains a success over the enemy. We have been calumniated, you and I. Those who are incapable of judging you have seen in the proofs of devotion you have given me a

zeal of which I was the sole object; let your future successes show that it was above all our country you served in obeying me, and that if I own a share of your affections I owe it to my ardent love for France, our common Mother. Save the honour, the independence, of the French, remain till the end such as I have known you during twenty years, and you will be invincible.

Poor Josephine! I cannot get used to being here without her. It seems as though I may see her coming out of an alley at any moment, picking some of these flowers that she loved so much!

I want to leave France now. Let them give me the two frigates I asked for, and I shall start at once for Rochefort.

29th. They are still afraid of me! I wanted to make one last effort to save France. They would not let me!

5 P. M. Departure for Rochefort.

July 14th, Island of Aix:
(To the Prince Regent of England.) Your Royal Highness: Exposed to the factions that divide my country and to the enmity of the powers of Europe, I have closed my political career, and I come, like Themistocles, to claim hospitality at the hearth of the British people. I place myself under the protection of their laws, which I demand from Your Royal Highness, as from the most powerful, the most constant, and the most generous of my foes.

15th, on the bridge of the *Epervier, 6 A. M.:*
General Beker, return to the island of Aix. It must not be said that France handed me over to the English.

Departure for H. M. S. *Bellerophon.*
(To Captain Maitland.) I come on board your ship to place myself under the protection of the laws of England.

August 4th, on board H. M. S. *Bellerophon:*
I solemnly protest here, in the face of heaven and of men, against the violation of my most sacred rights, in disposing of my person and of my liberty by force. I came on board the *Bellerophon* freely; I am not the prisoner, I am the guest of

England. From the instant I boarded the *Bellerophon* I was at the hearth of the British people. I appeal to History! It will place on record that an enemy who during twenty years waged war against the British people came freely in his misfortune to seek a refuge under their laws; and what, more striking proof could he display of his esteem and of his trust? And how did England reply to such magnanimity? She pretended to hold out the hand of hospitality to her enemy, and when he had placed himself in her power, she slew him!

Whatever shall we do in that remote spot? Well, we will write our Memoirs. Yes, we shall have to work; and work is the scythe of time. After all, a man must accomplish his destiny; that is my great doctrine. Well, let mine be fulfilled!

7th, on board H. M. S. *Northumberland*; departure for St. Helena.
Here I am, Admiral, at your orders!

They can call me what they like (General Bonaparte), they cannot prevent me from being myself.

13th, at sea:
What time is it?—Let's play *vingt et un*.

September 4th. *Vendémiaire*, even Montenotte, did not convince me that I was a really great man; it was only after Lodi that the idea took possession of me that I might easily become a decisive actor on our political stage. Then flashed the first spark of high ambition.

6th. I returned from the campaign of Italy not worth more than 300,000 francs of my own; I might easily have brought back ten or twelve millions, and I should have earned them; I never handed in any accounts, nor was I ever asked for any. I expected, on my return, some great national reward; but the Directoire put the matter on one side. My proclivity was for creating and not for possessing. My property lay in glory and fame: the Simplon for the people; the Louvre for the foreigners, were to me more of a property than the private domains. I bought diamonds for the Crown; I repaired the royal palaces; I crammed them full of furniture; and I found myself on occasion thinking that the money spent by Josephine on her hothouses or gallery was a positive injury for my Botanical Gardens or my Paris Museum.

14th. I did not usurp the crown; it was in the gutter and I picked it out; the people placed it on my head: their act must be respected.

18th. What latitude are we in? What longitude? What is the run since yesterday?

28th. In revolutions a man can be sure of nothing except what he is doing; it would not be reasonable to affirm that things might not have turned out differently.

October 8th. The men of 1815 were not the men of 1792. The generals were afraid of everything. I needed some one to lead the Guard: had Bessières or Lannes been there I should not have been defeated. Soult didn't have a good staff.

17th. *Landing at St. Helena.*

St. Helena

October 24th, 1815. What infamous treatment they have held in store for us! This is the agony of death! To injustice, to violence, they add insult and slow torture! If I was so dangerous, why didn't they get rid of me? A few bullets in my heart or in my head would have settled it; there would have been some courage at least in such a crime! If it were not for you and for your wives I would refuse everything here save a soldier's rations. How can the Sovereigns of Europe permit the sacred nature of sovereignty to be attainted in me? Can't they see that they are killing themselves at St. Helena? I have entered their capitals as a conqueror; had I been moved by such motives, what would have become of them? They all called me their brother, and I had become so by the will of the people, the sanction of victory, the character of religion, the alliances of policy and of family.

November 16th. You don't know men; they are difficult to judge precisely. Do they know, do they realize themselves fully? Had I continued prosperous, most of those who abandoned me would probably never have suspected their own treachery. In any case, I was more deserted than betrayed; there was more weakness about me than treason; they were the regiment of St. Peter,—repentance and tears may stand at the gates! Apart from that, who has there been in history with more partisans, more friends? Who has been more popular, more beloved? Who ever left behind more ardent regrets? Look at France: might not one say that from this rock of mine I still reign over her?

25th. When I returned from Moscow, from Leipzig, it was reported in Paris that my hair had turned white; but you see it is not so, and I expect to stand worse things than those!

29th. My Code alone,because of its simplicity, has done more good in France than the sum total of all the laws that preceded it. My schools are preparing unknown generations. And so during my reign crime diminished rapidly, whilst on the contrary among our neighbours in England it increased with frightful rapidity. And that is enough, I think, to give a clear judgment on the two governments.

People take England on trust, and repeat that Shakespeare is the greatest of all authors. I have read him: there is nothing that compares with Racine or Corneille: his plays are unreadable, pitiful.

30th, in the garden:
It is certainly far from poor Toby here (a negro gardener) to a King Richard! And yet the crime is no less atrocious; for, after all, this man had a family, happiness, an individual existence. And it is a horrible crime to have sent him here to finish his days under the load of slavery. But I read your looks; you think there is a similar case at St. Helena! There is not the least comparison between the two; if the misdeed strikes higher, the victim can fall back on far greater resources. Our situation may even have good points! The Universe watches us! We stand as martyrs of an immortal cause! Millions of men weep with us, our country sighs, and glory has put on mourning! We struggle here against the tyranny of the gods, and the hopes of humanity are with us! Misfortune itself knows heroism, and glory! Only adversity was wanting to complete my career! Had I died on the throne, in the clouds of my almightiness, I would have remained a problem for many; as it is, thanks to my misfortunes, I can be judged naked.

December 6th. Well, we shall have sentries under our windows for dinner at Longwood; they would like to compel me to have a foreign officer at my table, in my room; I must not ride out on horseback without one; in a word we must not take one step, under penalty of an insult!

January 1, 1816. In this accursed island one cannot see the sun or the moon for the greater part of the year; always rain or fog. One can't ride a mile without being soaked; even the English, accustomed as they are to dampness, complain of it.

15th. We have no superfluity here, except of time.

22d. On my return from the army of Italy, Bernardin de St. Pierre came to call on me, and almost at once turned the conversation on the subject of his poverty. During my boyhood I had dreamed of nothing but Paul and Virginia, and, flattered by a confession that I assumed to be confidential and due to my great reputation, I speedily returned his call, and discreetly left a little roll of twenty-five louis on the mantelpiece.

February 7. News of the death of Murat at Pizzo.

The Calabrese have been more humane, more generous, than those who sent me here!

8th. It was fated that Murat should do us injury. I would have taken him to Waterloo, but the French army was so patriotic, so honest, that it is doubtful if it could have been brought to swallow the disgust and horror that was felt for those who were traitors. I did not think I had the power to maintain him there, and yet he might have meant victory. For what was it we lacked at certain moments of the day? To break in three or four English squares,—and Murat was admirable at that business, he was the very man for it; there was never seen a more determined, fearless, brilliant leader at the head of cavalry.

17th. If I hadn't been fool enough to get myself beaten at Waterloo, the business was done; even now I can't see how it happened—but there, don't let's talk about it any more!

March 3d. I frightened them pretty well with my invasion of England, didn't I? What was the public talk about it at the time? Well, you may have joked about it in Paris, but Pitt wasn't laughing in London. Never was the English oligarchy in greater peril!

I had made a landing possible; I had the finest army that ever existed, that of Austerlitz; what more can be said? In four days I could have reached London; I would not have entered as a conqueror but as a liberator; I would have acted the part of William III again, but with greater generosity. The discipline of my army would have been perfect; and it would have behaved in London as it might in Paris. From there I would have operated from south to north, under the colours of the Republic, the European regeneration which later I was on the point of effecting from north to south, under monarchical forms. The obstacles before which I failed did not proceed from men but from the elements: in the south it was the sea destroyed me; and in the north it was the fire of Moscow and the ice of winter; so there it is, water, air, fire, all nature and nothing but nature; these were the opponents of a universal regeneration commanded by Nature herself! The problems of Nature are insoluble!

7th. Count Lascases Chambellan of the S. M. Longwood; into his polac: very press.

Count Lascases, Since sixt wek, y learn the english and y do not any progress. Sixt week do fourty and two day. If might have learn fivty word for day, i could know it two thousands and two hundred. It is in the dictionary more of fourty thousand; even he could most twenty; but much of tems. For know it or hundred and twenty week which do more two years. After this you shall agree that the study one tongue is a great labour who it must do into the young aged. Longwood, this morning the seven march thursday one thousand eight hundred sixteen after nativity the Lors Jesus Christ.

11th. The Emperor of Russia is intelligent, pleasing, well-educated, can fascinate easily; but one has to he on one's guard, he is a real Greek of the later Empire.

Greece awaits a liberator. What a splendid wreath of glory is there! He can inscribe his name for eternity with those of Homer, of Plato, of Epaminondas! I myself was perhaps not far from doing it! When at the time of my campaign of Italy I touched the shores of the Adriatic, I wrote to the Directoire that I could look out over the Empire of Alexander.

The French are all critical, turbulent: they are real weathervanes at the mercy of the winds; but this fault is free from any factor of self-interest, and that is their best excuse.

31st. With St. John of Acre captured, I could have reached Constantinople and India; I would have changed the face of the world!

April 1st. I can count thirty-one conspiracies on official record, without speaking of those that remain unknown; others invent such things, I have carefully concealed all I was able to. The risk to my life was a great one, especially between Marengo and the attempt of Georges and the affair of the Duke d'Enghien.

11th. Talleyrand's face is so impassive that it is impossible to interpret it; Lannes and Murat used to say of him jokingly that if, while he was speaking with you, some one kicked him from behind, his face would show nothing.

Fouché required intrigues just as he did food. He intrigued at all times, in all places, in all manners, with all people. He was always in everybody's boots.

(O'Meara: Which is the best of the French generals?)

It is difficult to say, but it seems to me that it is Suchet; formerly it was Masséna, but he may be considered a dead man. Suchet, Clausel, and Gérard are the best French generals, in my opinion. I made my generals out of mud.

18th. In my misfortunes, I sought an asylum, and instead I have found contempt, ill-treatment, and insult. Shortly after I came on board (Admiral Cockburn's) ship, as I did not wish to sit for two or three hours guzzling down wine to make myself drunk, I got up from table, and walked out upon deck. While I was going out, he said, in a contemptuous manner:—I believe the *general* has never read Lord Chesterfield; meaning, that I was deficient in politeness, and did not know how to conduct myself at table.

19th. I have no reason to complain of the English soldiers or sailors; on the contrary, they treat me with great respect, and even appear to feel for me. Moore was a brave soldier, an excellent officer, and a man of talent.

20th. England and France have held in their hands the fate of the world, especially that of European civilization. How we have injured one another!

21st. They want to know what I wish? I ask for my freedom, or for the executioner! Tell your Prince Regent what I say.' I no longer ask for news of my son since they have had the barbarism to leave my first request unanswered.

It is hard, all the same, to find myself without money; I might make arrangements to have an annual credit on Eugène of 7000 or 8000 napoleons. He could not very well refuse; he has had perhaps more than 40 millions from me, and it would be casting a slur on his personal character to doubt him.

26th. Well, after all said and done, circumstances might have led me to accept Islam, and as that excellent Queen of France used to say: How you do go on! But I should have wanted something worth my while,—at least up to the Euphrates. A change of religion, which is unpardonable for personal motives, may perhaps be accepted when immense political results depend on it. Henry IV rightly said:

Paris is worth a mass. To think that the Empire of the East, perhaps the dominion of all Asia, was the matter of a turban and a pair of baggy trousers; for really that was all it came to.

Constantinople alone is an Empire; whoever possesses it can rule the world.

28th. Had I not won at Austerlitz, I would have had the whole of Prussia on my back. Had I not triumphed at Jena, Austria and Spain would have risen behind me. Had I not succeeded at Wagram, a far less decisive victory, I had to fear that Russia would abandon me, that Prussia would revolt, and the English were already in front of Antwerp. I made a great mistake after Wagram in not striking Austria down even lower. She remained too powerful for our security; she eventually destroyed us. Austria had come into my family; and yet this marriage was fatal to me. I stepped on to an abyss covered with flowers.

29th. My dear friend, you and I, in this place, are already in the next world; we are conversing in the Elysian Fields.

May 1st. They may change, and chop, and suppress, but after all they will find it pretty difficult to make me disappear altogether. A French historian cannot very easily avoid dealing with the Empire; and, if he has a heart, he will have to give me back something of my own. I sealed the gulf of anarchy, and I unravelled chaos. I purified the revolution, raised the people, and strengthened monarchy. I stimulated every ambition, rewarded every merit, and pushed back the bounds of glory! All that amounts to something!

10th. It is most remarkable how the revolution suddenly produced so many great generals, Pichegru, Kléber, Masséna, Marceau, Desaix, Hoche; and nearly all of them rankers; but there the effort of Nature seemed to stop, she has produced nothing since.

16th. Well, my dear fellow, things got pretty hot; I was angry! They have sent me something worse than a gaoler; Sir Hudson Lowe is an executioner! Well, I received him to-day with my face of thunder, head down, and ears back! We stared like two rams on the point of butting at one another; and my emotions must have been quite violent, for I felt my left calf twitching. That is a great symptom with me, and hadn't occurred for a long time.

You say, sir, that your instructions are more terrible than those of the Admiral. Are they to kill me by the sword, or by poison? I am prepared for anything from your Minister; here I am, slaughter your victim! I don't know how you can manage the poison; but as for the sword you have already found the way. I warn you that if, as you have threatened, you intrude on my privacy, the brave 53d will not pass in except over my body. On learning of your arrival I flattered myself that I should find in you an army officer who, having been on the Continent and having witnessed its great struggles, would have behaved with propriety towards me; I made a profound mistake. Your nation, your government, you yourself, will be covered with opprobrium because of me; and your children too; that will be the verdict of posterity. What subtlety of barbarism could go further, sir, than that which led you a few days ago to invite me to your table under the qualification of General Bonaparte, to make me the amusement and the laughing-stock of your guests? Would you have cut your courtesy to the rank you were pleased to assign me? I am not General Bonaparte for you, sir; you have no more right than any other person on earth to take from me the qualifications that are mine!

They will kill me here, my dear fellow, that is quite certain!

19th. When sleeping together it is not easy to lose touch; but otherwise people are quickly strangers. And so it was that so long as that habit lasted, none of my thoughts, none of my actions, escaped Josephine; she seized, guessed, kept track of everything, which was sometimes quite awkward for me and for business. A passing quarrel put an end to it at the time of the camp of Boulogne.

Josephine was always thinking of the future, and was alarmed at her barrenness. She realized fully that no marriage is complete and real without children; and she had married when no longer able to have any. As prosperity came, her anxiety increased; she had recourse to the medical art; she frequently pretended that success had resulted. Josephine had the excessive extravagance and disorderliness of the Creoles. Her accounts never could be balanced; she was always in debt; and we always quarrelled vigorously when the moment came for settling those debts. Even at Elba Josephine's accounts were showered on me from every part of Italy.

Another characteristic trait of Josephine was her constant attitude of negation. At any moment, at any question made to her, her first instinct was to deny, her first word was *no*; and the no was not exactly a lie, it was a precaution, a mere defensive; and it is just that which differentiates us from you, ladies, a fundamental distinction of sex and of education: you are made for love, and you are taught to say no. We, on the contrary, glory in saying yes, even when we should not. And there is the key of our difference in conduct. We are not and cannot be of the same sort in life.

If I were starting at night in a chaise for a distant journey, to my great astonishment there would Josephine be, waiting in it ready dressed, although it had not been arranged that she should go.—But you can't possibly come! I am going too far; it would fatigue you too much!—Not in the least, answered Josephine.—And I must start at once.—Well, I'm quite ready.—But you need a whole paraphernalia.—Not at all, she said; I have everything.—And generally I had to give in.

After all said and done, Josephine gave her husband happiness, and was always his tenderest friend, always and in all events showing submission, devotion, absolute self-sacrifice. And I have always thought of her with tender affection and keen gratitude.

Madame (Mère) was too parsimonious; it was ridiculous. I even offered her a large monthly allowance if only she would disburse it. She was quite ready to take it, but on condition she could keep it. In reality it was all merely an excess of prudence on her part; she was always afraid of finding herself penniless some day. She had known necessity, and could never free her mind from the memory of that terrible time. It is only fair to say, however, that she gave a great deal of money to her children in secret; she is such a good mother!

And yet this same woman from whom it is so difficult to extract a five franc piece would have given her all to help my return from Elba; and after Waterloo she would have given me all she possessed to help reëstablish my affairs; she offered it me; she would have sentenced herself to black bread without a murmur.

20th. I am sad, bored, ill; sit in that armchair, keep me company.

21st. What shall we read to-night? You all agree on the Bible? It is really most edifying; they wouldn't guess what we're doing, in Europe!

June 1st. When any one of my ministers, or other high personages, had blundered badly, and it was necessary to get annoyed, really angry, furious, I always took care to have a third party present at the scene; my rule was that when I had decided to strike, the blow should fall on a good many; the one on whom it fell was neither more nor less resentful; while the witness, whose face and embarrassment were worth seeing, would go off and discreetly spread far and wide what he had seen and heard: a healthy terror circulated through the veins of the social body. Things went better; I had to punish less frequently; I profited much and without doing much harm.

4th. I have been scolded for my laziness to-day, so here I, am back at work to attack several points at once; there will be something for everybody. I shall tackle the Consulate with Montholon, Gourgaud can have some other epoch, or separate battles, and little Emmanuel (Las Cases) can prepare the documents and materials for the period of the coronation.

8th. Everything proclaims the existence of a God; that is beyond doubt; but all our religions are clearly the offspring of men. A man can swear to nothing that he will do in his last moments; yet undoubtedly my belief is that I shall die without a confessor. Assuredly I am far from being an atheist; yet I cannot believe all that is taught, in spite of reason, without being dishonest and a hypocrite. Under the Empire, and particularly after the marriage with Maria Louisa, the greatest efforts were made to persuade me to go to Notre Dame in full state for communion, after the manner of our kings; I refused flatly; my faith was not strong enough for it to do me any good, and yet was too great to commit a sacrilege in cold blood. To know whence I come, what I am, whither I go, is beyond me, and yet there it is! I am the clock that exists but does not know itself. I can appear before God's tribunal, I can await his judgment without fear. I worked only for the glory, the power, the splendour of France; there all my faculties, my efforts, my time were given. That could not be a crime; to me it appeared a virtue!

10th. Fox came to France immediately after the treaty of Amiens. He was working at a history of the Stuarts, and asked my permission to search in our diplomatic archives. I ordered that he should be given access to everything. I received him frequently; I knew of his talents by reputation; I quickly found in him a lofty soul, a good heart, large, generous, liberal views, an ornament of humankind; I became attached to him. We conversed freely, leaving prejudices aside, on a variety of subjects, and when I wanted to rub it in I would remind him of the infernal machine, I would say that his Ministers had tried to assassinate me; he used to get quite heated arguing against me, and would always finish by saying in his bad French: *Premier Consul, ôtez vous donc cela de votre tête!*

13th. The terrible *Moniteur* that has ruined so many reputations is constantly useful and favourable for me alone. Reasonable men, men of real talent, will write history from the official documents; but these documents are full of me, and it is they I invoke and stand by.

18th. An inconceivable battle! An unheard of concurrence of fatal events! Grouchy—Ney—d'Erlon! Was it nothing worse than misfortune? Ah, unhappy France! Extraordinary campaign in which in less than a week I three times saw success slip out of my hands! Had it not been for the desertion of a traitor I would have crushed the enemy at the beginning of the campaign. I would have crushed them at Ligny had my left done its duty. Again, I would have crushed them at Waterloo had my right not failed me.

21st. They will always fear me! Pitt told them truly: there is no safety for you with a man who carries a whole invasion in his head. In any case, what is there to fear? That I should make war? I am too old. That I should run after glory? I am gorged with it, I turned it into litter.

July 12th. *A questa casa, o in questo luogo tristo, non voglio niente di lui.* I hate this Longwood. The sight of it makes me melancholy. Let him put me in some place where there is shade, verdure, and water. Here it either blows a furious wind, loaded with rain and fog, *che mi taglia l'anima;* or, if that is wanting, *il sole mi brucia il cervello,* through the want of shade when I go out.

15th. I had resolved to renew at Cherbourg the marvels of Egypt: I had already erected my pyramid in the sea; I would also have had my lake Moeris. My grand object was to be able to concentrate all our naval forces so as to aim a great stroke at the enemy. I was, so to speak, laying out the field so that the two nations could grapple with one another bodily; and the result could not be in doubt, for we would have been more than forty millions of French against fifteen millions of English; the end would have been a battle of Actium.

16th. (To Hudson Lowe.) Shall I tell you what we think of you? We believe you capable of anything, I mean anything; and so long as you live with your hatred, we shall live with our thoughts. The most evil deed of your Minister was not sending me to St. Helena, but making you its governor. You are a greater plague than all the afflictions of this hideous rock!

21st. The English trembled when we occupied Egypt. We were revealing to Europe the real way of taking India from them. They are not quite easy yet, and they are quite right.

22d. Man loves the supernatural. He meets deception halfway. The fact is that everything about us is a miracle. Strictly speaking, there are no phenomena, for in nature everything is a phenomenon: my existence is a phenomenon; this log that is being put into the chimney is a phenomenon; this light that illuminates me is a phenomenon; my intelligence, my faculties, are phenomena; for they all exist, yet we cannot define them, I leave you here, and I am in Paris, entering the Opera; I bow to the spectators, I hear the acclamations, I see the actors, I hear the music. Now if I can span the space from St. Helena, why not that of the centuries? Why should I not see the future like the past? Would the one be more extraordinary, more marvellous than the other? No, but in fact it is not so.

25th. Can it be possible that the Emperor of Austria, whose daughter I married, who solicited that marriage on his knees, to whom I twice restored his capital, who has in his keeping my wife and my son, should send a commissioner here without one single line for me, without the least little scrap of a bulletin on the health of my son?

29th, at dinner:
Gentlemen, Santini there, wanted to murder the governor?

What, thief? You meant to kill the governor? If that idea gets into your head again, you will have me to deal with; you'll see what I'll do to you!

August 4th. A man must have accomplished all that I have, to realize fully the difficulty of doing good. It sometimes needed all my power to succeed. If it was a question of extending the Tuileries gardens, of repairing the sewers, of carrying through a public improvement, all my energy was necessary; I had to write six, ten letters a day, and get hot and angry. I have spent as much as 30 millions on sewers which nobody will ever thank me for. Archimedes would promise anything if only he could place his lever; I would have done as much wherever I could place my energy, my perseverance, and my budgets. With budgets one could create the world.

18th. (Hudson Lowe: But, sir, you don't know me!)

Eh! And where could I have known you indeed? I have not met you on a field of battle. You were only good for hiring murderers. Look at that camp where your soldiers are. It I went to them and said: The oldest soldier of Europe asks you for a bit of your rations,—I should get a share of their dinner. I, who have governed the world, know what sort of people are employed on such duties. Only men with no sense of honour accept them. You do well to ask to be relieved. It will be good for you, and for me!

(To Admiral Cockburn.) Lowe's faults come from his ways of life. He has only commanded foreign deserters, Piedmontese, Corsicans, Sicilians, all renegades, traitors to their country, the lees, the scum of Europe. Had he commanded men, Englishmen, he would treat with respect those who are entitled to honour. All these details are degrading. Were you to stretch me on the burning coals of Montezuma or of Guatemozin you could not extract from me gold I do not possess. In any case, who is asking anything of you? Who has asked you to feed me? If you stopped your provisions and I were hungry, these brave soldiers would take compassion on me. I could go to the mess of their grenadiers, and I am sure they would not deny the first, the oldest soldier of Europe. In a few years your Lord Castlereagh, your Lord Bathurst and the others, you who are speaking, will be buried in dust and forgotten; or, if your names are known it will only be for the insults you have heaped upon me.

19th. That governor came here yesterday to annoy me. He saw me walking in the garden, and in consequence I could not refuse to see him. He wanted to enter into some details with me, about reducing the expenses of the establishment. He had the audacity to tell me that things were as he found them, and that he came up to justify himself: that he had come up two or three times before, to do so, but that I was in a bath. I replied: No, sir, I was not in a bath, but I ordered one on purpose not to see you.

28th. (Mme. de Montholon: Which were the best troops?)

Those that win battles, madam. And they are fickle, they must be taken on their day, like you ladies. The best troops have been, the Carthaginians under Hannibal, the Romans under the Scipios, the Macedonians under Alexander, the Prus-

.ians under Frederick. Some day my army of Italy and that of Austerlitz may be equalled, but, surely, never surpassed.

September 2d. I was the keystone of an edifice that was new, and had such weak foundations! If I had been beaten at Marengo, you would have had all 1814 then, less the glorious miracles that followed and that remain immortal. The same holds good for Austerlitz, for Jena, for Eylau, and elsewhere.

24th. My force of character has often been praised; yet for my own family I was nothing but a mollycoddle, and they knew it. The first storm over, their perseverance, their obstinacy, always carried the day; and, from sheer lassitude, they did what they liked with me. I made some great errors there. I did not have the luck Gengis Khan had with his four sons, who knew no emulation save that of serving him well. When I created a king, he at once considered himself by the grace of God. A delusion seized all of them that they were adored, preferred to me.

27th. That's it; work is my element; I was born, I was made for work. I have reached the limit with my legs; I have reached the limit with my eyes; but never in my work. And so I almost killed poor Méneval; I had to relieve him and put him out as a convalescent with Marie Louise, with whom his duties were a real sinecure.

29th. You want to know the treasures of Napoleon? They are enormous, it is true, but in full view. Here they are: the splendid harbour of Antwerp, that of Flushing, capable of holding the largest fleets; the docks and dykes of Dunkirk, of Havre, of Nice; the gigantic harbour of Cherbourg; the harbour works at Venice; the great roads from Antwerp to Amsterdam, from Mainz to Metz, from Bordeaux to Bayonne; the passes of the Simplon, of Mont Cenis, of Mont Genèvre, of the Corniche, that give four openings through the Alps; in that alone you might reckon 800 millions. The roads from the Pyrenees to the Alps, from Parma to Spezzia, from Savona to Piedmont; the bridges of Jena, of Austerlitz, of the Arts, of Sèvres, of Tours, of Lyons, of Turin, of the Isère, of the Durance, of Bordeaux, of Rouen; the canal from the Rhine to the Rhone, joining the waters of Holland to the Mediterranean; the canal that joins the Scheldt and the Somme, connecting Amsterdam and Paris; that which joins the Rance and the Vilaine; the canal of Arles, of Pavia, of the Rhine; the draining of the marshes of Bourgoing, of the Cotentin, of Rochefort; the rebuilding of most of the churches pulled down during the Revolution, the building of new ones; the construction of many

industrial establishments for putting an end to pauperism; the construction of the
Louvre, of the public granaries, of the Bank, of the canal of the Ourcq; the water
system of the city of Paris, the numerous sewers, the quays, the embellishments
and monuments of that great city; the public improvements of Rome; the
reëstablishment of the manufactories of Lyons. Fifty millions spent on repairing
and improving the Crown residences; sixty millions' worth of furniture placed in
the palaces of France and Holland, at Turin, at Rome; sixty millions' worth of
Crown diamonds, all of it the money of Napoleon; even the Regent, the only
missing one of the old diamonds of the Crown of France, purchased from Berlin
Jews with whom it was pledged for three millions; the Napoleon Museum, valued
at more than 400 millions.

These are monuments to confound calumny! History will relate that all this was
accomplished in the midst of continuous wars, without raising a loan, and with
the public debt actually decreasing day by day.

October 21st. After all said and done, Mme. de Staël is a woman of great talent,
very distinguished, of very keen intelligence: she has won her place. It might be
said that if, instead of carping at me, she had taken my side, it would have been
useful to me.

30th. I must admit that I was spoiled; I always gave orders; from my birth power
was mine, I already rejected a master or a law.

November 6th. I was always searching for a man for my navy, without ever finding him. That business has about it a certain technicality, a certain specialness,
that always held up my plans. The instant I put forward any new idea, immediately Ganteaume and the whole of the naval section were on my back.—Sire, you
can't do that.—And why?—I was pulled up sharp. How can one maintain a discussion with people who speak a different language? How often have I
reproached them with the abuse of this in the Council of State! To hear them one
would have to be born in the navy to understand anything about it. It was in vain
I struggled, I had to give in to their unanimity, not, however, without warning
them that I left it on their consciences.

9th. Sidney Smith is a brave officer. He is active, intelligent, intriguing, and indefatigable; but I believe that he is half insane. Had it not been for that, I would
have taken Acre in spite of him. He dispersed proclamations amongst my troops,

which certainly shook some of them, and I therefore published an order stating that he was mad, and forbidding all communication with him. Some days after he sent, by means of a flag of truce, a lieutenant with a letter containing a challenge to me to meet him at some place he pointed out, in order to fight a duel. I laughed at this and sent him back an intimation that when he brought Marlborough to fight with me, I would meet him. Notwithstanding this, I like the character of the man.

11th. Democracy may run mad, but it has a heart, it can be moved; an aristocracy always remains cold, and never forgives.

16th. I am assured that it is through (Wellington) that I am here, and I believe it. I certainly gave him a bad quarter of an hour. That usually would appeal to a great soul; but his has not responded. Ah! old Blücher was worth a fine candle; without him I don't know where His Grace would be now; but at all events I would not be here.

25th. I have spent the day working out fortification problems with Bertrand, and it has seemed a very short one.

December 10th. I have never witnessed such a passion as that of Berthier for Mme. Visconti! In Egypt he would gaze at the moon at the very instant that she was doing the same. In the midst of the desert there was a tent sacred to her; her portrait was there, and he burned incense in front of it. Three mules were told off to carry it and the baggage. I would often go in, throwing myself on the sofa in my boots. It made Berthier furious; to him it was the desecration of his sanctuary. He loved her so that he would stir me up to speak of her although I always abused her; he didn't mind, he was delighted to be able to talk about her. If I had left him as commander-in-chief in Egypt, he would have evacuated the country immediately.

11th. My dear Count Las Cases, I am touched by what you are suffering; dragged from my side two weeks ago, you are locked up, unable to communicate or to receive communications, or even to have your own servant with you. I am gratified to have this opportunity of saying that your conduct at St. Helena has been, like your whole life, honourable and without reproach. Your company was a necessity for me. You alone read, speak, understand English. How often have you watched by me through nights of illness? However, I advise you, and if necessary order you, to ask the governor of this place to send you back to Europe. It would be a consolation for me to know that you were on your way to happier climes. If, some day, you should see my wife and my son, embrace them; it is now two years since I heard from them, directly or indirectly.

Console yourself, and console my friends. My body, it is true, is delivered over to the hatred of my enemies; they omit nothing that may satisfy their revenge; they are killing me by pin pricks; but Providence will not permit this to continue much longer.

As all the indications are that you will not be allowed to see me before you leave, receive my embrace, the assurance of my esteem and of my friendship. Be happy!

Your devoted, NAPOLEON.

29th. This governor is totally unfit to fill the situation he holds. He would employ cunning in saying, Good-day! I think he would eat his breakfast the same way.

30th. Ah, Warden, how do you do?

I certainly enjoy a good state of health. With respect to the English language I have been very diligent: I now read your newspapers with ease. In one paper I am called a liar, in another a tyrant, in a third a monster, and in one of them, which I really did not expect, a coward!

January 1st, 1817. To bear misfortune was the only thing wanting to my fame. I have worn the imperial crown of France, the iron crown of Italy; England has now given me a greater and more glorious one,—for it is that worn by the Saviour of the world,—the crown of thorns.

6th. What is electricity, galvanism, magnetism? There lies the great secret of nature. Galvanism works in silence. I believe that man is the product of these fluids and of the atmosphere; that the brain pumps in these fluids and produces life; that the soul is made up of them, and that after death they return to the ether whence other brains pump them.

)th. The Paris police terrifies more than it hurts. The post-office is a good source
of information, but I am not sure that the advantage compensates the evil. It was
not possible to read every letter, but those of the persons I specified and of my
ministers were unsealed. Fouché, Talleyrand, never wrote; but their friends, their
creatures, wrote, and by (such a person's) letter one could see what Talleyrand or
Fouché had in mind.

February 3d. The Bishop of Nantes was an excellent confessor for Maria Louisa;
he gave her good advice, explained how it was I could eat meat on fast days, and
when I pushed the Empress hard she would tell me all that passed between them.
Fesch said to her: if he eats meat, throw your plate at his head!—And Fesch
would more likely have made me a Turk than a Christian. If I had had to be converted, I think that the Bishop of Nantes is the only man who could have succeeded; but I have read too much history and handled too many religious for
that!

6th. My life here, were we in Europe and were I not a slave, would suit me very
well. I would like to live in the country and develop my estate. It is the best life
there is: A sick sheep supplies food for conversation. At the island of Elba, with
plenty of money and means of entertaining, living in the midst of the scientific
men of Europe as their centre, I would have been very happy.

28th. He must indeed be a barbarian who would deny to a husband and a father
the consolation of conversing with a person who had lately seen, spoken to, and
touched his wife and child, from whose embraces he is for ever separated by the
cruel policy of a few. The Anthropophagi of the South Seas would not do it. Previous to devouring their victims, they would allow them the consolation of seeing
and conversing with each other. The cruelties which are practised here would be
disavowed by cannibals!

Nature in forming some men, intended that they should always remain in a sub-
ordinate situation. Such was Berthier. There was not so good a chief of staff in
the world; but change his occupation, and he was not fit to command five hundred men.

March 3d. In spite of all the libels, I have no fear whatever about my fame. Posterity will do me justice. The truth will be known; and the good I have done will
be compared with the faults I have committed. I am not uneasy as to the result.

Had I succeeded, I would have died with the reputation of the greatest man that ever existed. As it is, although I have failed, I shall be considered as an extraordinary man: my elevation was unparalleled, because unaccompanied by crime. I have fought fifty pitched battles, almost all of which I have won. I have framed and carried into effect a code of laws that will bear my name to the most distant posterity. I raised myself from nothing to be the most powerful monarch in the world. Europe was at my feet. I have always been of opinion that the sovereignty lay in the people. In fact, the imperial government was a kind of republic. Called to the head of it by the voice of the nation, my maxim was, *la carrière est ouverte aux talens* without distinction of birth or fortune, and this system of equality is the reason that your oligarchy hates me so much.

6th. I was afraid there was bad news about my wife. Perhaps it's about my son; when you go into town tomorrow, try to see all the papers, and read them carefully.

April 3d. You English are aristocrats. You keep a great distance between yourselves and the *popolo*. Nature formed all men equal. It was always my custom to go amongst the soldiers and the rabble, to converse with them, hear their little histories, and speak kindly to them. This I found to be of the greatest benefit to me.

May 3d. Once for all, Admiral, I am bound to tell you what I think. With you English a foreigner is always a dog; one can expect neither help nor politeness. What! There was a botanist here, who had seen my wife and my child, and he was forbidden to give me any news of them; he is being prosecuted because he gave my valet a lock of my son's hair! If Hudson Lowe asks to see me, I shall refuse!

5th. Yes, I tasted happiness as First Consul, at the time of my marriage, of the birth of the King of Rome, but I was not quite secure then. Perhaps Tilsit was the (best) moment; I had had difficulties, worries, Eylau among others, and I was victorious, imposing my will, with emperors and kings to court me! Perhaps I felt more after my victories in Italy; what enthusiasm, what cheers for the liberator of Italy! At twenty-five years of age! From that moment I foresaw what I might become! I could see the world moving from under my footsteps as though I were sailing through the air.

16th. When I was at Tilsit with the Emperor Alexander and the King of Prussia, I was the most ignorant of the three in military affairs! These two sovereigns, especially the King of Prussia, were completely *au fait* as to the number of buttons there ought to be in front of a jacket, how many behind, and the manner in which the skirts ought to be cut. Not a tailor in the army knew better than King Frederick how many measures of cloth it took to make a jacket. In fact, I was nobody in comparison with them. They continually tormented me with questions about matters belonging to tailors, of which I was entirely ignorant, though, in order not to affront them, I answered just as gravely as if the fate of an army depended upon the cut of a jacket. The King of Prussia changed his fashion every day. He was a tall, dry looking fellow, and would give a good idea of Don Quixote. At Jena, his army performed the finest and most showy manœuvres possible, but I soon put a stop to their *coglionerie,* and taught them that to fight and to execute dazzling manœuvres and wear splendid uniforms were very different affairs. If the French army had been commanded by a tailor, the King of Prussia would certainly have gained the day, from his superior knowledge in that art!

Women, when they are bad, are worse than men. The softer sex, when degraded, falls lower than the other. Women are always much better or much worse than men.

21st. I can't sleep.

23d. Gourgaud, my friend, I can't walk any longer.

June 2d. A singular thing about me is my memory. As a boy I knew the logarithms of thirty or forty numbers; in France I not only knew the names of the officers of all the regiments, but where the corps had been recruited, had distinguished themselves; I even knew their spirit.

3d. The 32d demi-brigade would have laid down its life for me because, after Lonato, I wrote: The 32d was there: I was easy.—The influence of words over men is astounding!

13th. My own opinion is that I ought to have died at Waterloo; perhaps a little earlier. Had I died at Moscow, I should probably have had the reputation of the greatest conqueror ever known. But the smiles of fortune were at an end. The misfortune is that when a man seeks the most for death, he cannot find it. Men were killed around me, before, behind, everywhere, but no bullet for me.

14th. Marching on Landshut I met Bessières retreating. I ordered him to march forward. He objected that the enemy were in force.—Go ahead,—said I, and he advanced. The enemy seeing him take the offensive thought he was stronger than they and retreated. In war that is the way everything goes. It is moral I force more than numbers that wins the victory.

17th. Hudson Lowe says that I am the most subtle man in the world. I know how to put on a mild little expression when I want to get around anybody. That is how I won over O'Meara. I shammed sick to receive Lord Amherst so that, as he was just leaving, the governor couldn't undo the effect of all that I had said to him; I won his Lordship, whom I knew to be a not very intelligent person.

I wish to have no relations with Sir Hudson. Let him leave me in peace, for in ages to come his children will blush at their own name. Ah! good Heavens! how mistaken you are, nobody could be less subtle than I! On the contrary, my failing is that I am too easy-going. Ah! rascally governor!

August 3d. Hudson Lowe formerly thought that nothing which passed here would be known in Europe. He might as well have attempted to obscure the light of the sun with his hat. There are still millions in the world who are interested in me.

It is not the coat makes the gaoler, but manners and point of view.

24th. Misfortunes, you see, follow one another, and when misfortune comes, everything goes wrong. If only the battle of Vittoria had come earlier I would have signed peace, but it came at the very moment when I was bound not to. When the Allies saw that I had lost the battle, my artillery, my baggage, and that the English were marching into France, they concluded that I was lost. The French did not do much for me then. At the time of Cannæ the Romans redoubled their efforts, but that was because every individual stood in fear of death, of rape, of pillage. That is making war, but in modern campaigns everything is sprinkled with rosewater.

28th. Jesus was hanged, like so many a fanatic who posed as a prophet, a messiah; here were several every year. What is certain is that at that epoch opinion was setting towards a single God, and those who first preached the doctrine were well received: circumstances made for it. It is just as in my case, sprang from the lower ranks of society I became an emperor, because circumstances, opinion, were with me.

September 3d. If (Hudson Lowe) had his will, he would order me to breakfast at a certain hour, dine at another, go to bed at a time prescribed by him, and come himself to see it carried into execution. All will fall upon himself one day. He does not realize that what happens here will be recorded in history.

28th. O'Meara bearded Hudson Lowe and told him that in his opinion I had not six months to live. It's a good thing to have such a witness, it annoys the governor.

29th. St. Napoleon ought to bevery much obliged to me, and do everything in his powe r for me in the world to come. Poor fellow; nobody knew him before. He had not even a day in the calendar. I got him one, and persuaded the Pope to give him the fifteenth of August, my birthday.

November 2d. I could listen to the intelligence of the death of my wife, of my son, or of all my family, without a change of feature. Not the slightest sign of emotion, or alteration of countenance, would be visible. Everything would appear indifferent and calm. But when alone in my room, then I suffer. Then the feelings of the man burst forth.

30th. The King of Bavaria did not wish to give his daughter to Eugène, declaring that he did not know what adoption meant, and that he could only consider him as Viscount de Beauharnais. Josephine had had to put up with some slights at Munich, where they openly discussed in her presence the affection between the princess and the Prince of Baden. When I reached Munich the Elector came to see me in my study with a veiled lady. He raised the veil; it was his daughter; I found her charming, and was, I confess, somewhat embarrassed. I made the young woman sit down, and afterwards read a lecture to her governess. Should princesses fall in love? They are merely political merchandise.

The Queen of Bavaria was pretty, I enjoyed her society. One hunting-day the King started early, I promised to join him, but I went to see the Queen and staid an hour and a half. It caused talk, and the King was very angry, and when they met again he scolded her. She replied: Should I have shown him the door? I paid dear for my gallantry afterwards, for they followed me on my journey to Italy, where they were always after me; they had carriages that were breaking down every minute: I had to take them into mine; they were with me at Venice, yet, in reality, I was not annoyed because it gave me a following of kings.

December 21st. Whatever they say, I can make or unmake the reputation of the governor. All I choose to say of him, of his bad behaviour, of his ideas of poisoning me, will be believed.

25th. War is a singular art; I can assure you that fighting sixty battles taught me nothing I did not know at the first one. The essential quality of the general is firmness, and that is a gift from heaven.

January 7th, 1818. What I admire in Alexander the Great is not his campaigns, which we have no means of judging, but his political instinct. His going to Ammon was a profound political stroke; he thereby conquered Egypt. Had I remained in the East, I would probably have founded an Empire, like Alexander, by going to Mecca as a pilgrim, where I would have bowed the knee and offered prayers, but only if it had been worth while!

13th. What weariness every day! What martyrdom!

29th. To be a good general a man must know mathematics; it is of daily help in straightening one's ideas. Perhaps I owe my success to my mathematical conceptions; a general must never imagine things, that is the most fatal of all. My great talent, the thing that marks me most, is that I see things clearly; it is the same with my eloquence, for I can distinguish what is essential in a question from every angle. The great art in battle is to change the line of operations during the course of the engagement; that is an idea of my own, and quite new.

The art of war does not requite complicated manœuvres; the simplest are the best, and common sense is fundamental. From which one might wonder how it is generals make blunders; it is because they try to be clever. The most difficult thing is to guess the enemy's plan, to sift the truth from all the reports that come

n. The rest merely requires common sense; it's like a boxing-match, the more you punch the better it is. It is also necessary to read the map well.

February 18th. You have the impudence to talk of the conscription in France; it wounds your pride because it fell upon all ranks. Oh, how shocking, that a gentleman's son should be obliged to defend his country, just as if he were one of the mob!

The conscription did not crush a particular class like your press-gang, nor the rabble, because they were poor. My rabble would have become the best educated in the world. All my exertions were directed to illuminate the mass of the nation instead of brutalizing them by ignorance and superstition.

May 14th. (To O'Meara.) So you are going to leave us, doctor? Will the world believe that they have been cowardly enough to attack my doctor?

July 25th. (To O'Meara.) The crime will be accomplished more quickly. I have lived too long for them. Your ministry does not lack courage; when the Pope was in France, I would sooner have cut off my right arm than have signed an order for the removal of his surgeon.

When you arrive in Europe you will either go yourself or send to my brother Joseph. You will inform him that I desire that he shall give you the parcel containing the private and confidential letters of the Emperors Alexander and Francis, the King of Prussia, and the other sovereigns of Europe, which I delivered to his care at Rochefort. You will publish them, to cover those sovereigns with shame. When I was strong, and in power, they begged for my protection, and licked the dust from under my feet. Now, in my old age, they basely oppress me, and take my wife and child from me. Farewell, O'Meara, we shall never meet again. Be happy!

September 26th. Place that dear child next to his mother, there, on the right, nearer to my chimney. You recognise her by her colour: it's Marie Louise; she holds her son in her arms. And the other,—you recognise it? It's the Prince Imperial. The other two are of Josephine: I loved her so dearly! You are examining that big clock? It was the great Frederick's alarum; I took it from Potsdam,—that was all Prussia was worth! My mantelpiece is not very sumptuous, as you see. My son's bust, two chandeliers, two silver gilt cups, two decanters for eau de

Cologne, nail scissors, a small lookingglass. It is far from the spleadour of the Tuileries: but what of it, if I have fallen from power, I have not lost my glory.—I keep my memories.

September 23, 1819. Well, doctor, what do you think of it? Am I likely to disturb the monarchs' digestions much longer?

(Antommarchi: You will survive them, sire.)

No, doctor, the work of the English is nearly done, the mainspring is broken.

28th. I close my door to your drugs until to-morrow. I have some problems of algebra to work out.

October 4th. My country! my country! If only St. Helena were France I could be happy on this accursed rock.

Ah! doctor, where is the blue sky of Corsica? Fate has decided that I must not see again the scenes to which the memories of childhood recall me.

5th. *Dottoraccio di Capo Corso!* Leave me alone? Go out without my permission? You are a novice, so I forgive you; but neither the Grand Marshal nor General Montholon, would have gone out until I had given them leave.

14th. I am uncomfortable: I would like to sleep, read, do something or other. Aere is Racine, doctor; you are on the stage; come; I am listening,—Andromache. It's the play of unhappy fathers.

> ("I went to the spot where is kept my son,
>
> Whom once in each day you permit me to see,
>
> All, all that is left both of Hector and Troy;
>
> I went there to mingle my tears with his,
>
> I had not yet embraced him to-day—")

Doctor, it moves me too much,—leave me!

28th. My patent of nobility dates from Millesimo, from Rivoli. My family's is older. Only the genealogist Joseph can trace its origin; he pretends that we descend from I don't know how many obscure tyrants. After my reverses, I was only a Jacobin.

November 18th. What can I do?

(Antommarchi: Exercise!)

Where? Among the redcoats? Never!—How else? Hoeing the earth? Yes, doctor, you are right; I will hoe the earth.

July 26th, 1820. You are very attached to me, doctor; you spare nothing to relieve me; but all that is not the same as a mother's care. Ah! mamma Letizia!

August 10th. Has a man the right to kill himself? Yes, if his death injures n one, and if life is a burden to him. When is life a burden to a man? When it yields him only suffering and grief, But as suffering and grief change constantly, there can be no moment at which a man has the right to kill himself. That moment could only be at death's very door, because only then could it be proved that life was but a tissue of affliction and suffering.

September 18th. Happiness lies in sleep; Our necessities disappear with insomnia.

October 2d. The second book of the Æneid is considered the masterpiece of that epic; it deserves its reputation from the point of view of style, but not at all from that of realism. The wooden horse May come from a popular tradition, but the tradition was absurd and unworthy of an epic poem. There is nothing of the sort in the Iliad, where everything conforms to reality and to the practice of war.

14th. The art of medicine, my dear doctor, is none other than that of putting the imagination to sleep, of soothing it. That is why the ancients decked themselves out in robes and gowns that catch the eye and impose on one. You have given up the gown, and it is a mistake. Who knows? If you yourself appeared before me suddenly with an enormous wig, a toque, a trailing robe, I might take you for the god of health, although you are only that of drugs.

22d. My power lasted only a flash of time, but never mind, it was full, it wa~~ gorged with useful institutions; I consecrated the revolution; I infused it into ou~~ laws.

25th. Perhaps death will soon put a term to my sufferings.

27th. Well, doctor, how do you think I am? a little better? The fact is the pills—They have done their work—The devil! doctor, you preach the (doctrine of) Pills with more unction than they do that of legitimity nowadays. Do you take any yourself?

(Antommarchi: Sire, there are well-tested drugs.)

Like those Corvisart used to give the Empress, breadcrumb pills that worked miracles just the same. Marie Louise used to praise their good effects to me every day. They are all the same.

(Antommarchi: No, sire.)

Eh! but I belong to your shop too! I have practised! Water, Air, cleanliness, that was the foundation of my dispensary. I never got much beyond those remedies. You laugh at my methods? All right, laugh away.

Your colleagues in Egypt did just the same; but experience proved that my flannel and brush were more use than their pills.

November 16th. Well, doctor, is this the end?—I am going to get well, I suppose? A doctor would rather die than not try to persuade a dying man that he is not ill!—What, pills? A quinine mixture, as at Mantua?

19th. What a pleasant thing is rest! My bed has become a place of happiness for me; I would not exchange it for all the thrones of the universe. What a change! How I have fallen! I, whose activity knew no bounds, whose mind never slumbered! I am plunged in a stupor, in a lethargy; I have to make an effort to raise my eyelids.

December 8th. Desaix was devoted, generous, tormented by the thirst for glory; his death was one of my misfortunes. He was skilful, alert, bold; he made light of atigue, and even less of death: he would have followed victory to the ends of the earth. Brave Desaix!

26th. You want to get me into the garden? Very well.—I am very weak, my trembling legs will hardly hold me up.

Ah, doctor, how tired I am! I feel this fresh air I breathe is doing me good. Never having been sick, never having taken medicine, I can hardly have an opinion about such matters; the state I am now in appears in fact so extraordinary to me that I can scarcely realize it.

The newspapers report the death of Princess Elisa. Well, you see, Elisa points the way; death which appeared to have forgotten our family, has begun to strike it; my turn cannot be long delayed. The first of our family who will follow Elisa to the grave is that great Napoleon who is bending under his load and who yet keeps Europe in alarm.

January 22d, 1821. Will you not confess that I am right, *dottoraccio maledetto?* Is not my medicine better than yours? These cursed doctors are all the same; when they want their patient to do anything they deceive him, and frighten him. Isn't it time, *dottoraccio?*—Well, all right; we must obey the faculty.

February 15th. Were you at Milan when I assumed the Iron Crown? And when I went to Venice? Venice had put all her gondolas on the water, and fringes, and plumes, and stuffs; all that was lovely and fashionable had gathered at Fusine. Never had the Adriatic witnessed a more gorgeous procession.

March 15th. Ah, doctor, how I suffer!

26th. A consultation? What's the good? You are all, blind playing with the blind. Another doctor would not see any better than you can what is going on in my body. In any case, who is there to consult? Englishmen who would be under the influence of Hudson Lowe? I won't have them; I have already said so; I prefer that the iniquity should be accomplished.

29th. *Quod scriptum scriptum;* can you doubt, doctor, that all that happens to us is written, that our hour is, marked?

(Antommarchi: But, sire, your medicine!)

It is incredible how I dislike medicine! I could face danger with indifference, and see death without a tremor, but, however great an effort I make, I cannot put to my lips a cup with the least medicine in it.

30th. Kléber! He was the god Mars in uniform!

April 2d. A comet! It was the omen foretold the death of Cæsar!

5th. Ah, why did the bullets spare my life if it was only to lose it in this wretched way?

6th. I have always shaved myself, never has any person placed a hand on my cheek. Now that I am helpless, I must make up my mind to it.

12th. Thanks for your services, doctor; it's lost labour.

Doctor Arnott, don't people die of weakness? How can a man live eating so little?

13th. (Antommarchi with pills.)

Are they well wrapped up, covered? They won't poison my mouth? Really? (To Marchand.) Well, here you are, rascal, swallow them. He needed medicine, didn't he, doctor, and my pills will do him good? Give him some more now; as for me, I won't touch them again.

15th. I have nothing but satisfaction to express with my beloved wife, Maria Louisa; I shall retain my tender sentiments for her till my last breath; I beg her to watch and protect my son from the pitfalls that still surround his young days.

I bequeath to my son the objects specified in the schedule hereto. I hope this slight legacy will be dear to him, as recalling the memory of a father whom the whole world will tell him of.

Marchand will keep my hair, and will have a bracelet made of it that is to be sent to the Empress Maria Louisa.

6th. I wish my ashes to rest by the banks of the Seine, in the midst of the people of France whom I loved so dearly.

I have written too much. Ah, what suffering! What oppression! I feel at the left end of the stomach a pain that is unbearable.—You ought to marry, doctor. Marry an Englishwoman, her ice-cold blood will moderate the fire that devours you; you will become less obstinate.—Give me the potion!

19th. You are not mistaken, my friends, I am better to-day; but none the less I feel the end drawing near. When I am dead you will all have the sweet consolation of returning to Europe. You will see your relatives, your friends there, while I shall meet the brave in the Elysian Fields. I will relate the last events of my life to them.

21st. I was born in the Catholic faith, I wish to carry out the duties it imposes and to receive the consolation it gives.

24th. I have written too much, doctor; I am collapsing, I can't go on.

25th. (To M. Lafitte.) Monsieur Lafitte: I handed you, in 1815, as I was leaving Paris, a sum of six millions for which you gave me a duplicate receipt; I have cancelled one, and I charge Count Montholon to present the other to you, in order that you may hand the said sum to him after my death.

28th. After my death, which cannot be far off, I want my body to be opened; I also want, I exact, that no English doctor shall touch me. I further wish you to take my heart, place it in spirits of wine, and take it to my dear Marie Louise at Parma. You will tell her that I loved her tenderly, you will relate to her all you have seen, all that concerns my situation here, and my death.

May 2d, *2 A. M.:*
Steingel! Desaix! Masséna! Ah, victory is ours; go, hasten, press home the charge; they are ours!

3d, *3 P. M.:*
You have shared my exile, you will be faithful to my memory, you will do nothing to injure it.

5th. *5.30 P. M.:*
…head…army…

5.50 P. M.:

THE END

Summary

In all the new kingdoms created by the emperor, the Code Napoléon was established as law. Feudalism and serfdom were abolished, and freedom of religion established (except in Spain). Each state was granted a constitution, providing for universal male suffrage and a parliament and containing a bill of rights. French-style administrative and judicial systems were required. Schools were put under centralized administration, and free public schools were envisioned. Higher education was opened to all who qualified, regardless of class or religion. Every state had an academy or institute for the promotion of the arts and sciences. Incomes were provided for eminent scholars, especially scientists. Constitutional government remained only a promise, but progress and increased efficiency were widely realized. Not until after Napoleon's fall did the common people of Europe, alienated from his governments by war taxes and military conscription, fully appreciate the benefits he had given them.

In 1812 Napoleon, whose alliance with Alexander I had disintegrated, launched an invasion of Russia that ended in a disastrous retreat from Moscow. Thereafter all Europe united against him, and although he fought on, and brilliantly, the odds were impossible. In April 1814, his marshals refused to continue the struggle. After the allies had rejected his stepping down in favor of his son, Napoleon abdicated unconditionally and was exiled to the Mediterranean island of Elba. Marie Louise and his son were put in the custody of her father, the emperor of Austria. Napoleon never saw either of them again. Napoleon himself, however, soon made a dramatic comeback. In March 1815, he escaped from Elba, reached France, and marched on Paris, winning over the troops sent to capture him. In Paris, he promulgated a new and more democratic constitution, and veterans of his old campaigns flocked to his support. Napoleon asked peace of the allies, but they outlawed him, and he decided to strike first. The result was a campaign into Belgium, which ended in defeat at the Battle of Waterloo on June 18, 1815. In Paris, crowds begged him to fight on, but the politicians withdrew their support. Napoleon fled to Rochefort, where he surrendered to the captain of the British battleship *Bellerophon*. He was then exiled to Saint Helena, a remote island in the south Atlantic Ocean, where he remained until his death on May 5, 1821.

The cult of Napoleon as the "man of destiny" began during his lifetime. In fact he had begun to cultivate it during his first Italian campaign by systematically publicizing his victories. As first consul and emperor, he had engaged the best writers and artists of France and Europe to glorify his deeds and had contributed to the cult himself by the elaborate ceremonies with which he celebrated his rule, picturing himself as the architect of France's greatest glory. He maintained that he had preserved the achievements of the Revolution in France and offered their benefits to Europe. His goal, he said, was to found a European state—a "federation of free peoples." Whatever the truth of this, he became the arch-hero of the French and a martyr to the world. In 1840 his remains were returned to Paris at the request of King Louis-Philippe and interred with great pomp and ceremony in the Invalides, where they still lie.

Napoleon's influence is evident in France even today. Reminders of him dot Paris—the most obvious being the Arc de Triomphe, the centerpiece of the city, which was built to commemorate his victories. His spirit pervades the constitution of the Fifth Republic; the country's basic law is still the Code Napoléon, and the administrative and judicial systems are essentially Napoleonic. A uniform state-regulated system of education persists. Napoleon's radical reforms in all parts of Europe cultivated the ground for the revolutions of the 19th century. Today, the impact of the Code Napoléon is apparent in the law of all European countries.

Napoleon was a driven man, never secure, never satisfied. "Power is my mistress," he said. His life was work-centered; even his social activities had a purpose. He could bear amusements or vacations only briefly. His tastes were for coarse food, bad wine, cheap snuff. He could be charming—hypnotically so—for a purpose. He had intense loyalties—to his family and old associates. Nothing and no one, however, were allowed to interfere with his work.

Napoleon was sometimes a tyrant and always an authoritarian, but one who believed in ruling by mandate of the people, expressed in plebiscites. He was also a great enlightened monarch—a civil executive of enormous capacity who changed French institutions and tried to reform the institutions of Europe and give the Continent a common law. Few deny that he was a military genius. At Saint Helena, he said, "Waterloo will erase the memory of all my victories." He was wrong; for better or worse, he is best remembered as a general, not for his nlightened government, but the latter must be counted if he is justly to be called Napoleon the Great.

0-595-34849-1

Printed in the United States
27520LVS00006B/89

9 780595 348497